Converted t̶ ... P9-DFJ-721 ...73 .

spiritually peacefull at last.

LWDeffenderfer

THE QUAKER READER

purchased on a bright sunny
February day! Life is good!

THE Quaker Reader

Selected and introduced by
Jessamyn West

Pendle Hill Publications • Wallingford, Pennsylvania

Copyright © 1962 by Jessamyn West
Copyright © renewed 1990 by Harry McPherson
Reprinted by permission of Russel & Volkening
50 West 29th Street, New York, New York, 10001
as agents for the author.

September 1992 Pendle Hill Publications
Wallingford, Pennsylvania 19086
1-800-742-3150

Cover Art by Nicholas La Para, artist,
from the collection of Reginald and Barbara Lowe
Cover Design by John Davis Gummere

Printed in the United States of America
by Haddon Craftsmen, Scranton, Pennsylvania

Library of Congress Cataloging-in-Publication Data
will be found at the end of this book.

The editor wishes to thank the following for their kind permission to reprint excerpts from the works listed below.

George Allen and Unwin Ltd.: *Little Book of Selections from the Children of Light* by Rufus Jones. *Science and the Unseen World* by Arthur Stanley Eddington. Copyright 1929 by The Macmillan Co.

Cassell & Co., Ltd.: *Quaker Ways* by A. Ruth Fry

Estate of Rufus Jones: *A Small Town Boy* by Rufus Jones. Copyright 1941 by The Macmillan Co.

Friends Home Service Committee: *The Appeal of Quakerism to the Non-Mystic* by William Littleboy

Harcourt, Brace & World, Inc.: *Philadelphia Quaker* by Hannah Whitall Smith. Copyright 1950 by Harcourt, Brace Inc.

Harper & Brothers: *Roads to Agreement* by Stuart Chase. Copyright 1951 by Stuart Chase

William Hubben: *Exiled Pilgrim* by William Hubben. Copyright 1943 by The Macmillan Co.

J. B. Lippincott Co.: *Friend of Life* by Elizabeth Gray Vining. Copyright 1958 by Elizabeth Gray Vining

Liveright Publishers: *Two Quaker Sisters* by Elizabeth Buffum Chace & Lucy Buffum Lovell. Copyright 1937 by Liveright Publishing Corp.

Macmillan Company, New York: *Finding the Trail of Life* by Rufus M. Jones Copyright 1926 by The Macmillan Co., © 1954 by Mary Hoxie Jones

Pendle Hill: *Christ in Catastrophe* by Emil Fuchs. *By-Ways in Quaker History* edited by Howard H. Brinton. Copyright 1944 by Pendle Hill

A. D. Peters: *The English Mystics* by Gerald Bullett. Copyright 1950 by Gerald Bullett. Published by Michael Joseph Ltd.

Henry Regnery Co.: *The World of Science* by Max Picard. Copyright 1952 by Regnery

Withers & Co.: *Unforgotten Years* by Logan Pearsall Smith. Copyright 1937, 1939 by Logan P. Smith

Yale University Press: *A Quaker Childhood* by Helen Thomas Flexner. Copyright 1940 by Helen Thomas Flexner

Every effort has been made to credit the sources of copyrighted material used in this book. If any such acknowledgment has been inadvertently omitted or miscredited, receipt of such information would be appreciated.

CONTENTS

v

The Convictions (1)

PART THREE

QUAKERS IN THE WORLD

Children of Birthright Quakers

The Convinced (2)

The Convictions (2)

A QUAKER CHRONOLOGY

DATES	QUAKER HISTORY	DATES	GENERAL HISTORY
1624	Birth of George Fox	1625	Accession of Charles I
		1630	Beginning of Puritan migration to Massachusetts
		1634	Founding of Maryland
		1636	Founding of Harvard College
		1642–46	First Civil War in England
1643	George Fox becomes a religious "seeker"		
1644	Birth of William Penn	1644	Milton's *Areopagitica*
1647	George Fox finds the Light Within, begins to preach		
		1648	Second Civil War
		1649	Execution of Charles I
1652	George Fox on Pendle Hill sees a vision of "a great people to be gathered": beginning of Quaker movement		
		1653–58	Oliver Cromwell Lord Protector of England
1655	James Nayler's entry into Bristol and trial by Parliament		
1656	First Quakers in North America		
1659–61	Four Quakers hanged in Boston		

Year		Year	
1661	Establishment of New England Yearly Meeting	1660	Restoration of Charles II
1662–88	Systematic persecution of Quakers in England	1662	Quaker Act (Quakers forbidden to meet)
		1663	Charter of the Carolinas
		1664	First Conventicle Act (directed against all Nonconformists)
		1666	Great fire of London
1667	"Convincement" of William Penn	1667	Milton's *Paradise Lost*
1668	First Quaker schools in England		
1670	Trial of William Penn and William Meade	1670	Second Conventicle Act (climax of persecution)
1671–73	George Fox in America		
1675	Quakers acquire West New Jersey		
1676	Robert Barclay's *Apology*, greatest work of Quaker theology		
	Meeting for Sufferings organized in London	1678	Bunyan's *Pilgrim's Progress*
1681	William Penn's charter for Pennsylvania		
1682	William Penn in America; beginning of "Holy Experiment" in Pennsylvania		
1683	First Quaker school in Pennsylvania	1685	Accession of James II

QUAKER HISTORY		GENERAL HISTORY
	1687	Sir Isaac Newton's *Principia Mathematica*
	1688-89	"Glorious Revolution" in England; accession of William and Mary
	1689	Toleration Act
	1690	Locke's *Essay Concerning Human Understanding*
Protest of Germantown Quakers against slavery	1688	
Death of George Fox	1691	
Penn's *Some Fruits of Solitude*	1693	
Publication of Fox's *Journal*	1694	
John Archdale Governor of Carolina	1695-96	
Penn's second visit to America	1699-1701	
	1702	Accession of Queen Anne
First written book of discipline of Philadelphia Yearly Meeting	1704	
	1714	Accession of George I
Death of William Penn	1718	
	1726	Swift's *Gulliver's Travels*
James Logan demonstrates function of pollen in fertilizing Indian corn	1727	
	1733	Pope's *Essay on Man*; Voltaire's *Letters Concerning the English Nation*; Founding of Georgia

1738	John Wesley's conversion; beginning of the Methodist movement
1740–45	Climax of Great Awakening (religious revival) in American colonies
1754–63	French and Indian War
1754	Jonathan Edwards' *Freedom of the Will*
1765	Stamp Act
1769	Richard Arkwright invents spinning frame James Watt invents steam engine
1773	Boston Tea Party
1775-83	American Revolution
1776	Declaration of Independence

1737	Adoption of "birthright membership" in England
1738	First written book of discipline in England
1751	John Bartram's *Observations*
1756	Quakers relinquish control of Pennsylvania legislature; end of "Holy Experiment"
1758	John Woolman persuades Philadelphia Yearly Meeting to condemn slaveholding by Friends
1774	Publication of John Woolman's *Journal*
1777	Seventeen Philadelphia Quakers exiled to Virginia for refusing to take oath of allegiance
1781	Formation of "Free Quakers" ("Fighting Quakers")

QUAKER HISTORY	GENERAL HISTORY
	1787 Constitutional Convention
	1788 George Washington elected President
	1789–99 French Revolution
1790 Moses Brown applies power-driven machinery to spinning of cotton yarn at Pawtucket, R.I.: beginning of Industrial Revolution in U.S.	
1791 William Bartram's *Travels* (influenced English Romantic poets)	
	1793 Invention of cotton gin
	1794 Thomas Paine's *Age of Reason*
1796 York Retreat, first modern mental hospital, founded by Friends in England	
	1798 *Lyrical Ballads* by Wordsworth and Coleridge
1799 Westtown School, first American Quaker boarding school, founded Beginning of Quaker migration to Northwest Territory	
	1800 Election of Thomas Jefferson
	1801 Climax of Great Revival on American frontier
	1803 Louisiana Purchase
	1804 Napoleon crowned Emperor of France

1806	First Quakers in Indiana (Whitewater, near Richmond)		
1807		Embargo Act
1808	John Dalton states atomic theory	1808	End of foreign slave trade in U.S.
		1812–14	War of 1812
1813	Elizabeth Fry begins prison reform work at Newgate	1814	First steam locomotive built by George Stephenson in England
1816	First Peace Society in England, founded by William Allen and Joseph T. Price		
1817	Friends Asylum, Frankford, Pa., first modern mental hospital in U.S.		
		1819	Washington Irving's *Sketch Book*
		1820	William E. Channing's "Baltimore sermon," manifesto of Unitarian movement
			Missouri Compromise
1821	Benjamin Lundy begins publication of *The Genius of Universal Emancipation*, antislavery periodical		
1825	Edward Pease opens Stockton and Darlington Railway, first passenger railroad		
1827–28	Hicksite-Orthodox "separation"		

QUAKER HISTORY		GENERAL HISTORY	
		1828	Repeal of Test Act in England allows nonconformists to hold public office
			Election of Andrew Jackson
		1831	William Lloyd Garrison begins publication of *The Liberator*
		1832	Great Reform Bill in England
1833	Joseph Pease, first Quaker elected to Parliament	1833	Emancipation of slaves in British colonies
	Whittier publishes *Justice and Expediency*, his first important antislavery tract		
	Haverford School (later college), Pennsylvania, founded		
1835	First Quakers in Iowa	1836	Emerson's *Nature*
		1837	Accession of Queen Victoria
1837	New Garden Boarding School (later Guilford College), North Carolina, founded		
		ca.1840–60	"Underground Railroad" at its height
1843	John Bright enters Parliament		
1845	Wilburite–Gurneyite "separation" in New England	1846–48	Mexican War
1846	Levi Coffin settles in Cincinnati, "President" of Underground Railroad	1846	Potato famine in Ireland
1846–47	Quaker famine relief in Ireland		

1847	Boarding School at Richmond, Indiana (later Earlham College), founded	1850	Fugitive Slave Law passed
1848	Lucretia Mott (with Elizabeth Cady Stanton) organizes first women's rights convention	1851	Melville's *Moby Dick*
		1852	Harriet Beecher Stowe's *Uncle Tom's Cabin*
		1854	Thoreau's *Walden*
1854	Wilburite-Gurneyite "separation" in Ohio	1854–55	Crimean War
		1855	Whitman's *Leaves of Grass*
		1859	Darwin's *Origin of Species*
		1860	Election of Abraham Lincoln
		1861–65	Civil War
1862	Quakers undertake relief and educational work for freed slaves	1863	Emancipation Proclamation
1864	Swarthmore College, Pennsylvania, founded		
1866	Whittier's *Snow-bound*	1865–77	Reconstruction in South
1869	American Friends undertake supervision of Indian agencies in Nebraska, Kansas, and Indian Territory	1867	Second Reform Bill in England
1870–71	British Quaker war relief in Franco-Prussian War	1870–71	Franco-Prussian War

	GENERAL HISTORY		QUAKER HISTORY
1873		1873	First Quaker meeting on Pacific Coast (San José, California)
		ca. 1875	Introduction of "pastoral system" in some Quaker meetings, especially in Midwest
1882	British intervention in Egypt	1882	John Bright resigns from British cabinet in protest against bombardment of Alexandria
		1891	Whittier College, California, founded
1898	Spanish-American War		
		1900	Friends General Conference (Hicksite) established
1901	Death of Queen Victoria		
		1902	Five Years Meeting (Orthodox-Gurneyite) established
		1903	Woodbrooke Settlement (adult school near Birmingham, England) established
1912	Election of Woodrow Wilson		
1914–18	First World War	1914	War Victims' Relief Committee established by English Friends
1917	U.S. enters First World War	1917	American Friends Service Committee established by Rufus M. Jones and others
1920	Founding of League of Nations	1920–22	Quaker child-feeding program in Germany
		1924	German child-feeding resumed
1929	Beginning of Great Depression		

1932	Election of Franklin D. Roosevelt
1939-45	Second World War
1941	Attack on Pearl Harbor, U.S. enters Second World War
1945	First atomic bomb exploded at Alamagordo, N.M.
	Charter of the United Nations
1950	Korean War

1930	Pendle Hill (adult school at Wallingford, Pennsylvania) established
1931	Quaker child-feeding program in American coal fields
1936	Wider Quaker Fellowship established (for "friends of the Friends")
1937-39	Non-partisan Quaker relief work in Spanish Civil War
1937	Friends World Committee for Consultation established
1939-46	American and British Friends carry on war relief in Europe and Asia
1943	Friends Committee on National Legislation established (to present Quaker viewpoints to Congress and to inform Friends on legislative issues)
1947	Nobel Peace Prize awarded to American Friends Service Committee and Friends Service Council (Great Britain)

INTRODUCTION

Editor's Note: In keeping with our Quaker concern to use words clearly, we have made some changes in the Introduction and the section headings from Jessamyn West's original ones. We have made changes: to update references she made about the 1960s, to delete information no longer accurate, to break long bodies of text, and to render language inclusive where Jessamyn West's intent to be inclusive seemed obvious. Our hope has been to support the spirit of her desire to orient readers felicitously to this rich volume of Quaker writings. In the texts she selected to include, we have left archaic spellings, grammar, diction, and inconsistencies as we found them.

The Religious Society of Friends came into being in the middle of the seventeenth century. Though George Fox was the leader of those "persons called Quakers" (so named because some trembled or "quaked" when overflowing with the Spirit within), he cannot be said to have founded the Society of Friends. Rather it formed itself almost spontaneously as more and more people accepted the professions and practices of George Fox, having discovered in them the means by which they could bring their lives into closer accord with God.

Nor did George Fox himself have any idea of "founding" a church. A church, to his mind, was simply a group of people whose common purpose it was to relate themselves in love to God and with each other. Such a group cannot be founded. But such a group can begin and grow and its members can develop characteristics sufficiently alike to justify their being called by a like name.

The birth and rapid growth of the Religious Society of Friends in the mid-part of the seventeenth century hinged: first of all, upon the God-hungriness of the seventeenth-century individual; upon the conviction that to have missed in life a right

1

relationship with God was to have missed what was most important in life. It is almost impossible for a twentieth-century world to understand the passionate seriousness with which the seventeenth-century people addressed themselves to this hunt for God. The books they read, the preachers they listened to, the controversies they entered and the prayers they made: all were done with one purpose—to know God.

There are several reasons why the seventeenth century should have been so absorbed in this quest for a living relationship with God. The chief of these is the Puritan revolution which preceded it. Queen Elizabeth, says John Richard Green in his *Short History of the English People*, opened a book for her people, and "England became the people of a book and that book was the Bible. . . . The whole nation became in fact a Church." People, reading for themselves, felt, as never before, that they had a personal responsibility for the state of their own soul; and they felt also a pressing need to receive the assurance of their own heart, rather than of any institution, that this state was healthy.

Following the Puritan revolution (and its counterpart in their own realms) were the scientific and political revolutions of the seventeenth century. In the seventeenth century, inquiring minds for the first time began to theorize after the fact instead of before it. The Royal Society was founded in 1645 with the stated purpose of inquiring into "Experimental Philosophy." (And the accord between Quaker temperament and scientific state of mind may be seen in the fact that in the eighteenth century a member of the Religious Society of Friends had five times a better chance of becoming a member of the Royal Society than had any non-Friend.)

The scientific revolution was the result of a change in the way people thought. Individuals, or at least some individuals, ceased examining objects and events for the purpose of placing them in a previously decided-upon order. Some even began to look at the object or event *itself;* and they began to distrust the existence of qualities supposedly inherent in the object but of which they themselves could find no evidence. Such open-mindedness, such willingness to learn from the fact itself was not easy then—or now. We want the facts to fit the preconceptions. When they don't, it is easier to ignore the facts than to change the preconceptions. Garrett Hardin, in *Nature and Man's Fate*, speaks of "living with uncertainty or living falsely." Before the scientific revolution, people had not faced this dilemma. They believed that they could live truthfully *and* with certainty.

Men and women still wanted this comfort in the nineteenth century. Customers for botanical specimens would not buy a specimen which did not fit neatly into the niche of a preconceived genus or species. "What they wanted," wrote Lyell, "was names, not things."

This might have been, in reverse, Fox's motto. "Seek things, not names." It was out of his dissatisfaction with names as substitutes for experience that he began his search for a God he could know "experimentally." This search, this desire to go beyond the name, constitutes the basis for the existential revolution in religion of which the Quakers are still the most extreme example. But before George Fox began his search, found his answer, and set forth upon his lifelong walk to tell people that "there was one, even Christ Jesus," who could speak to the seeker's condition, seventeenth-century England had been filled with men and women also searching for a means by which they could know God more immediately and personally.

Many such persons are represented in this volume. Very few came to Quakerism without some history of previous spiritual searching. Of those included here, Mary Penington's account is fullest. Not included in this volume, but recommended to all for its vivid picture of life in the seventeenth century, is Mary Penington's letter to her grandson in which she tells him of his grandfather, Sir William Springett. Mary Penington, before she married Isaac Penington, was Sir William's wife and the life of the two Springetts—young, wealthy, gifted, titled—was a search for reality.

Isaac Penington, Mary's second husband, became one of the early Quakers' most appealing writers—and spent, because of his convictions, many years in English jails. Penington was originally a member of that religious sect which called itself, with Christian humility, simply "Seekers." As a Seeker he had

considered the Quakers "a poor weak silly contemptible generation." But it was the Seeker's temperament, the desire to know
God experimentally, which caused him finally to listen to and
examine the truths published by the Quakers and, convinced by
them, to become a Quaker himself.

A REVOLUTION'S MESSAGE

Though not contributing directly to the rapid growth of the
Society of Friends, the political revolution and the advance
toward democracy which seventeenth-century England
experienced provided a climate suitable for the expansion of
the Society. The Puritan revolution, which had emphasized
afresh the individual's responsibility before God for his or her
own soul, made it seem reasonable that any man or woman who
could meet God without intermediaries, and who was dear to
God, need not be so bashful before kings and courtiers as to
refrain from voicing his or her deepest convictions. Though the
circumstances we have just been reviewing prepared the way for
Fox, they did no more than that. Without the determination of
seventeenth-century men and women to discover the best
means by which a close relation could be developed between
themselves and God; without the emphasis placed by science on
the thing itself rather than on the name; without the newly
developed regard for the individual in politics and in literature
(this was the century of the journal, the diary, and the personal
essay); without these, Fox and his message would have been
neither heard nor heeded with the same enthusiasm. But we
must not make the mistake of thinking that any message, any
gospel, any individual, would have succeeded. There were
hundreds of people and hundreds of messages; and of most of
them we hear no more. Fox was nurtured by the seventeenth
century; his idiom, his cast of mind was of his age. But he
succeeded as he did in the seventeenth century because people
felt then, as they feel now, that his message was not of or for a
single century, but was instead timeless.

That message may be read at first hand in Fox's *Journal*,
with which the Quaker writing in this volume begins. I shall do

no more than suggest what there was in it to draw so many men and women so quickly to it. The message was revolutionary and, though accepted today without the seventeenth-century hullabaloo, it is perhaps practiced with less ardency today than then. George Fox, says the historian G. M. Trevelyan, was the first to teach "that Christian qualities matter much more than Christian dogma." For their lack of dogma, seventeenth-century Quakers suffered; but by their Christian qualities they succeeded.

George Fox, who exemplified the qualities and attacked the dogma, was born in 1624, the son of a Leicestershire weaver. Like many another of his century, Fox was early absorbed in a study of the nature of an individual's relationship with God and the means by which this relationship might be so perfected as to permit each person to live here on earth in the full realization of what he or she was in truth: a child of God. Shocked by the discrepancy between the lives and the professions of those who professed to be Christians, he left his home at the age of nineteen, took to field and road, seeking help, advice, and consolation from the "professors" and "priests." Finding no help in them, he heard at last a voice which said, "There is one, even Christ Jesus, that can speak to thy condition." As his search continued he said, finally, that he had come to know God, "experimentally." By which he meant that he had learned of God—as Keats said all learning came to him, "on his pulses." He and the knowledge had become one; that is, it was not a cerebral "notional" knowledge, apprehended without participation, without "a becoming." In the spiritual realm, Fox said, nothing could be truly known from the outside, or on hearsay, no matter what the reputation of the sayer. To know "experimentally" in this realm was to become one of the elements of the experiment, to enter the crucible where the fusion takes place—and without this fusion there was no true knowledge.

He was sent, Fox said, to bring people to know the "truth in the heart," as opposed to what, unless experienced there, was not *known* at all, but was apprehended only as a "notion."

Specifically, Fox's preachings recommended from the first many of the practices which have since become identified with Friends. Friends worshiped together without paid clergy, and in silence unless a member of the meeting was "moved by the spirit" to speak. This does not mean that there was not considerable preaching at Quaker meetings, but it was a preaching for which all—men and women alike—were responsible. Fox not only valued the silence, the absence of what was cut-and-dried; he valued the effectiveness of the group's seeking together openings through which new insights concerning a person's relationship with God might be learned—and which could be learned only by the *group*.

Two of the practices of the early Quakers stemmed from their conviction that the only pertinent differences between individuals were spiritual ones. They kept their hats on their heads and refused to doff them even when they encountered their "betters." They used the familiar "thee" and "thou" to all persons, not, as did others, reserving "thee" and "thou" for familiars and inferiors. They refused to have one language which flattered and one which devaluated.

Since they believed that everyone was spiritually better off if the responsibility for preaching was assumed by the entire meeting, they could not, with the approval of their consciences, pay the state-required tithes to support a paid clergy; for thus they would help perpetuate that which hindered people's spiritual growth.

Likewise, believing that God is in everyone and "that the Light lighteth every man that cometh into the world," they could not subscribe to the superstition that God must be worshiped only in, as Fox called them, "steeplehouses." God was as much at home in house, field, or street, as in a building called a "church." A "church" was a people, not a building, and the Quakers refused to pay the tithes which kept up these buildings—and kept up with them a doctrine which denied the omnipresence of God.

Friends refused to take legal oaths, since by doing so they acquiesced in the assumption that, unless under oath, one was not obliged to tell the truth. They persisted in this, as some of the selections which follow will show, in spite of great suffering and enormous economic loss to themselves.

They believed that they could not do unto others as they would be done by, and kill, either as soldiers or as individuals. They believed that they could not be true followers of a Christ who said, "Turn the other cheek," "Love one another," "Blessed are the peacemakers," and use violence on any occasion. Hence they refused to serve in the army and made no effort to defend themselves when they met, as they constantly did, with personal violence.

They wore simple drab-colored clothes (although they did not do so because of any *rule* of the Society, as Margaret Fox pointed out later), as a sign that they believed that what was inward was more important than what was outward; and they did so because they had scruples from the first about spending time and energy for the production of unnecessary finery while others were without necessities. They also thought it important to let others know *who* they were. And Thomas Ellwood in his *Journal*, much of which is included here, writes of the courage it took to announce himself publicly to be a Quaker by wearing "Quaker" clothes. Quakers encountered the derision and mob violence reserved for people of color today. Their skins were the right color, but they voluntarily assumed a costume which wasn't. They became in their own day, to use Norman Mailer's phrase in a different context, "White Negroes."

Connected with this emphasis on simplicity—which extended beyond home and dress to the arts—was the conviction that people's faculties were not sufficiently strong to permit them both to seek God and to indulge in worldly vanities. In these matters folks had, they thought, to make their choice. The Quakers choose God.

QUAKER THEOLOGY

On matters of theology the Quakers were and are, in the minds of many, pitifully lacking. They had and have no systematized theological abstractions, no creeds, no articles of faith, no catechisms. Barclay, whose writing follows Penn's in this volume, is the only recognized Quaker theologian. The spiritual convictions which Quakers held made impossible the codifying of belief into the rigidity of "a theological system," under which, in the words of R. A. Knox (and for this reason he deplores it) one could "shelter." The Quakers had and wanted one shelter only, and that was a mutuality of love experienced between God and the people here on earth. Without this, dogma was sacrilegious; with it, it was unnecessary.

Fox did have deep spiritual convictions and these, as he tramped northward on his first preaching trip, he voiced. Because Fox's openings as to spiritual truths spoke to their own conditions, he drew thousands to him. First of all, he preached that there was in each person a "light," "that of God," sufficient—did one intensify and enlarge it, by turning it toward God, its source—to make that individual one with God. The degree to which this oneness could be achieved was a much-debated question between Fox and those who thought him wrong. "They," Fox said, "cried up sin." "He," they said of Fox, "by preaching the spiritual perfectibility of man and the omnipresence and potency of the Light, denies the potency of Christ the Saviour and His death on the Cross." He also, they believed, by calling the Bible not the "Word" of God, but "God's words," subtracted something from the glory of God and exposed men and women to the vagaries of their own unstable nature. Fox also, his critics said, detracted from the holiness of holy writ by his belief that individuals now were as capable of spiritual insights as were those who wrote the scriptures. Fox had declared that he himself had been given openings by which truths were revealed to him which later he found in holy writ, but of which he was unaware at the time of the revelation.

So Fox walked northward in the summer of 1647, telling people that nothing of the "outward," no sacrament of baptism or communion, of marriage or confession, of "prayers said in the will of man" or tithes paid in the will of the state, was of the least relevance in determining the nature of a person's relationship with God. And not only were these practices irrelevant, they were—in the degree to which they blinded people to their real need for an experimental relationship with God—sinful.

As he made nothing of steeplehouses (except a persistent cry against them), so he made nothing of holy days, fast days,

Sundays, Easters, Christmases, and the like. Each day and season, each house and hour was alike holy, and life itself was sacramental. God lived in each hour and house to the degree that God lived in the awareness of the women and men who occupied the houses and moved through the hours. We celebrate Sunday, but we should not do so in order to forget that the same celebration is due on the other six days. Hence the Quakers called Sunday simply First-Day.

Above all, Fox preached what has been called a "practical mysticism." He himself had experienced moments of intense vision; and contemplation—if not vision—was a part of the plan for Quaker worship. Since worship meant life, not something abstracted from life, for Fox, hours and days, vestments and rites were inconsequential—and worse, stumbling blocks separating the individual from God. But union with God was not an end in itself; it was not even truly experienced if the life people lived did not exemplify God's nature: which is love. So Fox and those who became his followers were, from the beginning, people who had what we now call a "social conscience." But in the seventeenth century conscience had not yet been departmentalized into bits useful for this or that while other bits were temporarily put out to grass. The Quakers were, whatever their peculiarities of practice, Christians who did not believe they could *be* so and ignore the Golden Rule. So from the beginning Quakers were noted for their good works.

In accounting for the great numbers of people who became Quakers in the decade which followed George Fox's first preaching journey into Yorkshire, another element in addition to the times and the doctrine itself should be taken into account—and that is the enormously confident, robust, convinced, courageous, and magnetic personality of Fox himself. But the three together—the man, the message, and the times made the Society of Friends.

That the blood of martyrs fertilizes causes is a truism, though there is probably as much cynicism as truth in the saying. While it is true that the willingness of human beings to die for the most outrageous causes would indicate that people are drawn by a death-wish to what promises death, yet it may be supposed that there are also people who value life too much not to risk it for the sake of those qualities which give life meaning to them.

Within fifteen years after the first preaching trip of George Fox, four thousand Quakers had been jailed; thirty-three had died in England as the result of prison abuses, and three in America had been hanged. The Quakers accepted, and those in power inflicted, punishment for offenses which seem to us trivial. The Quakers accepted because non-resistance was their policy, and those in power persecuted because what the Quakers stood for threatened their power.

Until the passage of the Conventicle Acts in 1664–70 which forbade the unauthorized meeting of more than five persons, the authorities had slender grounds upon which to base their arrests of Quakers. It is often asked, "Why did the Quakers persist in practices which appear to us to have been of little significance?" They persisted, and the authorities persecuted, because both knew that back of the symbolic act, performed or refused, tremendous issues were at stake. The Quakers had only to lift the hat, take the vow, bury and marry according to rule, pay the tithe, abjure the use of "thee" and "thou," cease meeting openly, refrain from "traveling without cause," on the Lord's Day, to escape trouble. But to examine one of these offenses only, "hat honor": the tremendous significance to seventeenth-century English society of this seemingly trivial act can be seen in Thomas Ellwood's history of his life. By refusing to doff the hat to their "betters," Quakers were saying, "Under God we have no betters save those of greater spirituality than we." And by punishing them for the refusal to doff it the authorities were saying, "Any such evaluating of persons would revolutionize the established social and political order."

By refusing to take oaths, Quakers were saying, "There should be no difference between official and personal truth." And by jailing Quakers for refusing the oath, authorities were saying (as we now say of the differences between personal and official violence) "The two cannot be judged by the same standards."

By refusing to pay tithes to the state church, Quakers were saying, "A man must not support with his money what he does not support with his conscience." And the authorities were saying, when they punished, "The state decides what a man does with his money and his conscience."

What was at stake for the orthodox, politically as well as religiously, was, as William C. Braithwaite writes in *The Beginnings of Quakerism*, craft. The same fear, says Braithwaite, "which caused the craftsmen of Diana at Ephesus to rise against Paul," caused the seventeenth-century orthodox, fearing "that their craft was in danger," to attack those who endangered it.

This fear explains a large part of the persecution. It does not explain the Quaker persistence in the practices which brought the persecution down about their ears.

True, George Fox had said that he had come to bring people "off" their old practices. But primarily the Quakers were hanging on to their own convictions, rather than attacking the "craft" of others. Braithwaite is also illuminating here. "With Fox and his followers, 'the determination to thou' all men was not a piece of capricious trifling. It flowed from the principle which pervaded his whole conduct, the desire of piercing through the husk and coating of forms in which men's hearts and souls were wrapped up and of dragging them out from their lurking places into the open light of day. By refusing the homage of the hat and the customary titles of honour, by using the plain language and declining to pledge healths Fox was witnessing for reality in life and was applying a test to the Puritan professors by which their patience and kindliness and moderation were tried. He was at the same time putting the followers of Quakerism to a test which inured them to reproach, taught them to despise the false standards of the world, and led them into the way of the cross.... The witness of Friends on points of speech and dress thus touched off some of the greatest issues of life and is not to be treated as an excrescence on their main message. We ought rather to feel that the main message, under the conditions of that age, could not have been uttered in its purity and force if Friends had shrunk from giving it fearless application to these parts of life."

That those who had the power to mete out punishment did so for other reasons than protection of "craft" must not be ignored. They were as truly of the seventeenth century as the

Friends and hence as concerned as Friends about the relationship of the individual and God. Under the Blasphemy Act of 1650 persons affirming themselves or any other creatures to be God, or God's equal, or affirming that the true God dwells in the creature and nowhere else were liable to imprisonment. Fox himself was imprisoned for blasphemy, and Quakers generally were in danger under this act because of their conviction concerning the light "that lighteth every man." Quakers did not deny the historical Jesus, but they did deny the efficacy of a Jesus who lived only in history and not in the hearts of human beings. And Fox, preaching perfection and the possibility of a life beyond sin, seemed to be saying that a person was capable of becoming as much a child of God as Jesus. Quakers, said Cotton Mather, "scoff at our imagined God beyond the stars." In a sense they did. A God *beyond* the stars they believed, was of little good to people who lived *under* the stars.

Fox addressed himself to "that of God in every one"; and the great response he received was, he believed, proof that "that of God in every one," could communicate and through the communication become more and more Godlike. To a people convinced that God could be approached, worshiped, and known only through the intermediary of priests, the participation in rites, and the subscription to certain formalized propositions about the nature of God, the individual, and their relationship, this bypassing of religious machinery appeared to be a denial of God as an entity. And not only was this blasphemous, since God, disregarded by the disregarding of the heavenly designed apparatus for knowing God, was slighted; but people's immortal souls were endangered by their failure to make use of the apparatus. And what happened to their bodies here on earth was of little moment beside the fate of the soul in eternity.

So people were, for the best of reasons, punished. They were, out of a care for their own and for other immortal souls, which by their practices might be infected, thrown into prisons (which were nearer cesspools than houses of correction), branded, maimed, beaten at cart tail, deported, despoiled of property; all in the honest and passionate desire to prove that people were not, and should not affirm themselves to be, the dwelling place less, so that the Gaol at Newgate was filled with them. An abundance of them died in prison and yet they continued their assemblies still—yea, many turned Quakers because the Quakers kept their meetings openly and went to prison for it cheerfully."

They may have gone cheerfully, but they did not go without contesting by every legal means the right of the state to send them to prison at all. The account of an eyewitness of the trial of William Penn and William Meade is a classic in the history of the jury system. The Quakers, while contending for their own rights, established precedents which guaranteed the rights of all. "The rise of the people called Quakers," wrote George Bancroft, "is one of the memorable events in the history of man. It marks the moment when intellectual freedom was claimed unconditionally by the people as an inalienable birthright."

And Brooks Adams, saying that "freedom of thought is the greatest triumph over tyranny that brave men have ever won," declares that the "battle of New England" was won by the martyred Quakers. Such battles are no doubt only skirmishes in the great war which must constantly be waged for "perfect liberty of thought and speech." But by 1700 the Quakers had won their own skirmish and had the legal right to keep their hats on; "affirm" rather than swear; use "thee" and "thou" to all or none as they liked; worship silently; attend their own meetings and travel to get there on Sunday; be buried in their own plots and married in their own way; and declare publicly that it was possible for people so to unite themselves in love with God that sin became impossible. All they had to do now was to prove it. All they had to do was to make the religious practices for which they had been willing to suffer, the means by which they could lead Godly lives—without the spur of suffering.

PRACTICAL MYSTICS

For Quakerism, as Howard Brinton says in *Friends for 300 Years*, is, like science, primarily a method. The central procedures of the method were established by the time of George Fox's death in 1691. And the central procedures remain the same today as then. This does not mean that there is anything

of God and capable of approaching God as individu
chief point of interest in this for us, in both the impo
bearing of suffering, is the proof it provides of the imp
all people, three centuries ago, of their relationship wit
the seventeenth century, says Gerald Bullett, "the nai
was in every man's mouth." George Fox entered a
heard two men "discoursing of the blood of Christ"
nary men, met to drink ale and eat cheese, neither p
maniacs. The word on every tongue today is not God
"bomb" or "sex" or "money." And discourse in in
blood is mentioned, has to do with traffic accident
These changes must be kept in mind as we reac
Friends. What seems trivial to us now was of eternal
both sides then.

As readers, we may find one practice of the Fr
seventeenth century greatly to our advantage. As p
increased, "meetings for suffering" were set up,
these being in London. To these meetings were
from the meetings for worship in other parts of Eng
of the sufferings of their members at the hands of th
These reports were later collected by Joseph Besse
we have eyewitness accounts of the clash between
the old, between a "religious society" and a poli
which was also in its own and different way "relig
accounts are almost all fascinating, and readers wi
whatsoever in Quakerism will find them excitin;
tive when read as history, as adventure, or as biogr
they are.

After the passage of the Toleration Act in 1
were permitted to meet and worship in comp
Meanwhile, by their resistance and by the blood
and by the manner in which they had shed it,
followers. Richard Baxter, the great Puritan pr
friend of Quakers, wrote, "the fanaticks calle
greatly relieve the sober people for a time; they v
and gloried in their constancy and suffering;
sembled openly—and were dragged away daily
Gaol, and yet desisted not, but the rest came ne>

sacrosanct in the method. Fox did not love method; he loved God, and the method was important only as it gave him and others a living experience of God. The method has remained more or less the same for three hundred years not because Fox introduced it and early Friends used it but because those persons who are temperamentally Quakers have found no other means so efficacious in uniting people, in love, with each other and with God. The "method" could not have been used except that it was vitalized by a belief. The belief was in the "Inner Light"; the belief that there existed in everyone "that of God"; the belief, as Fox stated it, that with the Light it was possible to "answer the Light in every one (which comes from Christ) though they hate it."

In this paragraph from Caroline Stephens' *Quaker Strongholds*, the belief is fully stated, the method touched upon.

The one cornerstone of belief upon which the Society of Friends is built is the conviction that God does indeed communicate with each of the spirits. He has made in a direct and living inbreathing of some measure of the breath of His own Life, that He never leaves Himself without a witness in the heart as well as in the surroundings of man; that measure of light, life or grace thus given increases by obedience; and that in order clearly to hear the Divine Voice speaking within us we need to be still; to be alone with Him in the secret place of His presence; that all flesh should keep silence before Him.

This practice, the practice of the group "in keeping silence before Him," Howard Brinton calls "group mysticism." Many people shy away from the word "mysticism." But they shy away even more from the purpose of the group in this mystical practice, which is to experience God directly. But it is here in this practice, call it by whatever name you like, that Quakerism must be understood—if it is to be understood at all. "Here," says John Sykes, in his study of the meeting for worship in his book *The Quakers*, "at the center of their corporate life, the start of all their works and testimonies and the connecting thread throughout their history," all effort to know the Quakers should begin.

From George Fox to Rufus Jones, there are included in this volume descriptions of the nature of the meeting for worship and testimonies as to its power to "induce," as Sykes says, "the Light of God to flood into the conscious mind, a therapy and occasion for praise and sometimes through grace for the practice of His Presence." And, as Sykes warns, the method is open to failure. "There is no recital of creed, no outward sacrament, to sustain the Quaker on his way: he relies on the silent pressure of the group feeling towards the Light, and upon occasion this fails. It requires the commitment of many years and preferably of a familiar group (which explains why Friends beg of each other to be constant in attending meetings) to see through such occasions to the experience that still abundantly waits." Though the meeting for worship, when successful, is characterized by a "silence of all flesh," it is also characterized when successful by occasions when the creature "stands like a trumpet through which the Lord speaks to his flock." "The intent of all speaking being," as Fox says, "to feel God's presence."

Samuel Bownas, a blacksmith's apprentice, was the first to consider at any length the problems of what the Quakers call "vocal ministry." He was a Quaker from youth, attended meetings, but slept the greater part of his time there. One day a Quaker preacher pointed her finger at him and said, "A traditional Quaker; thou comest to meeting as thou went from it and goes from it as thou came to it but art no better from thy coming; what wilt thou do in the end?"

This, says Bownas, was so pat to his condition that, like Saul, he was "smitten to the ground." From this awakening Bownas went on to write a study of the requirements for a gospel minister.

Lest there should be those who find in the word "mysticism" hints of esoteric trances and "private raptures," as Sykes puts it, William Littleboy's essay on Quakerism for the non-mystical has been included. God's presence may be experienced with a minimum of "feeling." The proof of the Presence is in the life lived. Two facts should now be clear. The first of these is that the method of Quakerism was established early in the life of the Society. The second fact is that the writings which follow those of the seventeenth-century Quakers in this volume are then necessarily either further expositions of the method by later members of the Society, or accounts of the "concerns," "insights," "openings," and "testimonies" (to use a variety of Quaker words) which came to the Quakers as a result of their "method"—that is, of their practice of "group mysticism" for purposes of experiencing the presence of God.

If all the reader wants to know is the nature of Quakerism, one can, having read Fox, Penn, Barclay, and Penington, put down the book. The gist of the matter is there. Further reading can do only two things: first, open up and clarify meanings through hearing them expressed differently; and second, satisfy that interest in cause and effect inherent in us all which, having heard a theory expressed, asks, "How did it work out in practice?"

No account of Quakerism, whatever the interest or lack of interest of the reader "in how it worked out," would be complete without a report of what Quakers did outside the meeting house. For no people have been more convinced than the Quakers that, if God is known "experimentally," God's love must be lived out in our relations with others. Any communion with God which does not bear this fruit of love in our lives cannot, in their opinion, have been viable. And the Quakers who have been called "mystics" have also been called "practical mystics," people who experience God for the purpose of knowing God's will and carrying it out here and now. Their "practice of the Presence" is for purposes not of *feeling* good, but of *being* good. And the good people act. They act, as Woolman says, "so as not to lessen the sweetness of life for others." They labor for "a perfect redemption from the spirit of oppression."

"I think," writes Caroline Stephen, "I cannot be wrong in saying that a greater value has from the first been attached by Friends to practice as compared with doctrine than is the case with other Christian bodies." Whether too much so in latter years, is a question Friends often ask themselves. But in any case much of this volume has to do with practice: with the efforts of Friends to ameliorate prison and asylum conditions; to establish work camps; to care for the distressed, displaced, and undernourished; to advance the cause of liberty, whether of minds or of persons. These practices are not, as Fox would say, "notional": they are not the results of policy; they are not pietistic; they do not stem from "social conscience"; they are not imitative; they are not the rational efforts of a commercial morality which sees that morality "pays off." They are, when they proceed from the heart of the meeting for worship, where they originated, an outward reflection into the world of that Light whose other name is love.

The individual, it is said, is what he or she does. This, I suppose, is no less true of a religious society. I have, nevertheless, not presented the Quakers as persons who oppose war, combat intolerance, and care for the distressed, by segregating under these heads their writing on these subjects. It is particularly important, it seems to me, in an era of ever increasing departmentalization and specialization, to make the attempt occasionally to see wholes and to understand what lies behind the exterior manifestations. And it is particularly important not to transfer to spiritual areas techniques of examination designed for and suited to mechanisms. The image of the Quaker, so easily arrived at by a superficial pigeonholing of activities, as a "do-gooder," or a "band" of "well-to-do reformers," as R. A. Knox calls them, obscures the fact that behind the deed lives the person; and behind the person, in the case of the Quaker, the meeting. And in the meeting, if it succeeds in any degree, is God. God is the other half of the meeting, its justification and the One met. If this, which is the central fact of Quakerism, be made clear, even though practices which grow out of the meeting are somewhat obscured, the failure of this volume to segregate the Quakers according to their practice will be justified.

When William Penn asked Fox what to do about the sword which he was accustomed, as a well-dressed seventeenth-century gentleman, to wear at his side, Fox reputedly replied, "Wear it as long as thee can." By which Fox meant: It is not the exterior trapping but the interior state which matters. Until you become a person who *cannot* contemplate the acts for which a sword was designed, and hence abhor the sword, swordlessness for you is an imitative and even lying state. It disguises the fact that you still have a sword in the heart.

So too with the humanitarian Quaker practices. Behind them, if they are anything more than acts of self-interest designed either to lay an uneasy conscience or to build up healthy markets—or both—is the union of lives with God.

QUAKER MONEY MAKERS

The first section of this volume has had to do largely with two matters: Quaker beliefs and the efforts of Quakers to preserve these beliefs and survive. The second and third sections have to do less with physical than with spiritual survival; less with accounts of the vividness of the realized Presence, and more with the practice of love in "the outward." It is quite natural that, as Quakers were required to spend less energy staying out of prison and absorbing physical punishment, they had more energy to give to ameliorating the conditions under which others lived. It is also quite natural that with energies freed, and practicing in business a kind of integrity new to business, the Quakers should flourish commercially. Fox himself had anticipated this; and non-Quakers had urged as one of the reasons for stamping out the Quakers, "If we let these people alone they will take the trading of the nation out of our hands." It was not quite that bad. But it was bad enough, many students of Quakerism feel, to make Quakers less willing than they had been to lose all for their beliefs. They had more to lose now and, this being true, they were less quick than they had been to stake everything on absolute righteousness. They no longer saw the need of such dangerous testimonies against public immorality and private greed as their forebearers had made in the seventeenth century. They practiced with increased rigidity the old, already won and increasingly meaningless acts: plain dress, plain speech, plain meeting houses, plain affirmations. But those were, increasingly—in another realm—no more than Penn's sword, the accouterments of a well-dressed eighteenth-century Quaker.

Except for John Woolman, says Sykes, "historians lose interest in the Quakers after seventeen hundred." They do so because Quakers were no longer contributing anything new to religious thought; nor were they putting the convictions they already had to work to serve new conceptions of state and personal morality. And Quakers were no longer doing these things, Sykes believes, because after seventeen hundred too much of their creative energy was going into money-making. The switch-over had not been intentional. The Quakers made their money in the first place by being good Quakers. But most lacked Woolman's insight, which revealed to him that human nature was not sufficiently rich to be thus divisible between God's work and Mammon's without God's suffering (to say nothing of Mortals); and he saw that, once money was acquired, people were loath to advocate that which would diminish it. Or, if they had these insights, most people lacked Woolman's courage to combat both dangers by limiting the time spent in acquiring money—"The business of our lives," Woolman wrote, "is to turn all the treasures we possess into the channel of universal love." And by "treasure" Woolman meant *all*, money and energy and talent.

Those inclined to gauge intensity in terms of a flamboyant vocabulary and a frenetic rhetoric may miss, in the simple prose of Woolman, the record of a life stretched taut by God-awareness toward as complete an expression of universal love as any of which we have knowledge. John Woolman had nothing he would call a "social conscience." When a man has turned the whole of his life into channels of universal love, named splinters of it are not recognizable in that flood. Nevertheless Woolman was for a time the "social conscience" of the world in the matter of slavery. A hundred years before the enslavement by human beings of other human beings came to bloody issue, Woolman not only saw the evil (to which others, profiting by the practice, were blind) and spoke out against it, but so lived his own life that he should not in any way profit by the use of men, women, and children treated as domestic animals.

John Woolman was all of a piece. The sword he did not wear was *not* in his heart. Nor was the act he performed, the word he spoke, outward only. They also came from the heart, so that a native American, after hearing Woolman speak, said, "I love to feel where words come from." The native speaker loved God, for Woolman's words came from the union of himself with God. It is a pity that George Fox did not live to know John Woolman, for no other person, not Fox himself, has more completely lived out the Quaker ideal of the dominance of self-will by "that of God."

Though historians may, as Sykes says, lose interest in the Quakers after seventeen hundred, humanitarians do not. The first hospital for the insane, treating patients as diseased persons rather than criminal clowns, was established by the Quaker Joseph Tuke in York in 1796. Elizabeth Fry began her work with prisoners. Schools for the poor were established. Political equality for women was advocated. Nevertheless it is true that these were ameliorating activities rather than a radical striking at the roots of abuses. "No Quaker," Sykes says, "was in prison at this time." True, it was not as easy to get in prison as it had been in the sixteen hundreds, but any Quakers as uncompromising in their efforts to establish the kingdom of heaven on earth as Fox had been could probably have made the grade. Elizabeth Fry, born a daughter of John Gurney of Earlham, of the banking Gurneys and married into another of the great Quaker banking families of the day, led the movement for prison reform—and did so often enough from the dinner tables of the heads of government responsible for the conditions that needed reforming. Fox, on the other hand, had refused to eat the bread of Cromwell. Elizabeth Fry in some ways anticipates Buchman as much as she recalls Fox.

Whatever the historian may feel, the reader finds the Quaker writing of the second period changed, and interest will wax or wane depending upon one's own nature. The "classics" of Quaker writing are products of the earlier period when the Quaker experience and temperament found in the forms which that age had developed and made its own—the personal essay, the journal, the diary, the memoir—the perfect means for the expression of religious life. Fox, Ellwood, Penn, Penington, Roberts, Barclay, Woolman, these are the great names in Quaker writing. Never, perhaps, has any people found at hand a means at once so suited to its own purpose and so popular with readers of the day. The new evaluation of the individual in the seventeenth century gave writers a new sense of the importance of their own lives; and non-writers, sharing this interest in the individual, were eager to find to what degree their own convictions and struggles had been experienced by others.

"Before 1725," says Luella Wright in her *Literary Life of the Early Friends*, "Quakers had published over eighty religious confessions and Journals, a number probably greater than all the non-Quaker autobiographies printed in Great Britain at that time." These are, for the most part, the work of people "without the learning of the schools," to use Penn's phrase; but those interested in the spiritual lives of men and women and who value "writing which impresses . . . by the style in which it is written," will turn, as Robertson Davies urges, to "the outpourings of some of the great religious enthusiasts of the Quaker persuasion."

The important word here for us is "outpourings." The memoir, the journal, the confession perfectly suited the individual with a burning experience to report, but little literary art. One had only to have had the experience, to have known something "experimentally," to have a fair sense of chronology, a good memory, and an obvious sincerity, and a seventeenth-century audience, God-hungry, and hungry especially for God as experienced by the individual, eagerly awaited the outpouring. Seventeenth-century readers devoured these accounts of people's encounters with God with the same avidity we had, at the end of World War II, for the first-hand accounts of men and women home from the wars. The literary form instituted in the seventeenth century still prevails. It is only the subject matter which has changed.

In the second hundred years of Quakerism, two elements legislate against the production of Quaker classics. First of all, fewer Quakers seemed to be *having* burning religious experiences; and second, the novel was beginning to supplant the journal and the essay with readers. The novel is not well suited for the recounting of a religious experience—in which, of necessity, the leading character is God. The more God came into Tolstoi's writings, the worse his novels became. If, as Fox believed, the true relevance of God was "God in man," not "God beyond the stars," great novels which are also deeply religious might be written without giving offense to the imagination. But these have not yet appeared. Either God is still as far beyond the stars for most novelists as God was for Cotton Mather, or the hero irradiated with, or seeking the irradiation of, the Inner Light is too unlikely a character to hold the attention of the serious novelist.

However, some readers may, as I suggested, find the writings of later Quakers more sophisticated than those which preceded them. One element will be entirely missing: that of persecution and resistance. And another will be, in this middle period, in short supply: the burning experience of God. Now we have come to the time when Grace Church Meeting in London was attended by "the Richest Trading Men" in London; and when the predominance of "Rich Trading Men" in the Philadelphia meetings was, according to Sykes, even greater.

The Whittal-Smith-Thomas clan of Philadelphia was made up of just such traders; and since Hannah Whittal Smith, her son Logan Pearsall, and her niece Helen Thomas Flexner are all gifted writers, we can follow in their accounts the delineations of the "new Quaker" with unusual pleasure—whatever we feel about the "new Quaker" himself or herself. The "new Quaker" was no longer, as Colin Wilson labeled Fox, an "outsider." He or she was no longer, as the parson who requested Mark Rutherford not to read Fox's *Journal* to the Dorcas Society said of Fox, "not one of us." The new Quakers were, indeed, "of us"—and were frequently so wealthy, well educated, and sumptuously housed, that *we* were not of *them*.

In Hannah Whittal Smith's writings both the "new Quaker" and other attempts, through the technique of the popular nineteenth-century revival, to regain some of the spiritual awareness of the old Quaker can be seen. Accustomed as we are to thinking of the revival as a part of backwoods life, it is enlightening to see it against another background and affecting other people.

Rufus Jones, whose writings in this volume appear in the same section as those of Elizabeth Buffum Chace and the Smiths, is, though half of his life was spent in the nineteenth century, wholly of this century's Quakerism—and indeed this century's Quakerism owes more than a little of its emphasis to the example in writing and living of Rufus Jones, and that emphasis is on the Quaker strongholds (as Caroline Stephen designates them) of God within, strengthened through the meeting for worship and lived out in that "gateway to the effective practices of the Meeting for Worship . . . service for man." Rufus Jones, who said that he never doubted that his mission in life was to be "an interpreter of this religion of the inner way," was the man who went on to found—inasmuch as any one man could do so—the American Friends Service Committee. The influence of the work of this Committee may be to some extent gauged in the selections from Nora Waln and William Hubben included in this volume.

"LOVE GOD AND DO WHAT YOU PLEASE"

Rufus Jones faced, as a young man, "the pathetic deterioration of the Society—a process of cooling, hardening, stiffening, as lava once molten turns to rigid forms. A movement which had revolted against the stereotypes of secondhand religion adopted stereotypes, became too centrally concerned about minor legalisms of garb and speech and habit. The Quakers had started out to be a 'peculiar' people, open to fresh inspiration and leadership of the spirit, but their peculiarities became externalized, institutionalized, legalized. In his later years Rufus Jones looked back with half-incredulous amazement on the situation he had known in earlier years. We can hardly imagine that state of mind that would have a Monthly Meeting to disown a high-minded Friend because he owned a piano. It is difficult for us to believe the fact that 100,000 Friends were dropped from membership for marrying out of Meeting."

The preceding paragraph by Harry Emerson Fosdick is taken from his introduction to a Rufus Jones anthology. While none of Jones's writings advocating the reforms which make the Society what it is today are included in this volume, all the writings of the last section undoubtedly were influenced by his opinions and attitudes. In all of them the Quaker is envisaged once again as the person "who practices the presence" of God—

not as one who eschews pianos or espouses any individualized garb or manner. "Love God and do what you please" is again the Quaker motto.

It is an odd fact that a generation which has demonstrated so much interest in Zen Buddhism, Existentialism, and the writings of Martin Buber should not have noticed the many areas of likeness between these and Quakerism; if this interest in Zen, Buber, and Existentialism represents any true longing for a new and more satisfying way of life, one would think that Quakerism, so near at hand and so suited to our needs as members of the Western world, would have been examined. The "near at hand" may explain the lack of appeal. Because people think they know a little about the Quakers (and that little as often as not having to do with Mennonites, Shakers, or Dunkards; one woman told me, "I understand you attend a French Meeting") they are not drawn to a study of Quakerism.

Nevertheless nine-tenths of what is said by and about Zen Buddhists could be said by and about Quakers, and a very entertaining parlor game could be arranged—the purpose to guess the subject of a hundred statements: "——— is above all direct; no intermediaries, no mediators between God and man, no symbolism." Zen or Quakerism? "Zen," says R. H. Blyth in *Zen in English Literature and Oriental Classics*.

" 'Thy will be done on earth as it is in heaven' is the heart of ———?" "Zen," says Blyth again.

"The essentials of ——— can never be accurately and fully formulated, being an experience and not a set of ideas. . . ." Zen or Quakerism? "Zen," says Alan Watts.

"It is not an intellectual proof, a reasoned sequence of thoughts. It is the fact that men experience ———." Satori or God? "The presence of God," says Thomas Kelly.

"All willed morality is atrocious." Quaker or Zen? "Quaker," Pierre Cérésole.

"When the will is struggling with itself and is in conflict with itself it is paralyzed. . . ." Quaker or Zen? "Zen," says Alan Watts.

"The most fundamental distractions are not without; they are within us." Quaker or Zen? "Zen," says Robert Linssen in *Living Zen*.

This game could go on endlessly, but here are two final illustrations of the many similarities between Zen and Quakerism:

"The object of ——— is to make us intuitively sure that we have discovered in the depth of our soul the entity which goes beyond and takes the place of all individual differences and temporary changes." Zen or Quakerism? "Zen," says Anesaki.

"This is why ——— does not preach. Sermons remain words. It waits until people become stifled and insecure, driven by a secret longing." Quakerism or Zen? "Zen Buddhism," says Eugen Herregel.

The game can be terminated at once by quotations from the Quaker writers. Zen methods and Quaker methods have many similarities. The use by both of questions, for instance, which has not been discussed; but those interested in this similarity need only consult the *Quaker Book of Discipline* and any standard author on Zen. But the difference between the two can be seen at once in Ruth Fuller Sasaki's title *Zen: A Method for Religious Awakening*. Now Quakerism has also been called a "method," and surely no Friend would deny that Quakerism involves a religious awakening. But to be "awake religiously" is for the Friend no more an end in itself than being awake imaginatively, ethically, or amorously, is an end. It is what one does when he or she ceases to sleep that matters. "A man," says William Penn, "is like a watch to be valued for his going." To sit with face uncovered is not enough. "Religion itself," Penn continues, "is nothing else but Love to God and Man. He that lives in Love, lives in God. Love is above all; and when it prevails in us all, we shall all be Lovely, and in Love with God and one with another." A religious awakening which does not awaken the sleeper to love has roused the person in vain.

"Zen does not hold," writes Mrs. Sasaki, "that there is a god apart from the universe." And this she considers "the primary hindrance in understanding Zen" by Westerners. It is not a primary hindrance for Quakers, who long ago ceased to worship, with Cotton Mather, a god "beyond the stars." True, Zen, as Mrs. Sasaki says, considers a person "a cell . . . in the body of the Great Self," while Quakers reverse the imagery to say that God dwells in *our* bodies. But God dwells there, expressed or denied, as we "live in love." And it is interesting to note that Penn describes those who live in God not as Godly, but as Lovely. We have only to substitute "lovely" for "Godly" in the phrase "he was a Godly man," to see the image of a person change—change, because alas! people called Christian have too often forgotten that "to live in God is to live in Love"; so that men and women of pride and anger, of cruelty and self-righteousness, could be called "Godly."

QUAKERS AS EXISTENTIAL CHRISTIANS

Quakers are Existential Christians, and Fox, though he had not the philosophical equipment of Sören Kierkegaard, attacked in his life, the illusion against which Kierkegaard preached: "The illusion that there is such a 'thing' as Christianity, or that any 'thing,' be it creed, history, code or organization can be Christian. Only the subjective individual can be a Christian." Thus Richard Niebuhr describes Kierkegaard, and with the same words he might as truly have spoken of Fox.

Kierkegaard was in many respects waging Fox's battle two hundred years after Fox, and Niebuhr recognizes this fact when he says that at times Kierkegaard "speaks like a sixteenth-century sectarian." He speaks at times in the very words of a seventeenth-century sectarian, George Fox, and if the game of quotations had not already been carried on at so great a length it could be played once again with these two. The difference between them, who both saw so clearly that Christianity could not be "an objective something—a system of teachings, a church, a code of ethics," lies in the fact that Fox, convinced of this in his early twenties, knew "experimentally" what Christianity *could* be, and that was, in his own words, "to know a Fellowship with Christ..." "an inward light, spirit and grace. . . ." And knowing this, he preached, "directing all to the Spirit of God in themselves that they . . . might come to know Christ to be their teacher to instruct them, their counsellor to direct them, their shepherd to feed them, their bishop to oversee them; and might know their bodies to be prepared, sanctified and made fit temples for God and Christ to dwell in."

"Existentialism...involves...more what you do than what you think. . . ." This is Carl Michalson's comment on Existentialism, but it could be Fox's on Christianity, for he ceaselessly railed against a "notional" Christianity, a Christianity of definitions, creeds, and dogmas, against the conviction that Christianity could be anything less than a lived life.

There is so much to be found in Buber which is in the spirit of Quakerism that I am going to choose two quotations only from him: "All real living is meeting"; and "Every particular Thou is a glimpse through to Eternal Thou."

It is no coincidence that Friends also use the word "meeting" as descriptive of the basic act of their corporate religious life: they "meet" one another and God. They meet, a gathering of "particular Thous"; and in that gathered meeting, each Thou is an archway through which the "Eternal Thou" can be seen in a new and perhaps more vivid focusing than a Thou outside the meeting could manage.

The final section of this anthology, which could very easily, so rich is the material, have been taken up entirely with accounts of Quakers engaged in good works, is instead given over to the writings of those who have newly discovered Quakerism; or to "old" Quakers discovering anew the basic convictions of Quakers—and considering how these convictions can be so lived out as to make us all "Lovely and in Love with God and one another." That is the problem, and Quakerism is nothing else but an attempt to solve it. It is not an easy problem, for, as Penn says, "Love is the hardest lesson in Christianity."

But we have a new impetus today to search for an answer: the impetus of the knowledge that, if we fail the problem, we will very soon have a solution which will destroy the tardy solvers. Then we will all be unlovely together—a great and final meeting for suffering.

Jessamyn West
1962
Revised 1992 by Ellen Michaud

Part One

THE

BEGINNINGS

ENGLAND

IN THE

SEVENTEENTH CENTURY

The name of God was in every man's mouth.
—GERALD BULLETT

"By Their Gods Ye Shall Know Them"

[FROM *The English Mystics*]

GERALD BULLETT

[*Gerald Bullett (1893–1958), was a poet, a novelist, and the compiler of two remarkable anthologies:* The English Galaxy, *a collection of poems; and* The Testament of Light, *an anthology, in his own words,* "testifying to the 'divinity' in man, the inwardness of authority, the redemptive power of that love (within us, not elsewhere) 'whose service is perfect freedom.' " *Bullett, who was no Quaker, opened his* Testament of Light *with that excerpt from the writings of the Quaker James Nayler which begins* "You are as prone to love as the sun is to shine. . . ."

So it is fitting that a Quaker Reader should begin with a selection from Bullett's, The English Mystics. *George Fox, the first Quaker (though Fox himself did not know this till well along in his career of preaching), Bullett considers a mystic: that is, a person who gives the impression that he or she has "enjoyed contact and communion with something more real than is given in everyday experience." And, Bullett continues, "The first thing to be remembered about him [Fox] is that he lived and died (1624–1691) in a period of unparalleled religious ferment."*

The selection from Bullett which follows can give only a hint of the vigor of that ferment. But unless that ferment is, if not understood, at least known to have existed, nothing which follows in this volume can be seen in anything like its true perspective. "It is not difficult," it has been said, "to understand past times. It is impossible." The seventeenth century is more difficult for us to imagine today than is the topography of the moon. The sterile moon may contain what we will be tomorrow. The living ferment of the seventeenth century certainly made us what we are today.|

———

In the seventeenth century religion and politics were inextricably mixed. To a degree which we of today find it difficult to imagine, the name of God was in every man's mouth as a sanction for whatever conscience, self-interest, or expediency prompted him to do. The indefatigable William Laud (nicknamed parva Laus by his Oxford contemporaries) had come near to establishing theocratic rule in England; the Royalists, when the conflict between Crown and Parliament began, held fast by the comparatively novel doctrine of Divine Right; the Parliamentarians opposed the Royalists for equally godly reasons; and almost all public speeches were plentifully larded with pious unction, more especially of course those of the so-called "lecturers" or licensed preachers (not priests) who frequented marketplaces and discoursed on Sunday afternoons—an institution dating from Elizabethan times. The nation was divided into warring religious factions, each of which, by an entertaining coincidence, was the sole repository of God's truth. Speciously composing these differences was the legal fiction that the whole population of England, estimated at something under five millions, belonged to the established Anglican Church, though obvious exceptions were confessed Papists (or Recusants) at one extreme and Puritan Separatists (or Dissenters) at the other. Inside the Church, among the clergy themselves, there were two main parties of opinion: (i) the non-separatist Puritans, eager for further reforms, alert to exclude all rites and ceremonies that might seem to savour of Popery, and in doctrine strongly inclined towards Calvinism; and (ii) the Prelatists or Episcopalians, who in the main detested Calvinism and were zealous defenders of the divine right of bishops, as well as of the king.

These are live issues for only a tiny minority of our countrymen today: to the rest of us it must seem that there was right and wrong on both sides, as in nearly all party disputes. If the Puritans' excessive fear of Romanism looks like a neurosis, it must be conceded that there was some historical basis for it, and that they had excellent reason to distrust the king and his cronies; and if the Prelatists were too eager in their pursuit of temporal power, it is at least to their credit that so many of them repudiated that central doctrine of John Calvin's which, in the words of Johann Kollmann, a Dutch opponent of the system, made God "both a tyrant and an executioner." The most formidable single opponent of Calvinism was the more celebrated Dutch theologian Arminius, who died some fifteen years before Charles's accession but whose teaching survived to be an influence in seventeenth-century English theology; "Arminian" and "Popish" seem to have been used as interchangeable terms of opprobrium by the English and Scottish Puritans of the time, though Arminius himself was far from being an adherent of Rome. The Synod of Dort (1619), in which English as well as Continental ecclesiastics took part, came down heavily on the side of the Calvinists; but, so far from silencing controversy, its effect in England was rather to widen the breach between the two parties. We are not concerned with the details of this historic quarrel, but we cannot begin to understand George Fox's position, still less the cruel hostility he encountered, without some notion of the main points in dispute.

Calvin (1509–1564) is one of the most influential and disastrous figures in religious history. He owed much to the earlier Reformer, Luther; but he excelled his master in dialectical skill, in personal austerity, and in the intolerant zeal with which he propagated his opinions and established in Geneva his theocratic tyranny. He and his followers took upon themselves the power of excommunication; required every citizen to subscribe publicly, on oath, to the twenty-one articles of what he was pleased to call Christian doctrine; and conducted a vigilant and punitive inquisition into private morals. It is said that the men he trained at Geneva carried his principles into almost every country in Europe; and this is incontestable. But the further statement that these principles "did much for the cause of civil liberty" is difficult to reconcile with the fact that the only liberty he allowed was the liberty to do and believe as he ordained. Everything he did, whether good or evil, was done conscientiously and for the glory of God—for the glory, however, of a God made in Calvin's own image. Though one can admire his courage, sincerity, and perseverance, and applaud at least some part of his considerable achievement, it is difficult not to see him as a man sadly self-deceived about his own motives.

The doctrine of Predestination, by which Calvin is chiefly remembered today, differs from Atheistic Determinism only in being infinitely more horrible, because it affirms the immortality of the soul and existence of an implacable Deity. His mind was dominated by two ideas: the transcendent sovereignty of God and the utter depravity of Man. God, the creator of men, had by an absolute and immutable decree predestined some of them to salvation and the rest to eternal punishment. Those that were to be saved were "called" to salvation and could not by any misbehavior forfeit their title. One can see how, at a time when life-after-death loomed large in men's minds, the persuasion of being among "the elect" must have been a prime source of confidence and power to those fortunate enough to have it. By ridding them of fear and uncertainty it would effect a great release of energy. Nor, though theoretically they could sin with comparative impunity, would they be likely to take advantage of that freedom: as God's elect they would feel it incumbent upon them to live a life of rectitude. But what of the others? What of those earnest believers who were unsure of their salvation and who knew that if in fact they were among the damned nothing they did could avert the ultimate doom? Such a one, in a later century, was the gentle-hearted Cowper.

Calvin was inexorably logical: more so indeed than most of his opponents. His doctrine of Predestination follows inescapably from assumptions which he and they had in common: it is logically implied in the notion that God the creator is an almighty omniscient person entirely separate from His creatures. He detested mysticism, as well he might; for the mystical intuition that identifies God with Love makes nonsense of his system. The God of Calvin's fancy has all the disadvantages of anthropomorphism with none of its compensations. He is personal but remote; transcendent, all-powerful, inscrutable; arbitrary in His acts and utterly indifferent to considerations of justice. Atheism is infinitely more reasonable than such a theology. "It were better to have no opinion of God at all," said Bacon, "than such an opinion as is unworthy of Him: for the one is unbelief, the other is contumely." To know God was for Calvin "the supreme end of human endeavor," though it is difficult to see what profit or satisfaction there could be in knowing a God who created men with the deliberate intention of tormenting forever all but an arbitrarily selected few of them. The position of a believer in doubt of his own "election" was indeed pitiable. God alone knew what fate God had decreed for him, and what God had decreed had been decreed before the beginning of time. Do what he might he was already destined for either salvation or damnation. Good works could not avert the one, nor works of wickedness impede the other. Even faith, though necessary to salvation, was no guarantee of it. Arguing so, many a harassed soul must have been driven to the verge of madness, and beyond it, by the hideous prospect of immortality.

Robert Barclay, the first apologist of Quakerism, says of the doctrine of Absolute Reprobation (of which he finds some traces, prior to Calvin, in Augustine and Dominicus) that "it is highly injurious to God because it makes Him the author of sin, which of all things, is most contrary to His nature." The point is sufficiently obvious, but Barclay's words are worth quoting. "If

God has decreed that the reprobated ones shall perish, without all respect to their evil deeds but only of His own pleasure, and if He hath also decreed long before they were in being or in a capacity to do good or evil that they should walk in those wicked ways by which, as by a secondary means, they are led to that end; who, I pray, is the first author and cause thereof but God, who so willed and decreed? This is as natural a consequence as can be; and therefore, although many of the preachers of this doctrine have sought out various strange, strained, and intricate distinctions to defend their opinion and avoid this horrid consequence, yet some, and that of the most eminent of them, have been so plain in the matter as they have put it beyond all doubt." He quotes Calvin himself in support of this statement. "I say," says Calvin, "that by the ordination and will of God, Adam fell. God would have man to fall. Man is blinded by the will and commandment of God. We refer the causes of hardening us to God. The highest or remote cause of hardening is the will of God. It followeth that the hidden counsel of God is the cause of hardening." There follows a citation from Calvin's friend Theodore Beza: "God hath predestinated not only unto damnation, but also unto the causes of it, whomsoever he saw meet. The decree of God cannot be excluded from the causes of corruption." In speaking of the "causes" of damnation Beza means the secondary causes, the first and sufficient cause being God's decree. The matter is prettily summed up by the last author whom Barclay quotes in this connection: "Reprobate persons are absolutely ordained to this twofold end, to undergo everlasting punishment, and necessarily to sin; and, therefore, to sin that they may be justly punished." The cream of the jest is in that word "justly."

Whatever may be the truth about God, it is clearly not here. Nor is it to be found in any intellectual formula. All that is said and written about God reveals to us, not God, but only, for good or ill, the minds and hearts of men. By their gods ye shall know them. We cannot positively assert that the full rigor of the Calvinistic logic was accepted by all the Puritan parsons to whom Fox resorted, first to seek their counsel and afterwards to controvert and exhort them; but undoubtedly the disease was widespread. It is of the essence of his historical situation that he found himself spiritually homeless, an exile among worldlings on the one hand, and on the other among men whose religion was (in his view) either empty or evil. The child of "godly" parents, in matters of conduct he was by training and inclination puritanical: this at least he had in common with the chief of his enemies. But in all else he was a protestant against the protestantism of his day. He was not, like his young apostle Robert Barclay, a student of theology. The whole point of his mission or ministry was to insist on the primacy of experience, to exalt spiritual "light" above mere "notions." He became, once he had found himself, a great disputer, a man of many words; but all his words amounted to little more than the assertion that religion, God, is nothing if not an inward experience: which is the testimony of the mystic in all ages. In seventeenth-century protestantism he found, and hotly repudiated, two stupidities which survive in an attenuated form even today: bibliolatry, the fetishistic worship of the Old and New Testaments; and that doctrine of total human depravity which implies the utter separation of man from God. Against these traditional tenets of protestantism he affirmed the inwardness of authority and the presence of God in every human soul. His opponents "could not endure to hear of purity [of conscience] and of victory over sin." Again and again he tells us of how the "professors"—by which he means professed believers in religion—"pleaded for sin." He found among these men no one who in the crisis of his young manhood could "speak to his condition." They seemed to him to be eaten up with "notions," concerned only with a mechanical observance of ceremonies and with preaching doctrines that were either plainly untrue or spiritually null and void.

It was probably his disgust with this state of affairs that led him to out-puritan the Puritans and with characteristic indiscrimination denounce sacramental ritual and refuse the name of "churches" to the buildings in which they preached. Notwithstanding his dislike of bibliolatry he could bandy texts as well as the next man and was always ready to cap quotation with quotation and beat the "professors" at their own game. He was quick, and shrewd, and deeply sincere; but being unschooled in things of the intellect, and having nothing but mother wit to guide him, he made no distinction between the essentials and the inessentials of his teaching and was as stubborn in trivial matters as in great. He put himself and others to much trouble by refusing to doff his hat in court; and would quote chapter and verse to justify the refusal, for he was always ready to argue your head off. The men he had to deal with were more incensed by this kind of intransigence than their successors in high places today would be, because, being men of their time, they took it seriously. Though they were resolved to subdue his turbulent spirit, and very ready to turn his scruples into a weapon against him, there is a sense in which they understood them better than we can; for they lived in the same mental world as he, a world of zealous opinionativeness and hairsplitting literalism in which the notion of mutual toleration had no part. In Charles the First's England a man was either right or wrong in his opinions; if wrong he must be corrected; if resolute in error he must be persecuted as a matter of course. That was taken for granted by all parties, just as today it is taken for granted by totalitarian governments. The same rule held during the period of the Commonwealth, despite Cromwell's promise of religious liberty; and it persisted after the Restoration despite Charles the Second's wish to be amiable; because neither Protector nor King proved able to control the persecuting lust of the dominant religio-political party, though it is true that each of them did, on occasion, intervene on Fox's behalf. Fox and his enemies understood each other because, in our slang sense of the phrase, they spoke the same language. To us, living three centuries later and in an utterly different intellectual climate, it is almost a foreign language.

THE MESSAGE OF
GEORGE FOX

. . . reaching that of God in every one.
—GEORGE FOX

"*That All May Know the Dealings of the Lord
with Me . . .*"

[FROM *Journal*]

GEORGE FOX

[*All that follows in this volume is but the long shadow cast by George Fox
(1624–1691), that "new and heavenly minded man," as William Penn
called him. He was "new and heavenly minded" in that he preached
and practiced, with greater conviction and vigor than any other
seventeenth-century preacher, the need to abandon "the concept of faith
as intellectual adherence to propositional beliefs." (This phrase, which
so exactly fits Fox, is from Carl Michalson's* The Hinge of History
*"an existential approach to the Christian Faith.") The range and
complexity of George Fox's nature is suggested in the fact that if you study
mysticism, you find George Fox; and if you approach Christianity
existentially, he is there also. That is, George Fox encompassed, in his
thrust toward the divine, ways earlier than his own, and ways which we
are only now beginning to understand and define.*

Fox has been called a saint. If so, he was a saint from whose muscled jaw, when he turned the other cheek, the attacker was liable to fall back, bruised. There are many records of Fox's life. The early Quakers, for all they practiced silence in worship, were (and perhaps because of it) untiring communicators outside the meeting house. Fox himself was, considering his life of action, a prodigious writer. His Journal *is one of the great documents of a century of masterpieces. Its contents were, for the most part, not set down from day to day as were those of Pepys'* Diary. *Instead, they were recalled from memory and from notes, and dictated to an amanuensis. A complete account of the manner in which the* Journal *was written, and has been preserved, is to be found in the Preface to the Cambridge University Press edition, edited by J. Nickalls, from which the selections in this volume have been taken.*

Fox, like any complex person, cannot be easily summed up. When he says in his Journal *of a man, "And the truth came so over him that he grew loving," he reveals in one sentence his life's aim. The truth Fox worked to bring to others was the possibility of a oneness with Christ; and those who experienced this "oneness" would demonstrate it by growing "loving."*]

———

That all may know the dealings of the Lord with me, and the various exercises, trials, and troubles through which he led me in order to prepare and fit me for the work unto which he had appointed me, and may thereby be drawn to admire and glorify his infinite wisdom and goodness, I think fit (before I proceed to set forth my public travels in the service of Truth), briefly to mention how it was with me in my youth, and how the work of the Lord was begun and gradually carried on in me, even from my childhood.

I was born in the month called July in the year 1624, at Drayton-in-the-Clay in Leicestershire. My father's name was Christopher Fox; he was by profession a weaver, an honest man, and there was a Seed of God in him. The neighbours called him "Righteous Christer." My mother was an upright woman; her maiden name was Mary Lago, of the family of the Lagos and of the stock of the martyrs.

In my very young years I had a gravity and stayedness of mind and spirit not usual in children, insomuch that, when I have seen old men carry themselves lightly and wantonly towards each other, I have had a dislike thereof risen in my heart, and have said within myself, "If ever I come to be a man, surely I should not do so nor be so wanton."

When I came to eleven years of age, I knew pureness and righteousness; for while I was a child I was taught how to walk to be kept pure. The Lord taught me to be faithful in all things, and to act faithfully two ways, viz. inwardly to God and outwardly to man, and to keep to "yea" and "nay" in all things. For the Lord showed me that though the people of the world have mouths full of deceit and changeable words, yet I was to keep to "yea" and "nay" in all things; and that my words should be few and savoury, seasoned with grace; and that I might not eat and drink to make myself wanton but for health, using the creatures in their service, as servants in their places, to the glory of him that hath created them; they being in their covenant, and I being brought up into the covenant, as sanctified by the Word which was in the beginning, by which all things are upheld; wherein is unity with the creation.

But people being strangers to the covenant of life with God, they eat and drink to make themselves wanton with the creatures, devouring them upon their own lusts, and living in all filthiness, loving foul ways and devouring the creation; and all this in the world, in the pollutions thereof, without God; and therefore I was to shun all such.

Afterwards, as I grew up, my relations thought to have me a priest, but others persuaded to the contrary; whereupon I was put to a man, a shoemaker by trade, and that dealt in wool, and used grazing, and sold cattle; and a great deal went through my hands. While I was with him, he was blessed; but after I left him he broke, and came to nothing. I never wronged man or woman, in all that time, for the Lord's power was with me and over me, to preserve me. While I was in that service, I used in my dealings the word "verily," and it was a common saying among people that knew me, "If George says 'Verily' there is no altering him." When boys and rude people would laugh at me, I let them alone and went my way, but people had generally a love to me for my innocency and honesty.

When I came towards nineteen years of age, I being upon business at a fair, one of my cousins, whose name was Bradford, being a professor and having another professor with him, came to me, and asked me to drink part of a jug of beer with them, and I, being thirsty, went in with them, for I loved any that had a sense of good, or that did seek after the Lord. And when we had drunk a glass apiece, they began to drink healths and called for more drink, agreeing together that he that would not drink should pay all. I was grieved that any that made profession of religion should offer to do so. They grieved me very much, having never had such a thing put to me before by any sort of people; wherefore I rose up to be gone, and putting my hand into my pocket I took out a groat and laid it down upon the table before them and said, "If it be so, I'll leave you." So I went away; and when I had done what business I had to do, I returned home, but did not go to bed that night, nor could not sleep, but sometimes walked up and down, and sometimes prayed and cried to the Lord, who said unto me, "Thou seest how young people go together into vanity and old people into the earth; and thou must forsake all, both young and old, and keep out of all, and be as a stranger unto all."

Then, at the command of God, on the 9th day of the Seventh Month [September] 1643, I left my relations and brake off all familiarity or fellowship with young or old. And I passed to Lutterworth, where I stayed some time; and from thence I went to Northampton, where also I made some stay, then passed from thence to Newport Pagnall in Buckinghamshire, where, after I had stayed awhile, I went unto Barnet, and came thither in the Fourth Month, called June, in the year 1644. And as I thus travelled through the countries, professors took notice of me and sought to be acquainted with me, but I was afraid of them for I was sensible they did not possess what they professed.

Now during the time that I was at Barnet a strong temptation to despair came upon me. And then I saw how Christ was tempted, and mighty troubles I was in. And sometimes I kept myself retired in my chamber, and often walked solitary in the

Chase there, to wait upon the Lord. And I wondered why these things should come to me; and I looked upon myself and said, "Was I ever so before?" Then I thought, because I had forsaken my relations I had done amiss against them; so I was brought to call to mind all my time that I had spent and to consider whether I had wronged any. But temptations grew more and more and I was tempted almost to despair, and when Satan could not effect his design upon me that way, then he laid snares for me and baits to draw me to commit some sin, whereby he might take advantage to bring me to despair. I was about twenty years of age when these exercises came upon me, and some years I continued in that condition, in great trouble; and fain I would have put it from me. And I went to many a priest to look for comfort but found no comfort from them.

From Barnet I went to London, where I took a lodging, and was under great misery and trouble there, for I looked upon the great professors of the city of London, and I saw all was dark and under the chain of darkness. And I had an uncle there, one Pickering, a Baptist (and they were tender then), yet I could not impart my mind unto my parents and relations, lest I should grieve them, who, I understood, were troubled at my absence.

When I was come down into Leicestershire, my relations would have had me married, but I told them I was but a lad, and I must get wisdom. Others would have had me into the auxiliary band among the soldiery, but I refused; and I was grieved that they proferred such things to me, being a tender youth. Then I went to Coventry, where I took a chamber for a while at a professor's house till people began to be acquainted with me, for there were many tender people in that town.

And after some time I went into my own country again, and was there about a year, in great sorrows and troubles, and walked many nights by myself. Then the priest of Drayton, the town of my birth, whose name was Nathaniel Stephens, would come often to me, and I went often to him, and another priest sometimes would come with him; and they would have given place to me to hear me, and I would ask them questions and reason with them. And this priest Stephens asked me a question, why Christ cried out upon the Cross, "My God, my God, why has thou forsaken me?" and why he said, "If it be possible, let this cup pass from me, yet not my will but thine be done"? And I told him at that time the sins of all mankind were upon him, and their iniquities and transgressions with which he was wounded, which he was to bear, and to be an offering for them as he was man, but died not as he was God; and so, in that he died for all men, and tasted death for every man, he was an offering for the sins of the whole world. This I spoke, being at that time in a measure sensible of Christ's sufferings, and what he went through. And the priest said it was a very good full answer, and such an one as he had not heard. And at that time he would applaud and speak highly of me to others; and what I said in discourse to him on the week-days that he would preach of on the First-days, for which I did not like him. And this priest afterwards became my great persecutor. . . .

About the beginning of the year 1646, as I was going to Coventry, and entering towards the gate, a consideration arose in me, how it was said that all Christians are believers, both Protestants and Papists; and the Lord opened to me that, if all were believers, then they were all born of God and passed from death to life, and that none were true believers but such; and though others said they were believers, yet they were not. At another time, as I was walking in a field on a First-day morning, the Lord opened unto me that being bred at Oxford or Cambridge was not enough to fit and qualify men to be ministers of Christ; and I stranged at it because it was the common belief of people. But I saw clearly, as the Lord opened it to me, and was satisfied, and admired the goodness of the Lord who had opened this thing unto me that morning, which struck at Priest Stephens's ministry, namely, that to be bred at Oxford or Cambridge was not enough to make a man fit to be a minister of Christ. So that which opened in me, I saw, struck at the priest's ministry.

But my relations were much troubled at me that I would not go with them to hear the priest, for I would get into the orchard or the fields, with my Bible to myself. And I told them, "Did not the apostle say to believers that they needed no man to teach them, but as the anointing teacheth them?" And though they knew this was Scripture and that it was true, yet they would be grieved because I could not be subject in this matter to go to hear the priest with them. . . .

At another time it was opened in me that God, who made the world, did not dwell in temples made with hands. This, at the first, seemed a strange word because both priests and people use to call their temples or churches, dreadful places, and holy ground, and the temples of God. But the Lord showed me, so that I did see clearly that he did not dwell in these temples which men had commanded and set up, but in people's hearts; for both Stephen and the Apostle Paul bore testimony that he did not dwell in temples made with hands, not even in that which he had once commanded to be built, since he put an end to it; but that his people were his temple, and he dwelt in them. . . . And I had great openings concerning the things written in the Revelations; and when I spoke of them, the priests and professors would say that was a sealed-up book, and would have kept me out of it, but I told them Christ could open the seals, and that they were the nearest things to us, for the Epistles were written to the saints that lived in former ages, but the Revelations were written of things to come.

After this, I met with a sort of people that held women have no souls, adding in a light manner, no more than a goose. But I reproved them and told them that was not right, for Mary said, "My soul doth magnify the Lord, and my spirit hath rejoiced in God my Saviour." . . .

Now though I had great openings, yet great trouble and temptation came many times upon me, so that when it was day I wished for night, and when it was night I wished for day; and by reason of the openings I had in my troubles, I could say as David said, "Day unto day uttereth speech, and night unto night showeth knowledge." And when I had openings, they answered one another and answered the Scriptures, for I had great openings of the Scriptures; and when I was in troubles, one trouble also answered to another. . . .

And I fasted much, and walked abroad in solitary places many days, and often took my Bible and went and sat in hollow trees and lonesome places till night came on; and frequently in the night walked mournfully about by myself, for I was a man of sorrows in the times of the first workings of the Lord in me.

Now during all this time I was never joined in profession of religion with any, but gave up myself to the Lord, having forsaken all evil company, and taken leave of father and mother and all other relations, and travelled up and down as a stranger in the earth, which way the Lord inclined my heart, taking a chamber to myself in the town where I came, and tarrying sometimes a month, sometimes more, sometimes less in a place. For I durst not stay long in any place, being afraid both of professor and profane, lest, being a tender young man, I should be hurt by conversing much with either. For which reason I kept myself much as a stranger, seeking heavenly wisdom and getting knowledge from the Lord, and was brought off from outward things to rely wholly on the Lord alone. And though my exercises and troubles were very great, yet were they not so continual but that I had some intermissions, and was sometimes brought into such an heavenly joy that I thought I had been in Abraham's bosom. As I cannot declare the misery I was in, it was so great and heavy upon me, so neither can I set forth the mercies of God unto me in all my misery. Oh, the everlasting love of God to my soul when I was in great distress! When my troubles and torments were great, then was his love exceeding great. Thou, Lord, makest a fruitful field a barren wilderness, and a barren wilderness a fruitful field; thou bringest down and settest up; thou killest and makest alive; all honour and glory be to thee, O Lord of glory! The knowledge of thee in the spirit is life, but that knowledge which is fleshly works death. And while there is this knowledge in the flesh, deceit and self-will conform to anything, and will say, "Yes, yes," to that it doth not know. The knowledge which the world hath of what the prophets and apostles spake is a fleshly knowledge; and the apostates from the life in which the prophets and apostles were, have gotten their words, the Holy Scriptures, in a form, but not in their life nor spirit that gave them forth. And so they all lie in confusion and are making provision for the flesh, to fulfil the lusts thereof, but not to fulfil the law and command of Christ in his power and spirit; for that, they say, they cannot do, but to fulfil the lusts of the flesh, that they can do with delight.

Now after I had received that opening from the Lord that to be bred at Oxford or Cambridge was not sufficient to fit a man to be a minister of Christ, I regarded the priests less, and looked more after the dissenting people. And among them I saw there was some tenderness, and many of them came afterwards to be convinced, for they had some openings. But as I had forsaken all the priests, so I left the separate preachers also, and those called the most experienced people; for I saw there was none among them all that could speak to my condition. And when all my hopes in them and in all men were gone, so that I had nothing outwardly to help me, nor could tell what to do, then, Oh then, I heard a voice which said, "There is one, even Christ Jesus, that can speak to thy condition." And when I heard it my heart did leap for joy. Then the Lord did let me see why there was none upon the earth that could speak to my condition, namely, that I might give him all the glory; for all are concluded under sin, and shut up in unbelief as I had been, that Jesus Christ might have the pre-eminence, who enlightens, and gives grace, and faith, and power. Thus, when God doth work who shall let it? And this I knew experimentally.

My desires after the Lord grew stronger, and zeal in the pure knowledge of God and of Christ alone, without the help of any man, book, or writing. For though I read the Scriptures that spoke of Christ and of God, yet I knew him not but by revelation, as he who hath the key did open, and as the Father of life drew me to his Son by his spirit. And then the Lord did gently lead me along, and did let me see his love, which was endless and eternal, and surpasseth all the knowledge that men have in the natural state, or can get by history or books; and that love let me see myself as I was without him. And I was afraid of all company, for I saw them perfectly where they were, through the love of God which let me see myself. . . .

And I saw professors, priests, and people were whole and at ease in that condition which was my misery, and they loved that which I would have been rid of. But the Lord did stay my desires upon himself from whom my help came, and my care was cast upon him alone. Therefore, all wait patiently upon the Lord, whatsoever condition you be in; wait in the grace and truth that comes by Jesus; for if ye so do, there is a promise to you, and the Lord God will fulfil it in you. . . .

At another time I saw the great love of God, and I was filled with admiration at the infiniteness of it; and then I saw what was cast out from God, and what entered into God's kingdom, and how by Jesus, the opener of the door by his heavenly key, the entrance was given. And I saw death, how it had passed upon all men and oppressed the Seed of God in man and in me, and how I in the Seed came forth, and what the promise was to. Yet it was so with me that there seemed to be two pleading in me; and questionings arose in my mind about gifts and prophecies, and I was tempted again to despair, as if I had sinned against the Holy Ghost. And I was in great perplexity and trouble for many days, yet I gave up myself to the Lord still.

And one day when I had been walking solitarily abroad and was come home, I was taken up in the love of God, so that I could not but admire the greatness of his love. And while I was in that condition it was opened unto me by the eternal Light and power, and I therein saw clearly that all was done and to be done in and by Christ, and how he conquers and destroys this tempter, the Devil and all his works, and is atop of him, and that all these troubles were good for me, and temptations for the trial of my faith which Christ had given me. And the Lord opened me that I saw through all these troubles and temptations. My living faith was raised, that I saw all was done by Christ, the life, and my belief was in him. And when at any time my condition was veiled, my secret belief was stayed firm, and hope underneath held me, as an anchor in the bottom of the sea, and anchored my immortal soul to its Bishop, causing it to swim above the sea, the world where all the raging waves, foul weather, tempests, and temptations are. But oh, then did I see my troubles, trials, and temptations more than ever I had done! As the Light appeared, all appeared that is out of the Light, darkness, death, temptations, the unrighteous, the ungodly; all was manifest and seen in the Light. . . .

And passing on, I went among the professors at Dukenfield and Manchester, where I stayed a while and declared Truth among them. And there were some convinced, who received the Lord's teaching, by which they were confirmed and stood in the Truth. But the professors were in a rage, all pleading for sin and imperfection, and could not endure to hear talk of perfection, and of an holy and sinless life. But the Lord's power was over all; though they were chained under darkness and sin, which they pleaded for, and quenched the tender thing in them. . . .

And I went back into Nottinghamshire, and there the Lord shewed me that the natures of those things which were hurtful without were within, in the hearts and minds of wicked men. The natures of dogs, swine, vipers, of Sodom and Egypt, Pharaoh, Cain, Ishmael, Esau, etc. The natures of these I saw within, though people had been looking without. And I cried to the Lord, saying, "Why should I be thus, seeing I was never addicted to commit those evils?" And the Lord answered that it was needful I should have a sense of all conditions, how else should I speak to all conditions; and in this I saw the infinite love of God. I saw also that there was an ocean of darkness and death, but an infinite ocean of light and love, which flowed over the ocean of darkness. And in that also I saw the infinite love of God; and I had great openings.

And as I was walking by the steeplehouse side, in the town of Mansfield, the Lord said unto me, "That which people do trample upon must be thy food." And as the Lord spoke he opened it to me how that people and professors did trample upon the life, even the life of Christ was trampled upon; and they fed upon words, and fed one another with words, but trampled upon the life, and trampled underfoot the blood of the Son of God, which blood was my life, and they lived in their airy notions, talking of him. It seemed strange to me at the first that I should feed on that which the high professors trampled upon, but the Lord opened it clearly to me by his eternal spirit and power.

In Mansfield there came a priest who was looked upon to be above others, and all that professed themselves above the priests went to hear him and cried him up. I was against their going, and spoke to them against their going, and asked them if they had not a teacher within them: the anointing to teach them, and why would they go out to man. And then when they were gone to hear him, I was in sore travail, and it came upon me that I was moved to go to the steeplehouse to tell the people and the priest, and to bid them to cease from man whose breath was in their nostrils, and to tell them where their teacher was, within them, the spirit and the light of Jesus, and how God that made the world doth not dwell in temples made with hands. And many other things concerning the Trust I spake to them. And they were pretty moderate to hear the Truth, whereby, after, many were wrought upon. Then came people from far and near to see me; and I was fearful of being drawn out by them, yet I was made to speak and open things to them. . . .

In the year 1648, as I was sitting in a Friend's house in Nottinghamshire (for by this time the power of God had opened the hearts of some to receive the word of life and reconciliation), I saw there was a great crack to go throughout the earth, and a great smoke to go as the crack went; and that after the crack there should be a great shaking. This was the earth in people's hearts, which was to be shaken before the Seed of God was raised out of the earth. And it was so; for the Lord's power began to shake them, and great meetings we began to have, and a mighty power and work of God there was amongst people, to the astonishment of both people and priests. . . .

After this I went again to Mansfield, where was a great meeting of professors and people, and I was moved to pray, and the Lord's power was so great that the house seemed to be shaken. When I had done, some of the professors said it was now as in the days of the apostles, when the house was shaken where they were. After I had prayed, one of the professors would pray, which brought deadness and a veil over them. And others of the professors were grieved at him and told him it was a temptation upon him. Then he came to me, and desired that I would pray again, but I could not pray in man's will.

Soon after there was another great meeting of professors, and a captain, whose name was Amor Stoddard, came in. And they were discoursing of the blood of Christ and as they were discoursing of it, I saw, through the immediate opening of the invisible Spirit, the blood of Christ. And I cried out among them, and said, "Do ye not see the blood of Christ? see it in your hearts, to sprinkle your hearts and consciences from dead works to serve the living God?" for I saw it, the blood of the New Covenant, how it came into the heart. This startled the professors, who would have the blood only without them and not in them. But Captain Stoddard was reached, and said, "Let the youth speak; hear the youth speak," when he saw they endeavoured to bear me down with many words. . . .

In Leicestershire, as I was passing through the fields, I was moved to go to Leicester, and when I came there I heard of a great meeting for a dispute and that there were many to preach, Presbyterians, Independents, Baptists, and Common-prayer-men. The meeting was in a steeplehouse; and I was moved to go among them. And I heard their discourse and reasonings, some being in pews and the priest in the pulpit, abundance of people being gathered together. At last one woman asked a question out of Peter, what that birth was, viz. a being "born again of incorruptible seed, by the Word of God, that liveth and abideth for ever." And the priest said to her, "I permit not a woman to speak in the church"; though he had before given liberty for any to speak. Whereupon I was rapt up, as in a rapture, in the Lord's power; and I stepped up in a place and asked the priest, "Dost thou call this place a church? Or dost thou call this mixed multitude a church?" For the woman asking a question, he ought to have answered it, having given liberty for any to speak. But he did not answer me neither, but asked me what a church was. I told him the Church was the pillar and ground of Truth, made up of living stones, living members, a spiritual household which Christ was the head of, but he was not the head of a mixed multitude, or of an old house made up of lime, stones, and wood. . . .

And one morning, as I was sitting by the fire, a great cloud came over me, and a temptation beset me; but I sat still. And it was said, "All things come by nature"; and the elements and stars came over me so that I was in a manner quite clouded with it. But inasmuch as I sat, still and silent, the people of the house perceived nothing. And as I sat still under it and let it alone, a living hope arose in me, and a true voice, which said, "There is a living God who made all things." And immediately the cloud

and temptation vanished away, and life rose over it all, and my
heart was glad, and I praised the living God.

And after some time, I met with some people who had such
a notion that there was no God but that all things came by nature.
And I had great dispute with them and overturned them and
made some of them confess that there was a living God. Then
I saw that it was good that I had gone through that exercise. And
we had great meetings in those parts, for the power of the Lord
broke through in that side of the country. . . .

And at a certain time, when I was at Mansfield, there was a
sitting of the justices about hiring of servants; and it was upon
me from the Lord to go and speak to the justices that they should
not oppress the servants in their wages. So I walked towards the
inn where they sat but finding a company of fiddlers there, I did
not go in but thought to come in the morning, when I might have
a more serious opportunity to discourse with them, not thinking
that a seasonable time. But when I came again in the morning,
they were gone, and I was struck even blind that I could not see.
And I inquired of the innkeeper where the justices were to sit
that day and he told me at a town eight miles off. My sight began
to come to me again, and I went and ran thitherward as fast as I
could. And when I was come to the house where they were, and
many servants with them, I exhorted the justices not to oppress
the servants in their wages, but to do that which was right and
just to them; and I exhorted the servants to do their duties, and
serve honestly, etc. And they all received my exhortation
kindly, for I was moved of the Lord therein. . . .

Now was I come up in spirit through the flaming sword into
the paradise of God. All things were new, and all the creation
gave another smell unto me than before, beyond what words can
utter. I knew nothing but pureness, and innocency, and righteousness, being renewed up into the image of God by Christ
Jesus, so that I saw I was come up to the state of Adam which he
was in before he fell. The creation was opened to me, and it was
showed me how all things had their names given them according
to their nature and virtue. And I was at a stand in my mind
whether I should practise physic for the good of mankind, seeing
the nature and virtues of the creatures were so opened to me by

the Lord. But I was immediately taken up in spirit, to see into another or more steadfast state than Adam's innocency, even into a state in Christ Jesus, that should never fall. And the Lord showed me that such as were faithful to him in the power and light of Christ, should come up into that state in which Adam was before he fell, in which the admirable works of the creation, and the virtues thereof, may be known, through the openings of that divine Word of wisdom and power by which they were made. Great things did the Lord lead me into, and wonderful depths were opened unto me, beyond what can by words be declared; but as people come into subjection to the spirit of God, and grow up in the image and power of the Almighty, they may receive the Word of wisdom, that opens all things, and come to know the hidden unity in the Eternal Being. . . .

Now I was sent to turn people from darkness to the light that they might receive Christ Jesus, for to as many as should receive him in his light, I saw that he would give power to become the sons of God, which I had obtained by receiving Christ. And I was to direct people to the Spirit that gave forth the Scriptures, by which they might be led into all Truth, and so up to Christ and God, as they had been who gave them forth. And I was to turn them to the grace of God, and to the Truth in the heart, which came by Jesus, that by this grace they might be taught, which would bring them into salvation, that their hearts might be established by it, and their words might be seasoned, and all might come to know their salvation nigh. For I saw that Christ had died for all men, and was a propitiation for all, and had enlightened all men and women with his divine and saving light, and that none could be a true believer but who believed in it. I saw that the grace of God, which brings salvation, had appeared to all men, and that the manifestation of the Spirit of God was given to every man to profit withal. . . .

And I was to bring people off from all the world's religions, which are vain, that they might know the pure religion, and might visit the fatherless, the widows and the strangers, and keep themselves from the spots of the world. And then there would not be so many beggars, the sight of whom often grieved my heart, to see so much hard-heartedness amongst them that professed the name of Christ. And I was to bring them off from all the world's fellowships and prayings, and singings, which stood in forms without power, that their fellowships might be in the Holy Ghost, and in the eternal Spirit of God; that they might pray in the Holy Ghost, and sing in the spirit and with the grace that comes by Jesus, making melody in their hearts to the Lord who hath sent his beloved Son to be their Saviour, and caused his heavenly sun to shine upon all the world, and through them all, and his heavenly rain to fall upon the just and the unjust (as his outward rain doth fall, and his outward sun doth shine on all), which is God's unspeakable love to the world.

And I was to bring people off from Jewish ceremonies, and from heathenish fables, and from men's inventions and windy doctrines, by which they blowed the people about this way and the other way, from sect to sect; and all their beggarly rudiments, with their schools and colleges for making ministers of Christ, who are indeed ministers of their own making but not of Christ's; and from all their images and crosses, and sprinkling of infants, with all their holy days (so called) and all their vain traditions, which they had gotten up since the apostles' days, which the Lord's power was against, and in the dread and authority thereof I was moved to declare against them all, and against all that preached and not freely, as being such as had not received freely from Christ.

Moreover when the Lord sent me forth into the world, he forbade me to put off my hat to any, high or low; and I was required to "thee" and "thou" all men and women, without any respect to rich or poor, great or small. And as I travelled up and down, I was not to bid people "good morrow" or "good evening," neither might I bow or scrape with my leg to any one. . . .

But oh, the rage that then was in the priests, magistrates, professors, and people of all sorts, but especially in priests and professors! for, though "thou" to a single person was according to their own learning, their accidence and grammar rules, and according to the Bible, yet they could not bear to hear it, and the hat-honour, because I could not put off my hat to them, it set them all into a rage. But the Lord showed me that it was an honour below, which he would lay in the dust and stain it, an honour which proud flesh looked for, but sought not the honour which came from God only, that it was an honour invented by men in the Fall, and in the alienation from God, who were offended if it were not given them, and yet would be looked upon as saints, church-members, and great Christians. But Christ saith, "How can ye believe, who receive honour one of another, and seek not the honour that cometh from God only?" "And I," saith Christ, "receive not honour of men": showing that men have an honour, which men will receive and give, but Christ will have none of it. This is the honour which Christ will not receive, and which must be laid in the dust. Oh, the rage and scorn, the heat and fury that arose! Oh, the blows, punchings, beatings, and imprisonments that we underwent for not putting off our hats to men! For that soon tried all men's patience and sobriety, what it was. Some had their hats violently plucked off and thrown away so that they quite lost them. The bad language and evil usage we received on this account are hard to be expressed, besides the danger we were sometimes in of losing our lives for this matter, and that, by the great professors of Christianity, who thereby discovered that they were not true believers. And though it was but a small thing in the eye of man, yet a wonderful confusion it brought among all professors and priests. But, blessed be the Lord, many came to see the vanity of that custom of putting off the hat to men, and felt the weight of Truth's testimony against it.

About this time I was sorely exercised in going to their courts to cry for justice, and in speaking and writing to judges and justices to do justly, and in warning such as kept public houses for entertainment that they should not let people have more drink than would do them good, and in testifying against their wakes or feasts, their May-games, sports, plays, and shows, which trained up people to vanity and looseness, and led them from the fear of God, and the days they had set forth for holy-days were usually the times wherein they most dishonoured God by these things. In fairs also, and in markets, I was made to declare against their deceitful merchandise and cheating and cozening, warning all to deal justly, to speak the truth, to let their "yea" be "yea," and their "nay" be "nay"; and to do unto others as they would have others do unto them, and forewarning them of the great and terrible day of the Lord which would come upon them all. I was moved also to cry against all sorts of music, and against the mountebanks playing tricks on their stages, for they burdened the pure life and stirred up people's minds to vanity.

I was much exercised too, with school-masters and school-mistresses, warning them to teach their children sobriety in the fear of the Lord, that they might not be nursed and trained up in lightness, vanity, and wantonness. Likewise I was made to warn masters and mistresses, fathers and mothers in private families, to take care that their children and servants might be trained up in the fear of the Lord; and that they themselves should be therein examples and patterns of sobriety and virtue to them. For I saw that as the Jews were to teach their children the law of God and the old covenant, and to train them up in it, and their servants, yea the very strangers were to keep the Sabbath amongst them, and be circumcised, before they might eat of their sacrifices, so all Christians, and all that made a profession of Christianity, ought to train up their children and servants in the new covenant of light, Christ Jesus, who is God's salvation to the ends of the earth, that all may know their salvation. . . .

When I was a prisoner . . . there came a woman to me to the prison and two with her and said that she had been possessed two and thirty years. And the priests had kept her and had kept fasting days about her and could not do her any good, and she said the Lord said unto her, "Arise, for I have a sanctified people; haste and go to them, for thy redemption draweth nigh." And when I came out of prison I bade Friends have her to Mansfield. At that time our meetings were disturbed by wild people, and both they and the professors and priests said that we were false prophets and deceivers, and that there was witchcraft amongst us. The poor woman would make such a noise in roaring, and sometimes lying along upon her belly upon the ground with her spirit and roaring and voice, that it would set all Friends in a heat and sweat. And I said, "All Friends, keep to your own, lest that which is in her get into you," and so she affrighted the world from our meetings.

Then they said if that were cast out of her while she were with us, and were made well, then they would say that we were of God. This said the world, and I had said before that she should be set free.

Then it was upon me that we should have a meeting at Skegby at Elizabeth Hooton's house; and we had her there. And there were many Friends almost overcome by her with the stink that came out of her; roaring and tumbling on the ground, and the same day she was worse than ever she was. Another day we met about her, and about the first hour the Life rose in Friends and said it was done. She rose up, and her countenance changed and became white; and before it was wan and earthly; and she sat down at my thigh as I was sitting, and lifted up her hands and said "Ten thousand praise the Lord," and did not know where she was, and so she was well; and we kept her about a fortnight in the sight of the world and she wrought and did things, and then we sent her away to her friends. And then the world's professors, priests, and teachers never could call us any more false prophets, deceivers, or witches after, but it did a great deal of good in the country among people in relation to the Truth and to the stopping the mouths of the world and their slanderous aspersions. . . .

Now while I was at Mansfield-Woodhouse, I was moved to go to the steeplehouse there on a First-day, out of the meeting in Mansfield, and when the priest had done I declared the Truth to the priest and people. But the people fell upon me with their fists, books, and without compassion or mercy beat me down in the steeplehouse and almost smothered me in it, being under them. And sorely was I bruised in the steeplehouse, and they threw me against the walls and when that they had thrust and thrown me out of the steeplehouse, when I came into the yard I fell down, being so sorely bruised and beat among them. And I got up again and then they punched and thrust and struck me up and down and they set me in the stocks and brought a whip to whip me, but did not. And as I sat in the stocks they threw stones at me, and my head, arms, breast, shoulders, back, and sides were so bruised that I was mazed and dazzled with the blows. And I was hot when they put me in the stocks. After some time they had me before the magistrate, at a knight's house and examined me, where were many great persons, and I reasoned with them of the things of God and of God and his teachings, and Christ's, and how that God that made the world did not dwell in temples made with hands; and of divers things of the Truth I spake to them, and they, seeing how evilly I had been used, set me at liberty. The rude people were ready to fall upon me with staves but the constable kept them off. And when they had set me at liberty, they threatened me with pistols if ever I came again they would kill me and shoot me and they would carry their pistol to the steeplehouse. And with threatening I was freed. And I was scarce able to go or well to stand, by reason of ill-usage. Yet with much ado I got about a mile from the town, and as I was passing along the fields Friends met me. I was so bruised that I could not turn in my bed, and bruised inwardly at my heart, but after a while the power of the Lord went through me and healed me, that I was well, glory be to the Lord for ever. . . .

Passing away I heard of a people that were in prison in Coventry for religion. And as I walked towards the gaol, the word of the Lord came to me saying, "My love was always to thee, and thou art in my love." And I was ravished with the sense of the love of God and greatly strengthened in my inward man. But when I came into the gaol, where those prisoners were, a great power of darkness struck at me, and I sat still, having my spirit gathered into the love of God. At last these prisoners began to rant and vapour and blaspheme, at which my soul was greatly grieved. They said they were God, but another of them said "We could not bear such things." So when they were calm, I stood up and asked them whether they did such things by motion, or from Scripture; and they said, "From Scripture." Then, a Bible lying by, I asked them for that Scripture; and they showed me that place where the sheet was let down to Peter, and it was said to him, what was sanctified he should not call common or unclean. Now when I had showed them that that Scripture made nothing for their purpose, they brought another Scripture which spoke of God's reconciling all things to himself, things in heaven and things in earth. I told them I owned that Scripture also, but showed them that that was nothing to their purpose neither. Then seeing they said they were God, I asked them, if they knew whether it would rain tomorrow. They said they could not tell. I told them God could tell. Again, I asked them if they thought they should be always in that condition, or should change, and they answered they could not tell. Then said I unto them, "God can tell, and God doth not change. You say you are God, and yet you cannot tell whether you shall change or no." So they were confounded and quite brought down for the time. Then after I had reproved them for their blasphemous expressions, I went away, for I perceived they were Ranters, and I had met with none before. And I admired the goodness of the Lord in appearing so unto me before I went amongst them. Not long after this, one of these Ranters, whose name was Joseph Salmon, put forth a paper or book of recantation, upon which they were set at liberty. . . .

Now there was in that town a great man, that had long lain sick and was given over by the physicians; and some Friends in the town desired me to go to see him. And I went up to him and was moved to pray by him; spoke to him in his bed, and the power of the Lord entered him that he was loving and tender.

And I left him and came down among the family in the house, and spake a few words to the people that they should fear the Lord and repent and prize their time and the like words, and there came one of his servants with a naked sword and run at me ere I was aware of him, and set it to my side, and there held it, and I looked up at him in his face and said to him, "Alack for thee, it's no more to me than a straw." And then he went away in a rage, with threatening words, and I passed away, and the power of the Lord came over all, and his master mended, according to my belief and faith that I had seen before. And he then turned this man away that run at me with the sword, and afterwards he was very loving to Friends; and when I came to that town again both he and his wife came to see me. . . .

Then we passed through Friends to Derby and lay at a doctor's house. His wife was convinced and several in the town; and as I was walking in my chamber, the [steeplehouse] bell rung, and it struck at my life, at the very hearing of it; and I asked the woman of the house what the bell rung for, and she said there was to be a great lecture that day and abundance of the officers of the army, and priests, and preachers were to be there, and a colonel that was a preacher. I was moved of the Lord to go up to them, and when they had done, I spake to them what the Lord commanded me, of the Truth, and the day of the Lord, and the light within them, and the spirit to teach and lead them to God, and they were pretty quiet. There came an officer to me and took me by the hand and said I must go before the magistrates, and the other two that were with me, and so when we came before them about the first hour afternoon, they asked me why we came thither. I said God moved us to do so,...and I had many words with them. ... The power of God was thundered among them and they flew like chaff, and they put me in and out of the room from the first hour to the ninth hour at night in examinations, having me backward and forward, and, said in a deriding manner that I was taken up in raptures, as they called it.

At last they asked me whether I was sanctified.

I said, "Sanctified? yes," for I was in the Paradise of God.

They said, had I no sin?

"Sin?" said I, "Christ my saviour hath taken away my sin, and in him there is no sin."

They asked how we knew that Christ did abide in us. I said, "By his Spirit that he has given us."

They temptingly asked if any of us were Christ.

I answered, "Nay, we are nothing, Christ is all."

They said, "If a man steal is it no sin?"

I answered, "All unrighteousness is sin."

And many such like words they had with me. And so they committed me as a blasphemer and as a man that had no sin, and committed another man with me to the House of Correction in Derby for six months. ...

And then many people came from far and near to see a man that had no sin; and then did the priests roar up for sin, in their pulpits, and preach up sin, that people said never was the like heard. It was all their works to plead for it. ...

And some Friends would have removed me to the Parliament, it being then in the days of the Commonwealth. Then the priests and justices and professors and keeper were all in great rage against me. The keeper watched my words and asked me questions to ensnare me, sometimes would ask me such silly questions as whether the door was latched or not—things to get something to make sin of it. But I was kept watchful and chaste, and they admired at it. And several times I had motions from the Lord to go into the town, in time of fairs and markets, to speak to the people (though I was in prison), and I would tell the keeper and ask him to let me go, and he would not; and then I said to him, "Then let it be upon thee, the iniquity of the people be upon thee"; and the Lord said to me that I was not to be removed from that place yet, but was set as a king for the body's sake, and for the true hope that doth purify and the true faith that gives the victory and the true belief that overcomes the world. . . .

The keeper being a great professor was in a mighty rage against me, yet it pleased the Lord to strike him. So one day as I was walking in my chamber I heard a doleful noise, and I made a stand, and he was speaking to his wife how that he saw the day of judgment, and he saw George there and was afraid of him because that he had done him so much wrong, and spoke so much against him to professors, and justices, and the priests, and in taverns and alehouses. So, toward evening he came trembling up into my chamber and said to me, "I have been as a lion against you, but now I come like a lamb, and come like the gaoler in the Acts that came to Paul and Silas trembling." And he desired that he might lodge with me, and I told him I was in his power and he might do what he would, and he said, nay, he would have my leave, and he could desire to be always with me, but not to have me as a prisoner, and said that he had been plagued and his house was plagued, for my sake, like Pharaoh's and Abimelech's concerning Abraham and Isaac, and so I suffered him to lodge with me. Then he told me all his heart, and believed what I said to be true of the true faith, and hope, etc. . . .

And so the keeper confessed all to me, how that when I had the several motions from the Lord to go out and speak to people and he would not let me go, and when I laid it upon him, he was distracted and amazed for an hour afterward, and was much troubled and in such a condition for a time that one might have killed him with a crab, as he said. So when the morning came he went to the justices and told them he and his house had been plagued for my sake, and the justices said that the plagues were on them too for keeping me in prison. This was Justice Bennet of Derby that first called us Quakers because we bid them tremble at the word of God, and this was in the year 1650. And the justices gave leave that I should have liberty to go a mile. And I perceived their end, and I told the gaoler that if they would set me how far a mile was, I might walk in it sometimes, but it's like they thought I would go away. I told them I was not of that spirit; and the gaoler confessed it after, that they did it with that intent to have me gone away to ease the plague from them and they said I was an honest man. . . .

And when I had liberty I went into the market and streets and warned people to repentance, and so returned to prison again. I was allowed a mile to walk out by myself. . . .

And when I was in the House of Correction, there came a trooper to me and said, as he was sitting in the steeplehouse hearing the priest he was in an exceeding great trouble, and the voice of the Lord came to him saying, "What, dost not thou know that my servant is in prison? Go to him for directions." And he came, and I spake to his condition and opened his understanding, and settled his mind in the light and spirit of God in himself; and I told him, that which showed him his sin and troubled him, for it would show him his salvation; for he that shows a man his sins is he that takes it away. So the Lord's power opened to him, so that he began to have great understanding of the Lord's Truth and mercies, and began to speak boldly in his quarters amongst the soldiers and others concerning Truth. The Scriptures were very much opened to him so that he said that his two Colonels, Nathaniel Barton and Thomas Saunders, were as blind as Nebuchadnezzar to cast me, the servant of the Lord, into prison. For this they began also to have a spite and malice against him, that when he came to Worcester fight, and the two armies lay one nigh the other, and two came out of the King's army and challenged two out of the Parliament army to fight with them, his two Colonels made choice of him and another to go and fight with them. And they went forth to them, and his companion was killed; and after, he drove the two within musket shot of the town and never fired his own pistol at them. This he told me out of his own mouth; but when the fight was over he saw the deceit and hypocrisy of the officers and he laid down his arms and saw to the end of fighting, and how the Lord had miraculously preserved him.

My time being nearly out of being committed six months to the House of Correction, they filled the House of Correction with persons that they had taken up to be soldiers: and then they would have had me to be a captain of them and the soldiers cried they would have none but me. So the keeper of the House of Correction was commanded to bring me up before the Commissioners and soldiers in the market place; and there they proffered me that preferment because of my virtue, as they said, with many other compliments, and asked me if I would not take up arms for the Commonwealth against the King. But I told them I lived in the virtue of that life and power that took away the occasion of all wars, and I knew from whence all wars did rise, from the lust according to James's doctrine. Still they courted me to accept of their offer and thought that I did but compliment with them. But I told them I was come into the covenant of peace which was before wars and strifes were. And they said they offered it in love and kindness to me because of my virtue, and such like flattering words they used, and I told them if that were their love and kindness I trampled it under my feet. Then their rage got up and they said, "Take him away gaoler, and cast him into the dungeon amongst the rogues and felons"; which they then did and put me into the dungeon amongst thirty felons in a lousy, stinking low place in the ground without any bed. Here they kept me a close prisoner almost a half year, unless it were at times; and sometimes they would let me walk in the garden, for they had a belief of me that I would not go away. . . .

And there was a young woman that was to be put to death for robbing her master; and judgment was given and a grave made for her and she carried to execution. I was made to write to the judge and to the jury about her, and when she came there though they had her upon the ladder with a cloth bound over her face, ready to be turned off, yet they had not power to hang her (as by the paper which I sent to be read at the gallows may be seen), but she was brought back again. And they came with great rage against me into the prison. Afterwards in the prison this young woman came to be convinced of God's everlasting Truth.

And I also writ to the judges what a sore thing it was that prisoners should lie so long in gaol, and how that they learned badness one of another in talking of their bad deeds, and therefore speedy justice should have been done. For I was a tender youth and dwelt in the fear of God. I was grieved to hear their bad language and was made often to reprove them for their words and bad carriage each towards other. . . .

At length they were made to turn me out of gaol about the beginning of winter in the year 1651, who had been kept a year, within three weeks, in four prisons, the House of Correction, and at the town prison and the county gaol and dungeon, and then in the high gaol where I was kept till I was set freely at liberty. . . .

And as I was one time walking in a close with several Friends I lifted up my head and I espied three steeplehouse spires. They struck at my life and I asked Friends what they were, and they said, Lichfield. The word of the Lord came to me thither I might go, so, being come to the house we were going to I bid friends that were with me walk into the house from me; and they did and as soon as they were gone (for I said nothing to them whither I would go) I went over hedge and ditch till I came within a mile of Lichfield. When I came into a great field where there were shepherds keeping their sheep, I was commanded of the Lord to pull off my shoes of a sudden; and I stood still, and the word of the Lord was like a fire in me; and being winter, I untied my shoes and put them off; and when I had done I was commanded to give them to the shepherds and was to charge them to let no one have them except they paid for them. And the poor shepherds trembled and were astonished.

So I went about a mile till I came into the town, and as soon as I came within the town the word of the Lord came unto me again to cry, "Woe unto the bloody city of Lichfield!"; so I went up and down the streets crying, "Woe unto the bloody city of Lichfield!" Being market day I went into the market place and went up and down in several places of it and made stands, crying,

"Woe unto the bloody city of Lichfield!", and no one touched me nor laid hands on me. As I went down the town there ran like a channel of blood down the streets, and the market place was like a pool of blood.

And so at last some friends and friendly people came to me and said, "Alack George! where are thy shoes?" and I told them it was no matter; so when I had declared what was upon me and cleared myself, I came out of the town in peace about a mile to the shepherds: and there I went to them and took my shoes and gave them some money, but the fire of the Lord was so in my feet and all over me that I did not matter to put my shoes on any more and was at a stand whether I should or no till I felt freedom from the Lord so to do.

And so at last I came to a ditch and washed my feet and put on my shoes; and when I had done, I considered why I should go and cry against that city and call it a bloody city; for though the Parliament had the minster one while and the King another while, and much blood had been shed in the town, yet that could not be charged upon the town. . . .

But after, I came to see that there were a thousand martyrs in Lichfield in the Emperor Diocletian's time. And so I must go in my stockings through the channel of their blood in their market place. So I might raise up the blood of those martyrs that had been shed and lay cold in their streets, which had been shed above a thousand years before. So the sense of this blood was upon me, for which I obeyed the word of the Lord. And the ancient records will testify how many of the Christian Britons suffered there. . . .

And . . . I passed away through the country northwards and there were no Friends; and sometimes I lay out all night though in the winter-season and at night I came in my travels to a house, being weary, and there was a rude company of people and I asked the woman if she had any meat; and she was something strange because I said "thee" and "thou" to her; I asked her if she had any milk but she denied it and I asked her if she had any cream, though I did not greatly like such meat but only to try her and she denied it also. And there stood a churn in her house; and a little boy put his hand into the churn in which there was a great deal of cream, and plucked it down before my face, and it did run like a pool in the floor of the house; and so it manifested the woman to be a liar. The woman was amazed and took the child and whipped it sorely, and blessed herself; but I reproved her for her lying and deceit. So I walked out of her house after the Lord God had manifested her deceit and perverseness, and came to a stack of hay and lay in the haystack all night in the snow and rain, being but three days before the time called Christmas. . . .

And then I went to the steeplehouse, where was a high priest, that did much oppress the people with tithes. And when I spoke unto him, he fled away after I had laid his oppressing of the people upon him. For if the people went a hundred miles off a-fishing, he would make them pay the tithe money, though they catched the fish at such a distance and carried the fish to Yarmouth to sell. And the chief of the parish were very light and vain, so after I spoke the word of life to them I slighted their light spirits, seeing they did not receive it. But the word of the Lord stuck with some of them so that at night some of the heads of the parish came to me and were most of them convinced and satisfied, and confessed to Truth. So the Truth began to spread up and down the country and great meetings we had, that the priest began to rage, and the Ranters began to be stirred. They sent to me that they would have a dispute with me, both the oppressing priest and the leader of all the Ranters, and a day was set, and the Ranter, whose name was Thomas Bushel came and his company, and another priest, Levens. . . . And the priest that was convinced and a great number of people met, and so when we were set, the Ranter said to me that he had a vision of me: that I was sitting in a great chair, and that he was to come and put off his hat and bow down to the ground before me, and so he did; and many other flattering words he said. When he had done I told him it was his own figure: and said unto him, "Repent, thou beast." He said it was jealousy in me to say so. Then I asked him the ground of jealousy and how it came to be bred in man, and the nature of a heathen, what made it, and how that was bred in man; for I saw him directly in that nature of the beast and therefore I would have known from him how that came to be bred in him. So I told him he should give me an account of things done in the body before we came to discourse of things done out of the body. So I stopped up his mouth that he could say no more and all his fellow Ranters were stopped up, for he was the head of them. . . .

Yea, the Lord's everlasting power was over the world and did reach to the hearts of people, and made both priests and professors tremble. It shook the earthly and airy spirit, in which they held their profession of religion and worship, so that it was a dreadful thing unto them, when it was told them, "The man in leathern breeches is come." At the hearing thereof the priests, in many places, would get out of the way, they were so struck with the dread of the eternal power of God; and fear surprised the hypocrites. . . .

Some places where the priests were paid, they fled away from the town when as I came to it; and the people would break open the doors if I would go into the steeplehouse, if the churchwardens would not open it. But I would not let them, but spake to them in the yards or any where, the Truth of God, and in love it was received; and many justices were loving in Yorkshire, and the Truth spread. . . .

And so I turned into a town towards night, called Patrington; and as I was going along the town, preaching and speaking, I warned the priest that was in the street and people to repent and turn to the Lord. Some heard and others said that I was mad, and it grew dark before I came to the end of the town. And a great deal of people gathered about me and I declared the Truth and the word of life to them. And after, I went to an inn and desired them to let me have a lodging and they would not; and I desired them to let me have a little meat and milk and I would pay them for it, but they would not. So I walked out of the town and a company of fellows followed me and asked me what news, and I bid them repent and fear the Lord, and prize their time, for I saw their question was tempting.

And after I was passed a pretty way out of the town I came to another house and desired them to let me have a little meat and drink and lodging for my money, but they would not neither but denied me. And I came to another house and desired the same, but they refused me also; and then it grew so dark that I could not see the highway; but I discovered a ditch and got a little water and refreshed myself and got over the ditch and sat amongst the furze bushes, being weary with travelling, till it was day. . . .

And the next First-day I went to Tickhill and there the Friends of that side gathered together and there was a meeting; and a mighty brokenness with the power of God there was amongst the people. And when Friends were in the meeting and fresh and full of the power of God I was moved to go to the steeplehouse, and the priest had done. And he and most of the heads of the parish were got up into the chancel, and I went up among them. And when I began to speak, they fell upon me, and the clerk up with his Bible as I was speaking and hit me in the face that my face gushed out with blood, and it run off me in the steeplehouse. And then they cried, "Take him out of the church," and they punched me and thrust me out and beat me sore with books, fists and sticks, and threw me over a hedge into a close and there beat me and then threw me over again. And then they beat me into a house, punching me through the entry, and there I lost my hat and never had it again, and after dragged me into the street, stoning and beating me along, sorely blooded and bruised. And the priest beheld a great part of this his people's doings.

And so after a while I got into the meeting again amongst Friends, and the priest and people coming by the Friend's house, I went forth with Friends into the yard and there I spoke to the priest and people, they being in the street and I in the Friend's yard on a wall. My spirit was revived again by the power of God; for, through their bruising, beating, blooding, stoning, and throwing me down, I was almost mazed and my body sore bruised, but by the power of the Lord I was refreshed again, to him be the glory. And the priest scoffed at us and called us Quakers; but I declared to them the word of life and showed to them the fruits of their teachers and how they dishonoured Christianity. And the Lord's power was so over them all, and the word of life was declared in so much power and dread to them, that the priest fell a-trembling himself, so that one said unto him, "Look how the priest trembles and shakes, he is turned a Quaker also."

And Friends were very much abused that day by the priest and his people. The justices hearing of it, two or three of them came and sat to hear and examine the business; and he that had shed my blood was afraid of having his hand cut off for striking me in the steeplehouse, but I forgave him and did not appear against him. . . .

And so I passed away to the meeting where were a great many professors and friendly people gathered and a great convincement there was that day, and people satisfied with the Lord's teaching which they were turned to. Here we got some lodging for we had lain out, four of us, under a hedge the night before, for there were few Friends to receive us there.

And this priest's name was Christopher Marshall, whom the Lord not long after cut off in his wickedness. And James Nayler was a member of his church, whom he excommunicated not long after. And he raised a-many wicked slanders upon me, that I carried bottles and that I made people drink of my bottles, and that made them to follow me, and that I rid of a great black horse, and that I was seen in one country upon my black horse in one hour and in the same hour in another country three score miles off, and that I would give a fellow money to follow me when I was on my black horse. And with these hellish lies he fed his people to make them speak evil of the Truth which was in Jesus, that I had declared amongst them; for I went on foot and had no horse at that time, which the people generally knew. But by his lies he preached many of his hearers away from him, and the Lord's power came over them all and delivered us out of their hands. . . .

And so after the meeting was done I passed away to John Audland's and there came John Story to me, and lighted his pipe of tobacco, and, said he, "Will you take a pipe of tobacco," saying, "Come, all is ours"; and I looked upon him to be a forward, bold lad. Tobacco I did not take, but it came into my mind that the lad might think I had not unity with the creation, for I saw he had a flashy, empty notion of religion; so I took his pipe and put it to my mouth and gave it to him again to stop him lest his rude tongue should say I had not unity with the creation.

And from thence I came to Preston Patrick Chapel where there was a great meeting appointed. I went into it and had a large meeting amongst the people, and declared the word of life and the everlasting Truth to them, and showed them that the end of my coming into that place was not to hold it up no more than the apostles going into the Jewish synagogues and temple and Diana's was, but to bring them off all such things as they did: for the apostles brought the saints off the Jewish temple and Aaron's priesthood and told them that their bodies were the temples of God and that Christ was their teacher; and after, they met in houses. . . .

And in the morning I walked out after I had told them concerning the meeting, and they were in much reasoning and doubting of it and me, and as I was walking upon the top of the bank there came several poor people, travellers, that I saw were in necessity; and they gave them nothing but said they were cheats. But when they were gone in to their breakfast it grieved me to see such hard-heartedness amongst professors that I ran after the poor people a matter of a quarter of a mile and gave them some money. Meanwhile, some that were in the house came out again, and seeing me a quarter of a mile off they said I could not have gone so far in such an instant except I had wings; and then the meeting was like to have been stopped, they were so filled with strange thoughts, and that quite put the meeting out of their minds and they were against it; for they could not believe I could have gone so far in such a short space. And then there came Miles and Stephen Hubbersty, more simple hearted men, and they would have the meeting. I told them I ran after those poor people to give them some money and I was grieved at their hard-heartedness that gave them nothing. . . .

And the next day we passed on, warning people as we met them of the day of the Lord that was coming upon them. As we went I spied a great hill called Pendle Hill, and I went on the top of it with much ado, it was so steep; but I was moved of the Lord to go atop of it; and when I came atop of it I saw Lancashire sea; and there atop of the hill I was moved to sound the day of the Lord; and the Lord let me see atop of the hill in what places he had a great people to be gathered. As I went down, on the hillside, I found a spring of water and refreshed myself, for I had eaten little and drunk little for several days. . . .

And from thence I came to Ulverston and so to Swarthmoor to Judge Fell's.

And there came up priest Lampitt of Ulverston who I perceived had been and was still a Ranter in his mind, and had liberty to do anything, and I had a great deal of reasoning with him for he would talk of high notions and perfection and thereby deceived the people. He would have owned me but I could not own him nor join with him, he was so full of filth. For he said he was above John and made as though he knew all things, but I told him how that death reigned from Adam to Moses, and he was under that death and knew not Moses, for Moses saw the paradise of God; he neither knew Moses nor the prophets nor John, for that crooked nature stood in him and the rough, and the mountain of sin and corruptions. And the way was not prepared in him for the Lord. He confessed he had been under a cross in things but now he could sing psalms and do anything; and I told him now he could see a thief and join hand in hand with him, and he could not preach Moses, nor the prophets, nor Christ, nor John, except he was in the same spirit as they were in.

And so Margaret Fell had been abroad, and at night when she came home her children told her that priest Lampitt and I disagreed; and it struck something at her because she was in a profession with him, though he hid his dirty actions from them. So at night we had a great deal of reasoning and I declared the Truth to her and her family.

And the next day Lampitt came again and I had a great deal of discourse with him before Margaret Fell, who soon then discerned the priest clearly, and a convincement came upon her and her family of the Lord's Truth. And there was a humiliation day shortly after, within a day or two, kept at Ulverston, and Margaret Fell asked me to go to the steeplehouse with her, for she was not wholly come off, I said, "I must do as I am ordered by the Lord," so I left her and walked into the fields, and then the word of the Lord came to me to go to the steeplehouse after them and when I came the priest Lampitt was singing with his people. His spirit and his stuff was so foul that I was moved of the Lord to speak to him and the people after they had done singing; and the word of the Lord was to them. . . .

One Justice Sawrey cried out, "Take him away"; and Judge Fell's wife said to the officers, "Let him alone, why may not he speak as well as any other"; and Lampitt said for deceit, "Let him speak," and so at last when I had declared a pretty while, Justice John Sawrey, a rotten professor who was very full of hypocrisy, and deceit, and envy, caused me to be put out of the steeplehouse. I spoke to the people in the steeplehouse yard, and after came up to Swarthmoor Hall. . . .

And after this Judge Fell was come home, and Margaret sent for me to return thither, and so I came through the country back to Swarthmoor again; and the priests and professors, and that envious Justice Sawrey, had incensed Judge Fell and Captain Sandys much against the Truth with their lies; and after dinner I answered him all his objections and satisfied him by Scripture so as he was thoroughly satisfied and convinced in his judgment. . . . Judge Fell . . . came also to see by the spirit of God in his heart over all the priests and teachers of the world and did not go to hear them for some years before he died; for he knew it was the Truth, and that Christ was the teacher of his people and their saviour. He wished that I was awhile with Judge Bradshaw to convince him. There came over to Judge Fell that Captain Sandys, a wicked man, to incense him; and he was full of envy against me and yet he could use the apostles' words and say, "Behold I make all things new." I told him then he must have a new God for his god was his belly. . . .

And there was a captain stood up after the meeting was done and asked me where my leather breeches were, and I let the man run on awhile and at last I held up my coat and said "Here are my leather breeches which frighten all your priests and professors." . . .

And after, I came up to Swarthmoor again, and there came up four or five priests, and I asked them whether any of them could say they ever had a word from the Lord to go and speak to such or such a people and none of them durst say so. But one of them burst out into a passion and said he could speak his experiences as well as I; but I told him experience was one thing but to go with a message and a word from the Lord as the prophets and the apostles had and did, and as I had done to them, this was another thing.

Could any of them say they had such a command or word from the Lord at any time? But none of them could answer to it. But I told them the false prophets and false apostles and anti-christs could use the words and speak of other men's experiences that never knew or heard the voice of God and Christ; and such as they might get the good words and experience of others. This puzzled them much and laid them open.

And at another time there were several priests at Judge Fell's, and he was by; and I asked them the same question, whether ever they had heard the voice of God or Christ to bid them go to such or such a people to declare his word or message unto them, for any that could but read might declare the experiences of the prophets and apostles. Hereupon Thomas Taylor, an ancient priest, did ingenuously confess before Judge Fell that he had never heard the voice of God nor Christ, to send him to any people, but he spoke his experiences, and the experiences of the saints and preached that, which did astonish Judge Fell, for he and all people did look that they were sent from God and Christ. . . .

And after this, of a lecture day, I was moved to go again to Ulverston steeplehouse where there was abundance of professors, and priests, and friendly people to hear me, and queried if I would be there.

And I went up to Lampitt who was blustering on in his preaching: and . . . John Sawrey . . . came to me after the Lord had opened my mouth to speak, and took me by the hand, and asked me if I would speak, and I said, "Yes." And he said if I would speak according to the Scriptures I should speak and I stranged at him for speaking so to me, for I did speak according to the Scriptures. And I told him I would speak according to the Scriptures and bring the Scriptures to prove what I had to say, for I had some thing to speak to Lampitt and them; and then this Sawrey said I should not speak, contradicting his own saying where he said I should speak if I would speak according to Scriptures. Then the rude people said to the Justice, "Give him us!" and he did. So of a sudden all the people in the steeplehouse were in an outrage and an uproar, that they fell upon me in the steeplehouse before his face, with staves and fists and books, and knocked me down and kicked me and trampled upon me. And many people tumbled over their seats for fear and were knocked down, and the Justice and the priests among them. And at last the Justice said among the rude people, "Give him me!" and he came and took me from amongst the people again and led me out of the steeplehouse and put me into the hands of four officers and constables, and bid them whip me and put me out of town. And they led me about a quarter of a mile, some taking hold by my collar and some by the arms and shoulders and shook me by the head, and some by the hands, and dragged me through mire and dirt and water. And many friendly people that were come to the market, and some into the steeplehouse to hear me, many of them they knocked down, and broke their heads also. And the blood ran down several people so as I never saw the like in my life, as I looked at them when they were dragging me along. And Judge Fell's son running after to see what they would do with me, they threw him into a ditch of water and cried, "Knock out the teeth of his head!" And some got staves and some got hedge stakes and some got holme bushes and some got willows.

And when they had led me to the common moss, and a multitude of people following, the constables took me and gave me a wisk over the shoulders with their willow rods, and so thrust me amongst the rude multitude which then fell upon me with their hedge stakes and clubs and staves and beat me as hard as ever they could strike on my head and arms and shoulders, and it was a great while before they beat me down and mazed me, and at last I fell down upon the wet common. There I lay a pretty space, and when I recovered myself again, and saw myself lying on a watery common and all the people standing about me, I lay a little still, and the power of the Lord sprang through me, and the eternal refreshings refreshed me, that I stood up again in the eternal power of God and stretched out my arms amongst them all, and said again with a loud voice, "Strike again, here is my arms and my head and my cheeks." And there was a mason, a rude fellow, a professor called, he gave me a blow with all his might just a-top of my hand, as it was stretched out, with his walking rule-staff. And my hand and arm was so numbed and bruised that I could not draw it in unto me again but it stood out as it was. Then the people cried out, "He hath spoiled his hand, for ever having any use of it more." The skin was struck off my hand and a little blood came, and I looked at it in the love of God, and I was in the love of God to them all that had persecuted me.

And after a while the Lord's power sprang through me again, and through my hand and arm, that in a minute I recovered my hand and arm and strength in the face and sight of them all and it was as well as it was before, and I had never another blow afterward.

And then they began to fall out amongst themselves, and some of them came to me and said if I would give them money they would secure me from the rest; but I denied it. . . . And they said if I came into the town again they would kill me.

And so I was moved of the Lord to come up again through them and up into Ulverston market, and there meets me a man with a sword, a soldier. "Sir," said he, "I am your servant, I am ashamed that you should be thus abused, for you are a man," said he. He was grieved and said he would assist me in what he could, and I told him that it was no matter, the Lord's power was over all.

And so as I walked through the people in the market there was none of them had power to touch me. And this man with his sword was walking after me and some of the market people were striking up of Friends' heels in the market and I turned me about and I saw the soldier amongst them with his naked rapier; and I run amongst them and catched hold of his hand that his rapier was in and bid him put up his sword again if he would come along with me, for I was willing to draw him out from the company, lest some mischief should be done. . . .

And the next morning I went over in a boat to James Lancaster's, he being a Friend. But his wife, being an enemy to Truth, had gathered about forty rude fellows, fisherman and the like, for the people had persuaded James Lancaster's wife that I had bewitched her husband, and they had promised her that if she would let them know when I came hither, they would be my death. So as soon as I came to land they rushed out with staves, clubs and fishing poles and fell upon me with them, beating and punching and thrust me backward to the sea. And when they had thrust me almost into the sea, I saw they would have knocked me down there in the sea and thought to have sunk me down into the water. So I stood up and thrust up into the middle of them again. But they all laid at me again and knocked me down and mazed me. And when I was down and came to myself I looked up and I saw James Lancaster's wife throwing stones at my face and James Lancaster her husband was lying over my shoulders to save the blows and stones. I could hardly tell whether my head was cloven to pieces it was so bruised; nevertheless I was raised up by the power of God. Then they beat me down into the boat, and James Lancaster came into the boat to me and carried me over the water. But while we were on the water within their reach they struck at us with long poles and threw stones after us. We saw afterwards they were beating James Nayler, for while they were beating of me he walked up into a field and they never minded him till I was gone, and then they fell upon him and all their cry was "Kill him, kill him." Then James Lancaster went back again to look after James Nayler. And when I came on the other side of the water to the town where the man had bound himself with an oath to shoot me, all the town rose up with pitch-forks, staffs and flails and muck-hooks to keep me out of the town, and cried, "Kill him, knock him in the head, bring the cart and carry him away to the grave-yard." But they did not, but guarded me with all those weapons a pretty way off out of the town, but did not much abuse me and after a while left me. So I was alone and came to a ditch of water and washed me, for I was very dirty and wet and much bruised. So I walked a matter of three miles from that place where I washed me to Thomas Hutton's house at Rampside. . . . And I desired to have a little beer and I should go to bed, but when I was in bed I could turn me no more than a sucking child, I was so bruised, and the next day Margaret Fell hearing of it at Swarthmoor sent a horse for me, and as I was riding the horse knocked his foot against a stone and stumbled that it shook me and so pained me as it seemed worse to me than all my blows, my body was so tortured. So I came to Swarthmoor; and my body was exceedingly bruised. . . .

The charges against George Fox and his answers thereto.

1. That he did affirm that he had the divinity essentially in him.
ANSWER. For the word essentially, it is an expression of their own, but that the saints are the temples of God and God doth dwell in them, that I witness and the Scripture doth witness, and if God doth dwell in them the divinity dwelleth in them and the Scripture saith the saints shall be made partakers of the divine nature, this I witness. (2 Cor. vi. 15; Eph. iv. 6: 2 Pet. i. 4.)

2. Both baptism and the Lord's Supper are unlawful.
ANSWER. As for the word unlawful, it was not spoken by me, but the sprinkling of infants I deny, and there is no Scripture that speaketh of a sacrament; but that baptism that is in Christ with one spirit into one body, that I confess; and the bread that the saints break is the body of Christ and the cup that they drink is the blood of Jesus Christ, this I witness. (Gal. iii. 27; John vi. 13–58; 2 Cor. x. 16.)

3. He did dissuade men from reading the Scriptures telling them it was carnal.
ANSWER. For dissuading men from reading the Scriptures, it is false, for they were given to be read as they are not to be made a trade upon. But the letter is carnal and killeth, but that which gave it forth is spiritual and eternal and giveth life. This I witness. (2 Cor. iii. 6.)

4. That he was equal with God.
ANSWER. That was not so spoken, but he that sanctifieth and they that are sanctified are all of one in the Father and the Son, and that ye are the sons of God. The Father and the Son are one, and we of his flesh and of his bone; this the Scripture doth witness. (Heb. ii. 11; Eph. v. 31.)

5. That God taught deceit.
ANSWER. That is false, and never was so spoken by me.

6. That the Scriptures were anti-christ.
ANSWER. That is false and was never spoken by me; but they which profess the Scripture's spirit and live not in the life and

power of them, as they did which gave them forth, that I witness to be anti-christ.

7. That he was the judge of the world.
ANSWER. The saints shall judge the world, the Scripture doth witness, whereof I am one, and I witness the Scripture fulfilled. (1 Cor. vi. 2, 3.)

8. That he was as upright as Christ.
ANSWER. Those words were not so spoken by me, but as he is, so are we in this present world, and that the saints are made the righteousness of God; that the saints are one in the Father and the Son; that we shall be like him; that all teaching which is given forth by Christ is to bring the saints to perfection, even to the measure, stature, and fullness of Christ, this the Scripture doth witness, and this I do witness to be fulfilled. (1 John iii. 2; iv. 17; Eph. iv. 1–13.)

When once you deny the Truth then you are given over to believe lies and speak evil of them which live in the Truth, and your lies and envying lie upon them the righteous, you whose minds are envious and sow the seed of envy and make others envious. Oh, therefore, tremble before the Lord ye hypocrites, and mind the light of God in you, which shows you the deceit of your hearts, and obey that. Disobeying your teacher is your condemnation. Hating that light, you hate Christ.

And so I cleared all these things which they charged against me as aforesaid, and several other people that were at the meeting when they said I spoke those words they charged against me, they witnessed that the oath they had taken was altogether false and that no words like those they had sworn against me were spoken by me at that meeting. For indeed there was at that meeting most of the serious men of that side of the country at that time, who were at the Sessions and had heard me at the meeting aforesaid and at other meetings. . . .

And there came many to dispute in Northumberland, and pleaded against perfection. But I declared unto them that Adam and Eve were perfect before they fell, and all that God made was perfect, and the imperfection came by the Devil and the Fall. And Christ that came to destroy the Devil said, "Be ye perfect." But one of the professors said that Job said, "What! shall mortal man be more pure than his maker? The heavens are not clear in his sight. God charged his angels with folly." But I showed him his mistake, that it was not Job which said so, but those which contended against Job. For Job stood for perfection and his integrity; and they were called miserable comforters. And they said the outward body was the body of death and sin. But I let them see their mistakes, and how that Adam and Eve had a body before the body of death and sin got into them. And man and woman would have a body when the body of sin and death was put off again; when they were renewed up into the image of God again by Christ Jesus, that they were in before they fell. . . .

And the priests and the professors, they prophesied mightily against us about this time. For before, they prophesied we should all be knocked down within a month, as aforesaid. Then after, they prophesied within half a year; and their prophecies not coming to pass, they prophesied that we would eat one another out. For many times after the meetings, many tender people had a great way to go, and the houses not having beds, they stayed at the houses and lay in the hay mows. And Cain's fear possessed them, that when we had eaten one another out, we should all come to be maintained of the parishes ere long and that they would be troubled with us. But after this when they saw that the Lord blessed and increased Friends, as he did Abraham, both in the field and in the basket, and at their goings forth and comings in, risings up and lyings down, and that all things began to be blest unto them, then they saw the failings of all these their prophecies and that it was in vain to curse where God had blessed. . . .

Many Friends, being tradesmen of several sorts, lost their custom at the first; for the people would not trade with them nor trust them, and for a time Friends that were tradesmen could hardly get enough money to buy bread. But afterwards people came to see Friends' honesty and truthfulness and "yea" and "nay" at a word in their dealing, and their lives and conversations did preach and reach to the witness of God in all people, and they knew and saw that, for conscience sake towards God, they would not cozen and cheat them, and at last that they might send any child and be as well used as themselves, at any of their shops.

So then things altered so that all the enquiry was, where was a draper or shopkeeper or tailor or shoemaker or any other tradesman that was a Quaker; insomuch that Friends had double the trade, beyond any of their neighbours. And if there was any trading they had it, insomuch that then the cry of all the professors and others was "If we let these people alone they will take the trading of the nation out of our hands." . . .

And after a few days I was had before Oliver Cromwell by Captain Drury. . . .

He brought me in before him before he was dressed, and one Harvey (that had come amongst Friends but was disobedient) waited upon him.

And so when I came before him I was moved to say, "Peace be on this house"; and I bid him keep in the fear of God that he might receive wisdom, that by it he might be ordered, that with it he might order all things under his hand to God's glory. And I spake much to him of Truth, and a great deal of discourse I had with him about religion, wherein he carried himself very moderately; but he said we quarrelled with the priests, whom he called ministers; and I told him I did not quarrel with them, but they quarrelled with me and my friends. And such teachers, and prophets, and shepherds, that the prophets, Christ and the apostles declared against—if we owned the prophets, Christ, and the apostles, we could not hold them up but must declare against them by the same power and spirit. . . .

And many more words I had with him. And many people began to come in, that I drew a little backward, and as I was turning he catched me by the hand and said these words with tears in his eyes, "Come again to my house; for if thou and I were but an hour in a day together we should be nearer one to the other," and that he wished me no more ill than he did to his own soul. . . . So I went out, and he bid me come again. And then Captain Drury came out after me and told me his Lord Protector said I was at liberty and might go whither I would, "And," says he, "my Lord says you are not a fool," and said he never saw such a paper in his life as I had sent him before by him. Then I was brought into a great hall, where the Protector's gentlemen were to dine; and I asked them what they did bring me thither for. They said, it was by the Protector's order, that I might dine with them. I bid them let the Protector know I would not eat a bit of his bread, nor drink a sup of his drink. When he heard this, he said that there was a people risen, meaning us, that he could not win either with honour, high places or gifts, but all other people he could. For we did not seek any of their places, gifts, nor honours, but their salvation and eternal good, both in this nation and elsewhere. But it was told him again that we had forsook our own, and were not like to look for such things from him. . . .

And the next day we came to Launceston where Keate delivered us to the gaoler. Now there were no Friends nor friendly people near us then. And the town was a dark hardened town, that they made us to pay seven shillings a week for our horses and seven shillings a week for our diet a-piece. But at last several sober and friendly people came to see us and some of the town came to be convinced.

And there we lay nine weeks, under a very bad gaoler who much abused us, till the Assizes. . . .

Now the Assize being over, and we settled in prison upon such a commitment, that we were not likely to be soon released, we brake off from the gaoler, from giving a seven shillings a week for our horses and seven shillings a week a-piece for ourselves, and sent our horses into the country. And then he grew very devilish and wicked, and carried us and put us into Doomsdale, a nasty stinking place where they said few people came out alive; where they used to put witches and murderers before their execution; where the prisoners' excrements had not been carried out for scores of years, as it was said. It was all like mire and in some places at the top of the shoes in water and piss, and never a house of office in the place, nor chimney. The gaoler would not let us cleanse the place, nor let us have beds nor straw to lie on; but at night some friendly people of the town brought us a candle and a little straw, and we went to burn a little of our straw to take away the stink. The thieves were put over our heads and the head gaoler lay above with the thieves. It seems the smoke went up into the room and the gaoler was in such a rage that he stamped with his foot and stick and took the pots of excrements of the prisoners and poured it down a hole a-top of our heads in Doomsdale, so that we were so bespattered with the excrements that we could not touch ourselves nor one another, that our stink increased upon us. He quenched our straw with it. And he called us hatchet-faced dogs and such names as we never heard in our lives. What with the stink and what with the smoke, we were like to be choked and smothered, for we had the stink under our feet before but now we had it on our backs. In this manner we stood all night for we could not sit down the place being so full of the prisoners' excrements. And a great while he kept us of this manner before he would let us cleanse it or suffer us to have any victuals in but what we got through the grate.

And at one time a lass brought us a little meat and he arrested her for breaking his house, and had her into the town court for breaking the prison. And a great deal of trouble he brought the young woman to, so that we had much to do to get water, or drink, or victuals. And the noise was amongst the prisoners and people how the spirits haunted and walked in Doomsdale and how many died in it, but I told them and Friends that if all the spirits and devils in hell were there I was over them and feared no such thing, for Christ our priest would sanctify the walls from the house to us, that bruised the head of the Devil. For the priest under the law he was to cleanse the plague out of the walls of the house, which Christ our priest, ended, who sanctifies both inwardly and outwardly the walls of the house and the walls of the heart and all things to his people. . . .

And I was moved again to go and speak to Oliver Protector when there was a talk of making him King. And I met him in the Park and told him that they that would put him on an earthly crown would take away his life.

And he asked me, "What say you?"

And I said again, they that sought to put him on a crown would take away his life, and bid him mind the crown that was immortal.

And he thanked me after I had warned him of many dangers and how he would bring a shame and a ruin upon himself and his posterity, and bid me go to his house. And then I was moved to write to him and told him how he would ruin his family and posterity and bring darkness upon the nation if he did so. And several papers I was moved to write to him. . . .

And I was speaking of the heavenly divine light of Christ which he enlightens every one that cometh into the world withal, and turning them to it to give them the knowledge of the glory of God in the face of Christ Jesus their saviour.

This Priest Tombes cries out, "That is a natural light and a made light."

And then I desired all the people to take out their Bibles; for I would make the Scriptures bend him, and I asked them whether he did affirm that was a created, natural made light that John, a man that was sent from God to bear witness to it, did speak of who said, "In him was life," to wit the Word, "and this life was the light of men." (John i. 4.) And I asked him whether this light was that created, natural, made light he meant.

And he said, "Yes."

Then said I, "Before I have done with thee I will make thee bend to the Scriptures. The natural, created, made light is the sun, moon, and stars and this outward light. And dost thou say that God sent John to bear witness to the sun, moon, and stars which are the made lights?"

Then said he, "Did I say so?"

"Yes," said I, "thou said it was a natural, created, made light that John bare witness unto. And if thou dost not like thy words, take them again and mend them. For John came to bear witness to the light which was the life in the Word, by which all the natural lights were made and created, as sun, moon, and stars and the like. And in him, to wit, the Word, was life; and that life was the light of men."

And then he took at it again and said, that light I spoke of was a natural, created light, and so made it worse and worse in his argument.

And so I made manifest to the people how that in the

beginning was the Word and the Word was with God, and God was the Word, and all things that were made were made by him, and without him was not anything made that was made. So all natural created lights were made by Christ the Word. . . .

I had for some time felt drawings in my spirit to go into Scotland. . . .

And the people were opened to see, and a spring of life riz up amongst them, and many other Scriptures were opened concerning reprobation.

And these things came to the priests' ears, and the people that sat under their dark teachings began to see light and to come into the covenant of light, that the noise that I was come there was spread all over Scotland amongst the priests. And a great cry was amongst them that all was undone and that I had spoiled all the honest men and women in England, so that the worst was left to them. And they gathered great assemblies of priests together and drew up articles to be read in their parishes in the steeplehouses and that all the people should say Amen to them, which are as followeth in part: and the rest may be seen in the book of the Scotch priests' principles.

First: Cursed is he that saith every man hath a light within him sufficient to lead him to salvation and let all the people say, Amen.

Second: Cursed is he that saith faith is without sin and let all the people say, Amen.

Third: Cursed is he that denieth the sabbath day and let all the people say, Amen. . . .

And great sufferings we went through in these times of Oliver Protector and the Commonwealth, and many died in prisons. And they have thrown into our meetings wild fire and rotten eggs, and brought in drums beating, and kettles to make noises with; and the priests as rude as any, as you may see in the book of the fighting priests, a list of the priests that have beat and abused Friends. . . .

And after a while I passed to Reading, and was under great sufferings and exercises, and in a great travail in my spirit for ten weeks time. For I saw how the powers were plucking each other to pieces. And I saw how many men were destroying the simplicity and betraying the Truth. And a great deal of hypocrisy, deceit, and strife was got uppermost in people, that they were ready to sheath their swords in one another's bowels. There was a tenderness in people formerly, but when they were got up and had killed and taken possession, they came to be the worst of men; so that we had so much to do with them about our hats, and saying "Thou" and "Thee" to them, that they turned their profession of patience and moderation into rage and madness, and many of them were like distracted men for this hathonour. And this time, towards 1659, the powers had hardened themselves, persecuting Friends, and had many of them in prison, and were crucifying the Seed, Christ, both in themselves and others. And at last they fell a-biting and devouring one another until they were consumed one of another; who had turned against and judged that which God had wrought in them and showed them. So, God overthrew them, and turned them upside down, and brought the King over them; who were always complaining that the Quakers met together to bring in King Charles, whereas Friends did not concern themselves with the outward powers. But at last the Lord brought him in, and many of them when they saw he would be brought in voted at their meeting of the Parliament for the bringing in of King Charles. So with heart and voice praise the name of the Lord, to whom it doth belong being on them a-top, and over all hath the supreme. And the nations will he rock, being on them a-top. . . .

Much blood was shed this year, and many of them that had been the old King's judges were hanged, drawn and quartered. . . . A sad day it was, and a repaying of blood with blood. For in the time of Oliver Cromwell when several men were put to death by him, being hanged, drawn, and quartered for pretended treasons, I felt from the Lord God, that their blood would not be put up but would be required; and I said as much then to several. And now upon the King's return, several that had been against the King were put to death, as the others that were for the King had been before by Oliver. This was sad work, destroying of people, contrary to the nature of Christians who have the nature of lambs and sheep. . . . And then they complained that all these things that were come to pass were along of us.

And I was moved to write to those justices and to tell them did we ever resist them when they took our ploughs and plough-gear, our cows and horses, our corn and cattle, and kettles and platters from us, and whipped us, and set us in the stocks, and cast us in prison, and all this for serving and worshipping of God in spirit and truth and because we could not conform to their religions, manners, customs and fashions. Did we ever resist them? Did we not give them our backs and our cheeks and our faces to spit on, and our hair to pluck at? And had not their priests that prompted them on to such works plucked them into the ditch? Why would they say it was along of us when it was along of their priests, their blind prophets, that followed their own spirits and could foresee nothing of those times and things that were coming upon them, which we had long forewarned them of, as Jeremiah and Christ had forewarned Jerusalem. And they thought to have ruined and undone us, but they ruined themselves. But we could praise God, notwithstanding all their plundering of us, that we had a kettle, and a platter, and a horse, and plough still. And we do know that if the Presbyterians could get but the magistrates' staff to uphold them, and Judas's bag again, they would be as bad as ever they were; but our backs and cheeks were ready as aforesaid, and we could and can turn them to all the smiters on the earth; and we did not look for any help from men, but our helper was and is the Lord. . . .

Also before this time we received account from New England that they had made a law to banish the Quakers out of their colonies, upon pain of death in case they returned; and that several Friends, so banished, returning were taken and hanged, and that divers more were in prison, in danger of the like sentence. And when they were put to death, as I was in prison at Lancaster, I had a perfect sense of it, as though it had been myself, and as though the halter had been put about my neck.

But as soon as we heard of it, Edward Burrough went to the King, and told him there was a vein of innocent blood opened in his dominions, which, if it were not stopped would overrun all.

To which the King answered "But I will stop that vein." Edward Burrough said, "Then do it speedily, for we do not know how many may soon be put to death." The King answered "As speedily as ye will. Call," said he to some present, "the secretary, and I will do it presently." The secretary being called, a mandamus was forthwith granted. A day or two after, Edward Burrough going again to the King, to desire the matter might be expedited, the King said he had no occasion at present to send a ship thither, but if we would send one we might do it as soon as we would. Edward Burrough then asked the King if it would please him to grant his deputation to one called a Quaker, to carry the mandamus to New England. He said, "Yes, to whom ye will." Whereupon Edward Burrough named one Samuel Shattuck, (as I remember) who, being an inhabitant of New England, was banished by their law to be hanged if he came again; and to him the deputation was granted. Then we sent for one Ralph Goldsmith, an honest Friend, who was master of a good ship, and agreed with him for £300, goods or no goods, to sail in ten days. He forthwith prepared to set sail, and, with a prosperous gale, in about six weeks time arrived before the town of Boston in New England upon a First-day morning, called Sunday. With him went many passengers, both of New and Old England, that were Friends whom the Lord did move to go to bear their testimony against those bloody persecutors, who had exceeded all the world in that age in their persecutions.

The townsmen at Boston, seeing a ship come into the bay with English colours, soon came on board, and asked for the captain. Ralph Goldsmith told them he was the commander. They asked him if he had any letters. He said, "Yes." They asked if he would deliver them. He said, "No, not to-day." So they went a-shore and reported there was a ship full of Quakers, and that Samuel Shattuck was among them, who they knew was, by their law, to be put to death for coming again after banishment; but they knew not his errand, nor his authority.

So all being kept close that day, and none of the ship's company suffered to land, next morning, Samuel Shattuck, the King's deputy, and Ralph Goldsmith, the commander of the vessel, went on shore; and sending back to the ship the men that landed them, they two went through the town to the governor John Endicott's door, and knocked. He sent out a man to know their business. They sent him word their business was from the King of England, and they would deliver their message to none but the governor himself. Thereupon they were admitted to go in, and the governor came to them, and having received the deputation and the mandamus, he laid off his hat, and looked upon them. Then going out, he bid the Friends follow him. So he went to the deputy-governor, and after a short consultation, came out to the Friends, and said, "We shall obey his Majesty's commands," as by the order may be seen, and the relation in William Coddington's book, who is governor of Rhode Island and a Friend. After this, the master gave liberty to the passengers to come on shore, and presently the noise of the business flew about the town, and the Friends of the town and the passengers of the ship met together to offer up their praises and thanksgivings to God, who had so wonderfully delivered them from the teeth of the devourer. . . .

And there were many Papists and Jesuits in this year that made a boast and said that of all the sects the Quakers were the best and most self-denying people, and it was great pity that they did not return to the holy mother Church. And so they talked and made a buzz amongst people and said they would willingly discourse with Friends.

But Friends were loth because they were Jesuits and thought it was dangerous or might be esteemed so by others.

But I said to Friends, "Let us discourse with them, be they what they will." And so a meeting was appointed at Gerard Roberts's house, and there came two like courtiers.

And so they began to ask our names, and we told them we did not ask their names but understood they were called Papists and we were called Quakers.

Then I asked them the same question as I had formerly of a Jesuit, whether the Church of Rome was not degenerated from the Church in the primitive times, from the spirit, and power and practice that they were in in the apostles' time.

And one of them being subtle said he would not answer me, and I asked him why, but he would show no reason. But the

other said he would answer me. And he said they were not
degenerated from the Church in the primitive times. And I
asked the other whether he was of the same mind and he said
yes. So I bid them repeat their words over again, that we might
the better understand one another, whether the Church of
Rome now was in the same purity, practice, power, and spirit
that the Church was in in the apostles' times. When they saw
that we would be exact with them they flew off and denied that,
and said it was presumption for any to say they had the same
power and spirit the apostles had.

So then I showed them how different their fruits and
practices were from the fruits and practices of the apostles.

And therefore for them to meddle with Christ's and the
apostles' words and to make people believe they succeeded the
apostles, but not in the same power and spirit that the apostles
were in was all in a spirit of presumption, and rebuked by the
apostles' spirit.

Then one of them got up and said, "Ye are a company of
dreamers"; "Nay," said I, "you are the filthy dreamers that
despise the government of the spirit and the power that the
apostles were in, and defile your flesh and say it is presumption
for any to say they have the same power and spirit the apostles
were in, and if you have not the same power and spirit, then it
is manifest that you are led by another power and spirit than the
apostles and Church in the primitive times."

So I began to tell them how that evil spirit led them to pray
by beads and to images, and to put people to death for religion,
and to set up nunneries and friaries and monasteries.

And this practice of theirs was below the law and short of
the gospel, the power of God, in which was liberty.

They were soon weary of this discourse, went their ways
down the stairs and gave a charge to the Papists that they should
not dispute with us, or read none of our books for we were a
subtle people. . . .

The priests and professors of all sorts were much against
Friends' silent meetings, and sometimes the priests and professors would come to our meetings; and when they saw a hundred
or two hundred people all silent, waiting upon the Lord, they

would break out into a wondering and despising, and some of
them would say: "Look how these people sit mumming and
dumming. What edification is here where there are no words?
Come," would they say, "let us be gone, what! should we stay
here to see a people sit of this manner?" And they said they never
saw the like in their lives. Then it may be some Friends have
been moved to speak to them and say, "Didst thou never see the
like in thy life? Look in thy own parish and let the priest and thee
see there how your people sit mumming and dumming and
sleeping under your priests all their life time; who keep people
always under their teaching that they may be always paying.". . .

I was kept in prison till the Assizes, and at the Assizes there
was Judge Turner and Judge Twysden. And I was had before
Judge Twysden as may be seen in the papers of the examination
at large as followeth:

THE EXAMINATION OF GEORGE FOX BEFORE THE JUDGE AT
LANCASTER CONCERNING THE OATH OF ALLEGIANCE 1663

George Fox was called before Judge Twysden, being a prisoner
at the place aforesaid.
JUDGE: What! do you come into the Court with your hat on?
    Then the gaoler took it off.
GEORGE FOX: Peace be amongst you all. The hat is not the
honour that came down from God.
JUDGE: Will you take the Oath of Allegiance, George Fox?
G.F.: I never took an oath in my life, covenant, nor engagement.
JUDGE: Will you swear or no?
G.F.: Christ commands me not to swear at all, and the Apostle
James likewise. I am neither Turk nor Jew nor heathen, but a
Christian, and should show forth Christianity. Do you not know
that the Christians in primitive times refused swearing in the
days of the ten persecutions, and some of the martyrs in Queen
Mary's days because Christ and the apostles had forbidden it?
Have you not experience enough how many men at first swore
for the King and then against the King? Whether must I obey
God or man, I put it to thee, so judge thee.

JUDGE: I will not dispute with thee, George Fox. Come, read the oath to him.

And so the oath was read.

JUDGE: Give him the Book.

And so a man that stood by me held up the Book and said, "Lay your hands upon the Book."

G.F.: Give me the Book in my hand (which set them all a-gazing, as a hope I would have sworn; then when I got the Book in my hand, I held it up, and said) it is commanded in this Book not to swear at all. If it be a Bible, I will prove it.

And I saw it was a Bible, and I held it up, and then they plucked it out of my hand again, and cried, "Will you swear? Will you take the oath of Allegiance, yea or nay?"

G.F.: My allegiance to the King lieth not in oaths, but in truth and faithfulness, for I honour all men, much more the King, but Christ saith I must not swear, the great prophet, the saviour of the world, and the judge of the world; and thou sayest I must swear; whether must I obey Christ or thee? For it is in tenderness of conscience that I do not swear, in obedience to the command of Christ and the Apostle, and for his sake I suffer, and in obedience to his command do I stand this day. And we have the word of a King for tender consciences, besides his speeches and declarations at Breda. Dost thou own the King?

JUDGE: Yes, I own the King.

G.F.: Then why dost not thou own his speeches and declarations concerning tender conscience? (to the which he replied nothing; but I said), it is in obedience to Christ the saviour of the world, and the judge of the world, before whose judgment seat all must be brought that I do not swear, and I am a man of a tender conscience.

And then the judge stood up.

JUDGE: I will not be afraid of thee, George Fox, thou speakest so loud, thy voice drowns mine and the Court's; I must call for three or four criers to drown thy voice; thou hast good lungs.

G.F.: I am a prisoner here this day for the Lord Jesus Christ's sake, that made heaven and earth, and for his sake I suffer, and for him do I stand this day; and if my voice were five times louder, yet should I sound it out, and lift it up for Christ's sake, for whose cause sake I stand this day before your judgment seat, in obedience to Christ's command, who commands not to swear, before whose judgment seat you must all be brought and give an account.

Then he was moved and looked angrily at me.

JUDGE: Sirrah, will you take the oath?

G.F.: I am none of thy sirrahs, I am no sirrah, I am a Christian. Art thou a judge and sits there and gives names to prisoners? It does not become either thy gray hairs or thy office. Thou ought not to give names to prisoners.

JUDGE: I am a Christian too.

G.F.: Then do Christian works.

JUDGE: Sirrah, thou thinkest to frighten me with thy words (and looked aside and said, "I am saying so again").

G.F.: I speak in love to thee. That doth not become a judge, thou oughtest to instruct a prisoner of the law, and the Scripture, if he were ignorant, and out of the way.

JUDGE: George Fox, I speak in love to thee, too.

G.F.: Love gives no names.

JUDGE: Wilt thou swear? Wilt thou take the oath, yea or nay?

G.F.: As I said before, whether must I obey God or man, judge thee. Christ commands not to swear, and if thee or you, or any minister, or priest here will prove that ever Christ or the apostles, after they had forbidden swearing, commanded they should swear, then I will swear. And several priests being there never a one appeared or offered to speak. . . .

The 16th day of the same month, I was brought before the judge the second time, where he was a little offended at my hat; but being the last morning before he was to depart away and not many people, he made the less of it.

The judge read a paper to me, which was whether I would submit, stand mute, or traverse, and so have judgment passed. He spoke both these and many more words so very fast and in haste that we could not well tell what he said.

G.F.: I desire it may be traversed and tried, that I may have the liberty.

JUDGE: Take him away then, I will have no more with him; take him away.

G.F.: Live in the fear of God and do justice.

JUDGE: Why, have I not done you justice?

G.F.: That which thou hast done hath been against the commands of Christ. . . .

So he caused the oath to be read to me, and then when the oath was read he asked me whether I would take the oath or no, the grand jury standing by. . . .

And as I was turning them to the places and holding up the Bible, and telling them that I said as the book said, and that it and Christ forbid swearing, I wondered that the Bible was at liberty and that they did not imprison the book that forbids to swear. So I told them, "You may imprison the book."

The judge said, "But we will imprison George Fox."

I answered, Nay, you may imprison the book which saith, 'Swear not at all.' " Then they plucked the Bible out of my hand.

And this got abroad all over the country as a byword, that the Bible should be at liberty, and I in prison who said as the book said. . . .

Then the sheriff and the judge said the angel swore in the Revelation.

And I said, "I bring forth my first begotten son into the world, saith God; let all the angels in heaven worship him, who saith 'Swear not at all.' "

And the judge said he would not dispute.

And I said if they could not convince me, let the priests stand up and do it, there being many priests there; and if they could not do it let the bishop come and do it. But never a one of the priests made any answer. So then I spake much to the jury, how that which I did was for Christ's sake, and let none of them act contrary to that of God in their consciences, for before his judgment seat they must all be brought. "And as for all those things contained in the oath, as plots and persecuting about religion, and popery, I deny them in my heart, and shall show forth Christianity this day. It is for Christ's sake I stand. For it is Lo Tishshabiun becol dabar" [transliterated Hebrew for "Ye shall not swear by anything."] And they all gazed, and there was a great calm. . . .

And so they committed me again to close prison. And Colonel Kirkby gave order to the gaoler that no flesh alive must come at me for I was not fit to be discoursed with by men.

So I was put up in a smoky tower where the smoke of the other rooms came up and stood as a dew upon the walls, where it rained in also upon my bed and the smoke was so thick as I could hardly see a candle sometimes, and many times I was locked under three locks; and the under-gaoler would hardly come up to unlock one of the upper doors; the smoke was so thick that I was almost smothered with smoke and so starved with cold and rain that my body was almost numbed, and my body swelled with the cold.

And many times when I went to stop out the rain off me in the cold winter season, my shift would be as wet as muck with rain that came in upon me. And as fast as I stopped it the wind, being high and fierce, would blow it out again; and in this manner did I lie all that long cold winter till the next Assizes. . . .

And after a while John Whitehead brought an order from the King for my release.

For after I had lain prisoner above a year in Scarborough Castle, I sent a letter to the King, concerning my imprisonment, and bad usage in prison; and I was informed, no one could deliver me but he. . . .

So the governor received the order, and the officers gathered together, and discharged me without requiring bonds or sureties for my peaceable living, being satisfied that I was a man of a peaceable life. . . .

The first day I came out of that prison the fire broke out in London, that consumed most part of the city in three days time. And then I saw the Lord God was true and just in his word that he had showed me before in Lancaster Gaol. The people of London were forewarned of this fire; yet few people laid it to heart but grew rather more wicked and higher in pride.

We had a Friend that was moved to come out of Huntingdonshire before the fire, and to scatter his money up and down the streets, and to turn his horse loose in the streets and to untie his breeches' knees, and let his stockings fall, and to unbutton his doublet, and to tell the people so should they run up and down scattering their money and their goods half undressed like mad people, as he gave them a sign. And so they did when the fire broke out and the city was burning. . . .

And many have been moved to go naked in their streets as signs of their nakedness. And many men and women have been moved to go naked and in sackcloth, in the other power's days and since, as signs of their nakedness from the image of God and righteousness and holiness, and how that God would strip them and make them bare and naked as they were. But, instead of considering of it, they have many times whipped them and imprisoned them or abused them. . . .

And there was a great marriage of two Friends the next day. And there came some hundreds of beggars. And Friends refreshed them instead of the rich. And in the meeting before the marriage I was moved to open to the people the state of our marriages, how the people of God took one another in the assemblies of the elders, and how God did join man and woman together before the Fall. And man had joined in the Fall but it was God's joining again in the restoration, and never from Genesis to the Revelation did ever any priests marry any, as may be read in the Scriptures. And then I showed them the duty of man and wife how they should serve God, being heirs of life and grace together. . . .

And after a while I went to visit Esquire Marsh. And he was at dinner, and he sent for me up. And there were several great persons at dinner with him and he would have had me sit down with him to dinner but I was not free. And he said to a great Papist then there, "Here is a Quaker which you have not seen before."

And the Papist asked me whether I did own the christening of children.

And I told him there was no Scripture for any such practice.

"What!" said he, "not for christening children?"

And I said, "Nay," but if he meant the one baptism with the

spirit into one body, that we owned, but to throw a little water in a child's face and say it was baptised (or christened) there was no Scripture for that.

Then he asked me whether I did own the catholic faith.

I said, "Yes." But neither the Pope nor the Papists were in that catholic faith, for the true catholic faith works by love and purifies the heart; and if they were in that faith that gives victory, by which they might have access to God, they would not tell people of a purgatory after they were dead. So I would prove that neither Pope nor Papists that held up purgatory were in the true faith, for the true, precious, and divine faith, which Christ is the author of gives victory over the Devil and sin that had separated man and woman from God.

And if they were in the true faith they would never make racks, and prisons, gaols, and fires to persecute and force others that were not of their faith, for this was not the practice of the true faith of Christ that was witnessed and enjoyed by the apostles and primitive Church; neither had they any such command from Christ and the apostles. But it was the practice of the faithless Jews and heathen so to do.

And I said unto him, "Seeing thou art a great and leading man amongst the Papists and hast been taught and bred up under the Pope; and seeing thou says there is no salvation but in your Church, I have two questions to ask thee. The first is: "What is it that doth bring salvation to your Church?"

He answered, "A good life."

"And nothing else?" said I.

"Yes," said he, "good works."

"And is this it that brings salvation in your Church—a good life and good works? Is this your doctrine and principle?"

"Yes," said he.

Then I said, "Neither the Papists, Pope, nor thou dost know what it is that brings salvation."

Then he asked me what brought salvation in our Church.

I told him, "The same that brought salvation to the Church in the apostles' days, the same brought salvation to us and not another, which is the grace of God which brings salvation, which hath appeared unto all men; which taught the saints and teaches us then and now. And this grace is it which brings salvation, which teaches to live godily, righteously, and soberly, and to deny ungodliness and worldly lusts. So it is not good works, nor good life, that brings salvation but the grace."

"What!" said the Papist, "doth this grace that brings salvation appear unto all men?"

"Yes," said I.

"But I deny that," said the Papist.

Then I said, "I know ye Papists will deny that, and therefore ye are sect-makers and are not in the universal faith, grace, and truth, as the apostles were."

Then he spoke to me about the Mother Church. And I told him often the several sorts of sects in Christendom would accuse us and say we forsake our Mother Church.

And one while, the Papists would be charging of us for forsaking the Mother Church, who would say that Rome was the only Mother Church.

And another while, the Episcopalians; and they would be charging of us for forsaking the old Protestant religion, and they would say theirs was the reformed Mother Church.

And then again the Presbyterians and Independents; they would be accusing of us for forsaking of them, and they would say theirs was the right reformed Church.

And unto them all I answered that if we could own any outward city or place to be the Mother Church or any outward profession, we would own outward Jerusalem; where Christ and the Apostle preached and suffered and . . . where the first great conversion to Christianity was. . . .

And so after many words with them I went aside with Esquire Marsh into another room for he was a justice of peace at Limehouse, and being a courtier the other justices put off the management of matters more upon him.

Now he told me he was in a strait. And he said unto me, "You cannot swear, and so also say the Independent and Baptists and Monarchy people, that they cannot swear; therefore how shall I know how to distinguish betwixt you and them seeing they and you all say it is for conscience sake you cannot swear?"

Then I said, "I will show thee how to distinguish. These

thou speaks of can and do swear in some cases; but we cannot in any case. For if a man should take their cows or horses, if thou shouldst ask them whether they would swear they were theirs, they would readily do it. But if thou try our Friends, they cannot swear for their own goods, so when thou puttest the Oath of Allegiance to them, ask whether they can swear in any case, or for their cow or their horse; which they cannot do though they can bear witness to the Truth.

"For there was a thief stole two beasts from a Friend in Berkshire, which thief was taken and cast into prison. And the Friend appeared against him at the Assizes; and some people told the judge that the Friend that prosecuted was a Quaker and would not swear. And before he heard what he would say, 'Is he a Quaker?' said the judge, 'and won't he swear; then put the Oaths of Allegiance and Supremacy to him.' So they cast the Friend into prison and praemunired him and let the thief go at liberty that had stolen his goods."

Then said Esquire Marsh, "That judge was a wicked man."

"So," then I said, "thou must see that if we could swear in any case, we would take the Oath of Allegiance to the King who is to preserve the laws, which laws preserve every man in his estate. But they can swear for their own ends, or that such a man stole from them, to bring him to the law to preserve a part of their estates, and yet they will not take an oath to the King who is to preserve them in their whole estates and bodies also. So thou mayest easily distinguish, and put a difference betwixt us and other people." . . .

And after I had cleared myself of the Lord's service thataways, I passed away. And from thence we came through the country and had many precious meetings till we came to Bristol where I had many precious meetings. When I came to Bristol a letter met me there from John Stubbs in Ireland.

And there Margaret Fell and her daughters and sons-in-law met me, where we were married. Margaret Fell was come to visit her daughter Yeamans.

I had seen from the Lord a considerable time before that I should take Margaret Fell to be my wife. And when I first mentioned it to her she felt the answer of life from God thereunto. But though the Lord had opened this thing unto me, yet I had not received a command from the Lord for the accomplishment of it then. Wherefore I let the thing rest, and went on in the work and service of the Lord as before, according as the Lord led me, travelling up and down in this nation and through the nation of Ireland. But now, after I was come back from Ireland and was come to Bristol and found Margaret Fell there, it opened in me from the Lord that the thing should be now accomplished.

And after we had discoursed the thing together I told her if she also was satisfied with the accomplishing of it now she should first send for her children, which she did. And when the rest of her daughters were come I was moved to ask the children and her sons-in-law whether they were all satisfied and whether Margaret had answered them according to her husband's will to her children, she being a widow, and if her husband had left anything to her for the assistance of her children, in which if she married they might suffer loss, whether she had answered them in lieu of that and all other things. And the children made answer and said she had doubled it, and would not have me to speak of those things. I told them I was plain and would have all things done plainly, for I sought not any outward advantage to myself.

And so when I had thus acquainted the children with it and when it had been laid before several meetings both of the men and women, assembled together for that purpose, and all were satisfied, there was a large meeting appointed of purpose in the meeting house at Broad Mead in Bristol, the Lord joining us together in the honourable marriage in the everlasting covenant and immortal Seed of life, where there were several large testimonies borne by Friends. Then was a certificate, relating both the proceedings and the marriage, openly read and signed by the relations and by most of the ancient Friends of that city, besides many other Friends from divers parts of the nation. . . .

And there was one Walter Newton, a neighbour to my relations, who had been an ancient Puritan, said unto me he heard I was married, and asked the reason. And I told him, as a testimony, that all might come up into the marriage as was in the beginning, and as testimony that all might come up out of the wilderness to the marriage of the Lamb. And he said he thought marriage was only for the procreation of children, and I told him I never thought of any such thing but only in obedience to the power of the Lord. And I judged such things below me, though I saw such things and established marriages; but I looked on it as below me. And though I saw such a thing in the Seed yet I had no command to such a thing till a half year before, though people had long talked of it, and there was some jumble in some minds about it, but the Lord's power came over all and laid all their spirits; and some after confessed it. . . .

And the next day we passed away after I had finished my service for the Lord there; and as I was going towards Rochester I lighted and walked down a hill; and a great weight and oppression fell on my spirit. So I got on my horse again, but my weight and oppression remained so as I was hardly able to ride. So we came to Rochester; but I was very weak to ride, and very much loaden and burdened with the world's spirits, so that my life was oppressed under them.

I got to Gravesend and went to an inn but could hardly eat or sleep.

And the next day . . . I endeavoured to ride ten miles to Stratford, three miles off London, to an honest Friend's house, that had been a captain whose name was Williams; but I was exceeding weak. And several Friends came thither unto me from London.

But at last I lost my hearing and sight so as I could not see nor hear. And I said unto Friends that I should be as a sign to such as would not see, and such as would not hear the Truth. And in this condition I continued a pretty while. And several people came about me, but I felt their spirits and discerned, though I could not see them, who was honest hearted and who was not.

And several Friends that were doctors came and would have given me physic but I was not to meddle with their things. And under great sufferings and groans and travails, and sorrows and oppressions, I lay for several weeks. . . .

And the next morning I spoke to Friends to get a coach to carry me to Gerard Roberts about twelve miles off, and I called for my clothes, which put them into more fears and doubts, because people had used to desire a little before their departing to be changed; and so they said I had all the symptoms of death upon me and all their hopes were gone, except two or three. And when they thought to put me by concerning my clothes and made excuses, I perceived it and told them it was deceit, but at last they brought me my clothes and things and put them on. And so I spoke to the man and woman of the house and had a little glimmering sight, and I saw Edward Mann's wife putting up my clothes and told her she did well; and I felt the Lord's power was over all. So I went down a pair of stairs to the coach, and when I came to the coach I was like to have fallen down I was so weak and feeble, but I got up into the coach and some Friends with me and I could discern the people and fields and that was all.

And it was noised up and down in London that I was deceased but the next news they heard I was gone twelve miles in a coach to Gerard Roberts who was very weak, which astonished them to hear it. And I was moved to speak to him and encourage him, though I could hardly hear or see. And there I was about three weeks, and many times I could not tell when it was day or when it was night; and once I lay twenty-four hours, and asked them what day it was, and they said I had missed a day. . . .

And . . . I lay . . . all that winter, warring with the evil spirits, and could not endure the smell of any flesh meat.

And I saw all the religions and people that lived in them and the priests that held them up, as a company of men-eaters, and how they ate up the people like bread, gnawing the flesh off their bones. And great sufferings I was under at this time beyond words to declare, for I was come into the deep, and the men-eaters were about me and I warred with their spirits. . . .

And it was a cruel bloody persecuting time, but the Lord's power went over all, and his everlasting Seed. And as persecution began to cease I began to arise out of my sufferings. . . .

And at last I overcame these spirits and men-eaters though many times I was so weak that people knew not whether I was in the body or out. And many precious Friends came far and

nigh to see me and attended upon me and were with me; and
towards the spring I began to recover and to walk up and down,
to the astonishment of Friends and others. . . .

And I had a vision about the time that I was in this travail
and sufferings, that I was walking in the fields and many Friends
were with me, and I bid them dig in the earth, and they did and
I went down. And there was a mighty vault top-full of people
kept under the earth, rocks, and stones. So I bid them break
open the earth and let all the people out, and they did, and all the
people came forth to liberty; and it was a mighty place. And
when they had done I went on and bid them dig again. They did,
and there was a mighty vault full of people, and I bid them throw
it down and let all the people out, and so they did.

And I went on again and bid them dig again, and Friends
said unto me, "George, thou finds out all things," and so there
they digged, and I went down, and went along the vault; and
there sat a woman in white looking at time how it passed away.
And there followed me a woman down in the vault, in which
vault was the treasure; and so she laid her hand on the treasure
on my left hand and then time whisked on apace; but I clapped
my hand upon her and said, "Touch not the treasure." And then
time passed not so swift.

They that can read these things must have the earthy,
stony nature off them. And see how the stones and the earth
came upon man since the beginning, since he fell from the
image of God and righteousness and holiness. And much I could
speak of these things, but I leave them to the right eye and
reader to see and read. . . .

And there a Friend, John Jay of Barbados, that was with me
went to try a horse, and got on his back. And the horse ran and
cast him on his head and broke his neck as they called it, and the
people took him up dead, and carried him a good way, and laid
him on a tree. And I came to him and felt on him, and saw that
he was dead, and as I was pitying his family and him, for he was
one that was to pass with me through the woods to Maryland that
land journey, I took him by the hair of his head, and his head

turned like a cloth it was so loose. I threw away my stick and gloves, and took his head in both my hands, and set my knees against the tree and wrested his head and I did perceive it was not broken out that way. And I put my hand under his chin, and behind his head, and wrested his head two or three times with all my strength, and brought it in, and I did perceive his neck began to be stiff, and then he began to rattle, and after to breathe, and the people were amazed, and I bid them have a good heart and be of good faith, and carry him into the house, and then they set him by the fire, and I bid them get him some warm thing to drink and get him to bed. So after he had been in the house awhile, he began to speak, and did not know where he had been. So we bound up his neck warm with a napkin, and the next day we passed on and he with us, pretty well, about sixteen miles to a meeting at Middletown, and many hundreds of miles afterwards, through the woods and bogs. And we swam our horses over a river, and went over on a tree ourselves. And at the meeting was most of the town. And Friends were and are very well, blessed be the Lord, and a glorious meeting we had and the Truth was over all, blessed be the great Lord God for ever. . . .

(By the time I thought my wife could be got home, I wrote her the following letter.)

8th of 12th mo. 1673 (Feb., 1674)

Dear Heart,

Thou seemed to be much grieved when I was speaking of prisons, and when I was taken thou began to fall upon me with blaming of me, and I told thee that I was to bear it, and why could not thee be content with the will of God? And thou said some words and then was pretty quiet. And thou was loath to go to Parker, but it was well thou did, and it had been well thou had been more over it to me; for when I was at John Rous's I saw that I was taken prisoner, and when I was at Bray D'Oyly's as I sat at supper, I saw I was taken the night before I was.

The three pound thou sent up to me, in love, for it I did speak to a Friend to send thee as much Spanish black cloth as will make thee a gown and it did cost us a pretty deal of money.

And I saw I had a winepress to tread and the Lord's power

is over all, blessed be his name for ever; and not only so but the winepress is to be trodden among Friends where the life is not lived in.

I hear of a ship of Thomas Edmondson's is cast away, which I had a part in, but let it go; and Thomas can give you or thee an account of all things.   G.F.

Another time came a Common-Prayer priest, and some people with him, and he asked me if I was grown up to perfection.

I told him what I was, I was by the grace of God.

He replied, it was a modest and civil answer. Then he urged the words of John, "If we say that we have no sin, we deceive ourselves, and the truth is not in us." And he asked, what did I say to that.

I said, with the same apostle, "If we say that we have not sinned we make him a liar and his word is not in us"; who came to destroy sin, and to take away sin. So there is a time for people to see that they have sinned, and there is a time for them to see that they have sin; and there is a time for them to confess their sin, and forsake it, and to know "the blood of Christ to cleanse from all sin." Then the priest was asked whether Adam was not perfect before he fell, and whether all God's works were not perfect.

The priest said, there might be a perfection, as Adam had, and a falling from it.

But I told him, "There is a perfection in Christ, above Adam and beyond falling; and that it was the work of the ministers of Christ to present every man perfect in Christ; and for the perfecting of whom they had their gifts from Christ; therefore, they that denied perfection denied the work of the ministry, and the gifts which Christ gave for the perfecting of the saints."

The priest said, we must always be striving.

But I told him it was a sad and comfortless sort of striving, to strive with a belief that we should never overcome. I told him also that Paul, who cried out of the body of death, did also thank God who gave him the victory, through our Lord Jesus Christ. So there was a time of crying out for want of victory, and a time of praising God for the victory. And Paul said, "There is no condemnation to them that are in Christ Jesus." . . .

About this time I had a fit of sickness, which brought me very low and weak in my body; and I continued so a pretty while, insomuch that some Friends began to doubt of my recovery. I seemed myself to be amongst the graves and dead corpses; yet the invisible power did secretly support me, and conveyed refreshing strength into me, even when I was so weak that I was almost speechless. One night, as I was lying awake upon my bed in the glory of the Lord which was over all, it was said unto me that the Lord had a great deal more work for me to do for him before he took me to himself.

Endeavours were used to get me released, at least for a time, till I was grown stronger; but the way of effecting it proved difficult and tedious; for the King was not willing to release me by any other way than a pardon, being told he could not legally do it; and I was not willing to be released by a pardon, which he would readily have given me, because I did not look upon that way agreeable with the innocency of my cause. . . .

After this, my wife went to London, and spoke to the King, laying before him my long and unjust imprisonment, with the manner of my being taken, and the justices' proceedings against me in tendering me the oath as a snare, whereby they had praemunired me; so that I being now his prisoner, it was in his power and at his pleasure to release, which she desired. The King spoke kindly to her, and referred her to the lord-keeper, to whom she went, but could not obtain what she desired; for he said the King could not release me otherwise than by a pardon; and I was not free to receive a pardon, knowing I had not done evil. If I would have been freed by a pardon, I need not have lain so long, for the King was willing to give me pardon long before, and told Thomas Moore that I need not scruple being released by a pardon, for many a man that was as innocent as a child had had a pardon granted him. Yet I could not consent to have one. For I had rather have lain in prison all my days than have come out in any way dishonourable to truth; wherefore I chose to have validity of my indictment tried before the judges. . . .

THOMAS ELLWOOD'S ACCOUNT OF FOX'S DEATH

The 11th day of the 11th month [January 1691], and the first day of the week, he was at Gracechurch Street meeting, where he declared a long time very preciously and very audibly and went to prayer. And the meeting after departed, which was large. Thence he went to Henry Gouldney's, a Friend's house in Whitehart Court near the meeting-house. And he said he thought he felt the cold strike to his heart as he came out of the meeting, but was pretty cheery with Friends that came to him there, and said, "I am glad I was here. Now I am clear, I am fully clear." And after they were gone he lay down upon the bed (as he was wont to do after a meeting) twice. And at his risings, which were but for a little space, he still complained of cold. The latter time he was worse and groaned much, so that after a very little, being much out of order he was forced to go to bed, where he lay in much contentment and peace, and very sensible to the last.

And in about two hours after, his strength failed him very much, and so he continued spending. And as in the whole course of his life, his spirit in the universal love of God was set and bent for the exalting of Truth and righteousness, and the making known the way thereof to the nations and peoples afar off, so now in the time of his outward weakness, his mind was intent upon, and (as it were) wholly taken up with that. And some particular Friends he sent for, to whom he expressed his mind and desire for the spreading Friends' books, and Truth thereby in the world, and through the nations thereof. Divers Friends came to visit him in his illness, unto some of whom he said, "All is well. The Seed of God reigns over all, and over death itself. And though I am weak in body, yet the power of God is over all, and the Seed reigns over all disorderly spirits."

Thus lying in an heavenly frame of mind, his spirit wholly exercised towards the Lord, he grew weaker and weaker in his natural strength; and on the third day of that week, between the hours of nine and ten in the evening, he quietly departed this life in peace, and sweetly fell asleep in the Lord . . . on the 13th day of the 11th month, 1690 [January 1691], being then in the 67th year of his age.

THE FIRST PUBLISHERS
OF TRUTH

The doctrine they taught and the example they led. . .

—WILLIAM PENN

"For of Light Came Sight"

[FROM *"Preface to George Fox's* Journal*"*]

WILLIAM PENN

[*Asked to name a Quaker, most Americans, if they could answer at all,
would probably name William Penn. This has nothing to do with what
Penn did or wrote, but is the result of the chance that has left his name
on our land. Pennsylvania is Penn's Wood; and Philadelphia is the
"city of brotherly love."*

*Penn (1644–1718) was the son of a Cromwellian "General of the
Fleet" who, subsequently, was knighted by Charles II. Such a man
obviously knows how to get on in the world; and no son of his, except that
he had become a Quaker, would have exchanged money owed him by the
crown to provide a home in the New World for his fellow worshipers.*

*Penn was converted to Quakerism at the age of twenty-three, when
he heard the Quaker minister Thomas Loe preach on the text, "There is
a faith that is overcome by the world and a faith that overcomes the
world." Early Quakers, generally, were ready to (and, whether they*

107

were ready or not, often had to) renounce the world for their faith. Few of them had as much world to renounce as Penn; and though Penn's renunciation was complete, he had, up to the age of twenty-three, lived in the world, and he remained to the end in some sense a man of the world. Penn was, in the manner of his writing and in the balance of his mind, of the company of Montaigne, Franklin, Sir Thomas More, and La Rochefoucauld. Far from being the cliché Quaker of downcast eyes and sealed lips, Penn believed in discourse and declared that "they are next to unnatural that are not communicable."

Though they were one in Christ, it is this communicability which doubtless explains the sympathy and understanding which existed between men as unlike in background and upbringing as Fox and Penn. Fox, like Penn, was highly communicable. Penn, however, never doubted the superiority of Fox's spiritual gifts; and it is from Penn we have received the most complete picture of Fox and the clearest exposition by an early Quaker of the beliefs of early Quakers.]

———

Two things are to be considered: The doctrine they taught and the example they led among all people. I have already touched upon their fundamental principle, which is as the cornerstone of their fabric, and indeed, to speak eminently and properly, their characteristic or main distinguishing point or principle, viz., the light of Christ within, as God's gift for man's salvation. This, I say, is as the root of the goodly tree of doctrines that grew and branched out from it, which I shall now mention in their natural and experimental order.

First, repentance from dead works to serve the living God. Which comprehends three operations: first, a sight of sin; secondly, a sense and godly sorrow for sin; thirdly, an amendment for the time to come. This was the repentance they preached and pressed and a natural result from the principle they turned all people unto. For of light came sight, and of sight came sense and sorrow, and of sense and sorrow came amendment of life. . . . None can come to know Christ to be their sacrifice that reject Him as their sanctifier, the end of His coming being to save His people from the nature and defilement as well as guilt of sin; and . . . therefore those that resist His light and spirit make His coming and offering of none effect to them.

From hence sprang a second doctrine they were led to declare as the mark of the price of the high calling to all true Christians, viz., perfection from sin, according to the Scriptures of truth, which testify it to be the end of Christ's coming and the nature of His Kingdom, and for which His spirit was and is given, viz., to be perfect as our Heavenly Father is perfect, and holy because God is holy. . . .

Thirdly, this leads to an acknowledgment of eternal rewards and punishments, as they have good reason; for else of all people certainly they must be the most miserable, who for above forty years have been exceeding great sufferers for their profession, and in some cases treated worse than the worst of men, yea, as the refuse and offscouring of all things.

This was the purport of their doctrine and ministry, which, for the most part, is what other professors of Christianity pretend to hold in words and forms, but not in the power of godliness, which, generally speaking, has been long lost by men's departing from that principle and seed of life that is in man . . . and by which he can only be quickened in his mind to serve the living God in newness of life. . . .

THE QUAKER TESTIMONIES

Besides these general doctrines, as the larger branches, there sprang forth several particular doctrines, that did exemplify and further explain the truth and efficacy of the general doctrine before observed in their lives and examples. As,

I. Communion and loving one another. This is a noted mark in the mouth of all sorts of people concerning them: they will meet, they will help and stick one to another; whence it is common to hear some say, "Look how the Quakers love and take care of one another." Others, less moderate, will say, "The Quakers love none but themselves." And if loving one another and having an intimate communion in religion and constant care to meet to worship God and help one another be any mark of primitive Christianity, they had it, blessed be the Lord, in an ample manner.

II. To love enemies. This they both taught and practiced. For they did not only refuse to be revenged for injuries done them, and condemned it as of an unchristian spirit, but they did freely forgive, yea, help and relieve those that had been cruel to them when it was in their power to have been even with them (of which many and singular instances might be given), endeavoring through faith and patience to overcome all injustice and oppression and preaching this doctrine as Christian for others to follow.

III. Another was the sufficiency of truth-speaking, according to Christ's own form of sound words of Yea, yea, and Nay, nay, among Christians without swearing. . . .

IV. Not fighting, but suffering is another testimony peculiar to this people. They affirm that Christianity teacheth people to beat their swords into ploughshares, and their spears into pruning hooks, and to learn war no more, that so the wolf may lie down with the lamb and the lion with the calf, and nothing that destroys be entertained in the hearts of people. . . . Thus, as truth-speaking succeeded swearing, so faith and patience succeeded fighting in the doctrine and practice of this people. Nor ought they for this to be obnoxious to civil government, since if they cannot fight for it, neither can they fight against it, which is no mean security to any state. Nor is it reasonable that people should be blamed for not doing more for others than they can do for themselves. And, Christianity set aside, if the costs and fruits of war were well considered, peace with all its inconveniences is generally preferable. . . .

V. Another part of the character of this people was and is, they refuse to pay tithes or maintenance to a national ministry, and that for two reasons. The one is, they believe all compelled maintenance, even to gospel ministers to be unlawful, because expressly contrary to Christ's command, Who said, "Freely you have received, freely give"; at least, that the maintenance of gospel ministers should be free and not forced. The other reason of their refusal is, because those ministers are not gospel ones in that the Holy Ghost is not their foundation, but human arts and parts. So that it is not matter of humor or sullenness but pure conscience toward God that they cannot help to support national ministries where they dwell, which are but too much and too visibly become ways of worldly advantage and preferment.

VI. Not to respect persons was and is another of their doctrines and practices for which they are often buffeted and abused. They affirmed it to be sinful to give flattering titles or to use vain gestures and compliments of respect, though to virtue and authority they ever made a difference, but after their plain and homely manner, yet sincere and substantial way; well remembering . . . the command of their Lord and Master Jesus Christ, Who forbade His followers to call men Rabbi, which implies Lord or Master. . . .

VII. They also used the plain language of *thou* and *thee* to a single person, whatever was his degree among men.

And indeed the wisdom of God was much seen in bringing forth this people in so plain an appearance. For it was a close and distinguishing test upon the spirits of those they came among, showing their insides and what predominated, notwithstanding their high and great profession of religion. . . .

VIII. They recommended silence by their example, having very few words upon all occasions. They were at a word in dealing, nor could their customers [with] many words tempt them from it, having more regard to truth than custom, to example than gain. They sought solitude; but when in company they would neither use nor willingly hear unnecessary as well as unlawful discourses, whereby they preserved their minds pure and undisturbed from profitable thoughts and diversions. Nor could they humor the custom of "Good night, good morrow, Godspeed," for they knew the night was good and the day was good without wishing of either, and that in the other expression the holy name of God was too lightly and unthinkingly used and therefore taken in vain. Besides, they were words and wishes of course, and are usually as little meant as are love and service in the custom of cap and knee.

IX. For the same reason they forbore drinking to people or pledging of them, as the manner of the world is: a practice that is not only unnecessary, but, they thought, evil in the tendencies of it, being a provocation to drink more than did people good, as well as that it was in itself vain and heathenish.

X. Their way of marriage is peculiar to them, and shows a distinguishing care above other societies professing Christianity. They say that marriage is an ordinance of God, and that God only can rightly join man and woman in marriage. Therefore they use neither priest nor magistrate, but the man or woman concerned take each other as husband and wife in the presence of divers credible witnesses, promising unto each other, with God's assistance, to be loving and faithful in that relation till death shall separate them. . . . Which regular method has been, as it deserves, adjudged in courts of law a good marriage, where it has been by cross and ill people disputed and contested for want of the accustomed formality of priest and ring, etc. Ceremonies they have refused, not out of humor, but conscience reasonably grounded, inasmuch as no Scripture example tells us that the priest had any other part, of old time, than that of a witness among the rest before whom the Jews used to take one another; and therefore this people look upon it as an imposition to advance the power and profits of the clergy. And for the use of the ring, it is enough to say that it was a heathenish and vain custom, and never in practice among the people of God, Jews or primitive Christians. . . .

XI. It may not be unfit to say something here of their births and burials, which make up so much of the pomp and solemnity of too many called Christians. For births, the parents name their own children, which is usually some days after they are born, in the presence of the midwife if she can be there, and those that were at the birth, who afterward sign a certificate, for that purpose prepared, of the birth and name of the child or children, which is recorded in a proper book in the Monthly Meeting to which the parents belong, avoiding the accustomed ceremonies and festivals.

XII. Their burials are performed with the same simplicity. If the body of the deceased be near any public meeting place, it is usually carried thither for the more convenient reception of those that accompany it to the burying ground. And so it falls out sometimes that while the meeting is gathering for the burial some or other has a word of exhortation for the sake of the people there met together. After which the body is born away by the young men or those that are of their neighborhood or that were most of the intimacy of the deceased party, the corpse being in a plain coffin without any covering or furniture upon it. At the ground they pause some time before they put the body into its grave, that if anyone there should have anything upon them to exhort the people, they may not be disappointed, and that the relations may the more retiredly and solemnly take their last leave of the body of their departed kindred, and the spectators have a sense of mortality by the occasion then given them to reflect upon their own latter end. Otherwise, they have no set rites or ceremonies on those occasions. Neither do the kindred of the deceased ever wear mourning, they looking upon it as a worldly ceremony and piece of pomp; and that what mourning is fit for a Christian to have at the departure of a beloved relation or friend should be worn in the mind, which is only sensible of the loss; and the love they had to them and remembrance of them to be outwardly expressed by a respect to their advice and care of those they have left behind them, and their love of that they loved. . . .

These things, to be sure, gave them a rough and disagreeable appearance with the generality, who thought them turners of the world upside down, as indeed in some sense they were, but in no other than that wherein Paul was so charged, viz., to bring things back into their primitive and right order again. For these and such-like practices of theirs were not the result of humor or for civil distinction, as some have fancied, but a fruit of inward sense, which God through His holy fear had begotten in them. They did not consider how to contradict the world or distinguish themselves as a party from others, it being none of their business, as it was not their interest. . . . And though these things seemed trivial to some and rendered these people stingy and conceited in such persons' opinion, there was and is more in them than they were or are aware of.

It was not very easy to our primitive Friends to make themselves sights and spectacles and the scorn and derision of the world, which they easily foresaw must be the consequence of so unfashionable a conversation in it. But herein was the wisdom of God seen in the foolishness of these things. First, that they had discovered the satisfaction and concern that people had in and for the fashion of this world, notwithstanding their high pretenses to another. . . . Secondly, it seasonably and profitably divided conversation; for this making their society uneasy to their relations and acquaintance, it gave them the opportunity of more retirement and solitude, wherein they met with better company, even the Lord God their Redeemer, and grew strong in His love, power, and wisdom, and were thereby better qualified for his service. . . .

And though they were not great and learned in the esteem of this world (for then they had not wanted followers upon their own credit and authority), yet they were generally of the most sober of the several persuasions they were in and of the most repute for religion, and many of them of good capacity, substance, and account among men. And also some among them wanted not for parts, learning, or estate, though then, as of old, not many wise or noble, etc., were called or at least received the heavenly call, because of the cross that attended the profession of it in sincerity. But neither do parts or learning make men the better Christians, though the better orators and disputants; and it is the ignorance of people about the divine gift that causes that vulgar and mischievous mistake. . . .

THE CONVINCED (1)

We are resolved to meet, preach and pray.
—THOMAS SALTHOUSE

"The Little Quaking Lad . . ."

[FROM *The Sufferings of the Quakers*]

JOSEPH BESSE

[*George Fox, in 1656, estimated that there were not less than one thousand Quakers in English prisons, "for Truth's Testimony." The authorities cited other reasons for locking up Quakers. Fox himself spent seven years in prison on charges of interrupting a preacher, blasphemy, refusing to bear arms, attending Friends' meeting, disturbing the peace, refusing to swear; and on suspicion of plotting against Charles II. These charges, together with a refusal to doff the hat and pay tithes, and charges of traveling (to attend meeting) on Sunday were the common means of getting Quakers into prison. In addition to those who wanted them there for religious reasons, there was an even more determined band, the informers, who wanted them there for pecuniary reasons: the informers got a cut on fines levied and collected; they were the bounty hunters of their time.*

English prisons in the seventeenth century were cesspools; more than thirty Quakers died in prisons, to say nothing of those who died outside of prison but as the result of hardships suffered, and diseases

115

contracted, there. This number, compared with what the concentration camp did later, is paltry. However, those who died in the muck and darkness of seventeenth-century stinkholes had not the comfort of knowing that worse was to come.

Among the victims of prison hardship and cruelty was James Parnell (1637–1656). He died at nineteen and had been a Quaker minister since he was sixteen. The account of his imprisonment and death, which follows, is taken from Joseph Besse's The Sufferings of the Quakers.

In 1657 Fox advised each meeting to keep a careful record of its "sufferings": that is, of the fines, imprisonments, and abuses suffered by the individuals belonging to the meeting. These records were to be presented to the judges of the circuit, and to Cromwell himself, not only for purposes of keeping the record straight, but in hope of obtaining some redress. The meetings did, as Fox advised, keep such records; and Besse's Sufferings of the Quakers *is a collection of these.*

James Turner, in his study of martyrdom, Shrouds of Glory, *devotes a chapter to James Parnell. He takes Parnell to be a publicity-hungry boy; and he completely misunderstands the purpose of the records of suffering, speaking of them as though they were the work of some seventeenth-century publicity agent hired by the Quakers to get them a good press. Parnell, in Turner's eyes, offered up his life as a movie star offers up her measurements: for the record and for glory. Parnell, says Turner, did not want to live because "the devil's tongs were taking all the sweetness from the sugarbowl of earthly existence."*

Parnell himself states it more simply. "As I had a time to preach the Truth amongst you . . . so also now I have a time to seal the same with patient suffering. . . . Be willing that self shall suffer for the Truth and not Truth for self."

———

The first Sufferings in this County which occur to our Notice, were those of James Parnel, who, when sixteen Years of Age, was convinced of the Truth by the Ministry of George Fox, then Prisoner in the Dungeon at Carlisle. He gave early Proofs of his Patience and Constancy by suffering Imprisonment in Cambridgeshire, of which we have already made mention in our

Account of that County, pag. 86 foregoing. Being about eighteen Years of Age, he came into Essex, preaching the Doctrine of the Gospel with such Efficacy, that many were convinced, and among others Stephen Crisp, afterward an eminent Teacher of the same Doctrine. Parnel, as he was coming out of Nicholas Steeplehouse in *Colchester*, where he had been exhorting the People to Repentance, was met by a blind Zealot who struck him a violent Blow with a great Staff, saying, There, take that for Christ's Sake: To whom the innocent Sufferer meekly answered, Friend, I do receive it for Jesus Christ's Sake. From thence he went to Coggeshall, where the Independent Professors had appointed a Fast, on purpose to pray against the spreading of Error, by which they meant the Quakers Doctrine. The Priest, who officiated on that Occasion, uttered many Invectives against that People, such as Prejudice and Prepossession had furnished him with. James Parnel stood still till the Priest had done, and was coming down from his Pulpit, when, thinking it his Duty to undeceive the People, he said to the Priest, I am ready to prove that the Quakers are not on a Sandy Foundation, and that thou art a false Prophet and Deceiver. After some Words had passed, a Person standing by accused Parnel, saying, that he owned no Church: He replied, That's false. Then being asked, What Church he owned? He answered, The Church in God. Whereupon the Priest said, That was Nonsense. But Parnel taking a Bible out of his Pocket, shewed, that it was a Scripture Expression, and charged the Priest with Blasphemy in calling it Nonsense. On his coming out of the Steeple-house he was apprehended, and, after Examination, committed to Colchester Castle, by a Warrant signed by four Justices. . . .

Being in Prison he was closely confined, and at the Time of the next Assizes, held a few Weeks after at Chelmsford, he was fastned to a Chain with Felons and Murderers, and so led above twenty Miles through the Country, remaining chained both Night and Day.

At his Trial he was brought to the Bar hand-cuff'd, but the People exclaiming against that Cruelty, at his next Appearance the Manacles were taken off. The Judge seemed resolved against him, saying, that the Lord Protector had charged him to punish such Persons as should contemn either Magistrates or Ministers: And in his Charge to the Jury, he directed them to bring him in Guilty, which they readily did: He was fined 40 £. and sent again to Prison till Payment. And the Gaoler was ordered not to let any giddy-headed People, by which was meant his Friends, come at him.

The Gaoler observed his Orders, to which the Cruelty of his own Disposition also inclined him, for he would suffer none to come to him but such as abused him; and the Gaoler's Wife, equally cruel, not only ordered her Servant to beat him, but struck him with her own Hands, swearing she would have his Blood. When his Friends sent him Victuals, she ordered the other Prisoners to take it; and when a Bed was sent him, she refused to let him have it, but constrained him to lodge on the hard damp Stones. After this he was put into an Hole in the Castle-Wall, not so wide as some Bakers Ovens, which Hole being a great Heighth from the Ground, and a Ladder, used to go up by, being several Feet too short, he was obliged to climb up and down by a Rope to fetch his Victuals or other Necessaries: For when his Friends would have given him a Cord and a Basket to draw up his Food in, the cruel Keeper would not suffer it. By lying long in that damp Hole, his Limbs were benumbed; and as he was going up the Ladder with his Food in one Hand, attempting to lay hold on the Rope with the other, he missed his Aim, and fell down on the Stones, by which he was so wounded in his Head, and bruised in his Body, that he was taken up for dead. Then they put him into an Hole underneath the other, there being two Stories of such narrow vaulted Holes in the Wall: Here, when the Door was shut, was scarce any Air, there being no Window or Place beside to let it in. Thus bruised with the Fall, and shut up where he could hardly breathe, there was little Hope left of his Life. Whereupon two of his Friends, William Talcot and Edward Grant, wealthy Tradesmen of that Town, offered to be bound in sufficient Bonds, and Thomas Shortland, another of his Friends, offered to lie in Prison in his Stead, so that he might have Liberty to go to William Talcot's House till he might recover of his Bruises, but this was denied.

Nor would the Gaoler suffer him to walk sometimes in the Yard, as other Prisoners did. It happened once, that the Door of his Hole being open, he went forth into a narrow Yard between two high Walls, at which the Keeper in a Rage lockt up the Door and shut him out in the Yard all Night, in the cold Time of Winter. His Constitution being much impaired by cruel Usage and hard Imprisonment, after ten or eleven Months he fell sick and died. Two of his Friends, Thomas Shortland and Anne Langley, were present at his Departure. When Death approached, he said, that One Hour's Sleep would cure him of all. The last Words he was heard to speak were, Now I go, and then stretching himself out, slept about an Hour, and breathed his last. He died a Youth, about nineteen Years of Age, but approved himself a strong Man in Christ, and having an Eye to the Eternal Recompence of Reward set before him, persevered faithful to his End through manifold Sufferings, with a remarkable Innocence, Patience, and Magnanimity. His Persecutors, instead of repenting of their Cruelty, the apparent Cause of his Death, railed a slanderous Report of his hastning his own End by willfully abstaining from Food: but that Report was proved false by the Testimony of credible Witnesses, who were frequently with him during his Sickness; and to whom that groundless Calumny was a clear Indication of the deep-rooted Malice of those who invented it. . . .

So, finding that nothing but his body would Satisfy them, great application was made to them in a Superior authority but to no purpose. Thus he having Endured about ten months imprisonment, and having passed through many trials and Exercises, which the Lord Enabled him to bear with Courage and faithfulness, he laid down his head in peace and died a Prisoner and faithful Martyr for the Sake the Truth, under the hand of the persecuting generation in the year 1656.

"They Teach Dangerous Principles"

[FROM *Sufferings of the Quakers*]

JOSEPH BESSE

[*Judge Keeling was right about one thing. The Quakers were "a stubborn sect." David Masson, in his* Life of Milton, *says, "You may break in upon them, hoot at them, roar at them, drag them about. The meeting, if it is of any size, essentially still goes on till all the component individuals are murdered."*

Keeling is right about another thing. The Quakers did steadfastly refuse to accept what Keeling says was offered them: the right to worship God according to their consciences in their families. They refused because they believed that men and women had not only the right but the duty to worship in public, and that they should not desist because the manner of their worship was disapproved by the state.

The dangerous principle that Judge Keeling rightly sees—and fears—is not that of the individual who wants to worship God in some way strange to others but comfortable to oneself, but that of the individual who dares question the authority of the state over the person. And it is here the Quakers made their breakthrough for others beside themselves, became "an effective machine for legal and so for political reform," as John Sykes so clearly points out in his history of the movement.]

———

At the Sessions in the Old-Bailey, Judge Keeling made a Speech to the Grand Jury against the Quakers, as follows, *viz.*

"Because this Day was appointed for the Trial of these People, and inasmuch as many are come hither, expecting what will be done, I shall say something, concerning them and their Principles, that they might not be thought worthy of Pity, as suffering more than they deserve; for they are a stubborn Sect, and the King has been very merciful to them. It was hoped that the Purity of the Church of England would e'er this have convinced them, but they will not be reclaimed.

"They teach dangerous Principles, this for one, That it is not lawful to take an Oath. You must not think their Leaders believe this Doctrine, only they persuade these poor ignorant Souls so; but they have an Interest to carry on against the Government, and therefore they will not swear Subjection to it, and their End is Rebellion and Blood. You may easily know, that they do not believe themselves what they say, when they say it is not lawful to take an Oath, if you look into the Scriptures; that Text, (Mat. v.) where our Saviour saith, Swear not at all, will clear it self from such a Meaning as forbids Swearing, if you look but into the next Words, where it is said, Let your Communication be yea, yea, nay, nay; and it is said, An Oath is an End of all Strife; this for the New-Testament: And the *Old* is positive for Swearing: And they that deny Swearing, deny God a special Part of his Worship.

"Now you shall see how this Principle of Not Swearing tends to the Subversion of the Government; First, It denies the King the Security he ought to have of his Subjects for their Allegiance, which Oath they deny, and Security by Bond is not so good; for thereby they are not engaged in Conscience, and they will only wait for a convenient Season to forfeit their Bonds without Hazard, and make sure Work in overthrowing the present Government, and secure their own Securities; but an Oath binds the Conscience at all Times, and that they cannot abide. Again, This Principle tends to subvert the Government, because without Swearing we can have no Justice done, no Law executed, you may be robbed, your Houses broke open, your Goods taken away, and be injured in your Persons, and no Justice or Recompence can be had, because the Fact cannot be proved: The Truth is, no Government can stand without Swearing; and were these People to have a Government among themselves, they could not live without an Oath.

"Whereas they pretend in their Scribbles, that this Act against Conventicles doth not concern them, but such, as under Pretence of worshipping God, do at their Meetings conspire against the Government. This is a Mistake: for if they should conspire, they would then be guilty of Treason, and we should try them by other Laws: But this Act is against Meetings, to prevent them of such Conspiracy; for they meet to consult to know their Numbers, and to hold Correspondency, that they may in a short Time be up in Arms.

"I had the Honour to serve the King at York, upon the Trial of those wicked Plotters, and we found those Plots were hatched and carried on in these Meetings, and we hanged up four or five of the Speakers or Praters, whom we found to be the chief Leaders in that Rebellion. I warrant you their Leaders will keep themselves from the third Offence, we shall not take them: If we could catch their Leaders, we should try them by some other Law, which, if executed, will take away their Lives. This is a merciful Law, it takes not away from their Estates, it leaves them entire, only banishes them for seven Years, if they will not pay an Hundred Pounds: And this is not for worshipping God according to their Consciences, for that they may do in their Families, but forsooth they cannot do that, but they must have thirty, forty, or an hundred others to contrive their Designs withal."

"There Is a Spirit That Delights to Do No Evil"

[FROM *History of the People Called Quakers*]

WILLEM SEWEL

[*With the possible exception of Elias Hicks, James Nayler (1618–1660) has been the most controversial figure in Quaker history. George Fox believed in, and preached, the perfectibility of people: that is, through oneness with Christ, Christlikeness. The opening gambit of almost any questioning of Fox in court was "Do you believe yourself to be God?" Fox did not believe himself to be and was far too skilled a controversialist to let himself be trapped by such questions. If he was asked, "Are you a Son of God?" his answer was "Yes." But he never said he was "the" Son of God. Nor, however, would he admit that the "many who pleaded against perfection" were anything but wrong. Perfection was possible, if unlikely. (And it is here that Quakers are nearer to Catholics than to Protestants in their views.) And here also, curiously enough, Kenneth Rexroth, dean of the "beat generation," agrees with Fox, saying that with the exception of the Quakers "Christianity and the religions influenced by it teach . . . that it is very hard to be a good human being. This is simply not true."*

However, there was here, for early Quakers, a delicate line, and James Nayler, or at least some of the admiring women about him, crossed this line—with the results Sewel reports. R. A. Knox, in Enthusiasm, *looking at Nayler from the viewpoint of a monsignor in the Catholic church, points out that what the House of Commons, in trying Nayler, "was really debating, was the supreme crux of mysticism—whether the contemplative becomes wholly and literally identified with the Object of his contemplation."*

Knox finds, not surprisingly, that Nayler owed his downfall to the "women who kept telling him that in worshiping him they worshiped the God who was in him." And, Knox continues, "It is a singular thought that if Nayler had been grounded in a Catechism which had the phrase 'hypostatic union' in it, he could have avoided all his troubles."

Singular or not, it is obvious that all the Quakers could have avoided all their religious troubles by not being Quakers. And it is also obvious, right or wrong, that being "grounded in a Catechism" was not one of the ways by which they were willing to avoid trouble; to escape that, they were willing to suffer as Nayler did.]

———

This James Nayler was born of honest parents in the parish of Ardesley, near Wakefield in Yorkshire, about the year 1616. He had served in the parliament army, being a quartermaster in major-general Lambert's troop in Scotland; was a member of the

Independents; and afterwards, in the year 1651, he entered into the communion of the Quakers, so called.

He and Thomas Goodair were convinced by G. Fox, about Wakefield, anno 1651, as were also Richard Farnsworth, Thomas Aldam, William Dewsbury, and wife, about the same time. And in the beginning of the year following, as he was in the field at plough, meditating on the things of God, he heard a voice, bidding him go out from his kindred, and from his father's house; and had a promise given with it, that the Lord would be with him; whereupon he did exceedingly rejoice that he had heard the voice of God, whom he had professed from a child, and endeavored to serve; and when he went home he made preparation to go; but not being obedient, the wrath of God was upon him, so that he was made a wonder, and it was thought he would have died. Afterwards being made willing, and going out with a friend, not thinking then of a journey, he was commanded to go into the West, not knowing what he was to do there; but when he came, he had given him what to declare; and so he continued, not knowing one day what he was to do the next; and the promise of God, that he would be with him, he found made good to him every day.

He was a man of excellent natural parts, and at first did acquit himself well, both in word and writing among his friends, so that many came to receive the Truth by his ministry. He came to London towards the latter end of the year 1654, or beginning of 1655, and found there a meeting of Friends, which had already been gathered in that city, by the service of Edward Burrough, and Francis Howgill; and there he preached in such an eminent manner, that many admiring his great gift, began to esteem him much above his brethren, which as it brought him no benefit, so it gave occasion of some difference in the society; and this ran so high, that some forward and inconsiderate women, of whom Martha Simmons was the chief, assumed the boldness to dispute with F. Howgill and E. Burrough, openly in their preaching, and thus to disturb the meetings . . . whereupon they, who were truly excellent preachers, did not fail, according to their duty, to reprove this indiscretion. But these women were so disgusted, that Martha, and another woman, went and complained to J. Nayler, to incense him against F. Howgill and Edward Burrough; but this did not succeed, for he showed himself afraid to pass judgment upon his brethren, as they desired. Hereupon Martha fell into a passion, in a kind of moaning or weeping, and, bitterly crying out with a mournful shrill voice, said, "I looked for judgment, but behold a cry"; and with that cried aloud in a passionate lamenting manner, which so entered and pierced J. Nayler, that it smote him down into so much sorrow and sadness, that he was much dejected in spirit, or disconsolate. Fear and doubting then entered him, so that he came to be clouded in his understanding, bewildered, and at a loss in his judgment, and became estranged from his best friends, because they did not approve of his conduct; insomuch that he began to give ear to the flattering praises of some whimsical people, which he ought to have abhorred, and reproved them for. But his sorrowful fall ought to stand as a warning, even to those that are endued with great gifts, that they do not presume to be exalted, lest they also fall, but endeavor to continue in true humility, in which alone a Christian can be kept safe.

Hannah Stranger, whom I very well know, and have reason to believe a woman of high imaginations, at this time wrote to him several very extravagant letters; calling him the everlasting Son of Righteousness, Prince of Peace, the only begotten Son of God, the fairest of ten thousands, &c. In the letters of Jane Woodcock, John Stranger, and others, were expressions of the like extravagancy; the said Hannah Stranger, Martha Simmons, and Dorcas Erbury, arrived to that height of folly, that in the prison at Exeter, they kneeled before Nayler, and kissed his feet; but as to what hath been divulged concerning his committing of fornication, I never could find, though very inquisitive in the case, that he was in the least guilty thereof.

But for all that, he was already too much transported, and grew yet more exorbitant; for being released from that prison, and riding to Bristol in the beginning of November, he was accompanied by the aforesaid and other persons; and passing through the suburbs of Bristol, one Thomas Woodcock went bare-headed before him; one of the women led his horse;

Dorcas, Martha and Hannah, spread their scarfs and handkerchiefs before him, and the company sung, "Holy, holy, holy, is
the Lord God of hosts, Hosannah in the highest: holy, holy, holy,
is the Lord God of Israel." Thus these mad people sung, whilst
they were walking through the mire and dirt, till they came into
Bristol; where they were examined by the magistrates, and
committed to prison; and not long after Nayler was carried to
London, to be examined by the parliament. . . .

I believe that J. Nayler was clouded in his understanding in
all this transaction: but how grievous soever his fall was, yet it
pleased God, in his infinite mercy to raise him up again, and to
bring him to such sincere repentance, that, (as we may see in the
sequel,) he abhorred not only this whole business, but also
manifested his hearty sorrow, in pathetical expressions, which
were published, as will be shown in its proper place. . . .

On the 17th, after a long debate, they came to this resolution,

"That James Nayler be set on the pillory, with his head in
the pillory, in the Palace-yard, Westminster, during the space of
two hours, on Thursday next, and be whipped by the hangman
through the streets, from Westminster to the Old Exchange,
London; and there likewise be set on the pillory, with his head
in the pillory, for the space of two hours, between the hours of
eleven and one, on Saturday next, in each place wearing a paper
containing an inscription of his crimes; and that at the Old
Exchange his tongue be bored through with a hot iron, and that
he be there also stigmatized in the forehead with the letter B;
and that he be afterwards sent to Bristol, and be conveyed into,
and through the said city on horseback, with his face backward,
and there also publicly whipped the next marketday after he
comes thither; and that hence he be committed to prison in
Bridewell, London, and there restrained from the society of all
people, and there to labor hard till he shall be released by
parliament; and during that time he be debarred the use of pen,
ink and paper, and shall have no relief but what he earns by his
daily labor."

They were long ere they could agree on the sentence; for
suppose there was blasphemy committed, yet his tongue seemed

not properly guilty of it, since it was not proved that blasphemous words had been spoken by him.

Many thought it to be indeed a very severe judgment to be executed upon one whose crime seemed to proceed more from a clouded understanding, than any wilful intention of evil. . . .

The thing being thus far agreed upon, J. Nayler was brought up to the bar; when the speaker, Sir Thomas Widdrington, was about to pronounce the afore-mentioned sentence, Nayler said he did not know his offence. To which the speaker returned, he should know his offence by his punishment. After sentence was pronounced, though J. Nayler bore the same with great patience, yet it seemed he would have spoken something, but was denied liberty; nevertheless was heard to say, with a composed mind, "I pray God, he may not lay it to your charge."

The 18th of December, J. Nayler suffered part of the sentence; and after having stood full two hours with his head in the pillory, was stripped, and whipped at a cart's tail, from Palace-yard to the Old Exchange, and received three hundred and ten stripes; and the executioner would have given him one more (as he confessed to the sheriff), there being three hundred and eleven kennels, but his foot slipping, the stroke fell upon his own hand, which hurt him much. All this Nayler bore with so much patience and quietness, that it astonished many of the beholders, though his body was in a most pitiful condition: he was also much hurt with horses treading on his feet, whereon the print of the nails were seen. R. Travers, a grave person, who washed his wounds, in a certificate which was presented to the parliament, and afterwards printed, says, "There was not the space of a man's nail free from stripes and blood, from his shoulders, near to his waist, his right arm sorely striped, his hands much hurt with cords, that they bled, and were swelled: the blood and wounds of his back did very little appear at first sight, by reason of abundance of dirt that covered them, till it was washed off." . . . The 20th December was the time appointed for executing the other part of the sentence, viz. boring through his tongue, and stigmatizing in his forehead; but by reason of the most cruel whipping, he was brought to such a low ebb, that many persons of note, moved with compassion, presented petitions to the parliament on his behalf, who respited his further punishment for one week.

During this interval, several persons presented another petition, in which are these words:

"Your moderation and clemency in respiting the punishment of J. Nayler, in consideration of his illness of body, hath refreshed the hearts of many thousands in these cities, altogether unconcerned in his practice; wherefore we most humbly beg your pardon that are constrained to appear before you in such a suit, (not daring to do otherwise,) that you would remit the remaining part of our sentence against the said J. Nayler, leaving him to the Lord, and to such gospel remedies as he hath sanctified; and we are persuaded you will find such a course of love and forbearance more effectual to reclaim; and will leave a seal of your love and tenderness upon our spirits,

And we shall pray," &c.

This petition being presented at the bar of the house by about one hundred persons, on the behalf of the whole, was accordingly read and debated by them; but not being likely to produce the desired effect, the petitioners thought themselves in duty and conscience bound to address the Protector, for remitting the remaining part of the sentence; who, thereupon, sent a letter to the parliament, which occasioned some debate in the house. But the day for executing the remaining part of the sentence drawing near, the petitioners made a second address to the Protector. It was, indeed, very remarkable, that so many inhabitants that were not of the society of those called Quakers, showed themselves so much concerned in this business; but to me it seems to have proceeded merely from compassion towards the person of J. Nayler; whom they regarded as one that was rather fallen into error, through inconsiderateness, than to have been guilty of wilful blasphemy: for then he would not have deserved so much pity.

But, notwithstanding all these humble petitions, the public preachers, it seems, prevailed so much with Cromwell, that he could not resolve to put a stop to the intended execution. . . .

The execution of his sentence was . . . performed on the 27th of December. Robert Rich, that forward man, . . . was this day at the parliament door, from eight in the morning till about eleven, crying variously to the parliament men, as they passed by. . . . Then he went towards the Exchange, and got on the pillory, held Nayler by the hand while he was burned on the forehead, and bored through the tongue; and was not a little affected with Nayler's suffering, for he licked his wounds, thereby as it seems to allay the pain; and he led him by the hand from off the pillory. It was very remarkable that notwithstanding there might be many thousands of people, yet they were very quiet, and few heard to revile him, or seen to throw anything at him: and when he was burning, the people both before and behind him, and on both sides, with one consent stood bareheaded, as seeming generally moved with compassion and goodwill towards him.

Many now rejoiced, seeing how some few among the Quakers, as Rich, and the like sort of people, did side with Nayler, whilst the Quakers generally spoke against him and his doings; for those who hoped to see the downfall of them, signified not obscurely, that now things went as they would have, since the Quakers (as they said) were divided among themselves. But time showed that this pretended division soon came to an end, and those diviners and guessers overshot themselves. How it went with the execution of Nayler's sentence at Bristol, I am not informed. . . .

After this he was brought to Bridewell, London (as sentenced), where he continued prisoner about two years, during which confinement he came to a true repentance of his transgression; and having got the use of pen and ink, wrote several books and papers, condemning his error, which were published in print; and after his release, he published several others, one of which by way of recantation runs [in part] thus:

". . . Condemned forever be all those false worships with which any have idolized my person in the night of my temptation, when the power of darkness was above. All their casting of their clothes in the way, their bowings and singings, and all the rest of those wild actions which did any ways tend to dishonor the Lord, or draw the minds of any from the measure of Christ Jesus in themselves, to look at flesh, which is as grass, or to ascribe that to the visible, which belongs to Christ Jesus; all that I condemn, by which the pure name of the Lord hath been any ways blasphemed through me, in the time of temptation: or the spirits of any people grieved, that truly love the Lord Jesus, throughout the whole world, of what sort soever. This offence I confess, which hath been sorrow of heart, that the enemy of man's peace in Christ, should get this advantage in the night of my trial, to stir up wrath and offences in the creation of God; a thing the simplicity of my heart did not intend, the Lord knows; who in his endless love hath given me power over it, to condemn it. And also that letter which was sent me to Exeter, by John Stranger, when I was in prison, with these words, "Thy name shall be no more James Nayler, but Jesus," this I judge to be written from the imaginations; and a fear struck me when I first saw it, so I put it into my pocket, close, not intending any should see it; which they finding on me, spread it abroad, which the simplicity of my heart never owned. So this I deny also, that the name of Christ Jesus was received instead of James Nayler, or ascribed to him; for that name is to the promised seed of all generations; and he that hath the Son, hath the name, which is life and power, the salvation and the unction, into which name all the children of light are baptized. . . .

"And all those ranting wild spirits, which then gathered about me in that time of darkness; and all their wild actions and wicked words against the honor of God, and his pure spirit and people; I deny that bad spirit, the power and the works thereof; and as far as I gave advantage, through want of judgment, for that evil spirit in any to arise, I take shame to myself justly; having formerly had power over that spirit, in judgment and discerning, wherever it was; which darkness came over me through want of watchfulness and obedience to the pure eye of God, and diligently minding the reproof of life, which condemns the adulterous spirit. So the adversary got advantage, who ceases not to seek to devour; and being taken captive from the true light, I was walking in the night where none can work, as a wandering bird fit for a prey. And if the Lord of all my mercies had not rescued me, I had perished; for I was as one appointed to death and destruction, and there was none could deliver me.

And this I confess, that God may be justified in his judgment, and magnified in his mercies without end, who did not forsake his captive in the night, even when his spirit was daily provoked and grieved; but hath brought me forth to give glory to his name for ever. . . ."

THE DYING WORDS OF JAMES NAYLER

"There is a spirit which I feel that delights to do no evil, nor to revenge any wrong, but delights to endure all things, in hope to enjoy its own in the end. Its hope is to outlive all wrath and contention, and to weary out all exaltation and cruelty, or whatever is of a nature contrary to itself. It sees to the end of all temptations. As it bears no evil in itself, so it conceives none in thoughts to any other. If it be betrayed, it bears it, for its ground and spring is the mercies and forgiveness of God. Its crown is meekness, its life is everlasting love unfeigned; it takes its kingdom with entreaty and not with contention, and keeps it by lowliness of mind. In God alone it can rejoice, though none else regard it, or can own its life. It's conceived in sorrow, and brought forth without any to pity it, nor doth it murmur at grief and oppression. It never rejoiceth but through sufferings: for with the world's joy it is murdered. I found it alone, being forsaken. I have fellowship therein with them who live in dens and desolate places in the earth, who through death obtained this resurrection and eternal holy life.

"Thou wast with me when I fled from the face of mine enemies: then didst thou warn me in the night: thou carriedst me in thy power into the hiding-place thou hadst prepared for me; there thou coveredst me with thy hand, that in time thou mightst bring me forth a rock before all the world. When I was weak thou stayedst me with thy hand, that in thy time thou mightst present me to the world in thy strength in which I stand, and cannot be moved. Praise the Lord, O my soul. Let this be written for those that come after. Praise the Lord."

"I Durst Not Mock Him with a Form"

[FROM *Experiences in the Life of Mary Penington*]

MARY PENINGTON

[*Mary Penington (1616–1682), an extraordinary woman, did what extraordinary women frequently fail to do: she married two remarkable men. All who care about either good writing or vivid living should read the life of Sir William Springett, her first husband, which she wrote for his grandson, William Penn's son. There can have been few such attractive men in history. Sir William died at twenty-three of a fever caught at the close of some desperate campaigning. He relieved the tedium of dying by shooting with a crossbow out the opened window of his room.*

Any ordinary second husband would have lived in the shadow of this ardent young man. Isaac Penington, the son of a Lord Mayor of London, escaped this by shedding his own light of something very near to saintliness. He and Mary together discovered the Society of Friends, toward which Mary and Sir William had surely been traveling. The Peningtons, like Penn and Ellwood, had "to take up the cross to the language, fashions, customs, titles, honor and esteem in the world," in a way not demanded of most converts, who were innocent of the language, fashions, titles, and honors of the world.

Many of the seventeenth-century Quakers seem all of three centuries—and more—distant. Mary Penington does not. She is as contemporary as Franny Glass, and, like Franny with her "Jesus prayer," Mary had her period of praying incessantly until finally she was able "to swim in the life which overcame me." She comes nearer than any other woman of her time to telling us the meaning of this experience.]

———

The first scripture I remember to have taken notice of was, "Blessed are they that hunger and thirst after righteousness, for they shall be filled." This I heard taken for a text when I was about eight years of age, and under the care of people who were a kind of loose Protestants, that minded no more about religion than to go to their worship-house on first days, to hear a canonical priest preach in the morning, and read common prayers in the afternoon. They used common prayers in the family, and observed superstitious customs and times, days of feasting and fasting, Christmas (so-called), Good Friday, Lent, etc. About this time I was afraid, in the night, of such things as run in my mind by day, of spirits, thieves, etc. When alone in the fields, and possessed with fears, I accounted prayers my help and safety; so would often say (as I had been taught) the Lord's Prayer, hoping thereby to be delivered from the things I feared.

After some time I went to live with some that appeared to be more religious. They would not admit of sports on first days, calling first day the Sabbath. They went to hear two sermons a-day, from a priest that was not loose in his conversation: he used a form of prayer before his sermon, and read the common prayer after it. I was now about ten or eleven years of age. A maid-servant that waited on me and the rest of the children, was very zealous in their way: she used to read Smith's and Preston's sermons on first days, between the sermon times. I diligently heard her read, and at length liked not to use the Lord's Prayer alone, but got a prayer-book, and read prayers mornings and evenings; and that scripture of "howling on their beds," was much on my mind: by it I was checked from saying prayers in my bed.

About this time I began to be very serious about religion. One day, after we came from the place of public worship, the maid before mentioned read one of Preston's sermons, the text was: "Pray continually." In this sermon much was said respecting prayer: amongst other things, of the excellency of prayer, that it distinguished a saint from a sinner; that in many things the hypocrite could imitate the saint, but in this he could not. This thing wrought much on my mind. I found that I knew not what true prayer was; for what I used for prayer, an ungodly person could use as well as I, which was to read one out of a book, and this could not be the prayer he meant, which distinguished a saint from a wicked one. My mind was deeply exercised about this thing. When she had done reading, and all were gone out of the chamber, I shut the door, and in great distress I flung myself on the bed, and oppressedly cried out: "Lord, what is prayer?"

This exercise continued so on my mind, that at night, when I used to read a prayer out of a book, I could only weep, and remain in trouble. At this time I had never heard of any people that prayed any other way than by reading prayers out of a book, or composing themselves. I remember one morning it came into my mind that I would write a prayer of my own composing, and use it in the morning as soon as I was out of bed: which I did, though I could then scarcely join my letters, I had learnt so little a time to write. The prayer I wrote was something after this manner: "Lord, thou commandest the Israelites to offer a morning sacrifice, so I offer up the sacrifice of prayer, and desire to be preserved this day." The use of this prayer for a little while gave me some ease. I soon quite left my prayerbooks, and used to write prayers according to my several occasions. The second that I wrote was for the assurance of the pardon of my sins. I had heard one preach, "that God of his free grace pardoned David's sins." I was much affected by it, and, as I came from the worship place, I thought it would be a happy thing to be assured that one's past sins were pardoned. I wrote a pretty long prayer on that subject, and felt, that as pardon came through grace, I might receive it, though very unworthy of it. In said prayer I used many earnest expressions.

A little time after this, several persons spoke to me about the greatness of my memory, and praised me for it. I felt a fear of being puffed up, and wrote a prayer of thanks for that gift, and desired to be enabled to use it for the Lord, and that it might be sanctified to me.

These three prayers I used with some ease of mind, but not long, for I began again to question whether I prayed aright or not. I was much troubled about it, not knowing that any did pray extempore; but it sprung up in my mind, that to use words descriptive of the state I was in, was prayer, which I attempted to do, but could not. Sometimes I kneeled down a long time, and had not a word to say, which wrought great trouble in me. I had none to reveal my distress unto, or advise with; so, secretly bore a great burden a long time.

One day as I was sitting at work in the parlor, one called a gentleman (who was against the superstitions of the times) came in and looking sadly, said "it was a sad day: that Prynne, Bastwick and Burton, were sentenced to have their ears cut, and to be banished." This news sunk deep into my mind, and strong cries were raised in me for them, and the rest of the innocent people in the nation. I was unable to sit at my work, but was strongly inclined to go into a private room, which I did, and shutting the door, kneeled down and poured out my soul to the Lord in a very vehement manner. I was wonderfully melted and eased, and felt peace and acceptance with the Lord: and that this was true prayer, which I had never before been acquainted with.

Not long after this an account was brought to the house, that a neighbouring minister, who had been suspended by the bishops for not being subject to their canons, was returned to his flock again, and that he was to preach at the place where he did three years before (being suspended so long). I expressed a desire to go thither, but was reproved by those that had the care of my education, they saying that it was not fit to leave my parish church. I could not be easy without going, so I went. When I came there, he prayed fervently (he was one called a Puritan) and with great power. Then I felt that was true prayer, and what my mind pressed after, but could not come at in my own will, and had but just tasted of it the time before mentioned. And now I knew that this alone was prayer, I mourned solely because I kneeled down morning after morning, and night after night, and had not a word to say. My distress was so great, that I feared I should perish in the night, because I had not prayed; and I thought that by day my food would not nourish me, because I could not pray.

I was thus exercised a great while, and could not join in the common prayer that was read in the family every night; neither could I kneel down when I came to the worship-house, as I had been taught to do; and this scripture was much in my mind: "Be more ready to hear, than to offer the sacrifice of fools." I could only read the Bible, or some other book, whilst the priest read the common prayer. At last I could neither kneel nor stand up to join with the priest in his prayer before the sermon; neither

did I care to hear him preach, my mind being after the Noncon-
formist, the Puritan already mentioned.

By constraint I went with the family in the morning, but
could not be kept from the Puritan preacher in the afternoon. I
went through much suffering on this account, being forced to go
on foot between two and three miles, and no one permitted to
go with me; except sometimes a servant, out of compassion,
would run after me, lest I should be frightened going alone.
Though I was very young, I was so zealous that all the tried
reasonings and threatenings could not keep me back. In a short
time I refused to hear the priest of our parish at all, but went
constantly, all weathers, to the other place. In the family I used to
hear the Scripture read; but if I happened to go in before they had
done their prayers, I would sit down though they were kneeling.

These things wrought me much trouble in the family, and
there was none to take my part; yet at length two of the
maidservants were inclined to mind what I said against their
prayers, and so refused to join them, at which the governors of
the family were much disturbed, and made me the subject of
their discourse in company, saying that I would pray with the
spirit, and rejected godly men's prayers; that I was proud and
schismatic; and that I went to those places to meet young men,
and such like. At this time I suffered, not only from those
persons to whose care I was committed by my parents (who both
died when I was not above three years of age), but also from my
companions and kindred; yet, notwithstanding, in this zeal I
grew much, and sequestered myself from my former vain company, and refused playing at cards etc. I zealously kept the
Sabbath, not daring to eat or be clothed with such things as
occasioned much trouble, or took up much time on that day,
which I believe ought to be devoted to hearing, reading, and
praying. I disregarded those matches proposed to me by vain
persons, having desired of the Lord that if I married at all, it
might be a man that feared Him. I had a belief, that though I
then knew of none of my outward rank that was such a one, yet
that the Lord would provide such a one for me.

Possessed of this belief, I regarded not their reproaches,
that would say to me, that no gentleman was of this way, and that

I should marry some mean person or other. But they were disappointed, for the Lord touched the heart of him that was afterwards my husband, and my heart cleaved to him for the Lord's sake. He was of a good understanding, and had cast off those dead superstitions; which, that they were dead, was more clearly made manifest to him in that day, than any other person that I knew of, of his rank and years. He was but young, compared to the knowledge he had attained in the things of God. He was about twenty years old. We pressed much after the knowledge of the Lord, and walked in his fear; and though both very young, were joined together in the Lord; refusing the use of a ring, and such like things then used, and not denied by any that we knew of.

We lived together about two years and a month. We were zealously affected, and daily exercised in what we believed to be the service and worship of God. We scrupled many things then in use amongst those accounted honest people, viz: singing David's Psalms in metre. We tore out of our Bibles the common prayer, the form of prayer, and also the singing psalms, as being the inventions of vain poets, not being written for that use. We found that songs of praise must spring from the same source as prayers did; so we could not use any one's songs or prayers. We were also brought off from the use of bread and wine, and water baptism. We looked into the Independent way, but saw death there, and that there was not the thing our souls sought after.

In this state my dear husband died, hoping in the promises afar off, not seeing or knowing Him that is invisible to be so near him; and that it was He that showed unto him his thoughts, and made manifest the good and the evil. When he was taken from me, I was with child of my dear daughter Gulielma Maria Springett. It was often with me that I should not be able to consent to the thing being done to my child, which I saw no fruit of, and knew to be but a custom which men were engaged in by tradition, not having the true knowledge of that scripture in the last of the Galatians, of circumcision or uncircumcision availing nothing, but a new creature. This was often in my mind, and I resolved that it should not be done to my child. When I was delivered of her, I refused to have her sprinkled, which brought great reproach upon me; so I became a by-word and a hissing among the people of my own rank in the world; and a strange thing it was thought to be, among my relations and acquaintance; Such as were esteemed able ministers (and I formerly delighted to hear), were sent to persuade me; but I could not consent and be clear. My answer to them was: "He that doubteth is damned."

After some time I waded through this difficulty, but soon after I unhappily went from the simplicity into notions, and changed my ways often, and ran from one notion into another, not finding satisfaction nor assurance that I should obtain what my soul desired, in the several ways and notions which I sought satisfaction in. I was weary of prayers, and such like exercises, finding no peace therefrom; nor could I lift up my hands without doubting, nor call God father. In this state, and for this cause, I gave over all manner of religious exercises in my family and in private, with much grief, for my delight was in being exercised about religion. I left not those things in a loose mind, as some judged that kept in them; for had I found I performed thereby what the Lord required of me, and was well pleased with, I could gladly have continued in the practice of them; I being zealously affected about the several things that were accounted duties; a zealous Sabbath-keeper, and fasting often; praying in private, rarely less than three times a day, many times oftener; a hearer of sermons on all occasions, both lectures, fasts and thanksgiving. Most of the day was used to be spent in reading the scriptures or praying, or such like. I dared not to go to bed till I had prayed, nor pray till I had read scripture, and felt my heart warmed thereby, or by meditation. I had so great a zeal and delight in the exercise of religious duties, that when I questioned not but it was right, I have often in the day sought remote places to pray in, such as the fields, gardens, or outhouses, when I could not be private in the house. I was so vehement in prayer, that I thought no place too private to pray in, but I could not but be loud in the earnest pouring out of my soul. Oh! this was not parted with but because I found it polluted, and my rest must not be there.

I now had my conversation among a people that had no

religion, being ashamed to be thought religious, or do any thing that was called so, not finding my heart with the appearance. And now I loathed whatever profession any one made, and thought the professors of every sort worse than the profane, they boasted so much of what I knew they had not attained to; I having been zealous in all things which they pretended to, and could not find the purging of the heart, or answer of acceptance from the Lord.

In this restless state I entertained every sort of notion that arose in that day, and for a time applied myself to get out of them whatever I could; but still sorrow and trouble was the end of all, and I began to conclude that the Lord and his truth was, but that it was not made known to any upon earth; and I determined no more to enquire after Him or it, for it was in vain to seek Him, being not to be found. For some time, pursuant to my resolution, I thought nothing about religion, but minded recreations as they are called, and ran into many excesses and vanities; as foolish mirth, carding, dancing, singing, and frequenting of music meetings; and made many vain visits at jovial eatings and drinkings, to satisfy the extravagant appetite, and please the vain mind with curiosities; gratifying the lust of the eye, the lust of the flesh, and the pride of life. I also frequented other places of pleasure, where vain people resorted to show themselves, and to see others in the like excess of folly in apparel; riding about from place to place, in the airy mind. But in the midst of all this my heart was constantly sad, and pained beyond expression; and after a pretty long indulgence in such follies, I retired for several days, and was in great trouble and anguish.

To all this excess and folly I was not hurried by being captivated with such things, but sought in them relief from the discontent of my mind; not having found what I sought after, and longed for, in the practice of religious duties. I would often say to myself, What is all this to me? I could easily leave it all, for my heart is not satisfied therewith. I do these things because I am weary, and know not what else to do: it is not my delight, it hath not power over me. I had rather serve the Lord, if I knew how acceptably. . . .

In the situation I mentioned, of being wearied in seeking and not finding, I married my dear husband, Isaac Penington. My love was drawn towards him, because I found he saw the deceit of all notions, and lay as one that refused to be comforted by any appearance of religion, until He came to his temple, "who is truth and no lie." All things that appeared to be religion and were not so, were very manifest to him; so that, till then, he was sick and weary of all appearances. My heart became united to him, and I desired to be made serviceable to him in his disconsolate condition; for he was as one alone and miserable in this world. I gave up much to be a companion to him in his suffering state. And oh! the groans and cries in secret that were raised in me, that I might be visited of the Lord, and come to the knowledge of his way; and that my feet might be turned into that way, before I went hence, if I never walked one step in it, to my joy or peace; yet that I might know myself in it, or turned to it, though all my time were spent in sorrow and exercise.

I resolved never to go back to those things I had left, having discovered death and darkness to be in them; but would rather be without a religion, until the Lord taught me one. Many times, when alone, did I reason thus: "Why should I not know the way of life? For if the Lord would give me all in this world, it would not satisfy me." Nay, I would cry out: "I care not for a portion in this life: give it to those who care for it. I am miserable with it: it is acceptance with thee I desire, and that alone can satisfy me."

Whilst I was in this state I heard of a new people, called Quakers. I resolved not to enquire after them, nor what principles they held. For a year or more after I heard of them in the north, I heard nothing of their way, except that they used thee and thou; and I saw a book written in the plain language, by George Fox. I remember that I thought it very ridiculous, so minded neither the people nor the book, except that it was to scoff at them and it. Though I thus despised this people, I had sometimes a desire to go to one of their meetings, if I could, unknown, and to hear them pray, for I was quite weary of doctrines; but I believed if I was with them when they prayed, I should be able to feel whether they were of the Lord or not. I endeavoured to stifle this desire, not knowing how to get to one of their meetings unknown; and if it should be known, I thought it would be reported that I was one of them.

One day, as my husband and I were walking in a park, a man, that for a little time had frequented the Quakers' meetings, saw us as he rode by, in our gay, vain apparel. He cried out to us against our pride, etc., at which I scoffed, and said he was a public preacher indeed, who preached in the highways. He turned back again, saying he had a love for my husband, seeing grace in his looks.

He drew nigh to the pales, and spoke of the light and grace which had appeared to all men. My husband and he engaged in discourse. The man of the house coming up, invited the stranger in: he was but young, and my husband too hard for him in the fleshly wisdom. He told my husband he would bring a man to him the next day, that should answer all his questions, or objections, who, as I afterwards understood, was George Fox. He came again the next day, and left word that the friend he intended to bring could not well come; but some others, he believed, would be with us about the second hour: At which time came Thomas Curtis and William Simpson.

My mind was somewhat affected by the man who had discoursed with us the night before; and though I thought him weak in managing the arguments he endeavoured to support, yet many scriptures which he mentioned stuck with me very weightily: they were such as showed to me the vanity of many practices I was in: which made me very serious, and soberly inclined to hear what these men had to say. Their solid and weighty carriage struck a dread over me. I now knew that they came in the power and authority of the Lord, to visit us, and that the Lord was with them. All in the room were sensible of the Lord's power manifest in them. Thomas Curtis repeated this scripture: "He that will know my doctrine, must do my commands." Immediately it arose in my mind, that if I would know whether that was truth they had spoken or not, I must do what I knew to be the Lord's will. What was contrary to it was now set before me, as to be removed; and I must come into a state of entire obedience before I could be in a capacity to perceive or discover what it was which they laid down for their principles.

This wrought mightily in me. Things which I had slighted much, now seemed to have power over me. Terrible was the Lord against the vain and evil inclinations in me, which made me, night and day, to cry out; and if I did but cease a little, then I grieved for fear I should again be reconciled to the things which I felt under judgment, and had a just detestation of. Oh! how I did beg not to be left secure or quiet till the evil was done away. How often did this run through my mind: "Ye will not come to me, that ye may have life." "It is true I am undone if I come not to thee, but I cannot come, unless I leave that which cleaveth close unto me, and I cannot part with it."

I saw the Lord would be just in casting me off, and not giving me life; for I would not come from my beloved lusts, to Him, for life. Oh! the pain I felt still. The wrath of God was more than I could bear. Oh! in what bitterness and distress was I involved! A little time after the Friends' visit before mentioned, one night on my bed it was said unto me: "Be not hasty to join these people called Quakers." I never had peace or quiet from a sore exercise for many months, till I was, by the stroke of judgment, brought off from all those things, which I found the light made manifest to be deceit, bondage, and vanity, the spirit of the world, etc., and I given up to be a fool and a reproach, and to take up the cross to my honor and reputation in the world. The contemplation of those things cost me many tears, doleful nights and days; not now disputing against the doctrine preached by the Friends, but exercised against taking up the cross to the language, fashions, customs, titles, honor, and esteem in the world.

My relations made this cross very heavy; but as at length I happily gave up, divested of reasonings, not consulting how to provide for the flesh, I received strength to attend the meetings of these despised people which I never intended to meddle with, but found truly of the Lord, and my heart owned them. I longed to be one of them, and minded not the cost or pain; but judged it would be well worth my utmost cost and pain to witness such a change as I saw in them—such power over their corruptions. I had heard objected against them, that they wrought not miracles; but I said that they did great miracles, in that they turned them that were in the world and the fellowship of it, from all such things. Thus, by taking up the cross, I received strength against many things which I had thought impossible to deny; but many tears did I shed, and bitterness of soul did I experience, before I came thither; and often cried out: "I shall one day fall by the overpowering of the enemy." But oh! the joy that filled my soul in the first meeting ever held in our house at Chalfont. To this day I have a fresh remembrance of it. It was then the Lord enabled me to worship Him in that which was undoubtedly his own, and give up my whole strength, yea, to swim in the life which overcame me that day. Oh! long had I desired to worship Him with acceptation, and lift up my hands without doubting, which I witnessed that day in that assembly. I acknowledged his great mercy and wonderful kindness; for I could say, "This is it which I have longed and waited for, and feared I never should have experienced."

Many trials have I exercised with since, but they were all from the Lord, who strengthened my life in them. Yet, after all this, I suffered my mind to run out into prejudice against some particular Friends. This was a sore hurt unto me: but after a time of deep, secret sorrow, the Lord removed the wrong thing from me, blessing me with a large portion of his light, and the love and acceptance of his beloved ones. And He hath many times refreshed my soul in his presence, and given me assurance that I knew that estate in which He will never leave me, nor suffer me to be drawn from all which He has graciously fulfilled; for though various infirmities and temptations beset me, yet my heart cleaveth unto the Lord, in the everlasting bonds that can never be broken. In his light do I see those temptations and infirmities: there do I bemoan myself unto Him, and feel faith and strength, which give the victory. Though it keeps me low in the sense of my own weakness, yet it quickens in me a lively hope of seeing Satan trodden down under foot by his all-sufficient grace. I feel and know when I have slipped in word, deed, or thought; and also know where my help lieth, who is my advocate, and have recourse to Him who pardoned and heals, and gives me to overcome, setting me on my watch-tower: and though the enemy is suffered to prove me, in order more and

more to wean me from any dependance but upon the mighty
Jehovah, I believe he will never be able to prevail against me.
Oh! that I may keep on my watch continually: knowing, the
Lord only can make war with this dragon. Oh! that I may, by
discovering my own weakness, ever be tender of the tempted;
watching and praying, lest I also be tempted. Sweet is this state,
though low; for in it I receive my daily bread, and enjoy that
which He handeth forth continually; and live not, but as He
breatheth the breath of life upon me every moment.

====

"Now Was All My Former Life Ripped Up"

[FROM The History of the Life of Thomas Ellwood]

T H O M A S   E L L W O O D

[The Peningtons introduced Thomas Ellwood (1639–1714) to Quakerism. (He later was to become a secretary to Milton.) The "strict
gravity" which he found had replaced their usual "free, debonair, and
courtly" behavior, at first took him aback.
    Richenda Gurney, sister of Elizabeth Fry, said, when young, that
she would like to "bang all the old Quakers who look so triumphant and
disagreeable." Ellwood says nothing of "banging" but is "disappointed." Soon afterward the very gravity which had disappointed him
took hold of him, and the young man, as Edward Burrough said, "was
reached."
    Three matters are of particular interest in Ellwood's Life. First,
the unbelievable (to us) importance attached to "hat honor," "knee
honor," and the use, to one's betters, of "thee" and "thou." Second, the
trial it was for many converts to assume plain language and dress; the
trial, that is, of appearing unusual, apart from the actual physical trial

*of being knocked down by one's father, as a starter, for such innovations.
And third, and most important of all spiritually, is Ellwood's understanding and analysis of "will-worship" and the satisfactions people
take in the performance of religious exercises they have "willed"
themselves to perform. Hat honor, plain language and dress are
matters now of historical interest only to Quakers. "Will-worship," as
contrasted with "the movings of the Holy Spirit," lies still at the heart
of Quaker experience as a hindrance to spiritual growth.]*

I mentioned before, that during my father's abode in London,
in the time of the civil wars, he contracted a friendship with the
Lady Springett, then a widow, and afterwards married to Isaac
Penington, Esq., to continue which he sometimes visited them at
their Lodge, near Reading. And having heard that they were come
to live upon their own estate at Chalfont, in Buckinghamshire,
about fifteen miles from Crowell, he went one day to visit them
there, and to return at night, taking me with him.

But very much surprised we were when, being come thither,
we first heard, then found, they were become Quakers; a people
we had no knowledge of, and a name we had till then scarce
heard of.

So great a change, from a free, debonair, and courtly sort of
behaviour, which we formerly had found them in, to so strict a
gravity as they now received us with did not a little amuse us, and
disappoint our expectation of such a pleasant visit as we used to
have, and had now promised ourselves. Nor could my father
have any opportunity, by a private conference with them, to
understand the ground or occasion of this change, there being
some other strangers with them (related to Isaac Penington),
who came that morning from London to visit them also.

For my part I sought and at length found means to cast
myself into the company of the daughter, whom I found gathering some flowers in the garden, attended by her maid, who was
also a Quaker. But when I addressed myself to her after my
accustomed manner, with intention to engage her in some
discourse which might introduce conversation on the footing of

our former acquaintance, though she treated me with a courteous mien, yet, as young as she was, the gravity of her look and behaviour struck such an awe upon me, that I found myself not so much master of myself as to pursue any further converse with her.   Wherefore, asking pardon for my boldness in having intruded myself into her private walks, I withdrew, not without some disorder (as I thought at least) of mind.

We stayed dinner, which was very handsome, and lacked nothing to recommend it to me but the want of mirth and pleasant discourse, which we could neither have with them, nor by reason of them, with one another amongst ourselves; the weightiness that was upon their spirits and countenances keeping down the lightness that would have been up in us. We stayed, notwithstanding, till the rest of the company took leave of them, and then we also, doing the same, returned, not greatly satisfied with our journey, nor knowing what in particular to find fault with.

Yet this good effect that visit had upon my father, who was then in the Commission of the Peace, that it disposed him to a more favourable opinion of and carriage towards those people when they came in his, as not long after one of them did. . . .

Some time after this, my father, having gotten some further account of the people called Quakers, and being desirous to be informed concerning their principles, made another visit to Isaac Penington and his wife. . . .

It was in the tenth month, in the year 1659, that we went thither, where we found a very kind reception, and tarried some days; one day at least the longer, for that while we were there a meeting was appointed at a place about a mile from thence, to which we were invited to go, and willingly went.

It was held in a farm-house called the Grove, which having formerly been a gentleman's seat, had a very large hall, and that well filled.

To this meeting came Edward Burrough, besides other preachers, as Thomas Curtis and James Naylor, but none spoke there at that time but Edward Burrough, next to whom, as it were under him, it was my lot to sit on a stool by the side of a long table on which he sat, and I drank in his words with desire; for they not only answered my understanding, but warmed my heart with a certain heat, which I not till then felt from the ministry of any man.

When the meeting was ended, our friends took us home with them again; and after supper, the evenings being long, the servants of the family (who were Quakers) were called in, and we all sat down in silence. But long we had not so sat before Edward Burrough began to speak among us. And although he spoke not long, yet what he said did touch, as I suppose, my father's (religious) copyhold, as the phrase is. And he having been from his youth a professor, though not joined in that which is called close communion with any one sort, and valuing himself upon the knowledge he esteemed himself to have in the various notions of each profession, thought he had now a fair opportunity to display his knowledge, and thereupon began to make objections against what had been delivered.

The subject of the discourse was, "The universal free grace of God to all mankind," to which he opposed the Calvinistic tenet of particular and personal predestination; in defence of which indefensible notion he found himself more at a loss than he expected. Edward Burrough said not much to him upon it, though what he said was close and cogent; but James Naylor interposing, handled the subject with so much perspicuity and clear demonstration, that his reasoning seemed to be irresistible; and so I suppose my father found it, which made him willing to drop the discourse. . . .

The next morning we prepared to return home (that is, my father, my younger sister, and myself, for my elder sister was gone before by the stagecoach to London), and when, having taken our leaves of our friends, we went forth, they, with Edward Burrough, accompanying us to the gate, he there directed his speech in a few words to each of us severally, according to the sense he had of our several conditions. And when we were gone off, and they gone in again, they asking him what he thought of us, he answered them, as they afterwards told me, to this effect: "As for the old man, he is settled on his lees, and the young woman is light and airy; but the young man is reached, and may do well if he does not lose it." And surely that which he said to me, or rather that spirit in which he spoke it, took such fast hold on me, that I felt sadness and trouble come over me, though I did not distinctly understand what I was troubled for. I knew not what I ailed, but I knew I ailed something more than ordinary, and my heart was very heavy. . . .

I had a desire to go to another meeting of the Quakers, and bade my father's man inquire if there was any in the country thereabouts. He thereupon told me he had heard at Isaac Penington's that there was to be a meeting at High Wycombe on Thursday next.

Thither therefore I went, though it was seven miles from me; and that I might be rather thought to go out a-coursing than to a meeting, I let my greyhound run by my horse's side.

When I came there, and had set up my horse at an inn, I was at a loss how to find the house where the meeting was to be. I knew it not, and was ashamed to ask after it; wherefore, having ordered the ostler to take care of my dog, I went into the street and stood at the inn gate, musing with myself what course to take. But I had not stood long ere I saw a horseman riding along the street, whom I remembered I had seen before at Isaac Penington's, and he put up his horse at the same inn. Him therefore I resolved to follow, supposing he was going to the meeting, as indeed he was.

Being come to the house, which proved to be John Raunce's, I saw the people sitting together in an outer room; wherefore I stepped in and sat down on the first void seat, the end of a bench just within the door, having my sword by my side and black clothes on, which drew some eyes upon me. It was not long ere one stood up and spoke, whom I was afterwards well acquainted with; his name was Samuel Thornton, and what he said was very suitable and of good service to me, for it reached home as if it had been directed to me.

As soon as ever the meeting was ended and the people began to rise, I, being next the door, stepped out quickly, and hastening to my inn, took horse immediately homewards, and (so far as I remember) my having been gone was not taken notice of by my father.

This latter meeting was like the clinching of a nail, confirming and fastening in my mind those good principles which had sunk into me at the former. My understanding began to open, and I felt some stirrings in my breast, tending to the work of a new creation in me. The general trouble and confusion of mind, which had for some days lain heavy upon me and pressed me down, without a distinct discovery of the particular cause for which it came, began now to wear off, and some glimmerings of light began to break forth in me, which let me see my inward state and condition towards God. The light, which before had shone in my darkness, and the darkness could not comprehend it, began now to shine out of darkness, and in some measure discovered to me what it was that had before clouded me and brought that sadness and trouble upon me....

Now was all my former life ripped up, and my sins by degrees were set in order before me....

Now also did I receive a new law—an inward law superadded to the outward—the law of the spirit of life in Christ Jesus....

But as to myself and the work begun in me, I found it was not enough for me to cease to do evil, though that was a good and a great step. I had another lesson before me, which was to learn to do well; which I could by no means do till I had given up with full purpose of mind to cease from doing evil. And when I had done that, the enemy took advantage of my weakness to mislead me again....

I read abundantly in the Bible, and would set myself tasks in reading, enjoining myself to read so many chapters, sometimes a whole book or long epistle, at a time. And I thought that time well spent, though I was not much the wiser for what I had read, reading it too cursorily, and without the true Guide, the Holy Spirit, which alone could open the understanding and give the true sense of what was read.

I prayed often, and drew out my prayers to a great length, and appointed unto myself certain set times to pray at, and a certain number of prayers to say in a day: we knew not meanwhile what true prayer was....

This will-worship, which all is that is performed in the will of man and not in the movings of the Holy Spirit, was a great hurt to me, and hindrance of my spiritual growth in the way of truth.

But my heavenly Father, who knew the sincerity of my soul to Him and the hearty desire I had to serve Him, had compassion on me, and in due time was graciously pleased to illuminate my understanding further, and to open in me an eye to discern the false spirit, and its way of working from the true, and to reject the former and cleave to the latter.

But though the enemy had by his subtlety gained such advantages over me, yet I went on notwithstanding, and firmly persisted in my godly resolution of ceasing from and denying those things which I was now convinced in my conscience were evil. And on this account a great trial came quickly on me; for the general Quarter Sessions for the Peace coming on, my father, willing to excuse himself from a dirty journey, commanded me to get up betimes and go to Oxford, and deliver in the recognisances he had taken, and bring him an account what justices were on the bench, and what principal pleas were before them; which he knew I knew how to do, having often attended him on those services.

I, who knew how it stood with me better than he did, felt a weight come over me as soon as he had spoken the word; for I presently saw it would bring a very great exercise upon me. But having never resisted his will in anything that was lawful, as this was, I attempted not to make any excuse, but ordering a horse to be ready for me early in the morning, I went to bed, having great strugglings in my breast.

For the enemy came in upon me like a flood, and set many difficulties before me. . . .

He cast into my mind not only how I should behave myself in court and dispatch the business I was sent about, but how I should demean myself towards my acquaintance, of which I had many in that city, with whom I was wont to be jolly; whereas now I could not put off my hat, nor bow to any of them, nor give them their honorary titles (as they are called), nor use the corrupt language of *you* to any one of them, but must keep to the plain and true language of *thou* and *thee*. . . .

Early next morning I got up, and found my spirit pretty calm and quiet, yet not without a fear upon me lest I should slip and let fall the testimony which I had to bear. And as I rode a frequent cry ran through me to the Lord, in this wise: "Oh my God, preserve me faithful, whatever befalls me: suffer me not to be drawn into evil, how much scorn and contempt soever be cast upon me." . . .

When I had set up my horse I went directly to the hall where the sessions were held, where I had been but a very little while before a knot of my old acquaintances, espying me, came to me. One of these was a scholar in his gown, another a surgeon of that city (both my school-fellows and fellow-boarders at Thame school), and the third a country gentleman with whom I had long been very familiar.

When they were come up to me they all saluted me after the usual manner, pulling off their hats and bowing, and saying, "Your humble servant, sir," expecting no doubt the like from me. But when they saw me stand still, not moving my cap, nor bowing my knee in way of congee to them, they were amazed, and looked first one upon another, then upon me, and then one another again, for a while, without speaking a word.

At length the surgeon, a brisk young man, who stood nearest to me, clapping his hand in a familiar way upon my shoulder, and smiling on me, said, "What, Tom! a Quaker?" To which I readily and cheerfully answered, "Yes, a Quaker." And as the words passed out of my mouth I felt joy spring in my heart; for I rejoiced that I had not been drawn out by them into a compliance with them, and that I had strength and boldness given me to confess myself to be one of that despised people. . . .

But notwithstanding that it was thus with me, and that I found peace and acceptance with the Lord in some good degree, according to my obedience to the convictions I had received by His holy Spirit in me, yet was not the veil so done away, or fully rent, but that there still remained a cloud upon my understanding with respect to my carriage towards my father. And that notion which the enemy had brought into my mind, that I ought to put such a difference between him and all others as that, on account of the paternal relation, I should still deport myself towards him, both in gesture and language, as I had always heretofore done, did yet prevail with me. So that when I came home I went to my father bareheaded, as I used to do, and gave him a particular account of the business he had given me in command, in such manner that he, observing no alteration in my carriage towards him found no cause to take offence at me.

I had felt for some time before an earnest desire of mind to go again to Isaac Penington's, and I began to question whether, when my father should come (as I concluded ere long he would) to understand I inclined to settle among the people called Quakers, he would permit me the command of his horses, as before. Wherefore, in the morning when I went to Oxford I gave directions to a servant of his to go that day to a gentleman of my acquaintance, who I knew had a riding nag to put off either by sale or to be kept for his work, and desired him, in my name, to send him to me; which he did, and I found him in the stable when I came home.

On this nag I designed to ride next day to Isaac Penington's, and in order thereunto arose betimes and got myself ready for the journey; but because I would pay all due respect to my father, and not go without his consent, or knowledge at the least, I sent one up to him (for he was not yet stirring) to acquaint him that I had a purpose to go to Isaac Penington's, and desired to know if he pleased to command me any service to them. He sent me word he would speak with me before I went, and would have me come up to him, which did, and stood by his bedside.

Then, in a mild and gentle tone, he said: "I understand you have a mind to go to Mr. Penington's." I answered, "I have so."—"Why," said he, "I wonder why you should. You were there, you know, but a few days ago, and unless you had business with them, don't you think it will look oddly?"—I said, "I thought not."—"I doubt," said he, "you'll tire them with your company, and make them think they shall be troubled with you."—"If," replied I, "I find anything of that, I'll make the shorter stay."—"But," said he, "can you propose any sort of business with them, more than a mere visit?"—"Yes," said I, "I propose to myself not only to see them, but to have some discourse with them."—"Why," said he, in a tone a little harsher, "I hope you don't incline to be of their way."—"Truly," answered I, "I like them and their way very well, so far as I yet understand it; and I am willing to go to them that I may understand it better."

Thereupon he began to reckon up a beadroll of faults against the Quakers, telling me they were rude, unmannerly people, that would not give civil respect or honour to their superiors, no not to magistrates; that they held many dangerous principles; that they were an immodest shameless people; and that one of them stripped himself stark naked, and went in that unseemly manner about the streets, at fairs and on market days, in great towns.

To all the other charges I answered only, "That perhaps they might be either misreported or misunderstood, as the best of people had sometimes been." But to the last charge of going naked, a particular answer, by way of instance, was just then brought into my mind and put into my mouth, which I had not thought of before, and that was the example of Isaiah, who went naked among the people for a long time (Isaiah xx. 4). "Ay," said my father, "but you must consider that he was a prophet of the Lord, and had express command from God to go so."—"Yes, sir," replied I, "I do consider that; but I consider also, that the Jews, among whom he lived, did not own him for a prophet, nor believe that he had such a command from God. And," added I, "how know we but that this Quaker may be a prophet too, and might be commanded to do as he did, for some reason which we understand not?"

This put my father to a stand; so that, letting fall his charges against the Quakers, he only said, "I would wish you not to go so soon, but take a little time to consider of it; you may visit Mr. Penington hereafter."—"Nay, sir," replied I, "pray don't hinder my going now, for I have so strong a desire to go that I do not well know how to forbear." And as I spoke those words, I withdrew gently to the chamber door, and then hastening down stairs, went immediately to the stable, where finding my horse ready bridled, I forthwith mounted, and went off, lest I should receive a countermand. . . .

Before I went to bed they let me know that there was to be a meeting at Wycombe next day, and that some of the family would go to it. I was very glad of it, for I greatly desired to go to meetings, and this fell very aptly, it being in my way home. Next morning Isaac Penington himself went, having Anne Curtis with him, and I accompanied them. . . .

A very good meeting was this in itself and to me. Edward Burrough's ministry came forth among us in life and power, and the assembly was covered therewith. I also, according to my small capacity, had a share therein; for I felt some of that divine power working my spirit into a great tenderness, and not only confirming me in the course I had already entered, and strengthening me to go on therein, but rending also the veil somewhat further, and clearing my understanding in some other things which I had not seen before. For the Lord was pleased to make His discoveries to me by degrees, that the sight of too great a work, and too many enemies to encounter with at once, might not discourage me and make me faint.

When the meeting was ended, . . . Edward Burrough going home with Isaac Penington, he invited me to go back with him, which I willingly consented to, for the love I had more particularly to Edward Burrough, through whose ministry I had received the first awakening stroke, drew me to desire his company; and so away we rode together.

But I was somewhat disappointed of my expectation, for I hoped he would have given me both opportunity and encouragement to have opened myself to him, and to have poured forth my complaints, fears, doubts, and questionings into his bosom. But he, being sensible that I was truly reached, and that the witness of God was raised and the work of God rightly begun in me, chose to leave me to the guidance of the good Spirit in myself (the Counsellor that could resolve all doubts), that I might not have any dependence on man. Wherefore, although he was naturally of an open and free temper and carriage, and was afterwards always very familiar and affectionately kind to me, yet at this time he kept himself somewhat reserved, and showed only common kindness to me.

Next day we parted, he for London, I for home, under a very great weight and exercise upon my spirit. For I now saw, in and by the farther openings of the Divine light in me, that the enemy, by his false reasonings, had beguiled and misled me with respect to my carriage towards my father. For I now clearly saw that the honour due to parents did not consist in uncovering the head and bowing the body to them, but in a ready obedience to their lawful commands, and in performing all needful services unto them. Wherefore, as I was greatly troubled for what I already had done in that case, though it was through ignorance, so I plainly felt I could no longer continue therein without drawing upon myself the guilt of wilful disobedience, which I well knew would draw after it divine displeasure and judgment. . . .

Thus labouring under various exercises on the way, I at length got home, expecting I should have but a rough reception from my father. But when I came home, I understood my father was from home; wherefore I sat down by the fire in the kitchen, keeping my mind retired to the Lord, with breathings of spirit to Him, that I might be preserved from falling.

After some time I heard the coach drive in, which put me into a little fear, and a sort of shivering came over me. But by that time he was alighted and come in I had pretty well recovered myself; and as soon as I saw him I rose up and advanced a step or two towards him, with my head covered, and said, "Isaac Penington and his wife remember their loves to thee."

He made a step to hear what I said, and observing that I did not stand bare, and that I used the word *thee* to him, he, with a stern countenance, and tone that spake high displeasure, only said, "I shall talk with you, sir, another time"; and so hastening from me, went into the parlour, and I saw him no more that night. . . .

My spirit longed to be among friends, and to be at some meeting with them on the first day, which now drew on, this being the sixth-day night. Wherefore I purposed to go to Oxford on the morrow (which was the seventh day of the week), having heard there was a meeting there. Accordingly, having ordered my horse to be made ready betimes, I got up in the morning and made myself ready also. Yet before I would go (that I might be as observant to my father as possibly I could) I desired my sister to go up to him in his chamber, and acquaint him that I had a mind to go to Oxford, and desired to know if he pleased to command me any service there. He bid her tell me he would not

have me go till he had spoken with me; and getting up immediately, he hastened down to me before he was quite dressed.

As soon as he saw me standing with my hat on, his passion
transporting him, he fell upon me with both his fists, and having
by that means somewhat vented his anger, he plucked off my
hat and threw it away. Then stepping hastily out to the stable,
and seeing my borrowed nag stand ready saddled and bridled,
he asked his man whence that horse came; who telling him he
fetched it from Mr. Such-an-one's; "Then ride him presently
back," said my father, "and tell Mr. ———— I desire he will
never lend my son a horse again unless he brings a note from
me."

The poor fellow, who loved me well, would fain have made
excuses and delays; but my father was positive in his command,
and so urgent, that he would not let him stay so much as to take
his breakfast (though he had five miles to ride), nor would he
himself stir from the stable till he had seen the man mounted
and gone.

Then coming in, he went up into his chamber to make
himself more fully ready, thinking he had me safe enough now
my horse was gone; for I took so much delight in riding that I
seldom went on foot.

But while he was dressing himself in his chamber I (who
understood what had been done), changing my boots for shoes,
took another hat, and acquainting my sister, who loved me very
well, and whom I could confide in, whither I meant to go, went
out privately, and walked away to Wycombe, having seven long
miles thither, which yet seemed little and easy to me, from the
desire I had to be among friends.

As thus I travelled all alone, under a load of grief, from the
sense I had of the opposition and hardship I was to expect from
my father, the enemy took advantage to assault me again,
casting a doubt into my mind whether I had done well in thus
coming away from my father without his leave or knowledge. . . .

I considered thereupon the extent of paternal power, which
I found was not wholly arbitrary and unlimited, but had bounds
set unto it; so that as in civil matters it was restrained to things
lawful, so in spiritual and religious cases it had not a compulsory

power over conscience, which ought to be subject to the heavenly Father. And therefore, though obedience to parents be enjoined to children, yet it is with this limitation (*in the Lord*): "Children, obey your parents in the Lord; for this is right" (I Pet. vi. I). . . .

And yet I was not wholly free from some fluctuations of mind, from the besettings of the enemy. Wherefore, although I knew that outward signs did not properly belong to the gospel dispensation, yet for my better assurance I did, in fear and great humility, beseech the Lord that he would be pleased so far to condescend to the weakness of his servant as to give me a sign by which I might certainly know whether my way was right before Him or not.

The sign which I asked was, "That if I had done wrong in coming as I did, I might be rejected or but coldly received at the place I was going to; but if this mine undertaking was right in His sight, He would give me favour with them I went to, so that they should receive me with hearty kindness and demonstrations of love." Accordingly, when I came to John Raunce's house (which, being so much a stranger to all, I chose to go to, because I understood the meeting was commonly held there), they received me with more than ordinary kindness, especially Frances Raunce, John Raunce's then wife, who was both a grave and motherly woman, and had a hearty love to truth, and tenderness towards all that in sincerity sought after it. And this so kind reception, confirming me in the belief that my undertaking was approved of by the Lord, gave great satisfaction and ease to my mind; and I was thankful to the Lord therefor.

Thus it fared with me there; but at home it fared otherwise with my father. He, supposing I had betaken myself to my chamber when he took my hat from me, made no inquiry after me till evening came; and then, sitting by the fire and considering that the weather was very cold, he said to my sister, who sat by him: "Go up to your brother's chamber, and call him down; it may be he will sit there else, in a sullen fit, till he has caught cold." "Alas! sir," said she, "he is not in his chamber, nor in the house neither." At that my father, starting, said: "Why, where is he then?"—"I know not, sir," said she, "where he is; but I know that when he saw you had sent away his horse he put on shoes, and went out on foot, and I have not seen him since. And indeed, sir," added she, "I don't wonder at his going away, considering how you used him." This put my father into a great fright doubting I was gone quite away; and so great a passion of grief seized on him, that he forebore not to weep, and to cry out aloud, so that the family heard him: "Oh, my son! I shall never see him more; for he is of so bold and resolute a spirit that he will run himself into danger, and so may lie and die before I can hear of him." Then bidding her light him up to his chamber, he went immediately to bed, where he lay restless and groaning, and often bemoaning himself and me, for the greater part of the night.

Next morning my sister sent a man (whom for his love to me she knew she could trust) to give me this account; and though by him she sent me also fresh linen for my use, in case I should go farther or stay out longer, yet she desired me to come home as soon as I could.

This account was very uneasy to me. I was much grieved that I had occasioned so much grief to my father; and I would have returned that evening after the meeting, but the Friends would not permit it, for the meeting would in all likelihood end late, the days being short, and the way was long and dirty. And besides, John Raunce told me that he had something on his mind to speak to my father, and that if I would stay till the next day, he would go down with me, hoping, perhaps, that while my father was under this sorrow for me he might work some good upon him. Hereupon concluding to stay till the morrow, I dismissed the man with the things he had brought, bidding him tell my sister I intended, God willing, to return home tomorrow, and charging him not to let anybody else know that he had seen me, or where he had been.

Next morning John Raunce and I set out, and when we were come to the end of the town we agreed that he should go before and knock at the great gate, and I would come a little after, and go in by the back way. He did so; and when a servant came to open the gate he asked if the Justice was at home. She told him, Yes; and desiring him to come in and sit down in the hall, went and acquainted her master that there was one who desired to speak with him. He, supposing it was one that came for justice, went readily into the hall to him; but he was not a little surprised when he found it was a Quaker. Yet not knowing on what account he came, he stayed to hear his business; but when he found it was about me he fell somewhat sharply on him.

In this time I was come by the back way into the kitchen, and hearing my father's voice so loud, I began to doubt things wrought not well; but I was soon assured of that. For my father having quickly enough of a Quaker's company, left John Raunce in the hall, and came into the kitchen, where he was more surprised to find me.

The sight of my hat upon my head made him presently forget that I was that son of his whom he had so lately lamented as lost; and his passion of grief turning into anger, he could not contain himself, but running after me with both his hands, first violently snatched off my hat and threw it away, then giving me some buffets on my head, he said, "Sirrah, get you up to your chamber."

I forthwith went, he following me at the heels, and now and then giving me a whirret on the ear, which, the way to my chamber lying through the hall where John Raunce was, he, poor man, might see and be sorry for (as I doubt not but he was), but could not help me.

This was surely an unaccountable thing, that my father should but a day before express so high a sorrow for me, as fearing he should never see me any more, and yet now, so soon as he did see me, should fly upon me with such violence, and that only because I did not put off my hat, which he knew I did not put on in disrespect to him, but upon a religious principle. . . .

I had now lost one of my hats, and I had but one more. That therefore I put on, but did not keep it long; for the next time my father saw it on my head he tore it violently from me, and laid it up with the other, I knew not where. Wherefore I put on my montero-cap, which was all I had left to wear on my head, and it was but a very little while that I had that to wear, for as soon as my father came where I was I lost that also. And now I was forced to go bareheaded wherever I had occasion to go, within doors and without.

This was in the eleventh month, called January, and the weather sharp; so that I, who had been bred up more tenderly, took so great a cold in my head that my face and head were much swollen, and my gums had on them boils so sore that I could neither chew meat nor without difficulty swallow liquids. It held long, and I underwent much pain, without much pity except for my poor sister, who did what she could to give me ease; and at length, by frequent applications of figs and stoned raisins roasted, and laid to the boils as hot as I could bear them, they ripened fit for lancing, and soon after sunk; then I had ease.

Now was I laid up as a kind of prisoner for the rest of the winter, having no means to go forth among friends, nor they liberty to come to me. Wherefore I spent the time much in my chamber in waiting on the Lord, and in reading, mostly in the Bible.

But whenever I had occasion to speak to my father, though I had no hat now to offend him, yet my language did as much; for I durst not say "you" to him, but "thou" or "thee," as the occasion required, and then would he be sure to fall on me with his fists.

At one of these times, I remember, when he had beaten me in that manner, he commanded me, as he commonly did at such times, to go to my chamber, which I did, and he followed me to the bottom of the stairs. Being come thither, he gave me a parting blow, and in a very angry tone said: "Sirrah, if ever I hear you say 'thou' or 'thee' to me again, I'll strike your teeth down your throat." I was greatly grieved to hear him say so. And feeling a word rise in my heart unto him, I turned again, and calmly said unto him: "Would it not be just if God should serve thee so, when thou sayest Thou or Thee to Him?" Though his hand was up, I saw it sink and his countenance fall, and he turned away and left me standing there. But I, notwithstanding, went up into my chamber, and cried unto the Lord, earnestly beseeching Him that He would be pleased to open my father's eyes, that he might see whom he fought against, and for what; and that He would turn his heart.

After this I had a pretty time of rest and quiet from these disturbances, my father not saying anything to me, nor giving me occasion to say anything to him. But I was still under a kind of confinement, unless I would have run about the country bareheaded like a madman, which I did not see it was my place to do. . . .

But after some time a fresh storm, more fierce and sharp than any before, arose and fell upon me; the occasion thereof was this: My father, having been in his younger years, more especially while he lived in London, a constant hearer of those who are called Puritan preachers, had stored up a pretty stock of Scripture knowledge, did sometimes (not constantly, nor very often) cause his family to come together on a first day in the evening, and expound a chapter to them, and pray. His family now, as well as his estate, was lessened; for my mother was dead, my brother gone, and my elder sister at London; and having put off his husbandry, he had put off with it most of his servants, so that he had now but one man- and one maid-servant. It so fell out that on a first-day night he bade my sister, who sat with him in the parlour, call in the servants to prayer.

Whether this was done as a trial upon me or no, I know not, but a trial it proved to me; for they, loving me very well and disliking my father's carriage to me, made no haste to go in, but stayed a second summons. This so offended him that when at length they did go in, he, instead of going to prayer, examined them why they came not in when they were first called; and the answer they gave him being such as rather heightened than abated his displeasure, he with an angry tone said: "Call in that fellow" (meaning me, who was left alone in the kitchen), "for he is the cause of all this." They, as they were backward to go in themselves, so were not forward to call me in, fearing the effect of my father's displeasure would fall upon me, as soon it did, for I, hearing what was said, and not staying for the call, went in of myself. And as soon as I was come in, my father discharged his displeasure on me in very sharp and bitter expressions, which drew from me (in the grief of my heart, to see him so transported with passion) these few words: "They that can pray with such a spirit, let them; for my part, I cannot." With that my father flew upon me with both his fists, and not thinking that sufficient, stepped hastily to the place where his cane stood, and catching that up, laid on me, I thought, with all his strength. And I, being bareheaded, thought his blows must needs have broken my skull had I not laid mine arm over my head to defend it.

His man seeing this, and not able to contain himself, stepped in between us, and laying hold on the cane, by strength of hand held it so fast, that though he attempted not to take it away, yet he withheld my father from striking with it, which did but enrage him the more. I disliked this in the man, and bade him let go the cane and begone, which he immediately did, and turning to be gone, had a blow on his shoulders for his pains, which did not much hurt him.

But now my sister, fearing lest my father should fall upon me again, besought him to forbear, adding: "Indeed, sir, if you strike him any more, I will throw open the casement and cry out murder, for I am afraid you will kill my brother." This stopped his hand, and after some threatening speeches he commanded me to get to my chamber which I did, as I always did whenever he bade me.

Thither, soon after, my sister followed me, to see my arm and dress it, for it was indeed very much bruised and swelled between the wrist and the elbow, and in some places the skin was broken and beaten off. But though it was very sore, and I felt for some time much pain in it, yet I had peace and quietness in my mind, being more grieved for my father than for myself, who I knew had hurt himself more than me.

This was, so far as I remember, the last time that ever my father called his family to prayer; and this was also the last time that he ever fell, so severely at least, upon me. . . .

The rest of the winter I spent in a lonesome solitary life, having none to converse with, none to unbosom myself unto, none to ask counsel of, none to seek relief from, but the Lord alone, who yet was more than all. And yet the company and society of faithful and judicious friends would, I thought, have been very welcome as well as helpful to me in my spiritual travail, in which I thought I made slow progress, my soul breathing after further attainments, the sense of which drew from me the following lines:

The winter tree
Resembles me,
   Whose sap lies in its root:
The spring draws nigh;
As it, so I
   Shall bud, I hope, and shoot.

     ·   ·   ·   ·

Some little time before I went to Aylesbury prison I was desired by my quondam master, Milton, to take a house for him in the neighborhood where I dwelt, that he might go out of the city, for the safety of himself and his family, the pestilence then growing hot in London. I took a pretty box for him in Giles Chalfont, a mile from me, of which I gave him notice, and intended to have waited on him, and seen him well settled in it, but was prevented by that imprisonment.

But now being released and returned home, I soon made a visit to him, to welcome him into the country.

After some common discourses had passed between us, he called for a manuscript of his; which being brought he delivered to me, bidding me take it home with me, and read it at my leisure; and when I had so done, return it to him with my judgment thereupon.

When I came home, and had set myself to read it, I found it was that excellent poem which he entitled "Paradise Lost." After I had, with the best attention, read it through, I made him another visit, and returned him his book, with due acknowledgment of the favour he had done me in communicating it to me. He asked me how I liked it and what I thought of it, which I modestly but freely told him, and after some further discourse about it, I pleasantly said to him, "Thou hast said much here of 'Paradise Lost,' but what hast thou to say of 'Paradise Found'?" He made me no answer, but sat some time in a muse; then brake off that discourse, and fell upon another subject.

After the sickness was over, and the city well cleansed and become safely habitable again, he returned thither. And when afterwards I went to wait on him there, which I seldom failed of doing whenever my occasions drew me to London, he showed me his second poem, called "Paradise Regained," and in a pleasant tone said to me, "This is owing to you, for you put it into my head by the question you put to me at Chalfont, which before I had not thought of." . . .

I had always entertained so high a regard for marriage, as it was a divine institution, that I held it not lawful to make it a sort of political trade, to rise in the world by. And therefore as I could not but in my judgment blame such as I found made it their business to hunt after and endeavor to gain those who were accounted great fortunes, not so much regarding what she is as what she has, but making wealth the chief if not the only thing they aimed at; so I resolved to avoid, in my own practice, that course, and how much soever my condition might have prompted me, as well as others, to seek advantage that way, never to engage on account of riches, nor at all to marry till judicious affection drew me to it, which I now began to feel at work in my breast.

The object of this affection was a Friend whose name was Mary Ellis, whom for divers years I had had an acquaintance with, in the way of common friendship only, and in whom I thought I then saw those fair prints of truth and solid virtue which I afterwards found in a sublime degree in her; but what her condition in the world was as to estate, I was wholly a stranger to, nor desired to know. . . .

But some time, and that a good while after, I found my heart secretly drawn and inclining towards her, yet was I not hasty in proposing, but waited to feel a satisfactory settlement of mind therein, before I made any step thereto.

After some time I took an opportunity to open my mind therein unto my much-honoured friends Isaac and Mary Penington, who then stood *parentum loco* to me. They having solemnly weighed the matter, expressed their unity therewith; and indeed their approbation thereof was no small confirmation to me therein. Yet took I further deliberation, often retiring in spirit to the Lord, and crying to Him for direction, before I addressed myself to her. At length, as I was sitting all alone, waiting upon the Lord for counsel and guidance in this—in itself and to me—so important affair, I felt a word sweetly arise in me, as if I had heard a voice which said, "Go, and prevail." And faith springing in my heart with the word, I immediately arose and went, nothing doubting.

When I was come to her lodgings, which were about a mile from me, her maid told me she was in her chamber, for having been under some indisposition of body, which had obliged her to keep her chamber, she had not yet left it; wherefore I desired the maid to acquaint her mistress that I was come to give her a visit, whereupon I was invited to go up to her. And after some little time spent in common conversation, feeling my spirit weightily concerned, I solemnly opened my mind unto her with respect to the particular business I came about, which I soon perceived was a great surprise to her, for she had taken in an apprehension, as others also had done, that mine eye had been fixed elsewhere and nearer home.

I used not many words to her, but I felt a divine power went along with the words, and fixed the matter expressed by them so fast in her breast, that, as she afterwards acknowledged to me, she could not shut it out.

I made at that time but a short visit, for having told her I did not expect an answer from her now, but desired she would in the most solemn manner weigh the proposal made, and in due time give me such an answer thereunto as the Lord should give her, I took my leave of her and departed, leaving the issue to the Lord.

I had a journey then at hand, which I foresaw would take me up two weeks' time. Wherefore, the day before I was to set out I went to visit her again, to acquaint her with my journey, and excuse my absence, not yet pressing her for an answer, but assuring her that I felt in myself an increase of affection to her, and hoped to receive a suitable return from her in the Lord's time, to whom in the meantime I committed both her, myself, and the concern between us. And indeed I found at my return that I could not have left it in better hands; for the Lord had been my advocate in my absence, and had so far answered all her objections that when I came to her again she rather acquainted me with them than urged them.

From that time forward we entertained each other with affectionate kindness in order to marriage, which yet we did not hasten to, but went on deliberately. Neither did I use those vulgar ways of courtship, by making frequent and rich presents, not only for that my outward condition would not comport with the expense, but because I liked not to obtain by such means, but preferred an unbribed affection. . . .

From that time forward I continued my visits to my best beloved Friend until we married which was on the 28th day of the eighth month, called October, in the year 1669. We took each other in a select meeting of the ancient and grave Friends of that country, holden in a Friend's house, where in those times not only the monthly meeting for business but the public meeting for worship was sometimes kept. A very solemn meeting it was, and in a weighty frame of spirit we were, in which we sensibly felt the Lord with us, and joining us; the sense whereof remained with us all our lifetime, and was of good service and very comfortable to us on all occasions.

The Trial of William Penn

[FROM *The People's Ancient and Just Liberties Asserted*]

WILLIAM   PENN

[*We possess a report of the trial in 1670 of William Penn and William Mead because an unknown writer with a knowledge of shorthand was present, took down the proceedings verbatim, and published them immediately afterward. We are forever in that person's debt. Not only does the report of this trial give us unusual firsthand knowledge of the rip-snorting, knockabout methods of seventeenth-century trials, and provide,*

in addition, an important document in the history of the individuals'
long fight for civil rights: it, to cap the climax, and without reference to
history or civil rights, makes a stirring piece of reading matter.

Mead and Penn were brought to trial on the charge of causing a
riot. What they had done was to preach (though no one was certain that
this was what they were doing—the noise was too great to hear them)
outside the doors, locked against them, of Gracechurch Street Meeting
House. They came to their trial trying to stay out of jail and to defend
the right of Quakers to preach in public. They remained to champion
the jury system itself.

The words which follow are from John Sykes' The Quakers:
"William Penn and William Mead . . . pleaded 'Not Guilty' and Penn
. . . spoke to such effect that he and Mead were ushered out of court, and
the jury instructed in their absence. Next it was the jury's turn to offend.
They returned, from the Crown's point of view, an unsatisfactory
verdict. 'Gentlemen,' cried the irate Recorder, 'you have not given in
your verdict and you had as good say nothing. Therefore go and
consider it once more. . . .' They did so but again returned a verdict that
would acquit Penn. 'Gentlemen,' pursued the Recorder, now beside
himself with rage, 'you shall not be dismissed till we have a verdict the
court will accept and you shall be locked up without meat, drink, fire
and tobacco. . . .' Penn back at the bar called out to fortify them, . . . 'You
are Englishmen; mind your privilege, give not away your right.' 'Nor
will we ever do it,' sturdily replied the jury foreman.

"Nor did they. Shut up all night, bullied next day, finally thrown
into Newgate and fined for their pains, they still stood firm. Released
on a writ of habeas corpus, they promptly sued the Recorder for illegal
imprisonment; and won the case before a bench of twelve judges headed
by the Lord Chief Justice; and so established in English and American
courts the rightful independence of the jury. Bushel, the foreman, had
nerved his colleagues, but the inspiration for the whole spirited stand
had come from William Penn."]

———

. . . PENN: I affirm I have broken no law, nor am I guilty of the
indictment that is laid to my charge. And to the end the Bench,
the jury, and myself, with these that hear us, may have a more

direct understanding of this procedure, I desire you would let me know by what law it is you prosecute me, and upon what law you ground my indictment.

RECORDER: Upon the common law.

PENN: Where is that common law?

RECORDER: You must not think that I am able to run up so many years and over so many adjudged cases which we call common law to answer your curiosity.

PENN: This answer, I am sure, is very short of my question, for if it be common, it should not be so hard to produce.

RECORDER: Sir, will you plead to your indictment?

PENN: Shall I plead to an indictment that hath no foundation in law? If it contain that law you say I have broken, why should you decline to produce that law, since it will be impossible for the jury to determine or agree to bring in their verdict who have not the law produced by which they should measure the truth of this indictment, and the guilt or contrary of my fact.

RECORDER: You are a saucy fellow. Speak to the indictment.

PENN: I say it is my place to speak to matter of law. I am arraigned a prisoner; my liberty, which is next to life itself, is now concerned; you are many mouths and ears against me, and if I must not be allowed to make the best of my case, it is hard. I say again, unless you show me and the people the law you ground your indictment upon, I shall take it for granted your proceedings are merely arbitrary. (*At this time several upon the bench urged hard upon the prisoner to bear him down.*)

RECORDER: The question is whether you are guilty of this indictment.

PENN: The question is not whether I am guilty of this indictment, but whether this indictment be legal. It is too general and imperfect an answer to say it is the common law, unless we knew both where and what it is. For where there is no law there is no transgression, and that law which is not in being is so far from being common that it is no law at all.

RECORDER: You are an impertinent fellow. Will you teach the Court what law is? It's *lex non scripta,* that which many have studied thirty or forty years to know, and would you have me tell you in a moment?

PENN: Certainly if the common law be so hard to be understood, it's far from being very common; but if the Lord Coke in his *Institutes* be of any consideration, he tells us that common law is common right, and that common right is the Great Charter privileges, confirmed 9 Hen. III, c.29; 25 Edw. I, c.1; 2 Edw. III, c.8; 2 Coke *Inst.* 56.

RECORDER: Sir, you are a troublesome fellow, and it is not for the honor of the Court to suffer you to go on.

PENN: I have asked but one question, and you have not answered me, though the rights and privileges of every Englishman be concerned in it.

RECORDER: If I should suffer you to ask questions till tomorrow morning, you would be never the wiser.

PENN: That is according as the answers are.

RECORDER: Sir, we must not stand to hear you talk all night.

PENN: I design no affront to the Court, but to be heard in my just plea; and I must plainly tell you that if you will deny oyer of that law which you suggest I have broken, you do at once deny me an acknowledged right and evidence to the whole world your resolution to sacrifice the privileges of Englishmen to your sinister and arbitrary designs.

RECORDER: Take him away. My Lord, if you take not some course with this pestilent fellow to stop his mouth, we shall not be able to do anything tonight.

MAYOR: Take him away, take him away; turn him into the baildock.

PENN: These are but so many vain exclamations. Is this justice or true judgment? Must I therefore be taken away because I plead for the fundamental laws of England? However, this I leave upon your consciences, who are of the jury and my sole judges, that if these ancient fundamental laws, which relate to liberty and property, and are not limited to particular persuasions in matters of religion, must not be indispensably maintained and observed, who can say he hath right to the coat upon his back? Certainly our liberties are openly to be invaded, our wives to be ravished, our children slaved, our families ruined, and our estates led away in triumph by every sturdy beggar and malicious informer as their trophies, but our pretended forfeits for conscience' sake. The Lord of heaven and earth will be judge between us in this matter. . . .

[*The jury, having been exhorted to deliver a verdict of guilty, refused four times to do so, though they were kept all night without food, drink, or heat.*]

RECORDER: What is this to the purpose? I say I will have a verdict. (*And speaking to Edward Bushel, said:*) You are a factious fellow. I will set a mark upon you, and whilst I have any thing to do in the city, I will have an eye upon you.

MAYOR: Have you no more wit than to be led by such a pitiful fellow? I will cut his nose.

PENN: It is intolerable that my jury should be thus menaced. Is this according to the fundamental laws? Are not they my proper judges by the Great Charter of England? What hope is there of ever having justice done when juries are threatened and their verdicts rejected? I am concerned to speak and grieved to see such arbitrary proceedings. Did not the Lieutenant of the Tower render one of them worse than a felon? And do you not plainly seem to condemn such for factious fellows who answer not your ends? Unhappy are those juries who are threatened to be fined and starved and ruined if they give not in verdicts contrary to their consciences.

RECORDER: My Lord, you must take a course with that same fellow.

MAYOR: Stop his mouth, jailer; bring fetters and stake him to the ground.

PENN: Do your pleasure; I matter not your fetters.

RECORDER: Till now I never understood the reason of the policy and prudence of the Spaniards in suffering the Inquisition among them. And certainly it will never be well with us till something like the Spanish Inquisition be in England. . . .

PENN: I demand my liberty, being freed by the jury.

MAYOR: No, you are in for your fines.

PENN: Fines for what?

MAYOR: For contempt of the Court.

PENN: I ask if it be according to the fundamental laws of

England that any Englishmen should be fined or amerced but by the judgment of his peers or jury, since it expressly contradicts the Fourteenth and Twenty-ninth Chapters of the Great Charter of England, which say no freeman ought to be amerced but by the oath of good and lawful men of the vicinage?

RECORDER: Take him away, take him away, take him out of the Court.

PENN: I can never urge the fundamental laws of England but you cry, take him away, take him away. But 'tis no wonder, since the Spanish Inquisition hath so great a place in the Recorder's heart. God Almighty, who is just, will judge you all for these things.

(*They haled the prisoners into the bail-dock and from thence sent them to Newgate for non-payment of their fines, and so were their jury.*)

"Mary Dyer Did Hang as a Flag"

[FROM *Mary Dyer of Rhode Island*]

HORATIO ROGERS

[*The only Quakers ever to receive outright sentences of death (though prison sentences in England sometimes amounted to the same thing) were sentenced in America, and by those erstwhile lovers of religious liberty, the Puritans.*

Once again, as was William Penn, Mary Dyer (?–1660) was fighting—and gave up her life—for more than the right to be a Quaker. That right she had—outside of Massachusetts. She was fighting for and did finally die for religious freedom in Massachusetts.

Brooks Adams, in his The Emancipation of Massachusetts, *says of the Quakers, "We owe to their heroic devotion the most priceless of our treasures, our perfect liberty of thought and speech." Whether or not that liberty is "perfect" is debatable. That Mary Dyer did what she could to make it perfect cannot be debated.*]

———

Mary Dyer of Rhode Island, in the words of George Bishop, the old Quaker chronicler, written after her death, was "a Comely Grave Woman, and of a goodly Personage, and one of a good Report, having a Husband of an Estate, fearing the Lord, and a Mother of Children." Governor Winthrop of Massachusetts, a less friendly writer, refers to her, in 1638, as "the wife of one William Dyer, a milliner in the New Exchange, a very proper and fair woman, and both of them notoriously infected with Mrs. Hutchinson's errors, and very censorious and troublesome (she being of a very proud spirit, and much addicted to revelations)." Gerard Croese, a Dutch writer, states that she was reputed as a "person of no mean extract and parentage, of an estate pretty plentiful, of a comely stature and countenance, of a piercing knowledge in many things, of a wonderful sweet and pleasant discourse, so fit for great affairs, that she wanted nothing that was manly, except only the name and the sex." . . .

In 1652 William Dyer accompanied Roger Williams and John Clarke, who were sent from Rhode Island to England to obtain a revocation of the extraordinary powers granted to William Coddington; and Mrs. Dyer accompanied her husband. Though William Dyer returned home early in 1653, his wife remained abroad several years longer, becoming a convert to Quaker doctrines and a minister in that society. In 1657 she landed in Boston *en route* for her home in Rhode Island. The years before her coming, the arrival of the earliest Quakers in Boston had so wrought up the ministers and authorities of Massachusetts Bay that various repressive measures had been adopted, and hence when Mary Dyer, and a widow named Ann Burden who came to settle up her deceased husband's estate, set foot in Boston, they were arrested and cast into prison; for although Mary Dyer's sole business was to pass that way to Rhode Island, she was kept a close prisoner so that none might have communication with her, until her husband, hearing that she had arrived and was in prison, went after her. Then she was not released and suffered to depart until he had bound himself in a great penalty not to lodge her in any town of Massachusetts Bay, nor to permit any to have speech with her on her journey. . . .

In June, 1659, William Robinson, a merchant of London, and Marmaduke Stephenson, a countryman of the east part of Yorkshire, "were moved by the Lord," in Quaker phrase, to go from Rhode Island to Massachusetts to bear witness against the persecuting spirit existing there; and with them went Nicholas Davis of Plymouth Colony, and Patience Scott of Providence, Rhode Island, a girl of about eleven years of age. . . . During their incarceration Mary Dyer was moved of the Lord to go from Rhode Island to visit the prisoners, and she too was arrested and imprisoned. On September 12, 1659, the Court banished the four adults from Massachusetts upon pain of death, if after the 14th of September they should be found within the jurisdiction, but Patience Scott was discharged, as, in the words of the chronicler, "the child, it seems, was not of years, as to law, to deal with her by banishment."

Nicholas Davis and Mary Dyer departed to their homes without the jurisdiction of Massachusetts. . . . On October 8, within thirty days of her banishment, Mary Dyer with other Rhode Island Quakers went to Boston, . . . where she was again arrested and held for the action of the authorities. Five days later William Robinson and Marmaduke Stephenson, who had been travelling about spreading their doctrines through Massachusetts and Rhode Island since their release from prison, also went to Boston to look the bloody laws in the face, in the words of the Quaker chronicler; and they too were arrested and cast into prison [and subsequently sentenced to death]. . . .

Then Mary Dyer was brought to the bar of the Court, and the Governor pronounced sentence upon her as follows: "Mary Dyer, you shall go from hence to the place from whence you came, and from thence to the place of execution, and there be hanged till you be dead." To which she said, "The will of the Lord be done." — "Take her away, Marshal," quoth the Governor. She replied, "Yea, and joyfully I go." And on her way to prison she used similar words, with praises to the Lord. To the marshal who had her in custody, she said, "Let me alone, for I should go to prison without you." — "I believe you, Mrs. Dyer," he rejoined, "but I must do what I am commanded."

Great influence was brought to bear to prevent the execution of the sentences. Governor Winthrop of Connecticut appeared before the Massachusetts authorities, urging that the condemned be not put to death. He said that he would beg it of them on his bare knees that they would not do it. . . .

The 27th of October, 1659, was fixed for the triple execution, and elaborate preparations, for those days, were made for it. Popular excitement ran high, and the people resorted to the prison windows to hold communication with the condemned, so the male prisoners were put in irons, and a force was detailed, in the words of the order, "to watch with great care the towne, especially the prison." . . .

The eventful day having arrived, Captain Oliver and his military guard attended to receive the prisoners. The marshal and the jailer brought them forth, the men from the jail, and Mary Dyer from the House of Correction. They parted from their friends at the prison full of joy, thanking the Lord that he accounted them worthy to suffer for his name and had kept them faithful to the end. The condemned came forth hand in hand, Mary Dyer between the other two, and when the marshal asked her, "Whether she was not ashamed to walk hand in hand between two young men," for her companions were much younger than she, she replied, "It is an hour of the greatest joy I can enjoy in this world. No eye can see, no ear can hear, no tongue can speak, no heart can understand, the sweet incomes and refreshings of the spirit of the Lord which now I enjoy." The concourse of people was immense, the guard was strong and strict, and when the prisoners sought to speak the drums were caused to be beaten.

The method of execution was extremely simple in those days. A great elm upon Boston Common constituted the gallows. The halter having been adjusted round the prisoner's neck, he was forced to ascend a ladder affording an approach to the limb to be used for the fatal purpose, to which limb the other end of the halter was attached. Then the ladder was pulled away, and the execution, though rude, was complete. . . .

The prisoners took a tender leave of one another, and William Robinson, who was the first to suffer, said, as he was about to be turned off by the executioner, "I suffer for Christ, in whom I lived, and for whom I will die." Marmaduke Stephenson came next, and, being on the ladder, he said to the people, "Be it known unto all this day, that we suffer not as evil-doers, but for conscience sake." Next came Mary Dyer's turn. Expecting immediate death, she had been forced to wait at the foot of the fatal tree, with a rope about her neck, and witness the violent taking off of her friends. With their lifeless bodies hanging before her, she was made ready to be suspended beside them. Her arms and legs were bound, and her skirts secured about her feet; her face was covered with a handkerchief which the Rev. Mr. Wilson, who had been her pastor when she lived in Boston, had loaned the hangman. And there, made ready for death, with the halter round her neck, she stood upon the fatal ladder in calm serenity, expecting to die. . . .

Just then an order for a reprieve, upon the petition of her son all unknown to her, arrives. The halter is loosed from her neck and she is unbound and told to come down the ladder. She neither answered nor moved. In the words of the Quaker chronicler, "she was waiting on the Lord to know his pleasure in so sudden a change, having given herself up to dye." The people cried, "Pull her down." So earnest were they that she tried to prevail upon them to wait a little whilst she might consider and know of the Lord what to do. The people were pulling her and the ladder down together, when they were stopped, and the marshal took her down in his arms, and she was carried back to prison. . . .

It was a mere prearranged scheme, for before she set forth from the prison it had been determined that she was not to be executed, as shown by the reprieve itself, which reads as follows: "Whereas Mary Dyer is condemned by the Generall Court to be executed for hir offences, on the petition of William Dier, hir sonne, it is ordered that the sajd Mary Dyer shall have liberty for forty-eight howers after this day to depart out of this jurisdiction, after which tjme, being found therein, she is forthwith to be executed, and in the meane time that she be kept a close prisoner till hir sonne or some other be ready to carry hir away within the aforesajd tyme; and it is further ordered, that she shall be carrjed to the place of execution, and there to stand upon the gallowes, with a rope about her necke, till the rest be executed, and then to returne to the prison and remajne as aforesajd." . . .

When she returned to prison and understood the ground of the reprieve, she refused it, and the next morning she wrote to the General Court, again refusing to accept her life from her persecutors. She said: "My life is not accepted, neither availeth me, in comparison with the lives and liberty of the Truth and Servants of the living God, for which in the Bowels of Love and Meekness I sought you; yet nevertheless with wicked Hands have you put two of them to Death, which makes me to feel that the Mercies of the Wicked is cruelty: I rather chuse to Dye than to live, as from you, as Guilty of their Innocent Blood."

Such constancy and courage as the prisoners had displayed greatly excited the populace against the authorities, . . . so the day after the execution some officials came and took her in their arms and set her on horseback and conveyed her fifteen miles towards Rhode Island and left her with a horse and man to be conveyed further. Popular indignation was both loud and deep. . . .

Mary Dyer went to Rhode Island, where she did not tarry long, as she spent most of the winter on Long Island. Terribly in earnest was she; and her sufferings in no wise abated her purpose to combat, even unto death, the wicked persecution taking place in Massachusetts. . . . She therefore determined to go again to Boston, and again defy the authorities, forcing them either to practically annul their unjust laws, if they did not proceed against her, or else by her death to awaken popular indignation that would compel the repeal of them. She arrived in Boston May 21, 1660, and ten days later she was brought before the magistrates. "Are you the same Mary Dyer," inquired

Governor Endicott, "that was here before?"—"I am the same
Mary Dyer that was here the last General Court," she
undauntedly replied. "You will own yourself a Quaker," the
Governor inquired, "will you not?"—"I own myself to be
reproachfully so called," responded Mary Dyer.

Then the Governor said, "Sentence was passed upon you
the last General Court; and now likewise—you must return to
the prison, and there remain till tomorrow at nine o'clock;
then thence you must go to the gallows, and there be hanged
till you are dead." Mary Dyer replied, "This is no more than
what thou saidst before."—"But now," said the Governor, "it is
to be executed. Therefore prepare yourself tomorrow at nine
o'clock." Then she spoke thus: "I came in obedience to the will
of God the last General Court, desiring you to repeal your
unrighteous laws of banishment on pain of death; and that same
is my work now, and earnest request, although I told you that if
you refused to repeal them, the Lord would send others of his
servants to witness against them." Whereupon the Governor
sneeringly inquired if she was a prophetess? To which she
replied, she spoke the words the Lord spoke in her; and now the
thing was come to pass. She then proceeded to speak of her call,
when the Governor cried, "Away with her! away with her!" And
she was taken back to jail. Her husband, who was not a Quaker,
and did not share her views, wrote a letter of earnest intercession
for his wife's life to Governor Endicott, but in vain.

On June 1, 1660, at nine o'clock, Mary Dyer again set out
from the jail for the gallows on Boston Common, surrounded by
a strong military guard. As she stood upon the fatal ladder, she
was told if she would return home, she might come down and
save her life. "Nay," she replied, "I cannot; for in obedience to
the will of the Lord God I came, and in his will I abide faithful
to the death." Captain John Webb, the commander of the
military, said to her that she had been there before, and had the
sentence of banishment on pain of death, and had broken the
law in coming again now, as well as formerly, and therefore she
was guilty of her own blood. "Nay," she replied, "I came to
keep blood-guiltiness from you, desiring you to repeal the
unrighteous and unjust law of banishment upon pain of death,

made against the innocent servants of the Lord, therefore my blood will be required at your hands who wilfully do it; but for those that do it in the simplicity of their hearts, I do desire the Lord to forgive them. I came to do the will of my Father, and in obedience to his will I stand even to the death." Then her old Puritan pastor, the Rev. Mr. Wilson, bade her repent, and be not so deluded and carried away by the deceit of the devil. To which she replied, "Nay, man, I am not now to repent." ... And more she spake of the eternal happiness into which she was about to enter; and then, without tremor or trepidation, she was swung off, and the crown of martyrdom descended upon her head. Thus died brave Mary Dyer. ...

Roger Williams, the great apostle of Soul-Liberty, was thrust out of Massachusetts for conscience sake, but Mary Dyer ... persisted in remaining and watering it with her blood, and God gave the increase; so that nowhere on the face of the earth today is liberty of conscience more free or more highly revered than on the very spot where, in the words of General Atherton, one of her persecutors, "Mary Dyer did hang as a flag for others to take example by."

"I Ventured My Throat for My Religion"

[FROM *Some Memoirs of the Life of John Roberts*]

DANIEL ROBERTS

[*Oliver Wendell Holmes, who himself merits rediscovery, discovered Daniel Roberts' memoir of his father, John Roberts (?–1683), with delight. "It is so comforting," Holmes wrote, "to meet, even in a book, a man who is perfectly simple-hearted, clear-headed, and brave in all conditions. The story is admirably told, dramatically, vividly—one lives the whole scene over and knows the persons, who appear on it as if they had been his townsmen. . . ."*

Holmes puts his finger on this book's two great merits: the hero's character and the narrator's skill. But "brave, simplehearted, clear-headed" Quakers are easier to find in early Quaker history than writers able to tell a story "dramatically and vividly." Son Daniel practiced Boswell's art of letting a man reveal himself through his conversation, a hundred years before Boswell. And while Boswell, who observed that "many a man was a Quaker without knowing it," might have enjoyed his fellow biographer's acquaintance, Daniel Roberts would almost certainly have found Boswell, except when he was working on Johnson's biography, a dismaying companion.

Johnson and the older Roberts, however, have many characteristics in common. Roberts' clear-headedness would surely have pleased Johnson, who hated cant. And Roberts, who would not back down before church or king, would certainly have stood his ground with the great Cham. Johnson said that, though he did not care for the Quaker sect, he liked individual Quakers. Among these would surely have been (unless his verbal pride had been too badly wounded by the intrepid old charger) John Roberts.]

I have had it on my mind, for some years past, to commit to writing some memorable passages, the chief of which were transacted in my time; together with some short account of our family. . . .

In the year 1665, it pleased the Lord to send two women Friends out of the north to Cirencester; who, inquiring after such as feared God, were directed to my father, as the likeliest person to entertain them. They came to his house, and desired a meeting. He granted it, and invited several of his acquaintance to sit with them. After some time of silence, the Friends spake a few words, which had a good effect. After the meeting, my father endeavored to engage them in discourse; but they said little, only recommended him to Richard Farnsworth, then prisoner for the testimony of truth in Banbury jail, to whom they were going. Upon the recommendation my father went shortly after to the prison, in order to converse with Richard, where he met with the two women who had been at his house. The turnkey was denying them entrance, and telling them, "He had an order not to let any of those giddy-headed people in; and therefore, if they did go in, he would keep them there." But at my father's desire they were admitted in along with him, and conducted through several rooms, to a dungeon, where Richard Farnsworth was preaching through a grate to the people in the street. But soon after they came in, he desisted; and, after a little time of silence, turning to them, he spoke to this purpose: "That Zaccheus being a man of low stature, and having a mind to see Christ, ran before, and climbed up into a sycamore-tree: and our Saviour knowing his good desires, called to him, 'Zaccheus, come down! this day is salvation come to thy house.' Thus Zaccheus was like some in our day, who are climbing up into the tree of *Knowledge*, thinking to find Christ there. But the word is now, 'Zaccheus, come down! come down! for that which is to be known of God is manifested *within*.'" This, with more to the same purpose, was spoken in such authority, that, when my father came home, he told my mother, "He had seen Richard Farnsworth, who had spoke to his condition as if he had known him from his youth." And after this time he patiently bore the cross. . . .

He was afterwards cast into prison at Cirencester, by George Bull, vicar of Upper Siddington, for tithes; where was confined at the same time, upon the same account, Elizabeth Hewlings, a widow of Amney, near Cirencester. She was a good Christian, and so good a midwife, that her confinement was a loss to that side of the country; insomuch that Lady Dunch of Down-Amney, thought it would be an act of charity to the neighborhood to purchase her liberty, by paying the priest's demand; which she did. She likewise came to Cirencester in a coach, and sent her footman, Alexander Cornwall, to the prison, to bring Elizabeth to her. And while Elizabeth was making ready to go with the man, my father and he fell into a little discourse. He asked my father his name, and where his home was. . . . When he returned to his lady, he told her he had met with such a man in the prison, as he believed she would not suffer to lie in prison for conscience-sake; informing her withal who it was. She immediately bid him go back and fetch him to her. Accordingly he came to the jail, and told my father his lady wanted to speak with him. My father answered, "If any body would speak with me, they must come where I am; for I am a prisoner." "Oh," said Cornwall, "I'll get leave of the jailer for you to go." Which he did. And when they came before the lady, she put on a majestic air, to see how the *Quaker* would greet her. He went up towards her, and bluntly said, "Woman, wouldst thou speak with me?"

LADY: What's your name?

JOHN ROBERTS: My name is John Roberts; but I am commonly known by the name of John Hayward in the place where I live.

LADY: Where do you live?

J.R.: At a village called Siddington, about a mile distant from this town.

LADY: Are you the man that keeps conventicles at your house?

J.R.: The church of Christ do often meet at my house. I presume I am the man thou meanest.

LADY: What do you lie in prison for?

J.R.: Because, for conscience-sake, I can't pay a hireling priest what he demands of me; therefore he, like the false prophets of old prepares war against me, because I cannot put into his mouth.

LADY: By what I have heard of you, I took you to be a wise man; and if you could not pay him yourself, you might let somebody else pay him for you.

J.R.: That would be underhand dealings; and I had rather pay him myself than be such a hypocrite.

LADY: Then suppose some neighbor or friend should pay him for you, unknown to you, would you choose to lie in prison when you might have your liberty?

J.R.: I am very well content where I am, till it shall please God to make way for my freedom.

LADY: I have a mind to set you at liberty, that I may have some of your company, which I cannot well have while you are in prison.

Then speaking to her man, she bid him go to the priest's attorney, and tell him she would satisfy him; and then pay the jailer his fees, and get a horse for my father to go to Down-Amney with her.

J.R: If thou art a charitable woman, as I take thee to be, there are abroad in the world many real objects of charity, on whom to bestow thy bounty: but to feed such devourers as these, I don't think to be charity. They are like Pharaoh's lean kine; they eat up the fat and the goodly, and look not a whit the better.

LADY: Well, I would have you get ready to go with us.

J.R.: I don't know as thou art like to have me when thou hast bought and paid for me; for if I may have my liberty, I shall think it my place to be at home with my wife and family. But, if thou desirest it, I intend to come and see thee at Down-Amney some other time.

LADY: That will suit me better. But set your time, and I'll lay aside all other business to have your company.

J.R.: If it please God to give me life, health, and liberty, I intend to come on seventh day next, the day thou callest Saturday.

LADY: Is that as far as you used to promise?

J.R.: Yes.

According to his appointment, my father went; and found her very inquisitive about the things of God, and very attentive to the truths he delivered. She engaged him likewise a second time, and treated him with abundance of regard. A third time she bid her man Cornwall to go to him, and desire him to appoint a day when he would pay her another visit: And then ordered him to go to Priest Careless, of Cirencester, and desire him to come and take a dinner with her at the same time; and not let either of them know the other was to be there. On the day appointed, my father went; and when he had got within sight of her house, he heard a horse behind him, and looking back, he saw the priest following him; which made him conclude the lady had projected to bring them together. When the priest came up to him, "Well overtaken, John," said he; "how far are you going this way?" My father answered, "I believe we are both going to the same place." "What," said Careless, "are you going to the great house?" "Yes," said my father. "Come on then, John," said he. So then they went in together. And the lady being ill in bed, a servant went up and informed her they were come. "What," said she, "did they come together?" "Yes," answered the servant. "I admire that," said she. "But do you beckon John out, and bring him to me first up the back stairs." When my father came up, she told him she had been very ill in a fit of the stone; and said, "I have heard you done good in many distempers."

J.R.: I confess I have; but to this of the stone I am a stranger. Indeed I once knew a man, who lived at ease, and fared delicately, as thou mayst do, and whilst he continued in that practice he was much afflicted with that distemper. But it pleased the Lord to visit him with a knowledge of his blessed truth, which brought him to a more regular and temperate life, and this preserved him more free from it.

LADY: Oh! I know what you aim at. You want to have me a Quaker. And I confess if I could be such a one as you are, I would be a Quaker tomorrow. But I understand Mr. Careless is below; and though you are men of different persuasions, I account you both wise and godly men; and some moderate discourse of the things of God between you, I believe would do me good.

J.R.: If he ask me any questions, as the Lord shall enable me, I shall endeavour to give him an answer.

She then had the parson up; and after a compliment or two, said, "I made bold to send for you, to take an ordinary dinner with me, though I am disappointed of your company by my illness. But John Hayward and you, being persons of different persuasions (though I believe both good Christians), if you would soberly ask and answer each other a few questions, it would divert me, so that I should be less sensible of the pains I lie under."

PRIEST: An't please your ladyship, I see nothing in that.

LADY: Pray, Mr. Careless, ask John some questions.

PRIEST: It will not edify your ladyship; for I have discoursed John, and several others of his persuasion, divers times, and I have read their books, and all to no purpose; for they sprung from the Papists, and hold the same doctrine the Papists do. Let John deny it if he can.

J.R.: I find thou art setting us out in very black characters with design to affright me; but therein thou wilt be mistaken. I advise thee to say no worse of us than thou canst make out, and then make us as black as thou canst. And if thou canst prove me a

Papist in one thing, with the help of God I'll prove thee like them in ten. And this woman, who lies here in bed, shall be judge.

PRIEST: The Quakers hold that damnable doctrine, and dangerous tenet, of perfection in this life; and so do the Papists. If you go about to deny it, John, I can prove you hold it.

J.R.: I doubt now thou art going about to belie the Papists behind their backs, as thou hast heretofore done by us. For by what I have learnt of their principles, they do not believe a state of freedom from sin, and acceptance with God, possible on this side of the grave; and therefore they have imagined to themselves a place of purgation after death. But whether they believe such a state attainable or no, I do.

PRIEST: An't please your ladyship, John has confessed enough out of his own mouth; for that is a damnable doctrine, and dangerous tenet.

J.R.: I would ask thee one question: Dost thou own a purgatory?

PRIEST: No.

J.R. Then the Papists, in this case, are wiser than thou. They own the saying of Christ, who told the unbelieving Jews, if they died in their sins, whither he went they could not come. But, by thy discourse, thou, and thy followers, must needs go headlong to destruction; since thou neither ownest a place of purgation after death, nor such a preparation for heaven to be possible in this life, as is absolutely necessary, The scripture thou knowest tells us, "where death leaves us judgment will find us. If a tree falls towards the north or the south, there it must lie." And since "no unclean thing can enter the kingdom of heaven," pray tell this poor woman, whom thou hast been preaching to for thy belly, whether ever, or never, she must expect to be freed of her sins, and made fit for the kingdom of heaven; or whether the blind must lead the blind till both fall into the ditch.

PRIEST: No, John, you mistake me: I believe that God Almighty is able of his great mercy to forgive persons their sins, and fit them for heaven, a little before they depart of this life.

J.R.: I believe the same. But, if thou wilt limit the Holy One of Israel, how long wilt thou give the lord to fit a person for his glorious kingdom?

PRIEST: It may be an hour or two.

J.R.: My faith is a day or two, as well as an hour or two.

PRIEST: I believe so, too.

J.R.: Or a week or two.

And my father carried it to a month or two; and so gradually till he brought it to seven years, the priest confessing he believed the same. On which my father thus proceeded: how couldst thou accuse me of Popery, in holding this doctrine, which thou thyself hast confessed? If I am like a Papist, thou art, by thy own confession, as much a Papist as I am. And if it be a damnable doctrine and dangerous tenet in the Quakers, is it not the same in thyself? Thou told me I mistook thee: but hast not thou mistaken thyself, in condemning thy own acknowledged opinion when uttered by me? But notwithstanding thou hast failed in making me out to be a Papist in this particular, canst thou do it in anything else? Upon this the priest being mute, my father thus proceeded: Well, though thou hast failed in proving me like them, it need not hinder me from showing thee to be so in many things. For instance, you build houses and consecrate them, calling them churches; as do the Papists. You hang bells in them and consecrate them, calling them by the name of saints; so do they. The pope and the priests of the Romish church wear surplices, gowns, cassocks, &c., calling them their ornaments; here thou hast the like: And dost not thou style them thy ornaments? You consecrate the ground where you inter your dead, calling it holy ground; so do they. In short, thou art like a Papist in so many things, he had need be a wise man to distinguish betwixt them and thee.

At this the priest appeared uneasy, and said to the lady, "Madam, I must beg your excuse; for there's to be a lecture this afternoon, and I must be there." She pressed him to stay to dinner; but he earnestly desired to be excused. So a slice or two being cut off the spit, he ate, and took his leave. . . .

Some time after, my father had three conferences with ———— Nicholson, bishop of Gloucester, introduced in the following manner: An apparitor came to cite my father to appear at the bishop's court: but he told my father he could not encourage him to come, lest they should ensnare him and send him to prison. At the same time he cited a servant of my father's, named John Overall. My father went at the time appointed, without his servant; and when his name was called over, he answered to it. The discourse that occurred was in substance as follows:

BISHOP: What's your name?

J. ROBERTS: I have been called by my name, and answered to it.

BISHOP: I desire to hear it again.

J.R.: My name is John Roberts.

BISHOP: Well, you were born Roberts, but you were not born John. Pray who gave you that name?

J.R.: Thou hast asked me a very hard question, my name being given me before I was capable of remembering who gave it to me. But I believe it was my parents, they being the only persons who had a right to give me my name. That name they always called me by, and to that name I always answered; and I believe none need call it in question now.

BISHOP: No, no; but how many children have you?

J.R.: It hath pleased God to give me six children; three of whom he was pleased to take from me; the other three are still living.

BISHOP: And how many of them have been bishoped?

J.R.: None that I know of.

BISHOP: What reason can you give for that?

J.R.: A very good one, I think: most of my children were born in Oliver's days, when bishops were out of fashion. (*At this the court fell to laughing.*)

BISHOP: How many of them have been baptized?

J.R.: What dost thou mean by that?

BISHOP: What! don't you own baptism?

J.R.: Yes; but perhaps we may differ in that point.

BISHOP: What baptism do you own? That of the Spirit, I suppose.

J.R.: Yes. What other baptism should I own?

BISHOP: Do you own but one baptism?

J.R.: If one be enough, what needs any more? The apostle said, One Lord, one faith, one baptism. . . .

BISHOP: That is not our present business. You are here returned for not coming to church. What say you to that?

J.R.: I desire to see my accusers.

BISHOP: It is the minister and the churchwardens. Do you deny it?

J.R.: Yes, I do; for it was always my principle and practice to go to church.

BISHOP: And do you go to church?

J.R.: Yes; and sometimes the church comes to me.

BISHOP: The church comes to you? I don't understand you, friend.

J.R.: It may be so; 'tis often for want of a good understanding that the innocent are made to suffer.

APPARITOR: My lord, he keeps meetings at his house, and he calls that a church.

J.R.: No; I no more believe my house to be a church, than I believe what you call so to be one. I call the people of God the church of God, wheresoever they are met to worship him in spirit and in truth. . . .

BISHOP: We call it a church figuratively, meaning the place where the church meets.

J.R.: I fear you call it a church hypocritically and deceitfully, with design to awe the people into a veneration for the place, which is not due to it, as though your consecrations had made that house holier than others.

BISHOP: What do you call that which we call a church?

J.R.: It may properly enough be called a mass-house, it being formerly built for that purpose.

APPA.: Mr. Hayward, it is expected you should show more respect than you do in this place, in keeping on your hat.

J.R.: Who expects it?

APPA.: My Lord Bishop.

J.R.: I expect better things from him.

BISHOP: No, no, keep on your hat; I don't expect it from you.

A little after, the bishop said, "Well, friend, this is not a convenient time for you and me to dispute; but I may take you to my chamber, and convince you of your errors."

J.R.: I shall take it kindly of thee, or any man else to convince me of my errors that I hold, and would hold them no longer.

BISHOP: Call some others.

Then my father's man was called; who not appearing, the apparitor said, "Mr. Hayward, is John Overall here?"

J.R.: I believe not.

BISHOP: What is the reason he is not here?

J.R.: I think there are very good reasons for absence.

BISHOP: What are they? Mayn't I know?

J.R.: In the first place, he is an old man, and not of ability to undertake such a journey, except it was upon a very good account. In the second place, he is my servant; and I can't spare him out of my business in my absence.

BISHOP: Why does he not go to church then?

J.R.: He does go to church with me. (*At this the court fell a-laughing.*)

BISHOP: Call somebody else.

Then a Baptist preacher was called; who seeing the bishop's civility to my father, in suffering him to keep on his hat, thought to take the same liberty. At whom the bishop put on a stern countenance, and said, "Don't you know this is the king's court, and that I sit here to represent his majesty's person? and do you come here in an uncivil and irreverent manner, in contempt of his majesty and this court, with your hat on? I confess there are some men in this world who make a conscience of putting off their hats, to whom we ought to have some regard. But for you, who can put it off to every mechanic you meet, to come here, in contempt of authority, with it on, I'll assure you, friend, you shall speed never the better for it." I heard my father say, "These words came so honestly from the Bishop, that it did him good to hear him." . . .

Some time after the Bishop sent his bailiff to take my father; but he was then gone to Bristol with George Fox. . . . My father returning homewards, through Tedbury, was there informed that the bailiffs had been about his house almost ever since he went from home. He therefore contrived to come home after daylight. When he came into his own grounds, the moon shining bright, he spied the shadow of a man, and asked, "Who's there?" "It's I," said the man.

J. ROBERTS: Who? Sam. Stubbs?

SAM STUBBS: Yes, master.

J. ROBERTS: Hast thou anything against me? (*He was a bailiff.*)

S. STUBBS: No, master. I might; but I would not meddle. I have wronged you enough already, God forgive me. But those who now lie in wait for you are the Paytons, my lord bishop's bailiffs.

I would not have you fall into their hands, for they are merciless rogues. I would have you, master, take my counsel: "Ever while you live please a knave; for an honest man won't hurt you."

My father came home, and desired us not to let the bailiffs in upon him that night, that he might have an opportunity of taking counsel on his pillow. In the morning he told my mother what he had seen that night in a vision. "I thought," said he, "that I was walking in a fine, pleasant, green way; but it was narrow, and had a wall on each side of it. In my way lay something like a bear, but more dreadful. The sight of it put me to a stand. A man, seeing me surprised, came to me with a smiling countenance, and said, 'Why art afraid, friend? It is chained, and can't hurt thee.' I thought I made answer, 'The way is so narrow, I can't pass by but it may reach me.' 'Don't be afraid,' said the man, 'it can't hurt thee.' I saw he spake in great goodwill, and thought his face shone like the face of an angel. Upon which I took courage, and stepping forward, laid my hand upon his head." The construction he made of this to my mother was: "Truth is a narrow way; and this bishop lies in my way: I must go to him, whatever I suffer." So he arose, set forward, and called upon Amariah Drewett, a Friend of Cirencester, to accompany him. When they came to the bishop's house (at Cleave, near Gloucester), they found a butcher's wife of Cirencester, who was come to intercede for her husband, who was put into the bishop's court for killing meat on First Days. Two young sparks of the bishop's attendance were asking her if she knew John Hayward. She answered, "Yes, very well." "What is he for a man?" said they. "A very good man," said she, "setting aside his religion: but I have nothing to say to that." One of them said he would give five shillings to see him; the other offered eight. Upon which my father stepp'd up to them; but they said not one word to him. One of them presently informed the bishop he was come. Whereupon the bishop dismissed his company, and had him up stairs. My father found him seated in his chair, with his hat under his arm, assuming a majestic air. My father stood silent awhile; and seeing the bishop did not begin with him, he approached nearer, and thus accosted him: "Old man, my business is with thee."

BISHOP: What is your business with me?

J. ROBERTS: I have heard that thou hast sent out thy bailiffs to take me: but I rather chose to come myself, to know what wrong I have done thee. If it appear I have done thee any, I am ready to make thee satisfaction; but if, upon inquiry, I appear to be innocent, I desire thee for thy own soul's sake not to injure me.

BISHOP: You are misinformed, friend; I am not your adversary.

J.R.: Then I desire thee to tell me who is my adversary, that I may go and agree with him while I am in the way.

BISHOP: The king is your adversary. The king's laws you have broken; and to the king you shall answer.

J.R.: Our subjection to the laws is either active or passive. So that if a man can't for conscience-sake, *do* the thing the law requires, but passively *suffers* what the law inflicts, the law, I conceive, is as fully answered as if he had actually obeyed.

BISHOP: You are wrong in that too; for suppose a man steal an ox, and he be taken and hanged for the fact, what restitution is that to the owner?

J.R.: None at all. But though it is no restitution to the owner, yet the *law* is fully satisfied. Though the owner be a loser, the criminal has suffered the punishment the *law* inflicts, as an equivalent for the crime committed. But thou mayst see the corruptness of such laws, which put the life of a man upon a level with the life of a beast.

BISHOP: What! do such men as you find fault with the laws?

J.R.: Yes: and I'll tell thee plainly, 'tis high time wiser men were chosen, to make better laws. For if this thief was taken and sold for a proper term, according to the law of Moses, and the owner had four oxen for his ox, and four sheep for his sheep, he would be well satisfied, and the man's life preserved, that he might repent, and amend his ways. But I hope thou dost not accuse me of having stolen any man's ox or ass!

BISHOP: No, no; God forbid!

J.R.: Then, if thou pleasest to give me leave, I'll state a case more parallel to the matter in hand.

BISHOP: You may.

J.R.: There lived in the days past Nebuchadnezzar, king of Babylon, who set up an image, and made a decree, that all who would not bow down to it, should be cast the same hour into a burning fiery furnace. There were then three young men, who served the same God that I do now, and these durst not bow down to it; but passively submitted their bodies to the flames. Was that not a sufficient satisfaction to the unjust decree of the king?

BISHOP: Yes; God forbid else! For that was to worship the workmanship of men's hands; which is idolatry.

J.R.: Is that thy judgment, that to worship the workmanship of men's hands is idolatry?

BISHOP: Yes, certainly.

J.R.: Then give me leave to ask thee, by whose hands the Common Prayer-Book was made. I am sure it was made by somebody's hands, for it could not make itself.

BISHOP: Do you compare our Common Prayer-Book to Nebuchadnezzar's *image?*

J.R.: Yes, I do: that was his image, and this is thine. And be it known unto thee, I speak it in the dread of the God of heaven, I no more dare bow to thy Common Prayer-Book than the three children to Nebuchadnezzar's image.

BISHOP: Yours is a strange upstart religion of a very few years' standing; and you are grown so confident in it, that there is no beating you out of it.

J.R.: Out of my religion! God forbid! I was a long time seeking acquaintance with the living God amongst the dead forms of worship, and inquiring after the right way and worship of God, before I could find it; and now, I hope, neither thou nor any man living shall be able to persuade me out of it. But thou art very ignorant of the rise and antiquity of our religion.

BISHOP (*smiling*): Do you Quakers pretend antiquity for your religion?

J.R.: Yes; and I don't question but, with the help of God, I can make it appear, that our religion was many hundred years before thine was thought of.

BISHOP: You see I have given you liberty of discourse, and have not sought to ensnare you in your words; but if you can make the Quakers' religion appear to be many hundred years older than mine, you'll speed the better.

J.R.: If I do not, I seek no favour at thy hands; and in order to do it, I hope thou wilt give me liberty to ask a few sober questions.

BISHOP: You may.

J.R.: Then first I would ask thee, Where was thy religion in Oliver's days? The Common Prayer-Book was then become (even among the clergy) like an old almanac, very few regarding it in our country. There were two or three priests indeed who stood honestly to their principle, and suffered pretty much; but the far greater number turned with the tide, and we have reason to believe, that if Oliver would have put mass into their mouths, they would have conformed even to that for their bellies.

BISHOP: What would you have us do? Would you have had Oliver cut our throats?

J.R.: No, by no means. But what religion was that you were afraid to venture your throats for? Be it known to thee, I ventured my throat for my religion in Oliver's days, as I do now.

BISHOP: And I must tell you, though in Oliver's days I did not dare own it as I now do, yet I never owned any other religion.

J.R.: Then I suppose thou mad'st a conscience of it; and I should abundantly rather choose to fall in such a man's hands, than into the hands of one who makes no conscience towards God, but will conform to any thing for his belly. But if thou didst not think thy religion worth venturing thy throat for in Oliver's days, I desire thee to consider it, it is not worth cutting other men's throats now for not conforming to it.

BISHOP: You say right: I hope we shall have a care how we cut men's throats. (*Several others were now come into the room.*) But you know the Common Prayer-Book was before Oliver's days.

J.R.: Yes: I have a great deal of reason to know that; for I was bred up under a common prayer priest, and a poor drunken old man he was. Sometimes he was so drunk he could not say his prayers, and at best he could but say them; though I think he was by far a better man than he that is priest there now.

BISHOP: Who is your minister now?

J.R.: My minister is Christ Jesus, the minister of the everlasting covenant; but the present priest of the parish is George Bull. . . .

BISHOP: But I remember you said you would make it appear, that your religion was long before mine, and that is what I want to hear you make out.

J.R.: Our religion, as thou mayst read in the scripture (John iv) was set up by Christ himself, between sixteen and seventeen hundred years ago; and he had full power to establish the true religion in his church, when he told the woman of Samaria, that neither at that mountain, nor yet at Jerusalem, was the place of true worship; they worshipped they knew not what. For, said he, *God* is a *Spirit*, and they that worship him, must worship him in *spirit* and in *truth*. This is our religion, and hath ever been the religion of all those who have worshipped God acceptably through the several ages since, down to this time; and will be the religion of the true spiritual worshippers of God to the world's end; a religion performed by the assistance of the Spirit of God, because God is a Spirit; a religion established by Christ himself, before the mass-book, service-book, or directory, or any of those inventions or traditions of men, which, in the night of apostasy, were set up.

BISHOP: Are all the Quakers of the same opinion?

J.R.: Yes, they are. If any hold doctrines contrary to that taught by our Saviour to the woman of Samaria, they are not of us.

BISHOP: Do you own the Trinity?

J.R.: I don't remember such a word in the holy scriptures.

BISHOP: Do you own three persons?

J.R.: I believe, according to the scripture, that there are three that bear record in heaven, and that these three are one; thou mayst make as many persons of them as thou canst. But I would soberly ask thee, since the scriptures say, the heavens cannot contain him; and that he is incomprehensible, by what person or likeness canst thou comprehend the Almighty?

BISHOP: Yours is the strangest of all persuasions; for though there are many sects (*which he named*), and though they and we differ in some circumstances, yet in fundamentals we agree as one. But I observe you, of all others, strike at the very root and basis of our religion.

J.R.: Art thou sensible of that?

BISHOP: Yes, I am.

J.R.: I am glad of that; for the root is rottenness, and the truth strikes at the very foundation thereof. That little stone which Daniel saw cut out of the mountain without hands, will overturn all in God's due time, when you have done all you can to support it. But as to those others thou mentionest, there is so little difference between you, that wise men wonder why you differ at all; only we read, "The beast had many heads, and many horns, which push against each other." And yet I am fully persuaded there are in this day many true spiritual worshippers in all persuasions.

BISHOP: But you will not give us the same liberty you give a common mechanic, to call our tools by the same names.

J.R. I desire thee to explain thyself.

BISHOP: Why, you will give a carpenter leave to call his gimlet a gimlet and his gouge a gouge; but you call our church a mass-house.

J.R.: I wish you were half so honest men as carpenters.

BISHOP: Why do you upbraid us?

J.R.: I would not upbraid you; but I'll endeavor to show you wherein you fall short of carpenters. Suppose I have a son intended to learn the trade of carpenter; I indent with an honest man of that calling, in consideration of so much money, to teach my son his trade in such a term of years; at the end of which term my son may be as good, or perhaps a better workman than his master, and he shall be at liberty from him to follow the business for himself. Now will you be so honest as this carpenter? You are men who pretend to know more of light, life, and salvation, and things pertaining to the kingdom of heaven, than we do. I would ask in how long a time you would undertake to teach us as much as you know; and what shall we give you, that we may be once free from our masters? But here you keep us always learning, that we may be always paying you. Plainly, 'tis a very cheat. What! always learning, and never able to come to the knowledge of God! Miserable sinners you found us, and miserable sinners you leave us!

BISHOP: Are you against confession?

J.R.: No: for I believe those who confess and forsake their sins, shall find mercy at the hand of God; but those who persist in them shall be punished. But if ever you intend to be better, you must throw away your old book, and get a new one, or turn over a new leaf; for if you keep on in your old lesson, you must be always doing what you ought not, and leaving undone what you ought to do, and you can never do worse. I believe in my heart you mock God.

BISHOP: How dare you say so?

J.R.: I'll state the case, and thou shalt judge. Suppose thou hadst a son, and thou shouldst daily let him know what thou wouldst have him do, and he should, day by day, week by week, and year after year, provoke thee to thy face, and say, father, I have not done what thou commandest me to do; but have done quite the contrary; and continue to provoke thee to thy face in this manner once or oftener every week; wouldst thou not think him a rebellious child, and that his application to thee was mere mockery, and would it not occasion thee to disinherit him?

After some more discourse, my father told him, time was far spent; and, said he, if nothing will serve thee but my body in a prison, here it is in thy power; and if thou commandest me to deliver myself up, either to the sheriff, or to the jailer of Gloucester castle, as thy prisoner, I will go, and seek no other judge, advocate, or attorney to plead my cause, but the great Judge of heaven and earth, who knows I have nothing but love and goodwill in my heart to thee and all mankind.

BISHOP: No; you shall go home about your business. . . .

And the bishop being called out of the room, one Cuthbert, who took offence at my father's freedom with the bishop, said, "Hayward, you're afraid of nothing; I never met with such a man in my life. I'm afraid of my life, lest such fanatics as you should cut my throat as I sleep."

J.R.: I don't wonder that thou art afraid.

CUTHBERT: Why should I be afraid any more than you?

J.R.: Because I am under the protection of him who numbereth the very hairs of my head, and without whose providence a sparrow shall not fall to the ground; but thou hast Cain's mark of envy on thy forehead, and, like him, art afraid that whoever meets thee should kill thee.

CUTHBERT (*in a great rage*): If all the Quakers in England are not hanged in a month's time, I'll be hanged for them.

J.R. (*smiling*): Prithee, friend, remember, and be as good as thy word.

My father and his friend Amariah Drewett then took their leave, and returned home with the answer of peace in their bosoms.

Some time after this, the bishop and the chancellor, in their coaches, accompanied with Thomas Masters, Esq., in his coach, and about twenty clergymen on horseback, made my father's house in their way to the visitation, which was to be at Tedbury the next day. They stopp'd at the gate, and George Evans, the bishop's kinsman, rode into the yard to call my father; who coming to the bishop's coach-side, he put out his hand, (which my father respectfully took), saying, "I could not well go out of the county without seeing you." That's very kind, said my father; wilt thou please to alight and come in, with those who are along with thee?

BISHOP: I thank you, John; we are going to Tedbury, and time will not admit of it now; but I will drink with you if you please.

My father went in, and ordered some drink to be brought, and then returned to the coach-side.

GEO. EVANS: John, is your house free to entertain such men as we are?

J.R.: Yes, George; I entertain honest men, and sometimes others.

G. EVANS (*to the bishop*): My lord, John's friends are the honest men, and we are the others. . . .

At this the bishop smiled, and said, "John, I think your beer is long a coming."

J.R.: I suppose my wife is willing thou shouldst have the best, and therefore stays to broach a fresh vessel.

BISHOP: Nay, if it be for the best, we'll stay.

Presently my mother brought the drink; and when the bishop had drank, he said, "*I commend you*, John; you keep a cup of good beer in your house. I have not drank any that has pleased me better since I came from home." The chancellor drank next and the cup coming round again to my father's hand, 'Squire Masters said to him, "Now, old school-fellow, I hope you'll drink to me."

J.R.: Thou knowest it is not my practice to drink to any man; if it was, I would as soon drink to thee as another, being my old acquaintance and school-fellow; but if thou art pleased to drink, thou art very welcome.

The 'Squire, then taking his cup into his hand, said, "Now, John, before my lord and all those gentlemen, tell me what ceremony or compliment do you Quakers use when you drink to one another?"

J.R.: None at all. For me to drink to another and drink the liquor, is at best but a compliment and that borders much on a lie.

'SQUIRE MASTERS: What do you do then?

J.R.: Why if I have a mind to drink, I take the cup and drink; and if my friend pleases, he does the same; if not he may let it alone.

'SQUIRE MASTERS: Honest John, give me thy hand, here's to thee with all my heart; and, according to thy own compliment, if thou wilt drink, thou mayst, if not, thou mayst let it alone.

My father then offering the cup to Priest Bull, he refused it, saying, "It is full of hops and heresy." To which my father replied, "As for hops I cannot say much, not being at the brewing of it; but as for heresy, I do assure thee, neighbor Bull, there is none in my beer; and if thou art pleased to drink, thou art welcome; but if not, I desire thee to take notice, as good as thou will, and those who are as well able to judge of heresy. Here thy lord bishop hath drank of it, and commends it; he finds no heresy in the cup."

BISHOP (*leaning over the coach-door, and whispering to my father said*): John, I advise you to take care you don't offend against the higher powers. I have heard great complaints against you, that you are the ringleader of the Quakers in this country; and that if you are not suppressed, all will signify nothing. Therefore, pray, John, take care for the future, you don't offend any more.

J.R.: I like thy counsel very well, and intend to take it. But thou knowest God is the higher power; and you mortal men, however advanced in this world, are but the lower power; and it is only because I endeavour to be obedient to the will of the higher powers, that the lower powers are angry with me. But I hope, with the assistance of God, to take thy counsel, and be subject to the higher powers, let the lower powers do with me as it may please God to suffer them.

". . . Like Slobbering Beasts and Swine"

[FROM *Sufferings of the Quakers*]

JOSEPH   BESSE

[*The desire of the young to preserve, apart from any merit involved, the status quo, is always disconcerting. There is something vastly more unseemly in the sight of youth prematurely anticipating old age, than in old age aping, in a second childhood, youth.*

William Braithwaite, who believed that in 1658 the Oxford students were, by their barbarities, attempting to protect their "craft," quotes Hudibras *against them: they attempted to*

> *Prove their doctrine orthodox*
> *By apostolic blows and knocks.*

What is most appalling in the actions of the students is the illustration they give of the power of a difference in ideologies to blind one group of human beings to the humanity of another group, and of the fact that, when so blinded, people feel themselves exempted from every law of decency, to say nothing of every plea "to love one another."

A later student, the medieval historian G. G. Coulton, writes in his glorious autobiography, Fourscore: *"Again and again: Religion is experience! It is for each man the sum total of that man's truth seeking . . . nonetheless genuine for being individual."*

The seventeenth century saw the birth of individualism. But the university, by its nature a repository (if not a tomb) for the old, as much as it is a cradle for the new, was not ready in the seventeenth century to put anything as queer as a Quaker in its cradle.]

———

From the Narrative of the Cruelty of the Oxford Students:—
And the Scholars have come into the Meetings among the People of God and call'd for Wenches or Harlots, like Fellows that haunt Bawdy-houses.—And have brought Strong-Beer into

the Meetings, and drank to Friends, and because they have refused to drink, have thrown it on their Necks, and Clothes, and Bands.—And sung Bawdy-Songs, and curs'd and swore.—And several Times came into the Meetings, blowing and puffing with tobacco-Pipes in their Mouths, cursing, swearing, and stamping, making the House shake again.—And proffer'd to put their Hands under Woman's Aprons, and ask'd, If the Spirit were not there?—And the Scholars have come into the Meeting to act Tobit and his Dog, and one of them divided his filthy Stuff into Uses and Points, after the Manner of the Priests, and another rais'd Doctrines of a Tinker and a Cobler, and many more wicked Actions by Mockings, and Scoffings, and filthy Language.—And these Scholars have been so shameless, that after Meeting they have pressed in by Violence, and took Meat off from the Table, came into the House of the Friend where the Meeting was, and took the Bread, and the Pottage out of the Pot, like greedy Dogs, lapping them up, and have stolen and taken away the Books out of the House, and carried them away.—One of the Servants of the Lord going from a Meeting to his own Dwelling, and going by John's College, a great Company of Scholars drew him into the College, forc'd him up into their Hall, and by main Strength, and much Violence, thrust him into a Chair, and then used abominable and wicked Words, to have drawn the Friend's Mind out of the Fear of the Lord; but when they could not prevail, they brought Beer, and like slobbering Beasts and Swine, proffered to pour it down his Neck, and struck and beat him with many grievous Blows, and pinch'd him, insomuch as he was amazed, and his natural Sense taken away for a Time with their Cruelty; and this Man, about that Time, had not eaten a Bit of Bread in ten Days Time, being very weak; and they thrust Pins into his Flesh, and pinched him, and kept him in there with many wicked Scoffs, asking him, Whether the Spirit did not move him now.

"*. . . An Offer of Their Own Bodies*"

[FROM *Sufferings of the Quakers*]

J O S E P H   B E S S E

[*"Quakerism," writes John Morley in his life of Oliver Cromwell, "has undergone many developments but in all of them has been the most devout of all endeavours to turn Christianity into the religion of Christ."*

This offer by Quakers of a body for a body was an attempt (unsuccessful) by them to practice the religion of Christ. It would also have been a sound method, by substituting strong bodies for weak ones, of preserving Quakers. This, no doubt, occurred to the authorities, who refused the offer.]

────────

There was a printed Paper presented to the Parliament in 1659, *and subscribed by one Hundred and Sixty four of this People* [Quakers], *wherein they make an Offer of their own Bodies, Person for Person, to lie in Prison instead of such of their Brethren as were then under Confinement, and might be in Danger of their Lives through extreme Durance, which Paper was as follows,* viz.

Friends,

Who are called a Parliament of these Nations: We in Love to our Brethren that lie in Prisons, and Houses of Correction, and Dungeons, and many in Fetters and Irons, and have been cruelly beat by the cruel Gaolers, and many have been persecuted to Death, and have died in Prison, and many lie sick and weak in Prison, and on Straw. So we in Love to our Brethren do offer up our Bodies and Selves to you, for to put us as Lamps into the same Dungeons and Houses of Correction, and their Straw and nasty Holes and Prisons, and do stand ready a Sacrifice for to go into their Places in Love to our Brethren, that they may go forth, and that they may not die in Prison, as many of the Brethren are dead already: For we are willing to lay down our Lives for our Brethren, and to take their Sufferings upon us that you would inflict upon them: And if our Brethren suffer, we cannot but feel it: And Christ saith, It is he that suffereth and was not visited. This is our love towards God and Christ, and our Brethren, that we owe to them and our Enemies, who are Lovers of all your Souls and your eternal Good. . . .

THE CONVICTIONS (1)

. . . the bubbling of the everlasting springs.
—ISAAC PENINGTON

"The Utterance of Persons Who Were Plain . . ."

[FROM *Selections from the Children of Light*]

RUFUS M. JONES

[In what follows, Rufus Jones is speaking as the editor of an anthology of inspirational passages taken from the writings of Quakers. The present Reader, *to this point, has had to do with what Jones says, and truly, is scarce; that is, Quaker writing with "autobiographical touches." Though seventeenth-century Quakers produced many memoirs, journals, and diaries, these writings concerned themselves with what most interested the seventeenth-century Quaker: that is, the state of his or her soul. It is a rare journal or memoir which has in it as much an account of "the outward" as John Roberts' or Mary Penington's.*

The section which follows is made up of the kind of writing which is much less rare among early Quakers, and is also, alas, frequently much less interesting. However, the Quakers were not theologians; when they wrote of a religious experience they were not speaking of "intellectual adherence to propositional beliefs"; when they knew Christ, they knew Him "experimentally," so that there is more of the water of life and less of the dust of history in their reports than there is in most religious writing.

Also, by good chance, the work of Penn, Penington, and Barclay, three of the most gifted Quaker writers, is to be found in this section.]

———

I have already referred to a point of importance which needs emphasis, viz., that we have here the utterance of persons who were plain, simple, unsophisticated laymen. We must not expect to find here the bottomless profundity which we feel in Saint Augustine, in Meister Eckhart, or even in our English Walter Hilton. We are permitted here to get glimpses into the inner life of the average, everyday, common man—the labourer whose hands are more used to the plow than the pen. None of these books smell of the study and their margins are not crowded with references to the mystics of an earlier time. They "speak right on," in plain, blunt fashion and tell us in yeoman language of the inward battles which they have fought. We may prefer the more skillful pen, but it is worth while pausing a moment in reverence to hear what the common man has to say of the life of God in his soul, and to see how it makes him superior to the stress and strain of the world and triumphant over dungeons and death!

The "sacred words" of all these writers are "Light" and "Seed." This is their way of saying that there is something divine in the soul of man. They are not much skilled in metaphysics, and we should not go to them for sound theories of psychology. They did not critically analyze their experience and they do not tell us about it in the exact speech of the laboratory. They simply announced that they had discovered a Principle of new Life and new Light which they could not trace to any human origin, and which they could not account for on any natural basis. They hit upon two words which the New Testament gave them, and they made them voice the great idea which was supreme in their thought, viz., that something divine was working in them. Illumination had come and Life had come to them. It was as though the axis of their inner world had swung out of shadow into a blaze of sunlight. It was as though a germinating seed had lifted apart the hard clods of their heart, and the pushing tendrils had ramified all the recesses of their being: "We are born of the Eternal Seed," they tell us; "we have had a Birth of God within us," they repeat again and again.

They use all the Divine names indiscriminately, but always to tell the same fact, that God is within them and is an Immanuel. This Light, this Seed, is Christ, is the Holy Spirit, is the Everlasting Father. The Old and the New Testaments are ransacked for words to name this day-star experience, but through all the parable and symbolism there runs the one meaning, "God has come to my heart!"

The real test of the value of their experience must be sought, as always, not by measuring it with the foot rule of Church creeds, but in the practical fruits of life. It is a matter of little concern to us now what these men thought about the articles of faith over which their generation was so busy. We want to know whether this Light of God in their souls made them tender and loving and sympathetic, pushed them into contact with struggling humanity, gave them patience with their fellows, and faith in the onward march of the race; whether it put moral power into their strokes, enabled them to overcome the world and to live above circumstances and happenings.

On this test they ring very true. They were not always broad enough to see the element of truth in the position of their opponents and they sometimes jar us with their controversial jargon. We wish they had not asked us to look through such heaps of millet seed to find their occasional pearl, but we feel a kind of awe as we watch them suffer and endure for their precious truth, and we recognize in them a Higher Wisdom than that of the world, a Wisdom that carries them with the humble accuracy of instinct straight to the very heart of a moral issue. I verily believe they were "Children of the Light."

One of the most impressive characteristics of this mass of literature which they flung upon the world is its revelation of the *group-spirit* which pervaded and unified the movement. The individual appears to be quite swallowed up in the social group

and seems, in a unique degree, to be an organic member of a
larger whole which utters itself through each one. There are
almost no personal marks which differentiate one treatise from
another. Autobiographical touches are strikingly absent, and
the style is so similar that one scribe might conceivably have
produced almost the whole mass of writings.

Alexander Parker, writing to Margaret Fell, says: "Our life
is one, our food and raiment one—eating of one bread and
drinking of one cup in the Father's house." This "oneness" of
life runs through everything, and appears in every tract. They
have a common stock of ideas, a group-vocabulary, and their
views are as much *one* as their "raiment." It is what happens in
all pentecostal movements, where many are baptized into one
spirit and all are made to eat of one spiritual food and to drink of
one spiritual drink. They speak in a similar tongue, and have all
things in common. Religion in its intense form is always
contagious—it propagates itself almost or quite subconsciously—
it flows from life to life as if through subterranean springs. There
have been instances of isolated mystics, but they are always of
the intellectual or speculative type. The moment there appears
a person who is flooded with a joyous experience of God, the
flood overflows and waters and refreshes a "group." These
"Children of the Light" furnish a notable illustration of this fact.

All mystics insist on the use of particular methods for the
attainment of their desired goal—the experience of the Presence of God. These "Children of the Light" are no exception
to the rule. They all insist with much emphasis on the value of
silence. It is a method as old as the beginnings of inward religion.
There must be a hush from the din of the world's noises before
the soul can hear the inward Voice; there must be a closing of the
eyes to the glare and dazzle of the world's sights before the
inward eye can see that which is eternally Real and True. Isaac
Penington has beautifully expressed the idea in a letter to
Thomas Ellwood (both the writer of the letter and the receiver
of it being at the time in gaol):

"Oh that the eye and heart in thee which knoweth the value
of these things (Real Things) may be kept open, and that thou

mayest be kept close to the feelings of the life and that thou mayest be fresh in thy spirit in the midst of thy sufferings, and mayest reap the benefit of them; finding thereby that pared off which hindereth *the bubbling of the everlasting springs* and that which maketh unfit for the breaking forth and enjoyment of the Pure Power."

One sees at once that silence is no passive state, but that rather it is the highest activity of which the human spirit is capable, and the careful reader will note that these "Children of the Light" propose no easy way by which the soul is given a lazy holiday. All their words announce that silence is no mere absence of noise and talk, but the focusing of inner attention on the Will of God, the attuning of the human to the Divine. They are in full accord with the great saying of Meister Eckhart, the father of modern mysticism: "That a man should have a life of rest and peace in God is good; that he should have a painful life with patience is better; but that he should find his rest even in his painful life, that is best of all."

―――――――

". . . More Dispensations of Life and Mercy than One"

ISAAC PENINGTON

[Isaac Penington (1617–1679), the gifted son of a Lord Mayor of London, might have risen to a position of much prominence in the world. Instead, he married Mary Springett and with her made the hard, but for them inevitable, choice of Quakerism; as a result he spent fourteen years in various English jails, and wrote, finally, "The beginning of this

religion . . . is sweet, but the pure progress and going on of it much more pleasant." This in spite of the fact that "the pure progress and going on of it" had lost him his fortune, his freedom, and his health.

Isaac Penington might be called a "Quaker's Quaker," except that this has no meaning unless we understand what a Quaker is; and describing a Quaker is like describing a snowflake. Each Quaker, like each snowflake, has a unique, non-imitative form. They resemble one another, Quakers and snowflakes, only in their essence, not in their "outward." A scientist, faced with a mass of self-duplicating snowflakes, would know that he was in the presence of a synthetic product.

It is the same with Quakers. But the essence of Quakerism, in Fox's words, consists in the recognition of, and obedience to, "the spirit of God" in ourselves. And of this indwelling spirit of God, no other Quaker has written so limpidly as Isaac Penington; and at the same time none has obeyed it so implicitly.

Fox and Woolman lived as completely "in the pure progress and going on" of their religion as Penington, but they did not write so well— though it must be admitted that Penington never casts up sentences and phrases as pungent as some of Fox's. Nothing in Penington equals Fox's: "Stiff as a tree and pure as a bell. . . . I smiled in myself. . . . All creation gave another smell to me. . . . I am dead to it. . . . None of you be puddling in your own carnal knowledge. . . . So I left the North fresh and green under Christ their teacher. . . . When the priest had done his stuff . . . hot stuff . . . I could not pray in man's will. . . . Keep a-top that which will cumber the mind. . . . I told him I would not . . . put out his starlight if it were true light from the morning star."

Penn and Barclay write as well as Penington; but their subject matter is not consistently so near the heart of Quakerism as his, Penn being more worldly, Barclay more theological; and by chance their lives were also somewhat further removed from the "pure progress and going on of it." So of the five great Quaker writers, Fox, Penn, Penington, Barclay, and Woolman, I call Penington "the Quaker's Quaker."]

<hr>

What is the proper work of Man here in this world?

To fear God, and keep his commandments. This is all that God requires of him, and this is enough to make him happy.

What is God?

The fountain of beings and natures, the inward substance of all that appears; who createth, upholdeth, consumeth, and bringeth to nothing as he pleaseth.

How may I know that there is a God?

By sinking down into the principle of his own life, wherein he revealeth himself to the creature. There the soul receiveth such tastes and knowledge of him, as cannot be questioned by him that abideth there.

What is it to fear this God?

The spirit and soul of the creature standing in awe of his nature, and waiting to be kept in due subjection thereto, this is to fear him, and this is the proper means of preserving the spirit of the creature right in its motion towards him, attendance on him, and expectations from him.

What are his commandments?

They are such as are either general to all mankind, common to some sorts of men, or proper to particular persons.

What are those which are general to all mankind?

There are very many; but may all be referred to these two heads; to wit, to love God above all, and one's neighbor as one's self; even so in every respect doing to him, as one would be done by him in the like case.

How may man perform these?

Only by receiving a principle of life from God, and keeping close thereto.

How may a man come by a principle of Life from God?

God is near to every man with the breath of his life, breathing upon him at times according to his pleasure; which man's spirit opening unto, and drinking in, it becometh a seed or principle of life in him, overspreading and leavening him up to eternal life.

How may a man come to believe in this principle?

In feeling its nature, in waiting to feel somewhat begotten by it, in this its light springs, its life springs, its love springs, its hidden power appears, and its preserving wisdom and goodness is made manifest to the soul that clings to it in the living sense, which its presence and appearance begets in the soul.

How may a man come to obey this principle?

In the faith, in the eyeing of it, in the clinging to it, the strength issues from it into the creature, which maketh it able to perform all that it calleth for.

Are there other commands besides these, common to all men?

Yes; according to the dispensation of life and mercy unto which they are called, and into which they are admitted by the love and kindness of God, which overspreadeth all his works, and who forgetteth not his creatures in their estate of separation and alienation from him.

Are there then more dispensations of life and mercy than one?

Yes. For though the life and mercy in itself is but one; yet it hath several ways of seeking-out after, and gathering into itself, the lost sons of Adam.

But how may men know that these are true commands of the Lord and not imaginations or opinions of their own?

When the principle of life is known, and that which God hath begotten felt in the heart, the distinction between what God opens and requires there, and what springs up in man's wisdom, reason and imagination, is very manifest. . . .

". . . According as the Spirit Teaches"

ISAAC PENINGTON

The seed of God is the word of God; the seed of the kingdom is the word of the kingdom. It is a measure of the light and life, of the grace and truth, which is by Jesus Christ, whereof in his is the fulness. It is a heavenly talent, or manifestation of his spirit in the heart, which is given to man for him, in the virtue and strength of Christ, to improve for God. This which God hath placed in man, to witness for himself, and to guide man from evil unto good (in the pure breathing, quickenings, and shinings of it) this is the seed, which is freely bestowed on man, to spring up and remain in him, and to gather him out of himself into itself.

The pure, living, heavenly knowledge of the Father, and of his Son Christ Jesus, is wrapped up in this seed.

He that is united to the seed, to the measure of grace and truth from Christ . . . is united to God, and ingrafted into Christ; and as the seed is formed in him, Christ is formed in him; and as he is formed and new-created in the seed, he is the workmanship of God, formed and new-created in Christ.

What is the nature of the seed of God, or the seed of the kingdom?

It is of an immortal, incorruptible nature. . . .

It is of a gathering nature. . . .

It is of a purging, cleansing nature. . . .

It is of a seasoning, leavening, sanctifying nature. . . .

It is of an enriching nature. . . .

It is of an improving, growing nature, of a nature that will grow and be improved. . . .

Prayer is the breath of the living child to the Father of Life, in that spirit which quickened it, which giveth it the right sense of its wants, and suitable cries proportionate to its state, in the proper season thereof. . . . Prayer is wholly out of the will of the creature; wholly out of the time of the creature; wholly out of the power of the creature; in the spirit of the Father, who is the fountain of life, and giveth forth breathings of life to his child at his pleasure.

Lord, take care of all thy children. Oh thou tender Father, consider what they suffer for the testimony of thy truth and for thy name's thyself. Oh carry on thy glorious work which thy own mighty arm hath begun and cut it short in righteousness for thine Elect's sake, that it may be finished by thee, to thine own everlasting praise. . . .

Give over thine own willing, give over thine own running, give over thine own desiring to know or be anything, and sink down to the seed which God sows in thy heart and let that be in thee, and grow in thee, and breathe in thee, and act in thee, and thou shalt find by sweet experience that the Lord knows that and loves and owns that, and will lead it to the inheritance of life, which is his portion. . . .

And this is the manner of their worship. They are to wait upon the Lord, to meet in the silence of flesh, and to watch for the stirrings of his life, and the breaking forth of his power amongst them. And in the breakings forth of that power they may pray, speak, exhort, rebuke, sing or mourn, and so on, according as the spirit teaches, requires and gives utterance. But if the spirit do not require to speak, and give to utter, then everyone is to sit stiff in his place (in his heavenly place I mean) feeling his own measure, feeding thereupon, receiving therefrom (into his spirit) what the Lord giveth. Now in this is edifying, pure edifying, precious edifying; his soul who thus waits is hereby particularly edified by the spirit of the Lord at every meeting. And then also there is the life of the whole felt in every vessel that is turned to its measure; insomuch as the warmth of life in each vessel doth not only warm the particular, but they are like an heap of fresh and living coals, warming one another, insomuch as a great strength, freshness, and vigor of life flows into all. And if any be burdened, tempted, buffeted by Satan, bowed down, overborne, languishing, afflicted, distressed and so on, the estate of such is felt in spirit, and secret cries, or open (as the Lord pleaseth), ascend up to the Lord for them, and they many times find ease and relief, in a few words spoken, or without words, if it be the season of their help and relief with the Lord. . . . We wait on the Lord, either to feel him in words, or in silence of spirit without words, as he pleaseth. . .

"The Book of Cookery Has Outgrown the Bible"

[FROM *Fruits of an Active Life*]

WILLIAM PENN

As God's spirit is not tied to places, so all worship standing therein is truly catholic and public worship, in field or house, whether three or three thousand; convenient places being circumstantial, not essential, to God's worship. . . .

We say a measure of divine light is in every transgressor, even at the instant of his committing the vilest sin, yet it consents not to it, but stands a witness for the Lord God against the unrighteous soul. . . .

I would have every thing appear in its proper color: I love no apes in religion, and desire that foxes should appear in their own skins, and lambs in theirs. . . .

The scriptures we highly value. But we believe not the things we often quote thence to be true *only* because there, but for that we are witnesses of the same operation, and bring in our experimental testimonies to confirm the truth of theirs.

I know no religion that destroys courtesy, civility and kindness.

Death is a state without the living experimental knowledge of God and his work in the heart.

If you confine Christ's dwelling to a local heaven, you are ignorant of that which is the greatest joy that can be: Christ dwells in the heart.

O the rapes, fires, murders, and rivers of blood that lie at the doors of professed Christians! If this be godly, what's devilish? If this be christian, what's paganism? What's anti-christian, but to make God a party to their wickedness?

Time past is none of thine. 'Tis not what thou wast, but what thou art. God will be daily looked unto. Did'st thou eat yesterday? That feedeth thee not today.

One sigh, rightly begotten, outweigheth a whole volume of self-made prayers. For that which is born of flesh is flesh, and reacheth not to God's kingdom, he regardeth it not; and all that is not born of the spirit is flesh. But a sign or a groan arising from a living sense of God's work in the heart, it pierceth the clouds, it entereth the heavens; yea, the living God heareth it, his regard is to it, and his spirit helpeth the infirmity.

The book of cookery has outgrown the Bible, and I fear is read oftener; to be sure, it is more in use. . . .

The Church of England, Roman Catholics, Grecians, Lutherans, Presbyterians, Independents, Anabaptists, Quakers, Socinians: these I call so many orders of Christians, that unite in the text, and differ only in the comment; all owning the Deity, Savior and Judge, good works, rewards and punishments.

It shall be said at the last day "Not well professed, but well done, good and faithful servant, enter thou into the joy of thy Lord."

Nothing reaches the heart but what is from the heart, or pierces the conscience but what comes from a living conscience. . . .

They who are addicted to gaming are generally the most idle and useless people in any government. And give me leave to say that men are accountable to government for their time. There ought to be no idleness in the land.

I dare boldly affirm . . . there is not one instance to be found, where the hand of God was against a righteous nation, or where the hand of God was not against an unrighteous nation first or last.

For their learning be liberal; spare no cost, for by such parsimony all is lost that is saved; but let it be useful knowledge, such as is consistent with truth and godliness, not cherishing a vain conversation or idle mind, but ingenuity mixed with industry is good for the body and mind too. I recommend the useful parts of mathematics, as building houses or ships, measuring, surveying, dialling, navigation, etc.; but agriculture is especially in my eye; let my children be husbandmen and housewives; it is industrious, healthy, honest, and of good example.

If it be an evil to judge rashly or untruly of any single man, how much a greater sin it is to condemn a whole people.

There appears to me but three things upon which peace is broken, *viz.*, to keep, to recover, or to add. . . .

As you have intervals from your lawful occasions, delight to step home, within yourselves I mean, and commune with your own hearts, and be still. . . .

No man in England is born slave to another; neither hath one right to inherit the sweat of the other's brow, or reap the benefit of his labor, but by consent. Therefore, no man should be deprived of his property, unless he injure another man's, and then by legal judgment.

Liberty without obedience is confusion, and obedience without liberty is slavery.

Governments, as well as courts, change their fashions; the same clothes will not always serve. And politics made obsolete by new accidents are as unsafe to follow as antiquated clothes are ridiculous to wear.

That man cannot be said to have any religion, that takes it by another man's choice, not his own.

Force makes hypocrites, 'tis persuasion only that makes converts.

———————

"*I Am Your Loving Friend*"
[FROM *Fruits of an Active Life*]

WILLIAM PENN

LETTER TO THE INDIANS, DATED OCTOBER 18, 1681

My Friends,

There is one great God and power that hath made the world and all things therein, to whom you and I, and all people owe their being and well being, and to whom you and I must one day give an account, for all that we do in the world. This great God hath written his law in our hearts, by which we are taught and commanded to love, and help, and do good to one another and not do harm and mischief to one another.

Now this great God hath been pleased to make me concerned in your parts of the world, and the king of the country where I live, hath given unto me a great province; but I desire to enjoy it with your love and consent, that we may always live together as neighbours and friends, else what would the great God say to us, who hath made us not to devour and destroy one another but to live soberly and kindly together in the world? Now I would have you well observe, that I am very sensible of the unkindness and injustice that hath been too much exercised toward you by the people of these parts of the world, who sought themselves, and to make great advantages by you, rather than be examples of justice and goodness unto you, which I hear hath been matter of trouble to you, and caused great grudgings and animosities, sometimes to the shedding of blood, which hath made the great God angry. But I am not such a man, as is well known in my own country. I have great love and regard towards you, and I desire to win and gain your love and friendship, by a kind, just, and peaceable life; and the people I send are of the same mind, and shall in all things behave themselves accordingly; and if in any thing any shall offend you or your people, you shall have a full and speedy satisfaction for the same, by an equal number of just men on both sides that by no means you may have just occasion of being offended against them.

I shall shortly come to you myself. At which time we may more largely and freely confer and discourse of these matters. In the meantime, I have sent my commissioners to treat with you about land and a firm league of peace. Let me desire you to be kind to them and the people, and receive these presents and tokens which I have sent to you, as a testimony of my good will to you, and my resolution to live justly, peaceably, and friendly with you.

I am your loving friend,
WILLIAM PENN

"Love Is the Hardest Lesson in Christianity"

[FROM *Some Fruits of Solitude*]

WILLIAM PENN

[*Robert Louis Stevenson first discovered Penn's* Some Fruits of Solitude *in San Francisco in 1879. He describes himself at that time as a "mossy ruin." San Francisco's climate accounts for the moss; tuberculosis for the ruin.*

Two years later he gave the book to a friend, with these words: "If ever in all my human conduct I have done a better thing to any fellow creature than handing on to you this sweet, dignified and wholesome book, I know I shall hear of it on the last day."

Later he wrote the same friend that he had carried the book "in my pocket all about the San Francisco streets, read in street cars and ferryboats when I was sick unto death, and found it in all times and places a peaceful and sweet companion . . . for while just now we are so busy and intelligent, there is not the man living—no, nor recently dead—that could put, with so lovely a spirit, so much honest, kind wisdom into words."

Just now, as in Stevenson's day, "we are so busy and intelligent," and that busyness and intelligence may soon make "mossy ruins" of us all. Meanwhile, we might remember Penn's "To do evil, that good may come of it, is for Bunglers *in politicks, as well as morals."*

IGNORANCE

It is admirable to consider how many millions of people come into and go out of the world ignorant of themselves and of the world they have lived in.

If one went to see Windsor Castle or Hampton Court, it would be strange not to observe and remember the situation, the building, the gardens, fountains, etc, that make up the beauty and pleasure of such a seat; and yet few people know themselves—no, not their own bodies, the houses of their minds, the most curious structure of the world, a living, walking tabernacle; nor the world of which it was made and out of which it is fed, which would be so much to our benefit, as well as our pleasure, to know. We cannot doubt of this when we are told that the invisible things of God are brought to light by the things that are seen, and consequently we read our duty in them, as often as we look upon them, to Him that is the great and wise author of them, if we look as we should do.

The world is certainly a great and stately volume of natural things, and may be not improperly styled the hieroglyphics of a better. But alas, how very few leaves of it do we seriously turn over! This ought to be the subject of the education of our youth, who, at twenty, when they should be fit for business, know little or nothing of it.

EDUCATION

We are in pain to make them scholars but not men, to talk rather than to know, which is true canting.

The first thing obvious to children is what is sensible, and that we make no part of their rudiments.

We press their memory too soon, and puzzle, strain, and load them with words and rules, to know grammar and rhetoric and a strange tongue or two, that it is ten to one may never be useful to them, leaving their natural genius to mechanical and physical or natural knowledge uncultivated and neglected, which would be of exceeding use and pleasure to them through the whole course of their life.

To be sure, languages are not to be despised or neglected, but things are still to be preferred.

Children had rather be making of tools and instruments of play, shaping, drawing, framing, and building, etc., than getting some rules of propriety of speech by heart; and those also would follow with more judgment and less trouble and time.

It were happy if we studied nature more in natural things, and acted according to nature, whose rules are few, plain, and most reasonable.

Let us begin where she begins, go her pace, and close always where she ends, and we cannot miss of being good naturalists.

The creation would not be longer a riddle to us. The heavens, earth, and waters with their respective, various, and numerous inhabitants, their productions, natures, seasons, sympathies, and antipathies, their use, benefit, and pleasure, would be better understood by us; and an eternal wisdom, power, majesty, and goodness very conspicuous to us through those sensible and passing forms, the world wearing the mark of its Maker, Whose stamp is everywhere visible and the characters very legible to the children of wisdom.

And it would go a great way to caution and direct people in their use of the world that they were better studied and knowing in the creation of it.

For how could men find the confidence to abuse it while they should see the great Creator stare them in the face in all and every part thereof? . . .

DISCIPLINE

If thou wouldst be happy and easy in thy family, above all things observe discipline.

Everyone in it should know their duty, and there should be a time and place for everything; and whatever else is done or omitted, be sure to begin and end with God.

INDUSTRY

Love labor, for if thou dost not want it for food, thou mayest for physic. It is wholesome for thy body and good for thy mind. It prevents the fruits of idleness, which many times comes of nothing to do and leads too many to do what is worse than nothing.

A garden, a laboratory, a workhouse, improvements, and breeding are pleasant and profitable diversions to the idle and ingenious. For here they miss ill company and converse with nature and art, whose variety are equally grateful and instructing and preserve a good constitution of body and mind.

TEMPERANCE

To this a spare diet contributes much. Eat therefore to live and do not live to eat. That's like a man, but this below a beast.

Have wholesome but not costly food, and be rather cleanly than dainty in ordering it.

The recipes of cookery are swelled to a volume, but a good stomach excels them all, to which nothing contributes more than industry and temperance. . . .

If thou rise with an appetite, thou art sure never to sit down without one.

Rarely drink but when thou art dry; nor then, between meals, if it can be avoided. . . .

All excess is ill, but drunkenness is of the worst sort: it spoils health, dismounts the mind, and unmans men; it reveals secrets, is quarrelsome, lascivious, impudent, dangerous, and mad. In fine, he that is drunk is not a man, because he is so long void of reason, that distinguishes a man from a beast.

APPAREL

. . . It is said of the true church, "The King's daughter is all glorious within." Let our care therefore be of our minds more than of our bodies, if we would be of her communion.

We are told with truth that meekness and modesty are the rich and charming attire of the soul, and the plainer the dress, the more distinctly and with greater luster their beauty shines. . . .

RIGHT MARRIAGE

Never marry but for love, but see that thou lovest what is lovely. . . .

It is the difference betwixt lust and love that this is fixed, that volatile. Love grows, lust wastes by enjoyment; and the reason is that one springs from a union of souls, and the other from a union of sense. . . .

DEATH

I have often wondered at the unaccountableness of Man in this, among other things; that tho' he loves Changes so well, he should care so little to hear or think of his last, great, and best Change too, if he pleases.

Being, as to our Bodies, composed of changeable Elements, we with the World, are made up of, and subsist by Revolution: But our Souls being of another and nobler Nature, we should seek our Rest in a more induring Habitation.

The truest end of Life, is, to know the Life that never ends.

He that makes this his Care, will find it his Crown at last.

Life else, were a Misery rather than a Pleasure, a Judgment, not a Blessing.

For to Know, Regret and Resent; to Desire, Hope and Fear more than a Beast, and not live beyond him, is to make a Man less than a Beast.

And he that lives to live ever, never fears dying.

Nor can the Means be terrible to him that heartily believes the End.

For tho' Death be a Dark Passage, it leads to Immortality, and that's Recompence enough for Suffering of it.

And yet Faith Lights us, even through the Grave, being the Evidence of Things not seen.

And this is the Comfort of the Good, that the Grave cannot hold them, and that they live as soon as they die.

For Death is no more than a Turning of us over from Time to Eternity.

Death then, being the Way and Condition of Life, we cannot love to live, if we cannot bear to die. . . .

UNION OF FRIENDS

They that love beyond the World, cannot be separated by it.

Death cannot kill, what never dies.

Nor can Spirits ever be divided that love and live in the same Divine Principle; the Root and Record of their Friendship.

If Absence be not Death, neither is theirs. . . .

This is the Comfort of Friends, that though they may be said to Die, yet their Friendship and Society are, in the best Sense, ever present, because Immortal.

"... As If God Was an Old Man"

[FROM *No Cross, No Crown*]

WILLIAM PENN

That unlawful self in religion that ought to be mortified by the Cross of Christ is man's invention and performance of worship to God as divine which is not so either in its institution or performance. In this great error those people have the van of all that attribute to themselves the name of Christians that are most exterior, pompous, and superstitious in their worship; for they do not only miss exceedingly by a spiritual unpreparedness in the way of their performing worship to God Almighty, who is an eternal spirit, but the worship itself is composed of what is utterly inconsistent with the very form and practice of Christ's doctrine and the apostolical example. For whereas that was plain and spiritual, this is gaudy and worldly; Christ's most inward and mental, theirs most outward and corporal; that suited to the nature of God, who is a spirit, this accommodated to the most carnal part. So that instead of excluding flesh and blood, behold a worship calculated to gratify them, as if the business were not to present God with a worship to please him but to make one to please themselves, a worship dressed with such stately buildings and imagery, rich furnitures and garments, rare voices and musics, costly lamps, wax candles, and perfumes, and all acted with that most pleasing variety to the external senses that art can invent or cost procure, as if the world were to turn Jew or Egyptian again or that God was an old man indeed and Christ a little boy to be treated with a kind of religious masque, for so they picture them in their temples and too many in their minds. And the truth is [that] such a worship may very well suit such an idea of God; for when men can think him such a one as themselves, it is not to be wondered if they address to him and entertain him in a way that would be most pleasing from others to themselves. . . .

Nor is a recluse life (the boasted righteousness of some) much more commendable or one whit nearer to the nature of the true Cross; for if it be not lawful as other things are, 'tis unnatural, which true religion teaches not. The Christian convent and monastery are within, where the soul is encloistered from sin; and this religious house the true followers of Christ carry about with them, who exempt not themselves from the conversation of the world, though they keep themselves from the evil of the world in their conversation. This is a lazy, rusty, unprofitable self-denial, burdensome to others to feed their idleness, religious bedlams where people are kept up lest they should do mischief abroad: patience perforce, self-denial against their will, rather ignorant than virtuous, and out of the way of temptation than constant in it. No thanks if they commit not what they are not tempted to commit. What the eye views not the heart craves not, as well as rues not.

The Cross of Christ is of another nature: it truly overcomes the world and leads a life of purity in the face of its allurements. They that bear it are not thus chained up for fear they should bite nor locked up lest they should be stole away. No, they receive power from Christ, their captain, to resist the evil and do that which is good in the sight of God, to despise the world and love its reproach above its praise, and not only not to offend others but love those that offend them, though not for offending them. What a world we should have if everybody, for fear of transgressing, should mew himself up within four walls. No such matter; the perfection of Christian life extends to every honest labor or traffic used among men. . . .

"All in One Dress and One Colour . . ."

MARGARET FELL

[*Margaret Fell (1614–1702) has been called "the nursing mother" of Quakerism; and truly she gave the early Quakers sustenance, material, spiritual, and common-sensical.*

In 1652, when first she heard George Fox, Margaret Fell was thirty-eight, the wife of Judge Thomas Fell of Swarthmore Hall, and the mother of nine children. The first words Margaret Fell heard Fox say were: " 'He is not a Jew that is one outward . . . but he is a Jew that is one inward, and that is circumcision which is of the heart.' And so he went on," she writes, "and said, 'How that Christ was the Light of the world and lighteth every man that cometh into the world; and that by this Light they might be gathered to God, etc.' And I stood up in my pew and I wondered at his doctrine. . . . And then he went on, . . . 'The Scriptures were the prophets' words and Christ's . . . and what they spoke they enjoyed and possessed. . . . You will say, Christ saith this, and the apostles say this, but what canst thou say? Art thou a Child of Light and hast walked in the Light, and what thou speakest is it inwardly from God?' This opened me so that it cut me to the heart; and then I saw clearly we were all wrong. So I set me down in my pew again and cried bitterly. And I cried in my spirit to the Lord, 'We are all thieves, we are all thieves, we have taken the Scriptures in words and know nothing of them in ourselves.' "

Margaret Fell and eight of her nine children became Quakers. Judge Fell, though never himself convinced, permitted the use of Swarthmore Hall as a meeting place and refuge for Quakers. In 1669, eleven years after her husband's death, Margaret Fell married George Fox. They lived missionary lives, preaching and traveling, were more often separated than not, and were frequently, though never together, in prison. In one of his letters to his wife, George Fox mentions a length of scarlet cloth he is sending her.

Margaret Fox, who was ten years older than her husband, and who survived him for eleven years, lived to see a hardening of Quakerism into the formalism of rejecting all forms. Then perhaps she remembered, as well as the gift of scarlet cloth, her husband's first words, "the circumcision of the heart." He or she is not a Quaker who is one outward.

So she cried out against "these silly outside imaginary practices." But she died in 1702; and the eighteenth century, hearing no other voice with her authority speaking against these imaginings, practiced them as she had feared, "with great zeal."]

———

Friends, and Brethren, and Sisters,

We are the people of the living God, and God hath visited us and brought us out in an acceptable day of salvation, a Gospel day, in which the eternal God is gathering his elect from the four winds of heaven and from the four corners of the earth; and he hath shined from the throne of his glory in our hearts in his spiritual light, and given us the true knowledge of himself in the face and image of Jesus Christ. He hath made us partakers of his divine nature, and he hath given us his good and holy Spirit to lead us and to guide us into all truth in all things.

Now, dear Friends, brethren and sisters, let us all beware of limiting the Holy One of Israel, or tampering with anything contrary to this holy Spirit; for the grace of God is sufficient to teach us to deny all ungodliness and unrighteousness, and will teach us to live holily and righteously unto God and his truth in this present and evil world; and let us beware of meddling with the things of God, otherwise than his spirit leads and guides. Now there is a spirit got up amongst Friends in some places, that would make and model in their imaginations, in leading of Friends into things outwardly, which our Lord Jesus Christ never commanded. For he always testified against the Jews' manner of making and prescribing of things outwardly, for his testimony is in every heart to work inwardly, and make them the inside.

So let us beware of imitating and fashioning after the Jews' manner in outward things and ceremonies. For though it be said in Scripture that his people should dwell alone, that was in the time under the law, when he had chosen them out of all the families of the earth, yet he would punish them for their trangression.

But now our blessed Lord is come, and it's but a small thing for him to gather together the tribes of Israel and the dispersed of Judah. He is also given for a light to the Gentiles and to be for salvation to the ends of the earth: he would have all to be saved, and to come to the knowledge of his blessed truth: and he testified against the Pharisees, that said, I am more holy than thee. Let us beware of this, of separating or looking upon ourselves to be more holy than indeed and in truth we are. For what are we, but what we have received from God? And God is all-sufficient to bring in thousands into the same spirit and light, to lead and to guide them as he doth us. And let us frame and fashion ourselves unto the Apostle's doctrine and practice, who was in a glorious shining light (read I Corinthians, chapter 9, 19 ver., and so to the end).

Now see how contrary our practice is to the Apostle's, when we must not go to a burial of the people of the world, nor bid them to any of our burials, nor do that which is moderate and of a good report as to meat or drink, etc. Again, read I Corinthians, chapter 10, 27 ver.: "If any of them that believe not bid you to a feast, and ye be disposed to go; whatsoever is set before you, asking no question for conscience sake." This is more than a birth or burial, which is needful and necessary.

Away with these whimsical narrow imaginations, and let the Spirit of God which he hath given us lead us and guide us: and let us stand fast in that liberty wherewith Christ hath made us free, and not be entangled again into bondage in observing prescriptions, in outward things, which will not profit nor cleanse the inward man. It is the work of Christ Jesus in this his day, and by this let everyone do as they are persuaded in their own minds, for the Apostle saith he was not to rule over anyone's faith.

For it's now gone forty-seven years since we owned the truth, and all things has gone well and peaceably till now of late, that this narrowness and strictness is entering in, that many cannot tell what to do or not do.

Our monthly and quarterly meetings were set up for reproving and looking into superfluous or disorderly walking, and such to be admonished and instructed in the truth, and not private persons to take upon them to make orders, and say this must be done and the other must not be done: and can Friends think that those who are taught and guided of God can be subject and follow such low mean orders? So it's good for Friends of our country to leave these things to the Lord, who is become our leader, teacher and guider, and not to go abroad to spread them, for they will never do good, but has done hurt already: we are now coming into Jewism, into that which Christ cried woe against, minding altogether outward things, neglecting the inward work of almighty God in our hearts, if we can but frame according to outward prescriptions and orders, and deny eating and drinking with our neighbours, in so much that poor Friends is mangled in their minds, that they know not what to do. For one Friend says one way, and another another; but Christ Jesus saith that we must take no thought what we shall eat, or what we shall drink, or what we shall put on: but bids us consider the lilies, how they grow in more royalty than Solomon. But, contrary to this, we must look at no colours, nor make anything that is changeable colours as the hills are, nor sell them, nor wear them: but we must be all in one dress and one colour.

This is a silly poor gospel! It is more fit for us to be covered with God's eternal Spirit, and clothed with his eternal Light, which leads us and guides us into righteousness, and to live righteously and justly and holily in this present evil world. This is the clothing that God puts upon us, and likes, and will bless. This will make our light shine forth before men, that they may glorify our heavenly Father which is in Heaven, for we have God for our teacher, and we have his promises and doctrine, and we have the Apostles' practice in their day and generation: and we have God's holy Spirit, to lead us and guide us, and we have the blessed truth, that we are made partakers of, to be our practice. And why should we turn to men and woman teaching which is contrary to Christ Jesus' command, and the Apostles' practice? ... Friends, we have one God, and one mediator betwixt God and man, the man Christ Jesus; let us keep to him or we are undone.

This is not delightful to me that I have this occasion to write to you; for wherever I saw it appear I have stood against it several years; and now I dare neglect no longer. For I see that our blessed precious holy truth, that hath visited us from the beginning, is kept under, and these silly outside imaginary practices is coming up, and practised with great zeal, which hath often grieved my heart.

Now I have set before you life and death, and desire you to choose life, and God and his truth.

―――――――――

"Turn Thy Mind to the Light"

ROBERT BARCLAY

[*An Irish Quaker, it has been said, is a contradiction in terms. Yet statistically, in the seventeenth century, he was less so than a Scotch Quaker. Robert Barclay (1648–1690), a Scotch Quaker, came to the Society of Friends over the double hurdles of a Calvinistic inheritance and a Roman Catholic education. He was a student in Paris at the Scots' Theological College, whose purpose it was to prepare boys to return to their own countries as Roman Catholic missionaries. Barclay turned for a time toward Catholicism; but in both the Presbyterian and Catholic faiths he had, he says, "abundant occasions to receive impressions contrary to . . . the principle of Love." But, "When I came into the silent assemblies of God's people, I felt a secret power among them which touched my heart, and as I gave way unto it, I found the evil weakening in me and the good raised up. . . ."*

The convincement of Robert Barclay was a fortunate occurrence for the Quakers. He was well born and well educated, and few of their members had either his powers of logic or his gifts as a writer. "Fox," says Monsignor Knox, "did not theorize about the inner light; he walked in it." Barclay did both, and his theorizing in his An Apology for . . . the Principles and Doctrines of the People Called Quakers *remains the foremost theological expression of Quakerism.*

This book, written first in Latin, then translated into English by Barclay himself, is granted by Knox to be "courageously scholastic," though wrongheaded in asserting the "superiority of the inner light to tradition, scripture and reason itself."

Knox is right when he finds the immediate revelation of God's spirit to be the keystone of Robert Barclay's work. It must be, since, as Barclay's biographer, Christabel Cadbury, says, "it is the central point of the Quaker doctrine." "And it is also," says Barclay, "that which all professors of Christianity, of what-kind soever, are forced ultimately to recur to . . . the foundation of all Christian faith." Knox's quarrel with Barclay is only, then, one of time; are people today forbidden that "immediate revelation" which was permitted earlier people? Is "airy head-knowledge" to be preferred to "saving heart-knowledge"? Barclay thinks the two may go hand in hand, since "many things may further a work, which yet are not the main thing that makes the work go on."]

Seeing the height of all happiness is placed in the true knowledge of God (this is life eternal, to know thee the only true God, and Jesus Christ whom thou hast sent) the true and right understanding of this foundation and ground of knowledge is that which is most necessary to be known and believed in the first place.

IMMEDIATE REVELATION

We do distinguish betwixt the certain knowledge of God, and the uncertain; betwixt the spiritual knowledge, and the literal; the saving heart-knowledge, and the soaring, airy head-knowledge. The last, we confess, may be divers ways obtained; but the first, by no other way than the inward immediate manifestation and revelation of God's Spirit, shining in and upon the heart, enlightening and opening the understanding.

Knowledge then of Christ, which is not by the revelation of his own Spirit in the heart, is no more properly the knowledge of Christ, than the prattling of a parrot, which has been taught a few words, may be said to be the voice of a man; for as that, or some other bird, may be taught to sound or utter forth a rational sentence, as it hath learned it by the outward ear, and not from any living principle of reason actuating it; so just such is that knowledge of the things of God, which the natural and carnal man hath gathered from the words or writings of spiritual men.

But as the description of the light of the sun, or of curious colors to a blind man, who, though of the largest capacity, cannot so well understand it by the most acute and lively description, as a child can by seeing them; so neither can the natural man, of the largest capacity, by the best words, even scripture-words, so well understand the mysteries of God's kingdom, as the least and weakest child who tasteth them, by having them revealed inwardly and objectively by the Spirit.

What is proper in this place to be proved is, That Christians now are to be led inwardly and immediately by the Spirit of God, even in the same manner (though it befall not many to be led in the same measure) as the saints were of old.

I shall prove this first from the promise of Christ in these words, John xiv. 16, 17: "And I will pray the Father, and he will give you another Comforter, that he may abide with you forever. Even the Spirit of truth, whom the world cannot receive, because it seeth him not, neither knoweth him; but ye know him, for he dwelleth with you, and shall be in you."

That this Spirit is inward, in my opinion needs no interpretation or commentary. He dwelleth with you, and shall be in you. This indwelling of the Spirit in the saints, as it is a thing most needful to be known and believed, so is it as positively asserted in the scripture as anything else can be.

He then that acknowledges himself ignorant and a stranger to the inward in-being of the Spirit of Christ in his heart, doth thereby acknowledge himself to be yet in the carnal mind, which is enmity to God; and in short, whatever he may otherwise know or believe of Christ, or however much skilled or acquainted with the letter of the holy scripture, not yet to be, notwithstanding all that, attained to the least degree of a Christian; yea, not once to have embraced the Christian religion. For take but away the Spirit, and Christianity remains no more than the dead carcase of a man, when the soul and spirit is departed, remains a man; which the living can no more abide but do bury out of their sight, as a noisome and useless thing, however acceptable it hath been when actuated and moved by the soul. Lastly, whatsoever is excellent, whatsoever is noble, whatsoever is worthy, whatsoever is desirable in the Christian faith, is ascribed to this Spirit, without which it could no more subsist than the outward world without the sun. Hereunto have all true Christians, in all ages, attributed their strength and life.

And what shall I say more? For the time would fail me to tell of all those things which the holy men of old have declared, and the saints of this day do themselves enjoy, by the virtue and power of this Spirit dwelling in them. If therefore it be so, why should any be so foolish as to deny, or so unwise as not to seek after this Spirit, which Christ hath promised shall dwell in his children? They then that do suppose the indwelling and leading of his Spirit to be ceased, must also suppose Christianity to be ceased which cannot subsist without it.

Seeing then that Christ hath promised his Spirit to lead his children, and that every one of them both ought and may be led by it, if any depart from this certain guide in deeds, and yet in words pretend to be led by it, into things that are not good, it will not from thence follow, that the true guidance of the Spirit is uncertain, or ought not to be followed; no more than it will follow that the sun sheweth not light, because a blind man or one who wilfully shuts his eyes, falls into a ditch at noon-day for want of light; or that no words are spoken, because a deaf man hears them not; or that a garden full of fragrant flowers has no sweet smell, because he that has lost his smelling doth not smell it.

All these mistakes therefore are to be ascribed to the weakness or wickedness of men, and not to that Holy Spirit.

Moreover, these divine inward revelations, which we make absolutely necessary for the building up of true faith, neither do nor can ever contradict the outward testimony of the scriptures, or right and sound reason. Yet from hence it will not follow, that these divine revelations are to be subjected to the test, either of the outward testimony of the scriptures, or of the natural reason of man, as to a more noble or certain rule and touchstone; for this divine revelation, and inward illumination, is that which is evident and clear of itself, forcing, by its own evidence and clearness, the well-disposed understanding to assent.

THE SCRIPTURES

From these revelations of the Spirit of God to the saints have proceeded the Scriptures of Truth.

Because they are only a declaration of the fountain, and not the fountain itself, therefore they are not to be esteemed the principal ground of all truth, and knowledge, nor yet the adequate primary rule of faith and manners. Yet because they give a true and faithful testimony of the first foundation, they are and may be esteemed a secondary rule, subordinate to the Spirit, from which they have all their excellency and certainty; for as by the inward testimony of the Spirit we do alone truly know them, so they testify, that the Spirit is that Guide by which the saints are led into all Truth; therefore, according to the scriptures, the Spirit is the first and principal leader.

Through and by the clearness which that Spirit gives us it is that we are only best rid of those difficulties that occur to us concerning the scriptures. The real and undoubted experience whereof I myself have been a witness of, with great admiration of the love of God to his children in these latter days: for I have known some of my friends, who profess the same faith with me, faithful servants of the Most High God, and full of divine knowledge of his truth, as it was immediately and inwardly revealed to them, by the spirit, from a true and living experience, who not only were ignorant of the Greek and Hebrew, but even some of them could not read their own language, who being pressed by their adversaries with some citations out of the English translation, and finding them to disagree with the manifestation of truth in their own hearts, have boldly affirmed the Spirit of God never said so, and that it was certainly wrong; for they did not believe that any of the holy prophets or apostles had ever written so; which when I on this account seriously examined, I really found to be errors and corruptions of the translators; who (as in most translations) do not so much give us the genuine signification of the words, as strain them to express that which comes nearest to that opinion and notion they have of truth.

If it be then asked me, Whether I think hereby to render the scriptures altogether uncertain, or useless?

I answer: Not at all, provided that to the Spirit from which they came be but granted that place the scriptures themselves give it, I do freely concede to the scriptures the second place.

For tho' God doth principally and chiefly lead us by his Spirit, yet he sometimes conveys his comfort and consolation to us through his children, whom he raises up and inspires to speak or write a word in season, whereby the saints are made instruments in the hand of the Lord to strengthen and encourage one another, which doth also tend to perfect and make them wise unto salvation; and such as are led by the Spirit cannot neglect, but do naturally love, and are wonderfully cherished by, that which proceedeth from the same Spirit in another; because such mutual emanations of the heavenly life tend to quicken the mind, when at any time it is overtaken with heaviness.

Secondly, God hath seen meet that herein we should, as in a looking glass, see the conditions and experiences of the saints of old; that finding our experience answer to theirs, we might thereby be the more confirmed and comforted, and our hope of obtaining the same end strengthened; that observing the providences attending them, seeing the snares they were liable to, and beholding their deliverances, we may thereby be made wise unto salvation, and seasonably reproved and instructed in righteousness.

This is the great work of the scriptures, and their service to us, that we may witness them fulfilled in us, and so discern the stamp of God's spirit and ways upon them, by the inward acquaintance we have with the same Spirit and work in our hearts.

We have said how that a divine spiritual, and super-natural light is in all men; also how that, as it is received and closed within the heart, Christ comes to be formed and brought forth: but we are far from ever having said, that Christ is thus formed in all men, or in the wicked: for that is a great attainment, which the apostle travailed that it might be brought forth in the

Galatians. Neither is Christ in all men by way of union, or indeed, to speak strictly, by way of inhabitation; because this inhabitation, as it is generally taken, imports union, or the manner of Christ's being in the saints. But in regard Christ is in all men as in a seed, yea, and that he never is nor can be separate from that holy pure seed and light which is in all men; in this respect then, as he is in the seed which is in all men, we have said Christ is in all men, and have preached and directed all men to Christ in them, who lies crucified in them by their sins and iniquities, that they may look upon him whom they have pierced, and repent: whereby he that now lies as it were slain and buried in them, may come to be raised, and have dominion in their hearts, over all.

Though then this seed be small in its appearance, so that Christ compares it to a grain of mustard-seed, which is the least of all seeds, Matth. xiii. 31, 32 and that it be hid in the earthly part of man's heart; yet therein is life and salvation towards the sons of men wrapped up, which comes to be revealed as they give way to it. And this seed in the hearts of all men is the kingdom of God, as in capacity to be produced, or rather exhibited, according as it receives depth, is nourished, and not choaked. And as the whole body of a great tree is wrapped up potentially in the seed of the tree, and so is brought forth in due season, even so the kingdom of Jesus Christ, yea Jesus Christ himself, Christ within, who is the hope of glory, and becometh wisdom, righteousness, sanctification and redemption, is in every man's and woman's heart, in that little incorruptible seed, ready to be brought forth.

This leads me to speak concerning the manner of this seed or light's operation in the hearts of all men. To them then that ask us after this manner, If two men have equal sufficient light and grace, and the one be saved by it, the other not? is not then the will of man the cause of the one's salvation beyond the other?

I say, to such we thus answer: That as the grace and light in all is sufficient to save all, and of its own nature would save all; so it strives and wrestles with all in order to save them; he that resists its striving, is the cause of his own condemnation; he that resists it not, it becomes his salvation: for that in him that is saved, the working is of the grace, and not of the man; and it is a passiveness rather than an act; though afterwards, as man is wrought upon, there is a will raised in him, by which he comes to be a co-worker with the grace: for according to that of Augustine, He that made us without us, will not save us without us. So that the first step is not by man's working, but by his not contrary working. And we believe, that at these singular seasons of every man's visitation, as man is wholly unable of himself to work with the grace, neither can he move one step out of the natural condition, until the grace lay hold upon him; so it is possible for him to be passive, and not to resist it, as it is possible for him to resist it. So we say, the grace of God works in and upon man's nature; which, though of itself wholly corrupted and defiled, and prone to evil, yet is capable to be wrought upon by the grace of God; even as iron, though an hard and cold metal of itself, may be warmed and softened by the heat of the fire, and wax melted by the sun. And as iron or wax, when removed from the fire or sun, returneth to its former condition of coldness and hardness; so man's heart, as it resist or retires from the grace of God, returns to its former condition again.

REASON

It will manifestly appear by what is above said, that we understand not this divine principle to be any part of man's nature, nor yet to be any reliques of any good which Adam lost by his fall. For we certainly know that his light of which we speak is not only distinct but of a different nature from the soul of man, and its faculties. Indeed that man, as he is a rational creature, hath reason as a natural faculty of his soul, by which he can discern things that are rational, we deny not; for this is a property natural and essential to him, by which he can know and learn many arts and sciences, beyond what any other animal can do by the mere animal principle. Neither do we deny but by this rational principle man may apprehend in his brain, and in the notion, a knowledge of God and spiritual things; yet that not being the right organ, it cannot profit him towards salvation, but rather hindereth; and indeed the great cause of the apostasy hath been, that man hath sought to fathom the things of God in and by this natural and rational principle, and to build up a religion in it, neglecting and over-looking this principle and seed of God in the heart; so that herein, in the most universal and catholick sense, hath Anti-Christ in every man set up himself, and sitteth in the temple of God as God, and above every thing that is called God. For men being the temple of the Holy Ghost, as saith the apostle, I Cor. iii. 16 when the rational principle sets up itself there above the seed of God, to reign and rule as a prince in spiritual things, while the holy seed is wounded and bruised, there is Anti-Christ in every man, or somewhat exalted above and against Christ.

Nevertheless we do not hereby affirm as if man had received his reason to no purpose, or to be of no service unto him, in no wise; we look upon reason as fit to order and rule men in things natural. For as God gave two great Lights to rule the outward world, the sun and moon, the greater light to rule the day, and the lesser light to rule the night; so hath he given man the light of his Son, a spiritual divine light, to rule him in things spiritual, and the light of reason to rule him in things natural. And even as the moon borrows her light from the sun, so ought men, if they would be rightly and comfortably ordered in natural things, to have their reason enlightened by this divine and pure light. Which enlightened reason, in those that obey and follow this true light, we confess may be useful to man even in spiritual things, as even as the animal life in man, regulated and ordered by his reason, helps him in going about things that are rational.

CONSCIENCE

We do further rightly distinguish this from man's natural conscience; for conscience being that in man which ariseth from the natural faculties of man's soul, may be defiled and corrupted.

Now conscience, to define it truly, comes from conscire, and is that knowledge which ariseth in man's heart, from what agreeth, contradicteth, or is contrary to any thing believed by him, whereby he becomes conscious to himself that he transgresseth by doing that which is persuaded he ought not to do. So that the mind being once blinded or defiled with a wrong belief, there ariseth a conscience from that belief, which troubles him when he goes against it. As for example: A Turk who hath possessed himself with a false belief that it is unlawful for him to drink wine, if he do it, his conscience smites him for it; but though he keep many concubines, his conscience troubles him not, because his judgment is already defiled with a false opinion that it is lawful for him to do the one, and unlawful to do the other.

For conscience followeth judgment, doth not inform it; but this light, as it is received, removes the blindness of the judgment, opens the understanding, and rectifies both the judgment and conscience. So we confess also, that conscience is an excellent thing, where it is rightly informed and enlightened: wherefore some of us have fitly compared it to the lanthorn, and the light of Christ to a candle; a lanthorn is useful when a clear candle burns and shines in it: but otherwise of no use. To the light of Christ then in the conscience, and not to man's natural conscience, it is that we continually commend men.

JUSTIFICATION BY FAITH AND WORKS

As many as resist not this light, but receive the same, it becomes in them an holy, pure, and spiritual birth: by which holy birth, to wit, Jesus Christ formed within us, and working his works in us, as we are sanctified, so are we justified in the sight of God.

The works of the spirit of grace in the heart, wrought in conformity to the inward and spiritual law; which works are not wrought in man's will, nor by his power and ability, but in and by the power and Spirit of Christ in us, and therefore are pure and perfect in their kind (as shall hereafter be proved) and may be called Christ's works, for that he is the immediate author and worker of them: such works we affirm absolutely necessary to justification, so that a man cannot be justified without them; and all faith without them is dead and useless, as the apostle James saith. But faith, which worketh by love, is that which availeth, which is absolutely necessary: for faith, that worketh by love, cannot be without works.

PERFECTION

Since we have placed justification in the revelation of Jesus Christ formed and brought forth in the heart, there working his works of righteousness, and bringing forth the fruits of the Spirit, the question is, How far he may prevail in us while we are in this life, or we over our souls' enemies, in and by his strength?

We do believe, that to those in whom this pure and holy birth is fully brought forth, the body of death and sin comes to be crucified and removed, and their hearts united and subjected to the truth; so as not to obey any suggestions or temptations of the evil one, but to be free from actual sinning and transgressing of the law of God, and in that respect perfect.

By this we understand not such a perfection as may not daily admit of growth, and consequently mean not as if we were to be as pure, holy, and perfect as God in his divine attributes of wisdom, knowledge, and purity; but only a perfection proportionable and answerable to man's measure, whereby we are kept from transgressing the law of God, and enabled to answer what he requires of us; even as he that improved his two talents so as to make four of them, perfected his work, and was so accepted of his Lord as to be called a good and faithful servant, nothing less than he that made his five ten.

Though a man may witness this for a season, and therefore all ought to press after it; yet we do not affirm but those that have attained it in a measure may, by the wiles and temptations of the enemy, fall into iniquity, and lose it sometimes, if they be not watchful, and do not diligently attend to that of God in the heart. And we doubt not but many good and holy men, who have arrived to everlasting life, have had divers ebbings and flowings of this kind; for though every sin weakens a man in his spiritual condition, yet it doth not so as to destroy him altogether, or render him uncapable of rising again.

Nevertheless, I will not affirm that a state is not attainable in this life, in which to do righteousness may be so natural to the regenerate soul, that in the stability of that condition he cannot sin.

So then, if thou desirest to know this perfection and freedom from sin possible for thee, turn thy mind to the light and spiritual law of Christ in the heart, and suffer the reproofs thereof; so that that life that sometimes was alive in thee to this world, and the love and lusts thereof, may die, and a new life be raised, by which thou mayest live henceforward to God, and not to or for thyself; and with the apostle thou mayest say, Gal. ii. 20. "It is no more I, but Christ alive in me": And then thou wilt be a Christian indeed.

"We Are But Men Whom They Offend"

JOHN BELLERS

[*"Who hath wrote so much as the Quakers?" asked Francis Bugg— wearily, one imagines. John Bellers (1654–1725), before Bugg asked his question, gave the reason for the quantity: "He that doth not write whilst he is alive, can't speak when he is dead."*

Alive, Bellers wrote copiously; dead, he still speaks. Before the welfare state was dreamed of, Bellers was thinking of the welfare of citizens in terms of state action. He was both literal-minded and of an inventive turn of mind. Literally, it seemed to him that, if he were to love his neighbor as himself, he must make for his neighbor the same efforts he would make for himself—if he, Bellers, were imprisoned, ill, impoverished, uneducated, conscripted. And so thoroughly did he understand the commercial and mercantile temper of his age that the reforms he suggested were recommended not because they were Christian, but because they would bring England even greater prosperity.

But it was his inventives which suggested means for the establishment of workingmen's colleges, the rehabilitation of prisoners, the investment of private capital in projects for community betterment, state responsibility for the prevention of disease and the care of diseased, the possibility of settling international problems without the slaughter of nationals.

Bellers' estimate of the manner in which his ideas must be presented to the public, if they were to get a hearing, is sorrowful enough. Even more sorrowful has been the response. Though the reforms he suggested were clearly to the economic advantage of the public, the public has not been foresighted enough to be willing to part with today's penny in order to possess tomorrow's pound. So we still fight, die, sicken, and hang, much as in Bellers' day. We have not yet learned, in Bellers' words, to "run the way of His commandments with delight."|

————

SOME REASONS AGAINST PUTING FELLONS TO DEATH

I Having made some Essay to supply the Wants, and abate the Profaneness of the Age; I would say something of Fellons (most of whom rise from them two miserable Fountains), and of the Stain their untimely Death is to Religion and of the loss it is to the Kingdom. There are several sorts of Distractions, which all Men pities, and takes care of preserving from doing themselves or others harm: but Fellons are some of the worst sort of Mad Men, whom Charity therefore would oblige us to take some care to prevent their mischievous way of Living, and deplorable Deaths. The Idle and Profane Education of some, and the Necessities of others, brings Habits almost invincible; for such to conquer of themselves, without the State take them into their prudent management: But to put them into Bridewell or Newgate for a Month or two, and then turn them loose at their own Discressions (who have none) no more reclaims them, than baiting a Horse well with Provender makes him less able to Travel; they learn but more skill in their Trade, under the Tutors they meet with there.

The Scriptures saith, Watch; for the Devil your Adversary goes about like a roaring Lion, seeking which of you he may devour. What Consideration and Compassion then should be had of those unthinking, unwatchful People whose Pride, Lust, or Necessities, with the Devil's incitements of them is their sole Guide?

If a Man had a Child, or near Relation, that should fall into a capital Crime, he would use all his interest to preserve his Life, how much soever he abhorred his Fact, in hopes he might live to grow better, especially if he could have such a power of Confinement upon him as might prevent his acting such Enormities for the future.

And this Child, and near Relation, is every one to the Publick, whilst the cutting off by untimely Death of one able Man, may be reckoned 200 Pound loss out of the value of the Kingdom; for besides their Persons, they are commonly prevented of the Posterity which they might have (which is loss to all Generations), and if but one in a Succession, they may be valued at 10 £ a Year, at 20 Years Purchase, is 200 Pound.

How sincerely can we say the Lord's Prayer, Forgive us our Trespasses as we forgive them which Trespass against us; when for the loss, possibly of less than 20 Shillings, we Prosecute a Man to Death? Would it not be more natural and agreeable with our Prayers to God, to have Compassion on our deluded Fellow Creatures? We are but Men whom they offend, but God is infinitely above us, whom we have offended. . . .

"War and Christianity Are . . . Opposite Ends of a Balance"

[FROM "War: An Essay"]

JONATHAN DYMOND

[The classic statement by a Friend concerning war is George Fox's "I told them . . . that I lived in the virtue of that life and power that took away the occasion of all wars." And Fox's war against war was based on his effort to lead others into "the virtue of that life and power."

Jonathan Dymond (1798–1828) examined war itself and found that death was perhaps the least of its miseries. The chief horror of war is not the death of many—or few—physical men or women, but the death, in ninety-nine people out of a hundred, of Christian principle. Simply to "live at a period when scenes of horror and blood are frequent" makes one "callous to the feelings and sentiments of humanity."

What would Dymond think of us now? So inured are we to "scenes of horror and blood" that we use them as bedtime stories for our children and demand them for our own evening's relaxation and pleasure.]

———

To expatiate upon the miseries which War brings upon mankind, appears a trite and a needless employment. We all know that its evils are great and dreadful. Yet the very circumstance that the knowledge is familiar may make it inoperative upon our sentiments and our conduct. It is not the intensity of misery, it is not the extent of evil alone, which is necessary to animate us to that exertion which evil and misery should excite; if it were, surely we should be much more averse than we now are to contribute, in word or in action, to the promotion of War.

But there are mischiefs attendant upon the system which are not to every man thus familiar, and on which, for that reason, it is expedient to remark. In referring especially to some of those Moral consequences of War which commonly obtain little of our attention, it may be observed, that social and political considerations are necessarily involved in the moral tendency: for the happiness of society is always diminished by the diminution of morality; and enlightened policy knows that the greatest support of a state is the virtue of the people.

And yet the reader should bear in mind—what nothing but the frequency of the calamity can make him forget—the intense sufferings and irreparable deprivations which one battle inevitably entails upon private life. There are calamities of which the world thinks little, and which, if it thought of them, it could not remove. A father or a husband can seldom be replaced; a void is created in the domestic felicity which there is little hope that the future will fill. By the slaughter of a war, there are thousands who weep in unpitied and unnoticed secrecy, whom the world does not see; and thousands who retire in silence to hopeless poverty, for whom it does not care. To these the conquest of a kingdom is of little importance. The loss of a protector or of a friend is ill repaid by empty glory. An addition of territory may add titles to a king, but the brilliancy of a crown throws little light upon domestic gloom. It is not my intention to insist upon these calamities, intense and irreparable and unnumbered as they are; but those who begin a war without taking them into their estimates of its consequences, must be regarded as, at most, half-seeing politicians. The legitimate object of political measures is the good of the people;—and a great sum of good a war must produce, if it out-balances even *this* portion of its mischiefs.

DESTRUCTION OF HUMAN LIFE

Nor should we be forgetful of that dreadful part of all warfare, the destruction of mankind. The frequency with which this destruction is represented to our minds, has almost extinguished our perception of its awfulness and horror. Between the years 1141 and 1815, an interval of six hundred and seventy years, our country was at war with France alone *two hundred and sixty-six years*. If to this we add wars with other countries, probably we shall find that one-half of the last six or seven centuries has been spent by this country in war! A dreadful picture of human violence! How many of our fellow-men, of our fellow-Christians, have these centuries of slaughter cut off! What is the sum total of the misery of their deaths!

TAXATION

When political writers expatiate upon the extent and the evils of taxation, they do not sufficiently bear in mind the reflection that almost all our taxation is the effect of War. A man declaims upon national debts. He ought to declaim upon the parent of those debts. Do we reflect that if heavy taxation entails evils and misery upon the community, that misery and those evils are inflicted upon us by War? The amount of supplies in Queen

Anne's reign was about seventy millions; and of this about sixty-six millions was expended in War. Where is our equivalent good?

Such considerations ought, undoubtedly, to influence the conduct of public men in their disagreement with other states, even if higher considerations do not influence it. They ought to form part of the calculations of the evil of hostility. I believe that a greater mass of human suffering and loss of human enjoyment are occasioned by the pecuniary distresses of a war, than any ordinary advantages of a war compensate. But this consideration seems too remote to obtain our notice. Anger at offence, or hope of triumph, overpowers the sober calculations of reason, and outbalances the weight of after and long-continued calamities. The only question appears to be, whether taxes enough for a war can be raised, and whether a people will be willing to pay them. But the great question ought to be (setting questions of Christianity aside), whether the nation will gain as much by the war as they will lose by taxation and its other calamities.

If the happiness of the people were, what it ought to be, the primary and the ultimate object of national measures, I think that the policy which pursued this object, would often find that even the pecuniary distresses resulting from a war make a greater deduction from the quantum of felicity, than would those evils which the war may have been designed to avoid.

MORAL DEPRAVITY

"But War," says Erasmus, "does more harm to the morals of men than even to their property and persons." If, indeed, it depraves our morals more than it injures our persons and deducts from our property, how enormous must its mischiefs be!

I do not know whether the greater sum of moral evil resulting from War is suffered by those who are immediately engaged in it, or by the public. The mischief is most extensive upon the community, but upon the profession it is most intense. *Rara fides pietasque viris qui castra sequuntur.*—Lucan. No one pretends to applaud the morals of an army, and as for its religion, few think of it at all. The fact is too notorious to be insisted upon, that thousands who had filled their stations in life with propriety, and been virtuous from principle, have lost, by a military life, both the practice and the regard of morality; and when they have become habituated to the vices of War, have laughed at their honest and plodding brethren, who are still spiritless enough for virtue or stupid enough for piety.

Does any man ask, What occasions depravity in military life? I answer in the words of Robert Hall, "War reverses, with respect to its objects, all the rules of morality. It is nothing less than a temporary repeal of all the principles of virtue. It is a system out of which almost all the virtues are excluded, and in which nearly all the vices are incorporated." And it requires no sagacity to discover that those who are engaged in a practice which reverses all the rules of morality, which repeals all the principles of virtue, and in which nearly all the vices are incorporated, cannot, without the intervention of a miracle, retain their minds and morals undepraved.

FAMILIARITY WITH PLUNDER

Look, for illustration, to the familiarity with the plunder of property and the slaughter of mankind which War induces. He who plunders the citizen of another nation without remorse or reflection, and bears away the spoil with triumph, will inevitably lose something of his principles of probity. He who is familiar with slaughter, who has himself often perpetrated it, and who exults in the perpetration, will not retain undepraved the principles of virtue. His moral feelings are blunted; his moral vision is obscured; his principles are shaken; an inroad is made upon their integrity, and it is an inroad that makes after inroads the more easy. Mankind do not generally resist the influence of habit. If today we rob and shoot those who are "enemies" we are tomorrow in some degree prepared to shoot and rob those who are not enemies. Law may indeed still restrain us from violence; but the power and efficiency of Principle is diminished, and this alienation of the mind from the practice, the love, and the perception, of Christian purity, therefore, of necessity extends its influence to the other circumstances of life. *The whole evil* is imputable to War; and we say that this evil forms a powerful evidence to the abstract question of its lawfulness, or to the practical question of its expediency. *That* can scarcely be lawful which necessarily occasions such widespread immorality. *That* can scarcely be expedient, which is so pernicious to virtue, and therefore to the State.

IMPLICIT OBEDIENCE TO SUPERIORS

The economy of War requires of every soldier an implicit submission to his superior; and this submission is required of every gradation of rank to that above it. "I swear to obey the orders of the officers who are set over me: so help me, God." This system may be necessary to hostile operations, but I think it is unquestionably adverse to intellectual and moral excellence.

The very nature of unconditional obedience implies the relinquishment of the use of the reasoning powers. Little more is required of the soldier than that he be obedient and brave. His obedience is that of an animal which is moved by a goad or a bit without judgment of its own; and his bravery is that of a mastiff that fights whatever mastiff others put before it. It is obvious that in such agency the intellect and the understanding have little part. Now I think that this is important. He who, with whatever motive, resigns the direction of his conduct implicitly to another, surely cannot retain that erectness and independence of mind, that manly consciousness of mental freedom, which is one of the highest privileges of our nature. A British Captain declares that "the tendency of strict discipline, such as prevails on board ships of War, where almost every act of a man's life is regulated by the orders of his superiors, is to weaken the faculty of independent thought." Thus the rational being becomes reduced in the intellectual scale: an encroachment is made upon the integrity of its independence. God has given us, individually, capacities for the regulation of our individual conduct. To resign its direction, therefore, to the absolute disposal of another, appears to be an unmanly and unjustifiable relinquishment of the privileges which He has granted to us. And the effect is obviously bad; for although no character will apply universally to any large class of men, and although the intellectual character of the military profession does not result *only* from this unhappy subjection, yet it will not be disputed, that the honourable exercise of intellect amongst that profession is not relatively great. It is not from them that we expect, because it is not in them that we generally find, those vigorous exertions of intellect which dignify our nature, and which extend the boundaries of human knowledge.

RESIGNATION OF MORAL AGENCY

But the intellectual effects of military subjection form but a small portion of its evils. The great mischief is, that it requires the relinquishment of our moral agency; that it requires us to do what is opposed to our consciences, and what we know to be wrong. A soldier must obey, how criminal soever the command, and how criminal soever he knows it to be. It is certain that, of those who compose armies, many commit actions which they believe to be wicked, and which they would not commit but for the obligations of a military life. Although a soldier determinately believes that the war is unjust, although he is convinced that his particular part of the service is atrociously criminal, still he must proceed—he must prosecute the purposes of injustice or robbery, he must participate in the guilt, and be himself a robber.

To what a situation is a rational and responsible being reduced, who commits actions, good or bad, at the word of another? I can conceive no greater degradation. It is the lowest, the final abjectness of the moral nature. We see that it *is* this if we take away the glitter of War, and if we add this glitter it remains the same.

Such a resignation of our moral agency is not contended for, or tolerated, in any other circumstance of human life. War stands alone upon this pinnacle of depravity. She only, in the supremacy of crime, has told us that she has abolished even the obligation to be virtuous.

Some writers who have perceived the monstrousness of this system, have told us that a soldier should assure himself, before he engages in a war, that it is a lawful and just one; and they acknowledge that, if he does not feel this assurance, he is a "murderer." But how is he to know that the war is just? It is frequently difficult for the people distinctly to discover what the objects of a war are. And if the soldier knew that it was just in its commencement, how is he to know that it will continue just in its prosecution? Every war is, in some parts of its course, wicked and unjust; and who can tell what that course will be? You say, When he discovers any injustice or wickedness, let him withdraw: we answer, He cannot: and the truth is, that there is no way of avoiding the evil, but by avoiding the army.

It is an inquiry of much interest, under what circumstances of *responsibility* a man supposes himself to be placed, who thus abandons and violates his own sense of rectitude and of his duties. Either he is responsible for his actions, or he is not; and the question is a serious one to determine. Christianity has certainly never stated any cases in which personal responsibility ceases. If she admits such cases, she has at least not told us so; but she has told us, explicitly and repeatedly, that she does require individual obedience and impose individual responsibility. She has made no exceptions to the imperativeness of her obligations, whether we are required by others to neglect them or not; and I can discover in her sanctions no reason to suppose that in her final adjudications she admits the plea, *that another required us to do that which she required us to forbear.* But it may be feared, it may be *believed,* that how little soever Religion will abate of the responsibility of those who obey, she will impose not a little upon those who command. They, at least, are answerable for the enormities of War: unless, indeed, any one shall tell me that responsibility attaches nowhere; that that which would be wickedness in another man is innocence in a soldier; and that Heaven has granted to the directors of War a privileged immunity, by virtue of which crime incurs no guilt and receives no punishment.

BONDAGE AND DEGRADATION

Again, no one doubts that military power is essentially arbitrary. And what are the customary feelings of mankind with respect to a subjection to arbitrary power? How do we feel and think, when we hear of a person who is obliged to do whatever other men command, and who, the moment he refuses, is punished for attempting to be free? If a man orders his servant to do a given action, he is at liberty, if he think the action improper, or if, from any other cause, he choose not to do it, to refuse his obedience. Far other is the nature of military subjection. The soldier is compelled to obey, whatever be his inclination or his will. Being in the service, he has but one alternative—submission to arbitrary power, or punishment—the punishment of death perhaps—for refusing to submit. Let the reader imagine to himself any other cause or purpose for which freemen shall be subjected to such a condition, and he will then see that condition in its proper light. The influence of habit and the gloss of public opinion make situations that would otherwise be loathsome and revolting, not only tolerable but pleasurable. Take away this influence and this gloss from the situation of a soldier, and what should we call it? We should call it a state of degradation and of bondage. But habit and public opinion, although they may influence notions, cannot alter things. It *is* a state intellectually, morally, and politically, of bondage and degradation.

But the reader will say that this submission to arbitrary power is necessary to the prosecution of War. I know it, and that is the very point for observation. It is *because* it is necessary to War that it is noticed here: for a brief but clear argument results:—That custom to which such a state of mankind is necessary must inevitably be bad; it must inevitably be adverse to rectitude and to Christianity.

EFFECTS ON THE COMMUNITY

Yet I do not know whether the greatest moral evil on War is to be sought in its effects on the military character. Upon the community its effects are indeed less apparent, because they who are the secondary subjects of the immoral influence, are less intensely affected by it than the immediate agents of its diffusion. But whatever is deficient in the degree of evil, is probably more than compensated by its extent. The influence is like that of a continual and noxious vapour: we neither regard nor perceive it, but it secretly undermines the moral health.

Every one knows that vice is contagious. The depravity of one man has always a tendency to deprave his neighbours; and it therefore requires no unusual acuteness to discover, that the prodigious mass of immorality and crime which is accumulated by a war, must have a powerful effect in "demoralizing" the public. But there is one circumstance connected with the injurious influence of War, which makes it peculiarly operative and malignant. It is, that we do not hate or fear the influence, and do not fortify ourselves against it. Other vicious influences insinuate themselves into our minds by stealth; but this we receive with open embrace. Glory, and patriotism, and bravery, and conquest, are bright and glittering things. Who, when he is looking delighted upon these things, is armed against the mischiefs which they may veil?

The evil is in its own nature of almost universal operation. During a War, a whole people become familiarized with the utmost excesses of enormity—with the utmost intensity of human wickedness—and they rejoice and exult in them; so that there is probably not one man in a hundred who does not lose something of his Christian principles during a period of war.

"It is in my mind" said C. J. Fox, "no small misfortune to live at a period when scenes of horror and blood are frequent. . . . One of the most evil consequences of War is, that it tends to render the heart of mankind callous to the feelings and sentiments of humanity."

Those who know what the moral law of God is, and who feel an interest in the virtue and the happiness of the world, will not regard the bitterness and the restlessness of resentment which are produced by a war, as trifling evils. If anything be opposite to Christianity, it is retaliation and revenge. In the obligation to restrain these dispositions, much of the characteristic placability of Christianity consists. The very essence and spirit of our religion are abhorrent from resentment. The very essence and spirit of War are promotive of resentment; and what, then, must be their mutual adverseness? That War excites these passions needs not to be proved. When a war is in contemplation, or when it has been begun, what are the endeavours of its promoters? They animate us by every artifice of excitement to hatred and animosity. Pamphlets, placards, newspapers, caricatures— every agent is in requisition to irritate us into malignity. Nay, dreadful as it is, the pulpit has too often resounded with declamations to stimulate our too sluggish resentment, and to invite us to slaughter. And thus the most unchristianlike of all our passions, the passion which it is most the object of our religion to suppress, is excited and fostered. Christianity cannot be flourishing under circumstances like these. The more effectually we are animated to War, the more nearly we extinguish the dispositions of our religion. War and Christianity are like the opposite ends of a balance, of which one is depressed by the elevation of the other.

These are the consequences which make War dreadful to a State. Slaughter and devastation are sufficiently terrible, but their collateral evils are their greatest. It is the *immoral feeling* that War diffuses—it is *the depravation of Principle* which forms the mass of its mischief.

To attempt to pursue the consequences of War through all their ramifications of evil, were, however, both endless and vain. It is a moral gangrene, which diffuses its humours through the whole political and social system. To expose its mischief, is to exhibit all evil; for there is no evil which it does not occasion, and it has much that is peculiar to itself.

That, together with its multiplied evils, War produces some good, I have no wish to deny. I know that it sometimes elicits valuable qualities which had otherwise been concealed, and that it often produces collateral and adventitious, and sometimes immediate advantages. If all this could be denied, it would be needless to deny it; for it is of no consequence to the question whether it be proved. That any wide-extended system should not produce *some* benefits can never happen. In such a system, it were an unheard-of purity of evil, which was evil without any mixture of good. But, to compare the ascertained advantages of War with its ascertained mischiefs, and to maintain a question as to the preponderance of the balance, implies not ignorance, but disingenuousness, not incapacity to decide, but a voluntary concealment of truth.

And *why* do we insist upon these consequences of War? Because the review prepares the reader for a more accurate judgment respecting its lawfulness. Because it reminds him what War is, and because, knowing and remembering what it is, he will be the better able to compare it with the Standard of Rectitude.

Part Two

THE

QUAKERS

ESTABLISHED

"IN THE
SERVICE OF THE GOSPEL"

Henceforth I might not consider myself as a distinct or separate person.

—JOHN WOOLMAN

"*I Was Taught to Watch the Pure Opening*"

[FROM *Journal*]

JOHN WOOLMAN

[John Woolman (1720–1772) was a moral and religious genius. His life, in the realm of action, is to the lives of other individuals what a poet's use of words is to the nonpoetic. He was equipped with moral antennae which caused him to feel about slavery, and indeed about the conditions under which all people worked, what others would not feel for another century. He had insights about the use of time and of money and the waging of war which it may take most of us another thousand years to attain. One feels ashamed to understand Woolman's words without imitating his life.

He was no born idol-breaker like Fox, not natively courageous and built for buffetings. He was a frail man, often in poor health and with no stomach for facing warring peoples, traversing the wilderness, and telling others anything—*let alone that, by his lights, they were wrong. So before he could do any of these things he had to combat and conquer the naturally diffident, retiring, fearful Woolman. He did conquer him. Fox's belief—and bones—were so strong that, when beaten on the arm with a stave until the onlookers cried that he would never again have the use of his hand, he was able to control, within the hour, the injury and swelling. One feels that Woolman's arm would have been broken, that, as the crowd prophesied, he would never again have use of it—but that, nevertheless, he would have gone on, exactly as before.*

Fox, a man cast in the mold of the physical hero, and burning with a belief not yet completely voiced, preached the inner light. Woolman harkened to Fox, lived in that light, and disseminated it.

Woolman went to the native American tribes with a characteristically modest and honest statement. He intended to live with them, he said, not as a missionary but so that, "haply, I might receive some instruction from them, or they might in any degree be helped forward by my following the leadings of truth among them." If every missionary had approached the mission field with this concept, how different would have been the history of foreign missions. Woolman possessed no truth, extraneous to these people. He intended only, among this particular people, to follow "the leadings of truth." He would speak to their condition.

One Woolman in a hundred, one Woolman in a thousand, might be enough to change the face of the earth. Shall we see his like again? It was a part of Woolman's, as of Fox's, belief that perfection is possible to all. If they were right, we may.]

⸻

I have often felt a Motion of Love to leave some Hints in Writing of my Experience of the Goodness of God; and now, in the thirty-sixth Year of my Age, I begin this Work.

I was born in Northampton, in Burlington County, West Jersey, in the Year 1720; and before I was seven years old, I began to be acquainted with the Operations of divine Love. Through the Care of my Parents, I was taught to read nearly as soon as I was capable of it; and, as I went from School one seventh Day, I remember, while my Companions went to play by the Way, I went forward out of Sight, and, sitting down, I read the 22d Chapter of the Revelations: "He shewed me a pure River of Water of Life, clear as Chrystal, proceeding out of the Throne of God and of the Lamb, etc." and, in reading it, my Mind was drawn to seek after that pure Habitation, which, I then believed, God had prepared for his Servants. The Place where I sat, and the Sweetness that attended my Mind, remain fresh in my Memory.

This, and the like gracious Visitations, had that Effect upon me, that when Boys used ill Language it troubled me; and, through the continued Mercies of God, I was preserved from it.

The pious Instructions of my Parents were often fresh in my Mind when I happened to be among wicked Children, and were of Use to me. My Parents, having a large Family of Children, used frequently, on first Days after Meeting, to put us to read in the holy Scriptures, or some religious Books, one after another, the rest sitting by without much Conversation; which, I have since often thought, was a good Practice. From what I had read and heard, I believed there had been, in past Ages, People who walked in Uprightness before God, in a Degree exceeding any that I knew, or heard of, now living: And the Apprehension of there being less Steadiness and Firmness, amongst People in this Age than in past Ages, often troubled me while I was a Child.

A Thing remarkable in my Childhood was, that once, going to a Neighbour's House, I saw, on the Way, a Robin sitting on her Nest, and as I came near she went off, but, having young ones, flew about, and with many Cries expressed her Concern for them; I stood and threw Stones at her, till, one striking her, she fell down dead: At first I was pleased with the Exploit, but after a few Minutes was seized with Horror, as having, in a sportive Way, killed an innocent Creature while she was careful for her Young: I beheld her lying dead, and thought these young ones, for which she was so careful, must now perish for want of their Dam to nourish them; and, after some painful Considerations on the Subject, I climbed up the Tree, took all the young Birds, and killed them; supposing that better than to leave them to pine away and die miserably: And believed, in this Case, that Scripture-proverb was fulfilled, "The tender Mercies of the Wicked are cruel." I then went on my Errand, but, for some Hours, could think of little else but the Cruelties I had committed, and was much troubled. Thus he, whose tender Mercies are over all his Works, hath placed a Principle in the human Mind, which incited to exercise Goodness towards every living Creature; and this being singly attended to, People become tender hearted and sympathizing; but being frequently and totally rejected, the Mind becomes shut up in a contrary Disposition. . . .

Having attained the Age of sixteen Years, I began to love wanton Company; and though I was preserved from prophane Language, or scandalous Conduct, still I perceived a Plant in me which produced much wild Grapes; yet my merciful Father forsook me not utterly, but, at Times, through his Grace, I was brought seriously to consider my Ways; and the Sight of my Backslidings affected me with Sorrow; but, for want of rightly attending to the Reproofs of Instruction, Vanity was added to Vanity, and Repentance to Repentance: Upon the whole, my Mind was more and more alienated from the Truth, and I hastened toward Destruction. While I meditate on the Gulph towards which I travelled, and reflect on my youthful Disobedience, for these Things I weep, mine Eyes run down with Water.

Advancing in Age, the Number of my Acquaintances increased, and thereby my Way grew more difficult; though I had found Comfort in reading the holy Scriptures, and thinking on heavenly Things, I was now estranged therefrom: I knew I was going from the Flock of Christ, and had no Resolution to return; hence serious Reflections were uneasy to me, and youthful Vanities and Diversions my greatest Pleasure. Running in this Road I found many like myself; and we associated in that which is the reverse of true Friendship. . . .

Thus Time passed on: My Heart was replenished with Mirth and Wantonness, and pleasing Scenes of Vanity were presented to my Imagination, till I attained the Age of eighteen Years; near which Time I felt the Judgments of God, in my Soul, like a consuming Fire; and, looking over my past Life, the Prospect was moving. I was often sad, and longed to be delivered from those Vanities; then again, my Heart was strongly inclined to them, and there was in me a sore Conflict: At Times I turned to Folly, and then again, Sorrow and Confusion took hold of me. In a while, I resolved totally to leave off some of my Vanities; but there was a secret Reserve, in my Heart, of the more refined Part of them, and I was not low enough to find true Peace. Thus, for some Months, I had great Troubles; there remaining in me an unsubjected Will, which rendered my Labours fruitless, till at length, through the merciful Continuance of heavenly Visitations, I was made to bow down in Spirit before the Lord. I remember one Evening I had spent some Time in reading a pious Author; and walking out alone, I humbly prayed to the Lord for his Help, that I might be delivered from all those Vanities which so ensnared me. Thus, being brought low, he helped me; and, as I learned to bear the Cross, I felt Refreshment to come from his Presence; but, not keeping in that Strength which gave Victory, I lost Ground again; the Sense of which greatly affected me; and I sought Desarts and lonely Places, and there, with Tears, did confess my Sins to God, and humbly craved Help of him. And I may say with Reverence, he was near to me in my Troubles, and in those Times of Humiliation opened my Ear to Discipline. I was now led to look seriously at the Means by which I was drawn from the pure Truth, and learned this, that, if I would live in the Life which the faithful Servants of God lived in, I must not go into Company as heretofore in my own Will; but all the Cravings of Sense must be governed by a divine Principle. In Times of Sorrow and Abasement these Instructions were sealed upon me, and I felt the Power of Christ prevail over selfish Desires, so that I was preserved in a good degree of Steadiness; and, being young, and believing at that Time that a single Life was best for me, I was strengthened to keep from such Company as had often been a Snare to me.

I kept steadily to Meetings; spent First-day Afternoons chiefly in reading the Scriptures and other good Books; and was early convinced in Mind, that true Religion consisted in an inward Life, wherein the Heart doth love and reverence God the Creator, and learns to exercise true Justice and Goodness, not only toward all Men, but also toward the brute Creatures. That as the Mind was moved, by an inward Principle, to love God as an invisible incomprehensible Being, by the same Principle it was moved to love him in all his Manifestations in the visible World. That, as by his Breath the Flame of Life was kindled in all animal sensible Creatures, to say we love God, and, at the same Time exercise Cruelty toward the least Creature, is a Contradiction in itself.

I found no Narrowness respecting Sects and Opinions; but believed, that sincere upright-hearted People, in every Society, who truly love God, were accepted of him. . . .

All this Time I lived with my Parents, and wrought on the Plantation; and, having had Schooling pretty well for a Planter, I used to improve it in Winter Evenings, and other leisure Times; and, being now in the twenty-first Year of my Age, a Man, in much Business at shop-keeping and baking, asked me, if I would hire with him to tend Shop and keep Books. I acquainted my Father with the Proposal; and, after some Deliberation, it was agreed for me to go.

At Home I had lived retired; and now, having a Prospect of being much in the Way of Company, I felt frequent and fervent Cries in my Heart to God, the Father of Mercies, that he would preserve me from all Corruption; that in this more publick Employment, I might serve him, my gracious Redeemer, in that Humility and Self-denial, with which I had been, in a small Degree, exercised in a more private Life. The Man, who employed me, furnished a Shop in Mount-Holly, about five Miles from my Father's House, and six from his own; and there I lived alone, and tended his Shop. Shortly after my Settlement here I was visited by several young People, my former Acquaintance, who knew not but Vanities would be as agreeable to me now as ever; and, at these Times, I cried to the Lord in secret, for Wisdom and Strength; for I felt myself encompassed with Difficulties, and had fresh Occasion to bewail the Follies of Time past, in contracting a Familiarity with libertine People; and, as I now had left my Father's House outwardly, I found my heavenly Father to be merciful to me beyond what I can express. . . .

I went to Meetings in an awful Frame of Mind, and endeavoured to be inwardly acquainted with the Language of the true Shepherd; and, one Day, being under a strong Exercise of Spirit, I stood up, and said some Words in a Meeting; but, not keeping close to the divine Opening, I said more than was required of me; and being soon sensible of my Error, I was afflicted in Mind some Weeks, without any Light or Comfort, even to that Degree that I could not take Satisfaction in any Thing: I remembered God, and was troubled, and, in the Depth of my Distress, he had Pity upon me, and sent the Comforter: I then felt Forgiveness for my Offence, and my Mind became calm and quiet, being truly thankful to my gracious Redeemer for his Mercies; and, after this, feeling the Spring of divine Love opened, and a Concern to speak, I said a few Words in a Meeting, in which I found Peace; this, I believe, was about six Weeks from the first Time: And, as I was thus humbled and disciplined under the Cross, my Understanding became more strengthened to distinguish the pure Spirit which inwardly moves upon the Heart, and taught me to wait in Silence sometimes many Weeks together, until I felt that rise which prepares the Creature.

From an inward purifying, and stedfast abiding under it, springs a lively operative Desire for the Good of others: All the Faithful are not called to the public Ministry; but whoever are, are called to minister of that which they have tasted and handled spiritually. The outward Modes of Worship are various; but, wherever any are true Ministers of Jesus Christ, it is from the Operation of his Spirit upon their Hearts, first purifying them, and thus giving them a just Sense of the Conditions of others.

This Truth was clearly fixed in my Mind; and I was taught to watch the pure Opening, and to take Heed, lest, while I was standing to speak, my own Will should get uppermost, and cause me to utter Words from worldly Wisdom, and depart from the Channel of the true Gospel-Ministry. . . .

About the Time called Christmas, I observed many People from the Country, and Dwellers in Town, who, resorting to Public-Houses, spent their Time in drinking and vain Sports, tending to corrupt one another; on which Account I was much troubled. At one House, in particular, there was much Disorder; and I believed it was a Duty incumbent on me to go and speak to the Master of that House. I considered I was young, and that several elderly Friends in town had Opportunity to see these

Things; but though I would gladly have been excused, yet I could not feel my Mind clear.

The Exercise was heavy; and as I was reading what the Almighty said to Ezekiel, respecting his Duty as a Watchman, the Matter was set home more clearly; and then, with Prayers and Tears, I besought the Lord for his Assistance, who, in Loving-kindness, gave me a resigned Heart: Then, at a suitable Opportunity, I went to the Public-house, and, seeing the Man amongst much Company, I went to him, and told him, I wanted to speak with him; so we went aside, and there, in the Fear of the Almighty, I expressed to him what rested on my Mind; which he took kindly, and afterward shewed more Regard to me than before. In a few Years afterwards he died, middle-aged; and I often thought that, had I neglected my Duty in that Case, it would have given me great Trouble; and I was humbly thankful to my gracious Father, who had supported me herein.

My Employer having a Negro Woman, sold her, and desired me to write a Bill of Sale, the Man being waiting who bought her: The Thing was sudden; and, though the Thoughts of writing an Instrument of Slavery for one of my Fellow-creatures felt uneasy, yet I remembered I was hired by the Year, that it was my Master who directed me to do it, and that it was an elderly Man, a Member of our Society, who bought her; so, through Weakness, I gave way, and wrote; but, at the executing it, I was so afflicted in my Mind, that I said, before my Master and the Friend, that I believed Slave-keeping to be a Practice inconsistent with the Christian Religion: This in some Degree abated my Uneasiness; yet, as often as I reflected seriously upon it, I thought I should have been clearer, if I had desired to have been excused from it, as a Thing against my Conscience; for such it was. And, some Time after this, a young Man, of our Society, spoke to me to write a Conveyance of a Slave to him, he having lately taken a Negro into his House: I told him I was not easy to write it; for, though many of our Meeting and in other Places kept Slaves, I still believed the Practice was not right, and desired to be excused from the writing. I spoke to him in Good-will; and he told me that keeping Slaves was not altogether agreeable to his Mind; but that the Slave being a Gift to his Wife, he had accepted of her.

Having now been several Years with my Employer, and he doing less at Merchandize than heretofore, I was thoughtful of some other Way of Business; perceiving Merchandize to be attended with much Cumber, in the Way of trading in these Parts.

My Mind, through the Power of Truth, was in a good degree weaned from the Desire of outward Greatness, and I was learning to be content with real Conveniences, that were not costly; so that a Way of Life, free from much Entanglement, appeared best for me, though the Income might be small. I had several Offers of Business that appeared profitable, but did not see my Way clear to accept of them; as believing the Business proposed would be attended with more outward Care than was required of me to engage in.

I saw that a humble Man, with the blessing of the Lord, might live on a little; and that where the Heart was set on Greatness, Success in Business did not satisfy the craving; but that commonly, with an Increase of Wealth, the Desire of Wealth increased. There was a Care on my Mind so to pass my Time, that nothing might hinder me from the most steady Attention to the Voice of the true Shepherd.

My Employer, though now a Retailer of Goods, was by Trade a Taylor, and kept a Servant-man at that Business; and I began to think about learning the Trade, expecting that, if I should settle, I might, by this Trade and a little retailing of Goods, get a Living in a plain Way, without the Load of great Business: I mentioned it to my Employer, and we soon agreed on Terms; and then, when I had Leisure from the Affairs of Merchandize, I worked with his Man. . . .

A JOURNEY TO THE SOUTHERN STATES

Two Things were remarkable to me in this Journey; first, in Regard to my Entertainment, when I ate, drank, and lodged at free-cost, with People who lived in Ease on the hard Labour of their Slaves, I felt uneasy; and, as my Mind was inward to the Lord, I found, from Place to Place, this Uneasiness return upon me, at Times, through the whole Visit. Where the Masters bore a good Share of the Burthen, and lived frugally, so that their Servants were well provided for, and their Labour moderate, I felt more easy; but where they lived in a costly Way, and laid heavy Burthens on their Slaves, my Exercise was often great, and I frequently had Conversation with them, in private, concerning it. Secondly; this Trade of importing Slaves from their native Country being much encouraged amongst them, and the white People and their Children so generally living without much Labour, was frequently the Subject of my serious Thoughts: And I saw in these Southern Provinces so many Vices and Corruptions, increased by this Trade and this Way of Life, that it appeared to me as a Gloom over the Land; and though now many willingly run into it, yet, in future, the Consequence will be grievous to Posterity: I express it as it hath appeared to me, not at once nor twice, but as a Matter fixed on my Mind. . . .

About this Time, believing it good for me to settle, and thinking seriously about a Companion, my Heart was turned to the Lord with Desires that he would give me Wisdom to proceed therein agreeable to his Will; and he was pleased to give me a well-inclined Damsel, Sarah Ellis; to whom I was married the eighteenth Day of the eighth Month, in the Year 1749. . . .

Until this Year, 1756, I continued to retail Goods, besides following my Trade as a Taylor; about which Time, I grew uneasy on Account of my Business growing too cumbersome: I had begun with selling Trimmings for Garments, and from thence proceeded to sell Cloths and Linens; and, at length, having got a considerable Shop of Goods, my Trade increased every Year, and the Road to large Business appeared open; but I felt a Stop in my Mind.

Through the Mercies of the Almighty, I had, in a good degree, learned to be content with a plain Way of Living: I had but a small Family; and, on serious Consideration, I believed Truth did not require me to engage in much cumbering Affairs: It had been my general Practice to buy and sell Things really useful: Things that served chiefly to please the vain Mind in People, I was not easy to trade in; seldom did it; and, whenever I did, I found it weaken me as a Christian.

The Increase of Business became my Burthen; for, though my natural Inclination was toward Merchandize, yet I believed Truth required me to live more free from the outward Cumbers: and there was now a Strife in my Mind between the two; and in this Exercise my Prayers were put up to the Lord, who graciously heard me, and gave me a Heart resigned to his Holy Will: Then I lessened my outward Business; and, as I had Opportunity, told my Customers of my Intention, that they might consider what Shop to turn to: And, in a while wholly laid down Merchandize, following my Trade, as a Taylor, myself only, having no Apprentice. I also had a Nursery of Appletrees; in which I employed some of my Time in hoeing, grafting, trimming, and inoculating. In Merchandize it is the Custom, where I lived, to sell chiefly on Credit, and poor People often get in Debt; and when Payment is expected, not having wherewith to pay, their Creditors often sue for it at Law. Having often observed Occurrences of this Kind, I found it good for me to advise poor People to take such Goods as were most useful and not costly.

In the Time of Trading, I had an Opportunity of seeing, that the too liberal Use of spirituous Liquors, and the Custom of wearing too costly Apparel, led some People into great Inconveniences; and these two Things appear to be often connected; for, by not attending to that Use of Things which is consistent with universal Righteousness, here is an Increase of Labour which extends beyond what our heavenly Father intends for us: And by great Labour, and often by much Sweating, there is, even among such as are not Drunkards, a craving of some Liquors to revive the Spirits; that, partly by the luxurious Drinking of some, and partly by the Drinking of others (led to it through immoderate Labour), very great Quantities of Rum are every Year expended in our Colonies; the greater Part of which we should have no Need of, did we steadily attend to pure Wisdom. . . .

As every Degree of Luxury hath some Connection with Evil, those who profess to be Disciples of Christ, and are looked upon as Leaders of the People, should have that Mind in them which was also in Christ, and so stand separate from every Wrong Way, as a Means of Help to the Weaker. As I have sometimes been much spent in the Heat, and taken Spirits to revive me, I have found, by Experience, that in such Circumstances the Mind is not so calm, nor so fitly disposed for divine Meditation, as when all such Extremes are avoided; and I have felt an increasing Care to attend to that holy Spirit which sets Bounds to our Desires, and leads those, who faithfully follow it, to apply all the Gifts of divine Providence to the Purposes for which they were intended. Did such, as have the Care of great Estates, attend with Singleness of Heart to this heavenly Instructor, which so opens and enlarges the Mind, that Men love their Neighbours as themselves, they would have Wisdom given them to manage, without finding Occasion to employ some People in the Luxuries of Life, or to make it necessary for others to labour too hard; but, for want of steadily regarding this Principle of divine Love, a selfish Spirit takes Place in the Minds of People, which is attended with Darkness and manifold Confusion in the World. . . .

On the eleventh Day of the fifth Month, we crossed the Rivers Patowmack and Rapahannock, and lodged at Port-Royal; and on the Way we happening in Company with a Colonel of the Militia, who appeared to be a thoughtful Man, I took Occasion to remark on the Difference in general betwixt a People used to labour moderately for their Living, training up their Children in Frugality and Business, and those who live on the Labour of Slaves; the former, in my View, being the most happy Life: With which he concurred, and mentioned the Trouble arising from the untoward, slothful, Disposition of the Negroes; adding, that one of our Labourers would do as much in a Day as two of their Slaves. I replied, that free Men, whose Minds were properly on their Business, found a Satisfaction in improving, cultivating, and providing for their Families; but Negroes, labouring to support others who claim them as their Property, and expecting nothing but Slavery during Life, had not the like Inducement to be industrious.

After some farther Conversation, I said, that Men having Power too often misapplied it; that though we made Slaves of the Negroes, and the Turks made Slaves of the Christians, I believed that Liberty was the natural Right of all Men equally: Which he did not deny; but said, the Lives of the Negroes were so wretched in their own Country, that many of them lived better here than there: I only said, there are great odds, in regard to us, on what Principle we act; and so the Conversation on that Subject ended: And I may here add, that another Person, some Time afterward, mentioned the Wretchedness of the Negroes, occasioned by their intestine Wars, as an Argument in Favour of our fetching them away for Slaves: To which I then replied, if Compassion on the Africans, in Regard to their domestic Troubles, were the real Motive of our purchasing them, that Spirit of Tenderness, being attended to, would incite us to use them kindly; that, as Strangers brought out of Affliction, their Lives might be happy among us; and as they are human Creatures, whose Souls are as precious as ours, and who may receive the same Help and Comfort from the holy Scriptures as we do, we could not omit suitable Endeavours to instruct them therein: But while we manifest, by our Conduct, that our Views in purchasing them are to advance ourselves; and while our buying Captives taken in War animates those Parties to push on that War, and increase Desolation amongst them, to say they live unhappy in Africa, is far from being an Argument in our Favour: And I farther said, the present Circumstances of these Provinces to me appear difficult; that the Slaves look like a burthensome Stone to such who burthen themselves with them; and that if the white People retain a Resolution to prefer their outward Prospects of Gain to all other Considerations, and do not act conscientiously toward them as fellow Creatures, I believe that Burthen will grow heavier and heavier, till Times change in a Way disagreeable to us: At which the Person appeared very serious, and owned, that, in considering their Condition, and the Manner of their Treatment in these Provinces, he had sometimes thought it might be just in the Almighty so to order it. . . .

Having many Years felt Love in my Heart towards the Natives of this Land, who dwell far back in the Wilderness, whose Ancestors were the Owners and Possessors of the Land where we dwell; and who, for a very small Consideration, assigned their Inheritance to us; and, being at Philadelphia, in the eighth Month, 1761, in a Visit to some Friends who had

Slaves, I fell in Company with some of those Natives who lived on the East Branch of the River Susquehannah, at an Indian Town called Wehaloosing, two hundred Miles from Philadelphia, and, in Conversation with them by an Interpreter, as also by Observations on their Countenances and Conduct, I believed some of them were measurably acquainted with that divine Power which subjects the rough and forward Will of the Creature: And, at Times, I felt inward Drawings toward a Visit to that Place, of which I told none except my dear Wife, until it came to some Ripeness; and, then, in the Winter, 1762, I laid it before Friends at our Monthly and Quarterly, and afterwards at our general Spring-meeting; and, having the Unity of Friends, and being thoughtful about an Indian Pilot, there came a Man and three Women from a little beyond that Town to Philadelphia on Business: And I, being informed thereof by Letter, met them in Town in the fifth Month, 1763; and, after some Conversation, finding they were sober People, I, by the Concurrence of Friends in that Place, agreed to join with them as Companions in their Return; and, on the seventh Day of the sixth Month following, we appointed to meet at Samuel Foulk's, at Richland in Bucks County. . . .

I parted from Friends, expecting the next Morning, to proceed on my Journey, and, being weary, went early to Bed; and, after I had been asleep a short Time, I was awaked by a Man calling at my Door; and, arising, was invited to meet some Friends at a Publick-house in our Town, who came from Philadelphia so late, that Friends were generally gone to Bed: These Friends informed me, that an Express arrived the last Morning from Pittsburgh, and brought News that the Indians had taken a Fort from the English Westward, and slain and scalped English People in divers Places, some near the said Pittsburgh; and that some elderly Friends in Philadelphia, knowing the Time of my expecting to set off, had conferred together, and thought good to inform me of these Things, before I left Home, that I might consider them, and proceed as I believed best; so I, going again to Bed, told not my Wife till Morning. My Heart was turned to the Lord for his heavenly Instruction; and it was an humbling Time to me. When I told my dear Wife, she appeared to be

deeply concerned about it; but, in a few Hours Time, my Mind
became settled in a Belief, that it was my Duty to proceed on my
Journey; and she bore it with a good Degree of Resignation. In
this Conflict of Spirit, there were great Searchings of Heart, and
strong Cries to the Lord, that no Motion might be, in the least
Degree, attended to, but that of the pure Spirit of Truth. . . .

My own Will and Desires were now very much broken, and
my Heart, with much Earnestness, turned to the Lord, to whom
alone I looked for Help in the Dangers before me. I had a
Prospect of the English along the Coast, for upwards of nine
hundred Miles, where I had travelled; and the favourable Situation of the English, and the Difficulties attending the Natives
in many Places, and the Negroes, were open before me; and a
weighty and heavenly Care came over my Mind, and Love filled
my Heart toward all Mankind, in which I felt a strong Engagement, that we might be obedient to the Lord, while, in tender
Mercies, he is yet calling to us; and so attend to pure universal
Righteousness, as to give no just Cause of Offence to the
Gentiles, who do not profess Christianity, whether the Blacks
from Africa, or the native Inhabitants of this Continent: And
here I was led into a close laborious Enquiry, whether I, as an
Individual, kept clear from all Things which tended to stir up,
or were connected with Wars, either in this Land or Africa; and
my Heart was deeply concerned, that, in future, I might in all
Things keep steadily to the pure Truth, and live and walk in the
Plainness and Simplicity of a sincere Follower of Christ. And, in
this lonely Journey, I did, this Day, greatly bewail the Spreading
of a wrong Spirit, believing, that the prosperous, convenient
Situation of the English, requires a constant Attention to divine
Love and Wisdom to guide and support us in a Way answerable
to the Will of that good, gracious, and almighty Being, who hath
an equal Regard to all Mankind: And, here, Luxury and Covetousness, with the numerous Oppressions, and other Evils attending them, appeared very afflicting to me; and I felt in that
which is immutable, that the Seeds of great Calamity and
Desolation are sown and growing fast on this Continent: Nor
have I Words sufficient to set forth that Longing I then felt, that
we, who are placed along the Coast, and have tasted the Love

and Goodness of God, might arise in his Strength; and, like faithful Messengers, labour to check the Growth of these Seeds, that they may not ripen to the Ruin of our Posterity. . . .

On the eighteenth Day: We rested ourselves this Forenoon; and the Indians, knowing that the Moravian and I were of different religious Societies, and as some of their People had encouraged him to come and stay a While with them, were, I believe, concerned that no Jarring or Discord might be in their Meetings: And they, I suppose, having conferred together, acquainted me, that the People, at my Request, would, at any Time, come together, and hold Meetings; and also told me, that they expected the Moravian would speak in their settled Meetings, which are commonly held Morning and near Evening. So I found Liberty in my Heart to speak to the Moravian, and told him of the Care I felt on my Mind for the Good of these People; and that I believed no ill Effects would follow it, if I sometimes spake in their Meetings when Love engaged me thereto, without calling them together at Times when they did not meet of course: Whereupon he expressed his Good-will toward my speaking, at any Time, all that I found in my Heart to say: So, near Evening, I was at their Meeting, where the pure Gospel-love was felt, to the tendering some of our Hearts; and the Interpreters, endeavouring to acquaint the People with what I said in short Sentences, found some Difficulty, as none of them were quite perfect in the English and Delaware Tongues; so they helped one another, and we laboured along, divine Love attending: And afterwards, feeling my Mind covered with the Spirit of Prayer, I told the Interpreters that I found it in my Heart to pray to God, and believed, if I prayed aright, he would hear me, and expressed my Willingness for them to omit interpreting; so our Meeting ended with a Degree of divine Love: And, before the People went out, I observed Papunehang (the Man who had been zealous in labouring for a Reformation in that Town, being then very tender) spoke to one of the Interpreters; and I was afterwards told that he said in Substance as follows: "I love to feel where Words come from." . . .

In the Fall of this Year, having hired a Man to work, I perceived, in Conversation, that he had been a Soldier in the late

War on this Continent; and, in the Evening, giving a Narrative of his Captivity amongst the Indians, he informed me that he saw two of his Fellow-captives tortured to Death in a very cruel Manner.

This Relation affected me with Sadness, under which I went to Bed; and, the next Morning, soon after awoke, a fresh and living Sense of divine Love was spread over my Mind; in which I had a renewed Prospect of the Nature of that Wisdom from above, which leads to a right Use of all Gifts, both spiritual and temporal, and gives Content therein: Under a Feeling thereof, I wrote as follows:

"Hath he, who gave me a Being attended with many Wants unknown to Brute-creatures, given me a Capacity superior to theirs; and shewn me, that a moderate Application to Business is proper to my present Condition; and that this, attended with his Blessing, may supply all outward Wants, while they remain within the Bounds he hath fixed; and no imaginary Wants, proceeding from an evil Spirit, have any Place in me? Attend then, O My Soul! to this pure Wisdom, as thy sure Conductor through the manifold Dangers in this World.

"Doth Pride lead to Vanity? Doth Vanity form imaginary Wants? Do these Wants prompt Men to exert their Power in requiring that of others, which they themselves would rather be excused from, were the same required of them?

"Do these Proceedings beget hard Thoughts? Do hard Thoughts, when ripe, become Malice? Does Malice, when ripe, become revengeful; and, in the End, inflict terrible Pains on their Fellow-creatures, and spread Desolation in the World?

"Doth Mankind, walking in Uprightness, delight in each other's Happiness? And do these Creatures, capable of this Attainment, by giving way to an evil Spirit, employ their Wit and Strength to afflict and destroy one another?

"Remember then, O my Soul! the Quietude of those in whom Christ governs, and in all thy Proceedings feel after it.

"Doth he condescend to bless thee with his Presence? To move and influence to Action? To dwell in thee, and to walk in thee? Remember then thy Station, as a Being sacred to God; accept of the Strength freely offered thee; and take heed that no

Weakness, in conforming to expensive, unwise, and hardhearted Customs, gendering to Discord and Strife, be given way to. Doth he claim my Body as his Temple, and graciously grant that I may be sacred to him? O! that I may prize this Favour; and that my whole Life may be conformable to this Character!

"Remember, O my Soul! that the Prince of Peace is thy Lord: That he communicates his unmixed Wisdom to his Family; that they, living in perfect Simplicity, may give no just Cause of Offence to any Creature, but may walk as he walked." . . .

JOURNEY TO ENGLAND

As my lodging in the Steerage, now near a Week, hath afforded me sundry Opportunities of seeing, hearing, and feeling, with respect to the Life and Spirit of many poor Sailors, an inward Exercise of Soul hath attended me, in regard to placing our Children and Youth where they may be likely to be exampled and instructed in the pure Fear of the Lord; and I, being much amongst the Seamen, have, from a Motion of Love, sundry Times taken Opportunities, with one of them at a Time alone, and in a free Conversation laboured to turn their Minds toward the Fear of the Lord: And this Day we had a Meeting in the Cabbin, where my Heart was contrite under a Feeling of divine Love.

Now, concerning Lads being trained up as Seamen; I believe a Communication from one Part of the World to some other Parts of it, by Sea, is, at Times, consistent with the Will of our heavenly Father; and to educate some Youth in the Practice of sailing, I believe, may be right: But how lamentable is the present Corruption of the World! how impure are the Channels through which Trade hath a Conveyance! how great is that Danger, to which poor Lads are now exposed, when placed on shipboard to learn the Art of sailing!

O! that all may take Heed and beware of Covetousness! O that all may learn of Christ, who was meek and low of Heart! Then, in faithfully following him, he will teach us to be content with Food and Raiment, without respect to the Customs or Honours of this World.

Men, thus redeemed, will feel a tender Concern for their Fellow-creatures, and a Desire that those in the lowest Stations may be assisted and encouraged; and, where Owners of Ships attain to the perfect Law of Liberty, and are Doers of the Word, these will be blessed in their Deeds.

Rising to work in the Night is not commonly pleasant in any case; but, in dark rainy Nights, it is very disagreeable, even though each Man were furnished with all Conveniences: But, if Men must go out at Midnight, to help manage the Ship in the Rain, and, having small Room to sleep and lay their Garments in, are often beset to furnish themselves for the Watch, their Garments or something relating to their Business being wanting and not easily found, when, from the Urgency occasioned by high Winds, they are hastened and called up suddenly, here is a Trial of Patience on the poor Sailors and the poor Lads their Companions.

If, after they have been on Deck several Hours in the Night, and come down into the Steerage soaking wet, and are so close stowed that proper Convenience for change of Garment is not easily come at, but for Want of proper Room, their wet Garments are thrown in Heaps, and sometimes, through much crowding, are trodden under Foot in going to their Lodgings and getting out of them, and they have great Difficulties, at Times, each one to find his own, here are Trials on the poor Sailors.

Now, as I have been with them in my Lodge, my Heart hath often yearned for them, and tender Desires have been raised in me, that all Owners and Masters of Vessels may dwell in the Love of God, and therein act uprightly; and, by seeking less for Gain, and looking carefully to their Ways, may earnestly labour to remove all Cause of Provocation from the poor Seamen, either to fret or use Excess of Strong-drink; for, indeed, the poor Creatures, at Times, in the Wet and Cold, seem to apply to Strong-drink to supply the Want of other Convenience.

Great Reformation in the World is wanting; and the Necessity of it, amongst these who do Business on great Waters, hath, at this Time, been abundantly opened before me.

Stage-coaches frequently go upwards of an hundred miles in twenty-four hours; and I have heard Friends say, in several places, that it is common for horses to be killed with hard driving, and many others are driven until they grow blind.

Post-boys pursue their business, each one to his stage, all night through the winter: some boys who ride long stages, suffer greatly during winter nights; and at several places I have heard of their being frozen to death. So great is the hurry in the spirit of this world, that in aiming to do business quick and to gain wealth, the creation at this day doth loudly groan!

As my journey has been without a horse, I have had several offers of being assisted on my way in stage-coaches; but have not been in them; nor have I had freedom to send letters by these posts, in the present way of their riding; the stages being so fixed, and one boy dependent on another as to time, that they commonly go upward of one hundred miles in twenty-four hours; and in the cold long winter nights, the poor boys suffer much.

I heard in America of the way of these posts; and cautioned Friends in the General Meeting of ministers and elders of Philadelphia, and in the Yearly Meeting of ministers and elders at London, not to send letters to me on any common occasion by post. And though on this account I may be likely to hear more seldom from my family left behind, yet for righteousness sake, I am through Divine favor made content.

I have felt great distress of mind, since I came on this island, on account of the members of our Society being mixed with the world, in various sorts of business and traffic, carried on in impure channels. Great is the trade of Africa for slaves! and in loading these ships, abundance of people are employed in the factories; amongst whom are many of our Society. Friends in early times refused on a religious principle, to make or trade in superfluities, of which we have many large testimonies on record: but for want of faithfulness some gave way, even some whose examples were of note in our Society; and from thence others took more liberty. Members of our Society worked in superfluities, and bought and sold them; and thus dimness of sight came over many. At length, Friends got into the use of some superfluities in dress, and in the furniture of their houses; and this has spread from less to more, until superfluity of some kinds is common amongst us.

In this declining state, many look at the example one of another, and too much neglect the pure feeling of Truth. Of late years, a deep exercise has attended my mind, that Friends may dig deep, may carefully cast forth the loose matter, and get down to the Rock, the sure foundation, and there hearken to that Divine voice which gives a clear and certain sound. I have felt in that which doth not deceive, that if Friends who have known the Truth, keep in that tenderness of heart, where all views of outward gain are given up, and their trust is only on the Lord, he will graciously lead some to be patterns of deep self-denial in things relating to trade and handicraft labor; and that some who have plenty of the treasures of this world, will set an example of a plain frugal life, and pay wages to such whom they may hire, more liberally than is now customary in some places.

The 23d day of the month; was this day at Preston-Patrick, and had a comfortable meeting. I have several times been entertained at the houses of Friends, who had sundry things about them which had the appearance of outward greatness; and as I have kept inward, way has opened for conversation with such in private, in which Divine goodness has favored us together with heart-tendering times.

The 26th day of the month. Being now at George Crosfields, in the county of Westmoreland, I feel a concern to commit to writing that which to me hath been a case uncommon.

In a time of sickness with the pleurisy, a little upward of two years and a half ago, I was brought so near the gates of death, that I forgot my name: being then desirous to know who I was, I saw a mass of matter of a dull gloomy color, between the south and the east; and was informed, that this mass was human beings in as great misery as they could be, and live; and that I was mixed in with them, and that henceforth I might not consider myself as a distinct or separate being. In this state I remained several hours. I then heard a soft melodious voice, more pure and harmonious than any I had heard before. I believed it was the voice of an angel, who spake to the other angels, and the words were these, "John Woolman is dead." I soon remembered that I once was John Woolman; and being assured that I was alive in the body, I greatly wondered what that heavenly voice could mean.

I believed beyond doubting that it was the voice of an holy angel; but as yet it was a mystery to me.

I was then carried in spirit to the mines, where poor oppressed people were digging rich treasures for those called Christians; and I heard them blaspheme the name of Christ, at which I was grieved; for his name to me was precious.

Then I was informed, that these heathens were told, that those who oppressed them were the followers of Christ; and they said amongst themselves, If Christ directed them to use us in this sort, then Christ is a cruel tyrant.

All this time the song of the angel remained a mystery; and in the morning, my dear wife and some others coming to my bedside, I asked them if they knew who I was; and they telling me I was John Woolman, thought I was light-headed: for I told them not what the angel said, nor was I disposed to talk much to any one; but was very desirous to get so deep, that I might understand this mystery.

My tongue was often so dry, that I could not speak till I had moved it about and gathered some moisture, and as I lay still for a time, at length I felt Divine power prepare my mouth that I could speak; and then I said, "I am crucified with Christ, nevertheless I live; yet not I, but Christ liveth in me; and the life which I now live in the flesh, I live by the faith of the Son of God, who loved me, and gave himself for me."

Then the mystery was opened; and I perceived there was joy in heaven over a sinner who had repented; and that that language (John Woolman is dead) meant no more than the death of my own will. . . .

The like I afterwards went through in several Friends' houses in America, and have also in England, since I came here; and have cause, with humbly reverence, to acknowledge the lovingkindness of my heavenly Father, who hath preserved me in such a tender frame of mind, that none, I believe, have ever been offended at what I have said on that occasion.

After this sickness, I spake not in public meetings for worship for nearly one year; but my mind was very often in company with the oppressed slaves, as I sat in meetings; and though under this dispensation, I was shut up from speaking, yet the spring of the Gospel ministry was many times livingly opened in me; and the Divine gift operated by abundance of weeping, in feeling the oppression of this people. It being long since I passed through this dispensation, and the matter remaining fresh and livingly in my mind, I believe it safest for me to commit it to writing. . . .

I have sometimes felt a necessity to stand up, but that spirit which is of the world hath so much prevailed in many, and the pure life of Truth has been so pressed down, that I have gone forward, not as one travelling in a road cast up and well prepared, but as a man walking through a miry place, in which are stones here and there, safe to step on; but so situated that one step being taken, time is necessary to see where to step next.

I find that in the pure obedience, the mind learns contentment in appearing weak and foolish to that wisdom which is of the world; and in these lowly labors, they who stand in a low place, rightly exercised under the cross, will find nourishment.

The gift is pure, and while the eye is single in attending thereto, the understanding is preserved clear; self is kept out; and we rejoice in filling up that which remains of the afflictions of Christ, for his body's sake, which is the church.

The natural man loveth eloquence, and many love to hear eloquent orations; and if there is not a careful attention to the gift, men who have once labored in the pure Gospel ministry, growing weary of suffering, and ashamed of appearing weak, may kindle a fire, compass themselves about with sparks and walk in the light, not of Christ who is under suffering, but of that fire, which they going from the gift have kindled. And that in hearers which is gone from the meek suffering state into the worldly wisdom, may be warmed with this fire, and speak highly of these labors. That which is of God gathers to God; and that which is of the world is owned by the world. . . .

[A few days after writing these considerations, our dear friend in the course of his religious visits came to the City of York, and attended most of the sittings of the Quarterly Meeting there; but before it was over, was taken ill of the smallpox. Our friend Thomas Priestman and others who attended him, preserved the following minutes of his expressions in the time of his sickness, and of his decease.

First-day, the 27th of the ninth month, 1772. His disorder appeared to be the smallpox: being asked to have a doctor's advice, he signified he had not freedom or liberty in his mind so to do, standing wholly resigned to his will who gave him life, and whose power he had witnessed to raise and heal him in sickness before, when he seemed nigh unto death; and if he was to wind up now, he was perfectly resigned, having no will either to live or die, and did not choose any should be sent for to him. But a young man an apothecary coming of his own accord the next day, and desiring to do something for him, he said he found a freedom to confer with him and the other Friend, about him, and if anything should be proposed, as to medicines that did not come through defiled channels or oppressive hands, he should be willing to consider and take it, so far as he found freedom.

Second-day. He said he felt the disorder to affect his head, so that he could think little, and but as a child; and desired if his understanding should be more affected, to have nothing given him that those about him knew he had a testimony against. . . .

Fourth-day morning, being asked how he felt himself, he meekly answered, I don't know that I have slept this night. I feel the disorder making its progress, but my mind is mercifully preserved in stillness and peace.—Some time after he said he was sensible the pains of death must be hard to bear, but if he escaped them now, he must some time pass through them, and he did not know that he could be better prepared, but had no will in it. He said he had settled his outward affairs to his mind, and had taken leave of his wife and family as never to return, leaving them to the Divine protection; adding, "and though I feel them near to me at this time, yet I freely give them up, having a hope that they will be provided for." A little after he said, "This trial is made easier than I could have thought, my will being wholly taken away; for if I was anxious for the event, it would have been harder, but I am not, and my mind enjoys a perfect calm."

In the night a young woman having given him something to drink, he said, "My child, thou seems very kind to me, a poor creature, the Lord will reward thee for it." Awhile after he cried out with great earnestness of spirit, "Oh, my Father! my Father!" and soon after he said, "Oh, my Father! my Father! how comfortable art thou to my soul in this trying season." Being asked if he could take a little nourishment, after some pause he replied, "My child, I cannot tell what to say to it; I seem nearly arrived where my soul shall have rest from all its troubles." . . .

Another time he said, he had long had a view of visiting this nation, and some time before he came had a dream, in which he saw himself in the northern parts of it, and that the spring of the Gospel was opened in him much as in the beginning of Friends, such as George Fox and William Dewsbury; and he, saw the different states of the people as clearly as he had ever seen flowers in a garden; but in his going along he was suddenly stopped, though he could not see for what end; but looking toward home, fell into a flood of tears which waked him.

At another time he said, "My draught seemed strongest toward the North, and I mentioned in my own Monthly Meeting, that attending the Quarterly Meeting at York, and being there looked like home to me."

. . . Having repeatedly consented to take medicine with a view to settle his stomach, but without effect: the Friend then waiting on him, said through distress, "What shall I do now?" He answered with great composure, "Rejoice evermore, and in everything give thanks," but added a little after, "This is sometimes hard to come at." . . .

About the second hour on fourth-day morning he asked for pen and ink, and at several times with much difficulty wrote thus, "I believe my being here is in the wisdom of Christ, I know not as to life or death."

About a quarter before six o'clock the same morning he seemed to fall into an easy sleep, which continued about half an hour, when seeming to awake, he breathed a few times with more difficulty, and expired without sigh, groan, or struggle.]

THE QUAKER OBSERVED

An happier system could not have been devised.
—HECTOR ST. JOHN DE CRÈVECŒUR

The Religion of the Quakers

VOLTAIRE

[*Voltaire was by no means the first man to write about the Quakers. And the answer to F. Bugg's plaintive cry, "Who hath wrote so much as the Quakers?" is, "The anti-Quakers." They wrote more. There were more of them; and they were less inhibited, though this is saying a good deal. Fox himself wrote, "The pastor came and asked me who must be damned, being a high motionist and flashy man . . . and I was moved of a sudden to tell him that what spoke in him was to be damned."*

The present-day practice of avoiding the controversial would have struck a seventeenth-century person as simple-minded. Why waste words (unless you are young and in love) on what you both agree on? So anti-Quakers went "fanatic hunting"; and Quakers had what they called "threshing times"; and speakers rose in church, when the sermon was finished, to refute, if they could, the preacher; and after this set-to, members of the congregation ran out into the streets, crying (as we do baseball scores), "So-and-so has won the day."

"Much to be pitied," Voltaire wrote, "are they who need the help of religion to be honest men." This is not even half the truth. Even more to be pitied are those who need that help and don't get it. And finally,

and even more importantly, there are religious individuals whose honesty brought them to their religion—not vice versa.

Voltaire interviewed Andrew Pitt, the old Quaker of Hampstead, much in the spirit of present day TV interviewers who make the occasion one for the display of their personal superiority. Andrew Pitt was declaring something Voltaire had already shut himself off from—as the old Darwin had shut himself off from (and lamented it) music and poetry. He was declaring "heart-knowledge." In the words of Barclay, whom Pitt recommended to Voltaire, he was speaking of "what I have heard with the ears of my soul and seen with my inward eyes, and my hands have handled of the Word of Life, and what hath been inwardly manifested to me of the things of God."

Suave Voltaire tells us he "promised to peruse this piece; and my Quaker thought he had already made a convert." Voltaire knows we shall appreciate the irony of this. Voltaire a Quaker! Poor daft old Andrew Pitt!]

—————

Being of opinion that the doctrine and history of so extraordinary a sect as the Quakers were very well deserving the curiosity of every thinking man, I resolved to make myself acquainted with them, and for that purpose made a visit to one of the most eminent of that sect in England, who, after having been in trade for thirty years, had the wisdom to prescribe limits to his fortune, and to his desires, and withdrew to a small but pleasant retirement in the country, not many miles from London. Here it was that I made him my visit. His house was small, but neatly built, and with no other ornaments but those of decency and convenience. The Quaker himself was a hale, ruddy-complexioned old man, who had never suffered from sickness, because he had always been a stranger to passions and intemperance. I never in my life saw any one have a more noble, or a more engaging aspect. He was dressed after the fashion of those of his persuasion, in a plain coat, without plaits in the side, or buttons on the pockets and sleeves; and he wore a beaver hat, the brim of which flapped downward like those of our clergy. He advanced toward me without moving his hat, or making the least inclination of his body; but there appeared more real politeness in the open, humane air of his countenance, than in drawing one leg behind the other, and carrying that in the hand which is made to be worn on the head. "Friend," said he, "I perceive thou art a stranger, if I can do thee any service thou hast only to let me know it." "Sir," I replied, bowing my body, and sliding one leg toward him, as is the custom with us, "I flatter myself that my curiosity, which you will allow to be just, will not give you any offence, and that you will do me the honor to inform me of the particulars of your religion." "The people of thy country," answered the Quaker, "are too full of their bows and their compliments; but I never yet met with one of them who had so much curiosity as thyself. Come in and let us dine first together." I still continued to make some silly compliments, it not being easy to disengage at once oneself from habits we have been long accustomed to; and after taking part of a frugal meal, which began and ended with a prayer to God, I began to put questions to my plain host.

I opened with that which good Catholics have more than once made to Huguenots. "My dear sir," said I, "were you ever baptized?" "No, friend," replied the Quaker, "nor any of my brethren." "Zounds!" said I to him, "you are not Christians then!" "Friend," replied the old man, in a soft tone of voice, "do not swear; we are Christians, but we do not think that sprinkling a few drops of water on a child's head makes him a Christian." "My God!" exclaimed I, shocked at his impiety, "have you then forgotten that Christ was baptized by St. John?" "Friend," replied the mild Quaker, "once again, do not swear. Christ was baptized by John, but He Himself never baptized any one; now we profess ourselves disciples of Christ, and not of John." "Mercy on us," cried I, "what a fine subject you would be for the holy inquisitor! In the name of God, my good old man, let me baptize you." "Were that all," replied he very gravely, "we would submit cheerfully to be baptized, purely in compliance with thy weakness; for we do not condemn any person who uses that rite; but, on the other hand, we think that those who profess a religion of so holy and spiritual nature as that of Christ, ought to abstain to the utmost of their power from Jewish ceremonies."

"Why, there again!" said I, "baptism a Jewish ceremony!"
"Yes, my friend," said he, "and so truly Jewish, that many Jews
use the baptism of John to this day. Peruse ancient authors, and
they will show thee that John only revived this practice, and that
it was in use among the Hebrews long before his time, the same
as the pilgrimage to Mecca was among the Ishmaelites. Jesus
indeed submitted to be baptized of John, in the like manner as
He had undergone circumcision; but both the one and the other
ceremony were to end in the baptism of Christ, that baptism of
the spirit, that ablution of the soul which is the salvation of
mankind. Thus the forerunner John said, 'I indeed baptize you
with water unto repentance, but he that cometh after me is
mightier than I, whose shoes I am not worthy to bear: he shall
baptize you with the Holy Ghost, and with fire.' St. Paul
likewise, the great apostle of the Gentiles, writes thus to the
Corinthians: 'Christ sent me not to baptize but to preach the
gospel.' Accordingly Paul never baptized but two persons with
water, and that against his inclination. He circumcised his
disciple, Timothy; and the other apostles circumcised all those
who were desirous of it. Art thou circumcised?" added he. "I
really have not that honor," replied I. "Wilt thou, friend?"
replied the Quaker; "thou art a Christian without being circumcised, and I am one without being baptized."

Thus did my pious host make a false but very specious
application of three or four passages of Holy Writ, which seemed
to favor the tenets of his sect; but at the same time forgot, very
sincerely, above a hundred others that directly overturned
them. I resolved not to contend with him, as there is nothing to
be gained by arguing with an enthusiast: one should never
pretend to reveal to a lover his mistress' faults, to a lawyer the
weakness of one's cause, nor force the truth upon a fanatic.
Accordingly I proceeded to other questions.

"Pray," said I to him, "in what manner do you communicate?" "We have no such ceremony among us," replied he.
"How!" said I, "have you no communion?" "No," answered he;
"no other than that of hearts." He began to quote his texts of
Scripture, and read me a very curious lecture against the sacrament; and harangued with a tone of inspiration to prove that the

sacraments were mere human inventions, and that the word
"sacrament" was not once mentioned in the Scripture. "I must
ask thy excuse," said he, "for my ignorance; for I am sensible I
have not employed a hundredth part of the arguments that
might be made use of, to prove the truth of our religion: but thou
mayest see them all amply unfolded in the *Exposition of Our
Faith*, written by Robert Barclay. It is one of the best books that
ever came from the hand of man; our very adversaries confess it
is dangerous, and that is sufficient alone to prove its goodness."
I promised to peruse this piece; and my Quaker thought he had
already made a convert.

He then proceeded to give me a brief account of certain
singularities, which make this sect the contempt of others.
"Confess," said he, "that it was very difficult for thee to refrain
from laughing, when I answered all thy compliments without
uncovering my head, and at the same time spoke to thee only
with 'thee' and 'thou.' However, thou appearest to me too well
read not to know, that, in Christ's time, no nation was so
ridiculous as to use the plural for the singular. They said to
Augustus Caesar himself, 'I love thee,' 'I beseech thee,' 'I thank
thee'; and he would not even suffer himself to be called 'domine';
'sir.' It was not till long after his time that men took the
ridiculous notion of having themselves called 'you,' instead of
'thou,' as if they were double, and usurped the impertinent titles
of 'lordship,' 'eminence,' and 'holiness,' which poor reptiles
bestow on other reptiles like themselves; assuring them, that
they are, 'with the most profound respect,' and an infamous
falsehood, their 'most obedient humble servants.' It is the more
effectually to secure ourselves against this shameful traffic of
lies and flattery, that we 'thee' and 'thou' a king, with the
freedom as we do his meanest servant; and salute no person, as
owing mankind only charity, and respect only to the laws.

"We dress also differently from others, and this purely that
it may be a perpetual warning to us not to imitate them. While
others pride themselves on wearing the badges of their several
dignities, we confine ourselves to those of Christian humility.
We shun all the assemblies of the gay, we avoid places of
diversions of all kinds, and carefully abstain from gaming; for

wretched would be our state, indeed, were we to fill with such levities the heart that ought to be the habitation of God. We never swear, not even in a court of justice; being of opinion, that the name of the Most High ought not be prostituted in the frivolous contests between man and man. When we are obliged to appear before a magistrate, upon the concern of others—for lawsuits are unknown among the Friends—we affirm the truth by our 'yea' or 'nay' and they believe us on our simple affirmation, while other Christians are daily perjuring themselves on the blessed Gospels. We never take up arms, not that we are fearful of death; on the contrary, we bless the instant that unites us to the Being of beings. The reason is, that we are neither wolves, tigers, nor mastiffs, but men and Christians. Our God, who has commanded us to love our enemies, and to suffer without repining, can certainly not order us to cross the seas, and cut the throats of our fellow-creatures, as often as murderers, clothed in scarlet, and wearing caps two feet high, enlist peaceful citizens by a noise made with two sticks on an ass' skin extended. And when, after the gaining of a battle, all London blazes with illuminations, when the air glows with fireworks, and a noise is heard of thanksgivings, of bells, of organs, and of cannon, we groan in silence for the cruel havoc which occasions these public rejoicings."

Such was the substance of the conversation I had with this very singular person; and I was greatly surprised when, the Sunday following, he came to take me with him to one of their meetings. There are several of these in London; but that to which he carried me stands near the famous pillar called the Monument. The brethren were already assembled when I entered with my guide. There might be about four hundred men and three hundred women in the place. The women hid their faces with their hoods, and the men were covered with their broad-brimmed hats. All were sitting, and there was a universal silence amongst them. I passed through the midst of them; but not one lifted up his eyes to look at me. This silence lasted a quarter of an hour; when at last an old man rose up, took off his hat, and after making a number of wry faces, and groaning in a most lamentable manner, he, half-mouthing, half snuffling, threw out a heap of unaccountable stuff—taken, as he thought, from the Gospel—which neither himself nor any of his auditors understood. When this religious buffoon had ended his curious soliloquy, and the assembly broke up, very much edified, and very stupid, I asked my guide how it was possible the judicious part of them could suffer such incoherent prating? "We are obliged," said he, "to suffer it, because no one knows, when a brother rises up to hold forth, whether he will be moved by the spirit or by folly. In this uncertainty, we listen patiently to every one. We even allow our women to speak in public; two or three of them are often inspired at the same time, and then a most charming noise is heard in the Lord's house." "You have no priests, then?" said I. "No, no, friend," replied the Quaker; "heaven make us thankful!" Then opening one of the books of their sect, he read the following words in an emphatic tone: "'God forbid we should presume to ordain any one to receive the Holy Spirit on the Lord's day, in exclusion to the rest of the faithful!' Thanks to the Almighty, we are the only people upon earth that have no priests! Wouldst thou deprive us of so happy a distinction? Wherefore should we abandon our child to hireling nurses, when we ourselves have milk enough to nourish it? These mercenary creatures would quickly domineer in our houses, and oppress both the mother and the child. God has said, 'You have received freely, give as freely.' Shall we, after this injunction, barter, as it were, the Gospel; sell the Holy Spirit, and make of an assembly of Christians a mere shop of traders? We do not give money to a set of men, clothed in black, to assist our poor, to bury our dead, or to preach to the brethren; these holy offices are held in too high esteem by us to entrust them to others." "But how," said I, with some warmth; "how can you pretend to know whether your discourse is really inspired by the Almighty?" "Whosoever," replied my friend, "shall implore Christ to enlighten him, and shall publish the truths contained in the Gospel, of which he inwardly feels, such a one may be assured that he is inspired by the Lord." He then overwhelmed me with a multitude of Scripture quotations, which proved, as he imagined, that there is no such thing as Christianity, without an immediate revelation; and added these remarkable words:

"When thou movest one of thy limbs, is it moved by thy own power? Certainly not; for this limb is often liable to involuntary motions; consequently He who created thy body gives motion to this earthy tabernacle. Or are the several ideas, of which thy soul receives the impression, of thy own formation? Still less so; for they come upon thee whether thou wilt or no, consequently thou receivest thy ideas from Him who created thy soul. But as He leaves thy heart at full liberty, He gives thy mind such ideas as thy heart may deserve; if thou livest in God, thou actest and thinkest in God. After this, thou needest but open thine eyes to that light which enlightens all mankind, and then thou wilt perceive the truth, and make others perceive it." "Why, this," said I, "is our Malebranche's doctrine to a tittle." "I am acquainted with thy Malebranche," said he; "he had something of the Quaker in him; but he was not enough so."

These are the main particulars that I have been able to gather, concerning the doctrine of the Quakers. . . .

―――――――――

"... Gay without Levity, ... Cheerful without Loud Laughs."

[FROM *Letters from an American Farmer*]

HECTOR ST. JOHN DE CRÈVECŒUR

[*Hazlitt called Crèvecœur "one of the three notable writers" produced in the colonies in the eighteenth century. W. B. Blake, who edited the Everyman edition of* Letters from an American Farmer, *called Crèvecœur "an Eighteenth-century Thoreau." It is easier to agree with Hazlitt than with Blake. "I married," writes Crèvecœur, "and this perfectly reconciled me to my situation; my house . . . no longer appeared gloomy and solitary as before." Imagine a wife at Walden, "reconciling" Thoreau to his "situation." But there is much about Crèvecœur which would have pleased Thoreau. "After I have done my sawing . . . I prepare for a week's jaunt in the woods, not to hunt either the deer or the bears . . . but to catch the more harmless bees."*

And Thoreau would certainly have shared Crèvecœur's interest in Mr. Bertram, the botanist. While one feels that Thoreau would have had some sympathy with the Quakers (and while he, in a letter, expressed admiration for Fox), what he said on the subject does not reveal it. "There is a Quaker meetinghouse," he writes, "such an ugly shed, without a tree or bush about it. . . . It is altogether repulsive to me, like a powderhouse or grave. And even the quietness and perhaps unworldliness of an aged Quaker has something ghostly and saddening about it as it were a mere preparation for the grave." So Thoreau, on the day after Christmas, 1854, ends two sentences about Quakers with the word "grave."

Crèvecœur and Friend Ivan see nothing ghostly and saddening about the Quakers. Friend Ivan calls his visit with them "the golden days of my riper years." Crèvecœur had never before in his life seen "so much unaffected mirth." Is all in the eye of the beholder? Was that light by which Thoreau saw the lives of other men as "quiet desperation" one reflected outward from the gnawing fox-fire of his own misery?|

The manners of the Friends are entirely founded on that simplicity which is their boast, and their most distinguished characteristic; and those manners have acquired the authority of laws. Here they are strongly attached to plainness of dress, as well as to that of language; insomuch that though some part of it may be ungrammatical, yet should any person who was born and brought up here, attempt to speak more correctly, he would be looked upon as a fop or an innovator. On the other hand, should a stranger come here and adopt their idiom in all its purity (as they deem it) this accomplishment would immediately procure him the most cordial reception; and they would cherish him like an ancient member of their society. So many impositions have they suffered on this account, that they begin now indeed to grow more cautious. They are so tenacious of their ancient habits of industry and frugality, that if any of them were to be seen with a long coat made of English cloth, on any other than the first-day (Sunday), he would be greatly ridiculed and censured; he would be looked upon as a careless spendthrift, whom it would be unsafe to trust, and in vain to relieve. A few years ago two single-horse chairs were imported from Boston, to the great offence of these prudent citizens; nothing appeared to them more culpable than the use of such gaudy painted vehicles, in contempt of the more useful and more simple single-horse carts of their fathers. This piece of extravagant and unknown luxury almost caused a schism, and set every tongue a-going; some predicted the approaching ruin of those families that had imported them; others feared the dangers of example; never since the foundation of the town had there happened anything which so much alarmed this primitive community. One of the possessors of these profane chairs, filled with repentance, wisely sent it back to the continent; the other, more obstinate and perverse, in defiance to all remonstrances, persisted in the use of his chair until by degrees they became more reconciled to it; though I observed that the wealthiest and the most respectable people still go to meeting or to their farms in a single-horse cart with a decent awning fixed over it: indeed, if you consider their sandy soil, and the badness of their roads, these appear to be the best contrived vehicles for this island.

Idleness is the most heinous sin that can be committed in Nantucket: an idle man would soon be pointed out as an object of compassion: for idleness is considered as another word for want and hunger. This principle is so thoroughly well understood, and is become so universal, so prevailing a prejudice, that literally speaking, they are never idle. Even if they go to the market-place, which is (if I may be allowed the expression) the coffee-house of the town, either to transact business, or to converse with their friends; they always have a piece of cedar in their hands, and while they are talking, they will, as it were instinctively, employ themselves in converting it into something useful, either in making bungs or spoyls for their oil casks, or other useful articles. I must confess, that I have never seen more ingenuity in the use of the knife; thus the most idle moments of their lives become usefully employed. In the many hours of leisure which their long cruises afford them, they cut and carve a variety of boxes and pretty toys, in wood, adapted to different uses; which they bring home as testimonies of remembrance to their wives or sweethearts. They have showed me a variety of little bowls and other implements, executed cooper-wise, with the greatest neatness and elegance. You will be pleased to remember they are all brought up to the trade of coopers, be their future intentions or fortunes what they may; therefore almost every man in this island has always two knives in his pocket, one much larger than the other; and though they hold everything that is called fashion in the utmost contempt, yet they are as difficult to please, and as extravagant in the choice and price of their knives, as any young buck in Boston would be about his hat, buckles, or coat. As soon as a knife is injured, or superseded by a more convenient one, it is carefully laid up in some corner of their desk. I once saw upwards of fifty thus preserved at Mr. —————— 's, one of the worthiest men on this island; and among the whole, there was not one that perfectly resembled another. As the sea excursions are often very long, their wives in their absence are necessarily obliged to transact business, to settle accounts, and in short, to rule and provide for their families. These circumstances being often repeated, give women the abilities as well as a taste for that kind of superintendency, to which, by their prudence and good management, they seem to be in general very equal. This employment ripens their judgment, and justly entitles them to a rank superior to that of other wives; and this is the principal reason why those of Nantucket as well as those of Montreal are so fond of society, so affable, and so conversant with the affairs of the world. The men at their return, weary with the fatigues of the sea, full of confidence and love, cheerfully give their consent to every transaction that has happened during their absence, and all is joy and peace. "Wife, thee hast done well," is the general approbation they receive, for their application and industry. What would the men do without the agency of these faithful mates? The absence of so many of them at particular seasons, leaves the town quite desolate; and this mournful situation disposes the women to go to each other's house much oftener than when their husbands are at home; hence the custom of incessant visiting has infected every one, and even those whose husbands do not go abroad. The house is always cleaned before they set out, and with peculiar alacrity they pursue their intended visit, which consists of a social chat, a dish of tea, and an hearty supper. When the good man of the house returns from his labour, he peaceably goes after his wife and brings her home; meanwhile the young fellows, equally vigilant, easily find out which is the most convenient house, and there they assemble with the girls of the neighborhood. Instead of cards, musical instruments, or songs, they relate stories of their whaling voyages, their various sea adventures, and talk of the different coasts and people they have visited. "The island of Catharine in the Brazil," says one, "is a very droll island, it is inhabited by none but men; women are not permitted to come in sight of it; not a woman is there on the whole island. Who among us is not glad it is not so here? The Nantucket girls and boys beat the world." At this innocent sally the titter goes round, they whisper to one another their spontaneous reflections: puddings, pies, and custards never fail to be produced on such occasions; for I believe there never were any people in their circumstances, who live so well, even to superabundance. As inebriation is unknown, and music, singing, and dancing, are held in equal detestation, they never could fill all the vacant hours of their lives without the repast of the table. Thus these young people sit and talk, and divert themselves as well as they can; if any one has lately returned from a cruise, he is generally the speaker of the night; they often all laugh and talk together, but they are happy, and would not exchange their pleasures for those of the most brilliant assemblies in Europe. This lasts until the father and mother return; when all retire to their respective homes, the men re-conducting the partners of their affections.

Thus they spend many of the youthful evenings of their lives; no wonder therefore, that they marry so early. But no sooner have they undergone this ceremony than they cease to appear so cheerful and gay; the new rank they hold in the society impresses them with more serious ideas than were entertained before. The title of master of a family necessarily requires more

solid behavior and deportment; the new wife follows in the
trammels of Custom, which are as powerful as the tyranny of
fashion; she gradually advises and directs; the new husband goes
to sea, he leaves her to learn and exercise the new government,
in which she is entered. Those who stay at home are full as
passive in general, at least with regard to the inferior depart-
ments of the family. But you must imagine from this account
that the Nantucket wives are turbulent, of high temper, and
difficult to be ruled; on the contrary, the wives of Sherburn in so
doing, comply only with the prevailing custom of the island: the
husbands, equally submissive to the ancient and respectable
manners of their country, submit, without ever suspecting that
there can be any impropriety. Were they to behave otherwise,
they would be afraid of subverting the principles of their society
by altering its ancient rules; thus both parties are perfectly
satisfied, and all is peace and concord. . . .

To this dexterity in managing the husband's business
whilst he is absent, the Nantucket wives unite a great deal of
industry. They spin, or cause to be spun in their houses,
abundance of wool and flax; and would be for ever disgraced and
looked upon as idlers if all the family were not clad in good, neat,
and sufficient homespun cloth. First Days are the only seasons
when it is lawful for both sexes to exhibit some garments of
English manufacture; even these are of the most moderate
price, and of the gravest colours: there is no kind of difference
in their dress, they are clad alike, and resemble in that respect
the members of one family. . . .

Such an island inhabited as I have described, is not the
place where gay travellers should resort, in order to enjoy that
variety of pleasures the more splendid towns of this continent
afford. Not that they are wholly deprived of what we might call
recreations, and innocent pastimes; but opulence, instead of
luxuries and extravagancies, produces nothing more here than
an increase of business, an additional degree of hospitality,
greater neatness in the preparation of dishes, and better wines.
They often walk and converse with each other, as I have
observed before; and upon extraordinary occasions, will take a ride
to Palpus, where there is an house of entertainment; but these

rural amusements are conducted upon the same plan of moderation, as those in town. They are so simple as hardly to be described; the pleasure of going and returning together; of chatting and walking about, of throwing the bar, heaving stones, etc., are the only entertainments they are acquainted with. This is all they practise, and all they seem to desire. The house at Palpus is the general resort of those who possess the luxury of a horse and chaise, as well as of those who still retain, as the majority do, a predilection for their primitive vehicle. By resorting to that place they enjoy a change of air, they taste the pleasures of exercise; perhaps an exhilarating bowl, not at all improper in this climate, affords the chief indulgence known to these people, on the days of their greatest festivity. The mounting a horse, must afford a most pleasing exercise to those men who are so much at sea. I was once invited to that house, and had the satisfaction of conducting thither one of the many beauties of that island (for it abounds with handsome women) dressed in all the bewitching attire of the most charming simplicity: like the rest of the company, she was cheerful without loud laughs, and smiling without affectation. They all appeared gay without levity. I had never before in my life seen so much unaffected mirth, mixed with so much modesty. The pleasures of the day were enjoyed with the greatest liveliness and the most innocent freedom; no disgusting pruderies, no coquettish airs tarnished this enlivening assembly: they behaved according to their native dispositions, the only rules of decorum with which they were acquainted. What would an European visitor have done here without a fiddle, without a dance, without cards? He would have called it an insipid assembly, and ranked this among the dullest days he had ever spent. This rural excursion had a very great affinity to those practised in our province, with this difference only, that we have no objection to the sportive dance, though conducted by the rough accents of some self-taught African fiddler. We returned as happy as we went; and the brightness of the moon kindly lengthened a day which had past, like other agreeable ones, with singular rapidity. . . .

There are but two congregations in this town. They assemble every Sunday in meeting houses, as simple as the dwelling of the people; and there is but one priest on the whole island. What would a good Portuguese observe?—But one single priest to instruct a whole island, and to direct their consciences! It is even so; each individual knows how to guide his own, and is content to do it, as well as he can. This lonely clergyman is a Presbyterian minister, who has a very large and respectable congregation; the other is composed of Quakers, who you know admit of no particular person, who in consequence of being ordained becomes exclusively entitled to preach, to catechize, and to receive certain salaries for his trouble. Among them, every one may expound the Scriptures, who thinks he is called so to do; beside, as they admit of neither sacrament, baptism, nor any other outward forms whatever, such a man would be useless. Most of these people are continually at sea, and have often the most urgent reasons to worship the Parent of Nature in the midst of the storms which they encounter. These two sects live in perfect peace and harmony with each other; those ancient times of religious discords are now gone (I hope never to return) when each thought it meritorious, not only to damn the other, which would have been nothing, but to persecute and murther one another, for the glory of that Being, who requires no more of us, than that we should love one another and live! Every one goes to that place of worship which he likes best, and thinks not that his neighbour does wrong by not following him; each busily employed in their temporal affairs, is less vehement about spiritual ones, and fortunately you will find at Nantucket neither idle drones, voluptuous devotees, ranting enthusiasts, nor sour demagogues. I wish I had it in my power to send the most persecuting bigot I could find in _____ to the whale fisheries; in less than three or four years you would find him a much more tractable man, and therefore a better Christian. . . .

The Presbyterians live in great charity with them, and with one another; their minister as a true pastor of the gospel, inculcates to them the doctrines it contains, the rewards it promises, the punishments it holds out to those who shall commit injustice. Nothing can be more disencumbered likewise from useless ceremonies and trifling forms than their mode of worship; it might with great propriety have been called a truly primitive one, had that of the Quakers never appeared. As fellow Christians, obeying the same legislator, they love and mutually assist each other in all their wants; as fellow labourers they unite with cordiality and without the least rancour in all their temporal schemes: no other emulation appears among them but in their sea excursions, in the art of fitting out their vessels; in that of sailing, in harpooning the whale, and in bringing home the greatest harvest. As fellow subjects they cheerfully obey the same laws, and pay the same duties: but let me not forget another peculiar characteristic of this community: there is not a slave I believe on the whole island, at least among the Friends; whilst slavery prevails all around them, this society alone, lamenting that shocking insult offered to humanity, have given the world a singular example of moderation, disinterestedness, and Christian charity, in emancipating their Negroes. I shall explain to you farther, the singular virtue and merit to which it is so justly entitled by having set before the rest of their fellow-subjects, so pleasing, so edifying a reformation. Happy the people who are subject to so mild a government; happy the government which has to rule over such harmless, and such industrious subjects!

Comrade Iwan Visits Friend John Bertram

[FROM *Letters from an American Farmer*]

HECTOR ST. JOHN DE CRÈVECŒUR

From Mr. IW——N AL——Z, a Russian Gentleman; Describing the visit he paid at my request to Mr. John Bertram, the celebrated Pennsylvania botanist:

Examine this flourishing province, in whatever light you will, the eyes as well as the mind of an European traveller are equally delighted; because a diffusive happiness appears in every part: happiness which is established on the broadest basis. The name of *Penn*, that simple but illustrious citizen, does more honour to the English nation than those of many of their kings.

In order to convince you that I have not bestowed undeserved praises in my former letters on this celebrated government; and that either nature or the climate seems to be more favourable here to the arts and sciences, than to any other American province; let us together, agreeable to your desire, pay a visit to Mr. John Bertram, the first botanist, in this new hemisphere: become such by a native impulse of disposition. It is to this simple man that America is indebted for several useful discoveries, and the knowledge of many new plants. I had been greatly prepossessed in his favour by the extensive correspondence which I knew he held with the most eminent Scotch and French botanists; I knew also that he had been honoured with that of Queen Ulrica of Sweden.

His house is small, but decent; there was something peculiar in its first appearance, which seemed to distinguish it from those of his neighbours: a small tower in the middle of it, not only helped to strengthen it but afforded convenient room for a staircase. Every disposition of the fields, fences, and trees, seemed to bear the marks of perfect order and regularity, which in rural affairs, always indicate a prosperous industry.

I was received at the door by a woman dressed extremely neat and simple, who without courtesying, or any other ceremonial, asked me, with an air of benignity, who I wanted? I answered, I should be glad to see Mr. Bertram. If thee wilt step in and take a chair, I will send for him. No, I said, I had rather have the pleasure of walking through his farm, I shall easily find him out, with your directions. After a little time I perceived the Schuylkill, winding through delightful meadows, and soon cast my eyes on a new-made bank, which seemed greatly to confine its stream. After having walked on its top a considerable way I at last reached the place where ten men were at work. I asked, if any of them could tell me where Mr. Bertram was? An elderly looking man, with wide trousers and a large leather apron on, looking at me said, "My name is Bertram, dost thee want me?" Sir, I am come on purpose to converse with you, if you can be spared from your labour. "Very easily," he answered, "I direct and advise more than I work." We walked toward the house, where he made me take a chair while he went to put on clean clothes, after which he returned and sat down by me. The fame of your knowledge, said I, in American botany, and your well-known hospitality, have induced me to pay you a visit, which I hope you will not think troublesome: I should be glad to spend a few hours in your garden. "The greatest advantage," replied he, "which I receive from what thee callest my botanical fame, is the pleasure which it often procureth me in receiving the visits of friends and foreigners: but our jaunt into the garden must be postponed for the present, as the bell is ringing for dinner." We entered into a large hall, where there was a long table full of victuals; at the lowest part sat his Negroes, his hired men were next, then the family and myself; and at the head, the venerable father and his wife presided. Each reclined his head and said his prayers, divested of the tedious cant of some, and of the ostentatious style of others. "After the luxuries of our cities," observed he, "this plain fare must appear to thee a severe fast." By no means, Mr. Bertram, this honest country dinner convinces me, that you receive me as a friend and an old acquaintance. "I am glad of it, for thee art heartily welcome. I never knew how to use ceremonies; they are insufficient proofs of sincerity; our society, besides, are utterly strangers to what the world calleth polite expressions. We treat others as we treat ourselves." . . .

Pray, Mr. Bertram, what banks are those which you are making: to what purpose is so much expense and so much labour bestowed? "Friend Iwan, no branch of industry was ever more profitable to any country, as well as to the proprietors; the Schuylkill in its many windings once covered a great extent of ground, though its waters were but shallow even in our highest tides: and though some parts were always dry, yet the whole of this great tract presented to the eye nothing but a putrid swampy soil, useless either for the plough or for the scythe. The proprietors of these grounds are now incorporated; we yearly pay to the treasurer of the company a certain sum, which makes an aggregate, superior to the casualities that generally happen either by inundations or the musk squash. It is owing to this happy contrivance that so many thousand acres of meadows have been rescued from the Schuykill, which now both enricheth and embellisheth so much of the neighborhood of our city. Our brethren of Salem in New Jersey have carried the art of banking to a still higher degree of perfection." . . .

By this time the working part of the family had finished their dinner, and had retired with a decency and silence which pleased me much. Soon after I heard, as I thought, a distant concert of instruments.—However simple and pastoral your fare was, Mr. Bertram, this is the dessert of a prince; pray what is this I hear? "Thee must not be alarmed, it is of a piece with the rest of thy treatment, friend Iwan." Anxious I followed the sound, and by ascending the staircase, found that it was the effect of the wind through the strings of an Eolian harp; an instrument which I had never before seen. After dinner we quaffed an honest bottle of Madeira wine, without the irksome labour of toasts, healths, or sentiments; and then retired into his study. . . .

Our walks and botanical observations engrossed so much of our time, that the sun was almost down ere I thought of returning to Philadelphia; I regretted that the day had been so short, as I had not spent so rational a one for a long time before. I wanted to stay, yet was doubtful whether it would not appear improper, being an utter stranger. Knowing, however, that I was visiting the least ceremonious people in the world, I bluntly informed him of the pleasure I had enjoyed, and with the desire I had of staying a few days with him. "Thee art as welcome as if I was thy father; thee art no stranger; thy desire of knowledge, thy being a foreigner besides, entitleth thee to consider my house as thine own, as long as thee pleaseth: use thy time with the most perfect freedom; I too shall do so myself." I thankfully accepted the kind invitation.

We went to view his favourite bank; he showed me the principles and method on which it was erected; and we walked over the grounds which had been already drained. The whole store of nature's kind luxuriance seemed to have been exhausted on these beautiful meadows; he made me count the amazing number of cattle and horses now feeding on solid bottoms, which but a few years before had been covered with water. Thence we rambled through his fields, where the right-angular fences, the heaps of pitched stones, the flourishing clover, announced the best husbandry, as well as the most assiduous attention. His cows were then returning home, deep bellied, short legged, having udders ready to burst; seeking with seeming toil to be delivered from the great exuberance they contained: he next showed me his orchard, formerly planted on a barren sandy soil, but long since converted into one of the richest spots in that vicinage.

"This," said he, "is altogether the fruit of my own contrivance; I purchased some years ago the privilege of a small spring, about a mile and a half from hence, which at a considerable expense I have brought to this reservoir; therein I throw old lime, ashes, horse-dung, etc., and twice a week I let it run, thus impregnated; I regularly spread on this ground in the fall, old hay, straw, and whatever damaged fodder I have about my barn. By these simple means I mow, one year with another, fifty-three hundreds of excellent hay per acre, from a soil, which scarcely produced five-fingers (a small plant resembling strawberries) some years before." This is, Sir, a miracle in husbandry; happy the country which is cultivated by a society of men, whose application and taste lead them to prosecute and accomplish useful works. "I am not the only person who do these things," he said, "wherever water can be had it is always turned to that important use; wherever a farmer can water his meadows, the greatest crops of the best hay and excellent after-grass, are the sure rewards of his labours." . . .

Pray, Mr. Bertram, when did you imbibe the first wish to cultivate the science of botany; was you regularly bred to it in Philadelphia? "I have never received any other education than barely reading and writing; this small farm was all the patrimony my father left me, certain debts and the want of meadows kept me rather low in the beginning of my life; my wife brought me nothing in money, all her riches consisted in her good temper and great knowledge of housewifery. I scarcely know how to trace my steps in the botanical career; they appear to me now like unto a dream: but thee mayest rely on what I shall relate, though I know that some of our friends have laughed at it." I am not one of those people, Mr. Bertram, who aim at finding out the ridiculous in what is sincerely and honestly averred. "Well, then, I'll tell thee: One day I was very busy in holding my plough (for thee seest that I am but a ploughman) and being weary I ran under the shade of a tree to repose myself. I cast my eyes on a daisy, I plucked it mechanically and viewed it with more curiousity than common country farmers are wont to do; and observed therein very many distinct parts, some perpendicular, some horizontal. What a shame, said my mind, or something that inspired my mind, that thee shouldest have employed so many flowers and plants, without being acquainted with their struc-tures and their uses! This seeming inspiration suddenly awak-ened my curiousity, for these were not thoughts to which I had been accustomed. I returned to my team, but this new desire did not quit my mind; I mentioned it to my wife, who greatly discouraged me from prosecuting my new scheme, as she called it; I was not opulent enough, she said, to dedicate much of my time to studies and labours which might rob me of that portion of it which is the only wealth of the American farmer. However her prudent caution did not discourage me; I thought about it continually, at supper, in bed, and wherever I went. At last I could not resist the impulse; for on the fourth day of the following week, I hired a man to plough for me, and went to Philadelphia. Though I knew not what book to call for, I ingeniously told the bookseller my errand, who provided me with such as he thought best, and a Latin grammar beside. Next I applied to a neighbouring schoolmaster, who in three months taught me Latin enough to understand Linnaeus, which I purchased afterward. Then I began to botanize all over my farm; in a little time I became acquainted with every vegetable that grew in my neighbourhood; and next ventured into Maryland, living among the Friends: in proportion as I thought myself more learned I proceeded farther, and by a steady application of several years I have acquired a pretty general knowledge of every plant and tree to be found in our continent. In process of time I was applied to from the old countries, whither I every year send many collections. Being now made easy in my circumstances, I have ceased to labour, and am never so happy as when I see and converse with my friends. If among the many plants or shrubs I am acquainted with, there are any thee wantest to send to thy native country, I will cheerfully procure them, and give thee moreover whatever directions thee mayest want."

Thus I passed several days in ease, improvement, and pleasure; I observed in all the operations of his farm, as well as in the mutual correspondence between the master and the inferior members of his family, the greatest ease and decorum; not a word like command seemed to exceed the tone of a simple wish. The very Negroes themselves appeared to partake of such a decency of behaviour, and modesty of countenance, as I had never before observed. By what means, said I, Mr. Bertram, do you rule your slaves so well, that they seem to do their work with all the cheerfulness of white men? "Though our erroneous prejudices and opinions once induced us to look upon them as fit only for slavery, though ancient custom had very unfortunately taught us to keep them in bondage; yet of late, in consequence of the remonstrances of several Friends, and of the good books they have published on that subject, our society treats them very differently. With us they are now free. I give those thee didst see at my table, eighteen pounds a year, with victuals and clothes, and all other privileges which white men enjoy. Our society treats them now as the companions of our labours; and by this management, as well as by means of the education we have given them, they are in general become a new set of beings. Those whom I admit to my table, I have found to be good, trusty, moral men; when they do not what we think they should do, we dismiss them, which is all the punishment we inflict. Other societies of Christians keep them still as slaves, without teaching them any kind of religious principles: what motive beside fear can they have to behave well? In the first settlement of this province, we employed them as slaves, I acknowledge; but when we found that good example, gentle admonition, and religious principles could lead them to subordination and sobriety, we relinquished a method so contrary to the profession of Christianity. We gave them freedom, and yet few have quitted their ancient masters. The women breed in our families; and we become attached to one another. I taught mine to read and write; they love God, and fear his judgments. The oldest person among them transacts my business in Philadelphia, with a punctuality, from which he has never deviated. They constantly attend our meetings, they participate in health and sickness, infancy and old age, in the advantages our society affords. Such are the means we have made use of, to relieve them from that bondage and ignorance in which they were kept before. Thee perhaps hast been surprised to see them at my table, but by elevating them to the rank of freemen, they necessarily acquire that emulation without which we ourselves should fall into debasement and profligate ways." . . .

"Stitch Away, Thou Noble Fox"

[FROM *Sartor Resartus*]

THOMAS CARLYLE

[*At first thought, Carlyle seems the most un-Quakerly of men. The very look of a page of his writing appears anti-Quaker. This is because the later, pietistic, conforming Quaker has blotted out the image of the earlier, iconoclastic Quaker. For this earlier breed of Friend, Carlyle had much sympathy, and he shared a good many of his characteristics; it is not too fanciful to think of Fox as a Carlyle with a reliable digestive system, or of Carlyle as a Fox who never had a vision of Pendle Hill. And the cannonade of Carlyle's prose would have been admirable for purposes of seventeenth-century controversy. Carlyle, it has been said, "preached the gospel of silence in forty volumes." Some of the Quakers approached this record.*]

Fox squared very well with many of Carlyle's theories of the Hero, theories Fox would have denounced. And Carlyle believed in what Fox worked and suffered for: the death, in Carlyle's words, "of slavery, world-worship and the Mammon-god."

Carlyle is a slipshod reporter of the facts of Fox's exterior life. We have no reason to believe Fox made his own breeches. And he certainly never told a parson, as Carlyle reports, "My fat-faced friend, thou art a damned lie. Thou are pretending to serve God Almighty, and are really serving the devil." But Carlyle understood the interior facts of the Religious Society of Friends, and he, like Fox, preached "a righteous intolerance of the devil."]

"Perhaps the most remarkable incident in Modern History," says Teufelsdrockh, "is not the Diet of Worms, still less the Battle of Austerlitz, Waterloo, Peterloo, or any other Battle; but an incident passed carelessly over by most Historians, and treated with some degree of ridicule by others; namely, George Fox's making to himself a suit of Leather. This man, the first of the Quaker's and by trade a Shoemaker, was one of those, to whom, under ruder or purer form, the Divine Idea of the Universe is pleased to manifest itself; and, across all the hulls of Ignorance and earthly Degradation, shine through, in unspeakable Awfulness, unspeakable Beauty, on their souls: who therefore are rightly accounted Prophets, God-possessed; or even Gods, as in some periods it has chanced. Sitting in his stall; working on tanned hides, amid pincers, paste-horns, rosin, swine-bristles, and a nameless flood of rubbish, this youth had, nevertheless, a Living Spirit belonging to him; also an antique Inspired Volume, through which, as through a window, it could look upwards, and discern its celestial Home. The task of a daily pair of shoes, coupled even with some prospect of victuals, and an honourable Mastership in Cordwainery, and perhaps the post of Third-borough in his hundred, as the crown of long faithful sewing—was nowise satisfaction enough to such a mind; but ever amid the boring and hammering came tones from that far country, came Splendours and Terrors; for this poor Cordwainer, as we said, was a Man; and the Temple of Immensity, wherein as Man he had been sent to minister, was full of holy mystery to him.

"The Clergy of the neighbourhood, the ordained Watchers and Interpreters of that same holy mystery, listened with unaffected tedium to his consultations, and advised him, as the solution of such doubts, to 'drink beer and dance with the girls.' Blind leaders of the blind! For what end were their tithes levied and eaten; for what were their shovel-hats scooped-out, and their surplices and cassock-aprons girt-on; and such a church-repairing, and chaffering, and organing, and other racketing, held over that spot of God's Earth, if Man were but a Patent Digester, and the Belly with its adjuncts the grand Reality? Fox turned from them, with tears and a sacred scorn, back to his Leather-parings and his Bible. Mountains of encumbrance, higher than Ætna, had been heaped over that Spirit: but it was a Spirit, and would not lie buried there. Through long days and nights of silent agony, it struggled and wrestled, with a man's force, to be free: how its prison-mountains heaved and swayed tumultuously, as the giant spirit shook them to this hand and that, and emerged into the light of Heaven! That Leicester shoe-shop, had men known it, was a holier place than any Vatican or Loretto-shrine. 'So bandaged, and hampered, and hemmed in,' groaned he, 'with thousand requisitions, obligations, straps, tatters, and tagrags, I can neither see nor move: not my own am I, but the World's; and Time flies fast, and Heaven is high, and Hell is deep: Man! bethink thee, if thou hast power of Thought! Why not; what binds me here? Want, want!—Ha, of what? Will all the shoe-wages under the Moon ferry me across into that far Land of Light? Only Meditation can, and devout Prayer to God. I will to the woods: the hollow of a tree will lodge me, wild-berries feed me; and for Clothes, cannot I stitch myself one perennial suit of Leather!'

"Historical Oil-painting," continues Teufelsdrockh, "is one of the Arts I never practised; therefore shall I not decide whether this subject were easy of execution on the canvas. Yet often has it seemed to me as if such first outflashing of man's Freewill, to lighten, more and more into Day, the Chaotic Night that threatened to engulf him in its hindrances and its horrors,

were properly the only grandeur there is in History. Let some
living Angelo or Rosa, with seeing eye and understanding heart,
picture George Fox on that morning, when he spreads-out his
cutting-board for the last time, and cuts cowhides by unwonted
patterns, and stitches them together into one continuous all-
including Case, the farewell service of his awl! Stitch away, thou
noble Fox: every prick of that little instrument is pricking into
the heart of Slavery, and World-worship, and the Mammon-god.
Thy elbows jerk, and in strong swimmer-strokes, and every
stroke is bearing thee across the Prison-ditch, within which
Vanity holds her Work-house and Ragfair, into lands of true
Liberty; were the work done, there is in broad Europe one Free
Man, and thou are he!

"Thus from the lowest depth there is a path to the loftiest
height; and for the Poor also a Gospel has been published.
Surely if, as D'Alembert asserts, my illustrious namesake,
Diogenes, was the greatest man of Antiquity, only that he
wanted Decency, then by stronger reason is George Fox the
greatest of the Moderns; and greater than Diogenes himself: for
he too stands on the adamantine basis of his Manhood, casting
aside all props and shoars; yet not, in half-savage Pride, under-
valuing the Earth; valuing it rather, as a place to yield him
warmth and food, he looks Heavenward from his Earth, and
dwells in an element of Mercy and Worship, with a still Strength,
such as the Cynic's Tub did nowise witness. Great, truly, was
that Tub; a temple from which man's dignity and divinity was
scornfully preached abroad: but greater is the Leather Hull, for
the same sermon was preached there, and not in Scorn but in Love."

George Fox's "perennial suit," with all that it held, has
been worn quite into ashes for nigh two centuries: why, in a
discussion on the Perfectibility of Society, reproduce it now?
Not out of blind sectarian partisanship: Teufelsdrockh himself
is no Quaker; with all his pacific tendencies, did not we see him,
in that scene at the North Cape, with the Archangel Smuggler,
exhibit fire-arms?

For us, aware of his deep Sansculottism, there is more
meant in this passage than meets the ear. At the same time, who

can avoid smiling at the earnestness and Boeotian simplicity (if indeed there be not an underhand satire in it), with which that "Incident" is here brought forward; and, in the Professor's ambiguous way, as clearly perhaps as he durst in Weissnichtwo, recommended to imitation! Does Teufelsdrockh anticipate that, in this age of refinement, any considerable class of the community, by way of testifying against the "Mammon-god," and escaping from what he calls "Vanity's Workhouse and Ragfair," where doubtless some of them are toiled and whipped and hoodwinked sufficiently, will sheathe themselves in close-fitting cases of Leather? The idea is ridiculous in the extreme. Will Majesty lay aside its robes of state, and Beauty its frills and train-gowns, for a second-skin of tanned hide? By which change Huddersfield and Manchester, and Coventry and Paisley, and the Fancy-Bazaar, were reduced to hungry solitudes; and only Day and Martin could profit. For neither would Teufelsdrockh's mad daydream, here as we presume covertly intended, of levelling Society (levelling it indeed with a vengeance, into one huge drowned marsh!), and so attaining the political effects of Nudity without its frigorific or other consequences, be thereby realized. Would not the rich man purchase a waterproof suit of Russia Leather; and the high-born Belle step-forth in red or azure morocco, lined with shamoy: the black cowhide being left to the Drudges and Gibeonites of the world; and so all the Distinctions be re-established?

Or has the Professor his own deeper intention; and laughs in his sleeve at our strictures and glosses, which indeed are but a part thereof?

BIRTHRIGHT QUAKERS

Children whose parents are both members of the Society of Friends are, by birthright, members.
—BOOK OF DISCIPLINE, PHILADELPHIA YEARLY MEETING, 1927

First-Day Thoughts

JOHN GREENLEAF WHITTIER

In calm and cool and silence, once again
   I find my old accustomed place among
   My brethren, where, perchance, no human tongue
   Shall utter words; where never hymn is sung,
Nor deep-toned organ blown, nor censer swung,
Nor dim light falling through the pictured pane!
There, syllabled by silence, let me hear
The still small voice which reached the prophet's ear;
Read in my heart a still diviner law
Than Israel's leader on his tables saw!
There let me strive with each besetting sin,
   Recall my wandering fancies, and restrain
   The sore disquiet of a restless brain;
   And, as the path of duty is made plain,
May grace be given that I may walk therein,
   Not like the hireling, for his selfish gain,
With backward glances and reluctant tread,
Making a merit of his coward dread,
   But, cheerful, in the light around me thrown,
   Walking as one to pleasant service led;
   Doing God's will as if it were my own,
Yet trusting not in mine, but in His strength alone!

"It Must Be in the Spirit, Not of Judgment, but of Mercy"

ELIZABETH FRY

[*In their early history Quakers spent too much time behind bars themselves to make any concerted effort to ameliorate the conditions of prisons for others. Their immediate problem was to survive, though there are many instances of Quaker effort, from the beginning, to help individual fellow prisoners. But work for the imprisoned, as a "Quaker concern," began with Elizabeth Fry (1780–1845), born a Gurney of Earlham Hall in Norfolk, England. At seventeen she had written in her journal, "If some kind and great circumstance does not happen to me, I shall have my talent devoured by moth and rust."*

The "kind and great circumstance" happened, but not until she was thirty-three and already the mother of eight children. In 1813, at the suggestion of the American Quaker Stephen Grellet, she made her first visit to Newgate Prison. From that day on, her talents were in no danger from rust or moth. The reforms suggested by her spread across the world. Men prisoners were separated from women, and hardened criminals from first offenders. Provision was made for employment and instruction, for sanitation and exercise. Nor did Elizabeth Fry forget that prisoners had souls. The American Ambassador to England reported, "I have seen the two greatest sights in London; St. Paul's Cathedral and Mrs. Fry reading the Bible to prisoners at Newgate."

John Bellers, a hundred and fifty years earlier, had recommended all the reforms initiated by Elizabeth Fry—and more. It is a pity, the time lapse apart, that prison reform did not stem from Bellers' rationale of citizens' responsibility rather than from Mrs. Fry's personal efforts, capable of being interpreted as the kindly noblesse oblige assumed by the haves for the have-nots, something "the Quakers were taking care of." This was not Elizabeth Fry's attitude, nor did she assume any position of moral superiority.]

Sunday, 4th Feb. 1798. Today much has passed in my mind of a very serious nature. I have had a faint light spread over my mind; at least I believe it is something of that kind, owing to having been much with and heard much excellence from one who appears to me a true Christian. It has caused me to feel a little religion. I wish the state of enthusiasm I am now in may last, for today I felt there is a God. I have been devotional and my mind has been led away from the follies that it is mostly wrapped up in. . . .

Sunday, 17th March 1798. May I never lose the little religion I now have, but if I cannot feel religion and devotion I must not despair, for if I am truly warm and earnest in the cause it will come one day. In my idea true humility and lowness of heart is the first grand step towards true religion. . . .

20th April 1798. I do not know the course I am to run, all is hid in mystery, but I try to do right in everything. . . . Look up to true religion as the very first of blessings, cherish it, nourish and let it flourish and bloom in my heart; it wants taking care of, it is difficult to obtain. I must not despair or grow sceptical if I do not always feel religious. I felt God as it were, and I must seek to find Him again.

[*In 1843, when suffering acutely in an illness, Elizabeth Fry remarked to one of her daughters:*] My dear Rachel—I can say one thing: since my heart was touched at seventeen years old, I believe I never have awakened from sleep, in sickness or in health, by day or by night, without my first waking thought being how best I might serve my Lord.

[*Of her prison work she wrote:*] Much depends on the spirit in which the visitor enters upon her work. It must be in the spirit, not of judgment, but of mercy. She must not say in her heart "I am more holy than thou," but must rather keep in perpetual remembrance that "all have sinned and come short of the Glory of God." . . .

1844. My life has been one of great vicissitude: mine has been a hidden path, hidden from every human eye. I have had deep humiliations and sorrows to pass through. I can truly say I have "wandered in the wilderness in a solitary way, and found no city to dwell in"; and yet how wonderfully I have been sustained. I have passed through many and great dangers, many ways—I have been tried with the applause of the world, and none know how great a trial that has been, and the deep humiliations of it; and yet I fully believe it is not nearly so dangerous as being made much of in religious society. There is a snare even in religious unity, if we are not on the watch. I have sometimes felt that it was not so dangerous to be made much of in the world, as by those whom we think highly of in our own Society: the more I have been made much of by the world, the more I have been inwardly humbled. I could often adopt the words of Sir Francis Bacon—"When I have ascended before men, I have descended in humiliation before God."

"Treat Them as Brethren, and Not as Slaves"

[FROM *Account of a Journey to the Indian Country*]

JOSEPH CLARK

[*In the long history of the Quaker concern for native Americans, Joseph Clark's account of the attempted domestication of the young women of the tribe forms a serio-comic chapter. One knows not whether to laugh or cry. Clark is wise enough to see the Creek nation's point in rejecting the Princeton missionaries, trained though they were for primitive society by sleeping on rough boards, and primed though they were to preach salvation in and out of season. (The encounter of Princeton and the Creeks has an awesomely modern echo.) But Clark either does not see, or refrains from mentioning, flaws in the Quaker mission to the Oneidas.*

What appears to be missing, from Quakers and Princetonians alike, is Woolman's deep respect for the people with whom he deals. Woolman wanted to "feel and understand" the life of native Americans.

The tribes were not to be changed or "converted," but perhaps "helped forward"; not by preaching or roadbuilding or any outward technique whatsoever, but "by my following the leadings of truth among them."

This is the third time these words have appeared in these pages. They bear repetition amid a nation of self-elected torch-bearers and impatient do-gooders who find it much easier to preach "truth" than to follow its "leadings."]

———

In the year 1797, John Parrish, a friend and father in the church, suggested the advantage that might arise to the Indian natives, by bringing a few of their young females into this part of the country, in order to instruct them in the useful arts of domestic economy, by placing them in the families of suitable Friends, where they might be carefully educated.

This being a very weighty matter, claimed my serious attention, and was laid before the Committee appointed by the Yearly Meeting, for promoting the improvement and gradual civilization of the Indian natives. The proposal was acceded to by the Committee, who furnished me with a Certificate expressive of their unity therewith, and addressed to the Indians, as follows:

Brothers,

We received by our friend, Henry Simmons, a few lines from you. We were glad to hear from you, and that your young men were encouraged to walk in the good path, we recommended to you. It did our hearts good, when he told us that you had raised corn, wheat, and other grain, to supply yourselves till next crop. We wish you all to be sober and industrious, and learn to be good farmers.

Brothers, we understand that you are desirous, a few of your girls should be placed in the families of some of our Friends, and be taught what our daughters are. We rejoice at it, and are willing to take three of them; and our friend Joseph Clark, has agreed to assist in bringing them safe down. They (H. Simmons and J. Clark) will deliver you this. We also have agreed to take two girls from Oneida, and two from the Tuscaroras.

Brothers, we expect the girls you send us, will remain till they are eighteen years of age, as our daughters are placed by their parents or friends, to learn what we want your daughters should know; that is, spinning, weaving, how to make butter, and such other things as are useful on a farm. We shall place them in such families as will use them kindly, and instruct them in what is needful.

We remain your friends and brothers,

> John Drinker,
> H. Drinker,
> John Parrish,
> Thos. Stewardson,
> Thomas Wister,
> John Biddle.

Having laid the subject before my family, after about two weeks' consideration and preparation, I took an affectionate leave of them, on the 16th of the 10th month, 1797, and went to Bristol in Bucks county, where I met with my friend, Henry Simmons, jun. who was to be my companion in the journey, which was very satisfactory. But he was taken unwell, after travelling about twenty miles, and continued so all the journey.

When we arrived at New York, a number of articles were purchased, for clothing for the girls, and we prosecuted our journey till, in due season, we arrived at Oneida, in the state of New York, where we were received with marks of affection, by the Indians. I was taken to the house of one of the Chiefs, his wife having been informed concerning my coming.

On the 29th, Nicholas Cusick, Chief of the Tuscaroras, with his wife, made us a visit. He is an orderly and sensible man.

We also had a conference with the Stockbridge and Tuscarora Indians; at which we produced our certificates, and they were read, not only by paragraphs, but by sentences and words. Hendrick Apaumut was interpreter for the Stockbridge, and Nicholas Cusick for the Tuscaroras. Some warriors from Niagara, were also present. At this conference, the Indians seemed fully satisfied with the proposals made to them. We informed them that Friends had nothing but love for them and their children; and as it was their desire that we should take their children, we would do it at Friends' expense. On which information, they acknowledged Friends' love for them.

11th mo. 1st.—Had a conference with the principal Chief of the Oneidas, about the girls. He remarked, that those of the young Indians who go out, often learn wrong habits; and mentioned some instances in the neighbourhood. He further observed, that they would rather the sons of Onas (meaning of William Penn) should have their people or children, than any other people; but their judgment was, for our women to come and instruct them; which would better preserve their morals, and be of far greater utility amongst the Indians, and which they always understood would be the case, from the first proposal made by the Committee. In answer to all this, I replied, "Great trees grow slow"; meaning great matters take time to accomplish.

He called upon me twice after this, to write a piece for their nation. At first, I declined: but, upon the second application, I complied; well knowing that what they requested was the mind of Friends, and also of Government. When it was written, they conferred together about its contents; and next day I was informed by their Chief that they approved thereof. The purport of it was to warn off some bad tenants, who had settled on their land contrary to law. The Chief gave me a name, Onas, signifying the man who uses a pen, which I thought no way suitable for my small abilities.

Being frequently in company with the Stockbridge Indians, I was induced to believe they are superior, especially the women, to many under our name, who make a high profession of religion. . . .

7th.—A fine morning. My mind often felt the sweet influences of Divine Goodness; and I could behold its salutary effects among some of these inhabitants of the wilderness. Their penetration and judgment in religious matters, are very evident and striking, as may appear in the following narrative.

It appears that two young men were prepared at Princeton

college, to be sent as missionaries among the Indians. And in order to habituate themselves to the hardships that awaited them, they lodged upon boards. When they set out upon their mission, several persons of respectability accompanied them to the Creek Nation. When arrived, the Chiefs were called—a conference was held with them, and it was proposed to call a Council; which being met, the visitors informed them that they had brought two ministers of the gospel to preach salvation to them—and also a number of books, which would lead them the way to heaven. The Indians received the information, without apparent emotion; and said they would consider the subject; which should occupy the space of fourteen days. Meantime the young ministers proposed preaching; but the Indians would not suffer them, until their own conclusions were made. At the expiration of the fourteen days, the Indians made inquiry, whether they had any dark-coloured people among them, and whether they preached the gospel of salvation to them: whether they gave them these good books, which would show them the way to heaven; or, whether they treated them as slaves, or as brothers. Being answered accordingly, the Indians again spoke, "Go home, and preach the gospel of salvation to them; give them those good books, that will learn them the way to heaven—treat them as brethren, and not as slaves; then come and preach to us." In consequence of this refusal, the whole missionary company returned; and one of them who was in the station of a Congress-man, was so affected with the circumstance, that he emancipated all his slaves. When I came home, I called upon the person, and inquired more fully respecting the matter, when he readily, seriously, and fully confirmed the same.

I never experienced greater kindness than from the Indians. I had not only their horses to ride, but a guide from place to place. The natives would not permit me even to carry my portmanteau, nor scarcely to go over a bridge that was dangerous, but offered to carry me over in their arms; though I would not suffer them. When I lodged with the Indians, they would build a large fire at bed-time, in the room that I occupied, and always renewed it at midnight;—the family being remarkably still, whether up or a-bed. . . .

10th. This morning our Indian girls came, each one accompanied by her parent or guardian. The business of parting was conducted with great seriousness, for the Indians delivered their children to us with the utmost confidence and quietude: which brought over my mind a considerable weight of concern and care, that nothing on my part, might obstruct this great and important work. The girls manifested much stillness and composure, at taking leave of their parents, to go a long journey, with perfect strangers, to reside in a distant land. So we went to the Mohawk river, and they stepped into the boat, wrapped their faces in their blankets, and I do not remember that they uttered a word. We now had to pass down this river about one hundred miles, but got on very well the first day's voyage. . . .

At length we arrived safely in New York, and were kindly received by our friend Edmund Pryor; and may truly say, from the tenderness that was shown to us, and to the Indian girls, it was "like a brook by the way."

17th. A snowy morning. Friends manifested kindness towards us, particularly Joseph Delaplaine, who accompanied us to the vessel, and presented to each of the girls a piece of silver. We arrived safely at Brunswick about seven o'clock in the evening. There was here, at this time, a certain great man from Poland, who had never seen an Indian, and was desirous of being introduced to the girls. They being in a private room at supper, he walked in to take a view of them. When he beheld their orderly deportment, he seemed much surprised; and after walking round the table, where they were sitting, he said, "These are almost civilized already." I informed him that the father of one of them would not drink wine.

The same evening, the Poland general and his company came into the room, where my companion and I were sitting. In the course of the conversation, the word *thou* was used, which attracted the attention of a young man, who remarked in French to the general, that we, as a people, had a very uncouth way of speaking thou;—he apprehended, (as I suppose,) that we should not understand what he said in that language. However, I informed him, that it was the language of the Almighty to the first man, Adam; therefore bid him not reflect upon the people for using the language, which the Lord had taught them. He looked confused; and the Polander, who understood English, appeared to favour the observation. . . .

20th. Rode to Bristol, and next morning to Henry Simmons's, where the girls remained during my absence. Being equipped, we again set out, and arrived at my house about sunset. The girls continued with us for three days; during which time, they conducted themselves in an orderly manner; and occasionally read the Scriptures. Many Friends called to see them, and gave them a number of small presents.

The next concern was, to find suitable places for them. We accordingly set out for James Emlen's, in Delaware county, where we arrived safely, and were kindly treated.

On first-day, the 26th, we had them all taken to meeting, where they behaved in a becoming manner. In the course of a few days, we had them stationed at the Friends' houses, who were willing to take charge of them, and instruct them in the business of housewifery. Two of the girls were placed with Nathan Cooper and son;—one, with a woman Friend, who had a concern to take charge of one of the Indians;—one was placed with the family of William Jackson, and the remaining two with Isaac Jackson. At my taking leave of them, they wept considerably; and I felt much tenderness toward them, when I reflected upon the confidence which their parents had placed in me. On looking over this journey, I may thankfully acknowledge, that through adorable mercy, I have witnessed preservation; and may the great Preserver of men have the praise.

The President of the Underground R

"He Never Lost a Passenger"

[FROM *Southern Heroes*]

FERNANDO G. CARTLAND

[*"Quakers," says John Sykes in his stimulating study of the place of Quakers in society, "were prominent in the work of the Underground Railways, helping slaves north to Canada. But against them, the sedate, over-entrenched establishment of Orthodox Friends, especially on the Eastern seaboard, were anxious to tone down such activity. . . . In 1837 . . . at Newport in Rhode Island . . . the Yearly Meeting denied the use of its meeting house to abolitionist lecturers. . . . In Indiana . . . Friends favored doing nothing . . . 'lest if we over act the part called for at our hands, we injure the righteous cause, and suffer loss ourselves.' "*

This lukewarm attitude on the part of many Friends toward abolition needs to be mentioned, since it is often taken for granted that all Quakers were as outspoken against slavery as were Woolman, Whittier, and Levi Coffin.

Levi Coffin (1789–1877), "the President of the Underground Railway," saw three thousand passengers safely through his station alone. He practiced Quakerism while others debated whether or not they might "suffer loss." "True godliness don't turn men out of the world," said Penn. Nor does it send slaves back to the coffle and the auction block.]

———

We will here introduce to our readers Levi Coffin, the President of the Underground Railroad.

He was born in Guilford County, N.C., of Quaker parents and Nantucket ancestry. His father's farm was on the Salisbury road, near the Friends' meeting-house at New Garden, six miles from Greensboro. In this vicinity was fought the battle of Guilford Court House, between General Greene and Lord

Cornwallis, near the close of the war of the Revolution. Many of the soldiers slain in this battle were buried in the Friends' burying-ground, near their meeting-house, which was used as a hospital for the wounded. The houses of two Friends in the neighborhood, whose farms joined, were occupied by the officers of the opposing armies.

The road passing this meeting-house was traveled for many years by slave-traders going South with their human merchandise. The slaves were driven in what were called "coffles," two slaves being fastened on each side of a heavy chain, thus making four abreast. A little behind these were four more, and so on until all were thus fastened together. They were followed by a white man on horseback, carrying a long whip, which he sometimes used with as little mercy as a cruel driver might now show in driving cattle. A wagon followed containing supplies. Day after day in this manner the journey was continued, until the destination was reached or a sale was made. These coffles were never seen going North.

The owners of the rice swamps and cane and cotton fields of the extreme Southern States required more slaves than they could raise, and they depended mostly upon Maryland, Virginia, North Carolina, and Kentucky to supply the deficiency. The work of the more Southern States and often the greater cruelty in the treatment of the slaves shortened the years of labor, "as they toiled 'mid the cotton and the cane." Slaves from the upper States dreaded to be sold South more than anything else that could happen to them.

When about seven years of age, Levi Coffin was with his father by the roadside, and saw a coffle of slaves pass. His father pleasantly addressed them with the words, "Well, boys! why do they chain you?" One of them replied "They have taken us away from our wives and children, and they chain us lest we should make our escape and go back to them." The boy was much impressed with the dejected appearance of the company, and with the sad words that he heard, and asked his father many questions concerning them. His father explained as best he could the sad meaning of slavery, and thus Levi Coffin took his first lessons as an abolitionist.

A few years later he was at a corn husking, where the neighbors, white and colored, were assembled to "shuck the corn," which had been broken from the stalk in the field and piled in the yard. At several points surrounding the pile, posts were set in the ground with flat stones placed on the top, and here the resinous pine-knots, or "light-wood," were burned, shedding a bright light all around. The white people began at one end of the pile, the colored at the other; and with much story-telling, song, joke, and laughter they worked until the golden ears were stowed away.

On this occasion, while the white people were at supper, Levi remained with the colored folks. Among them he found one named Stephen, who had been free born and apprenticed to a Friend named Lloyd, living near Philadelphia. He was engaged in helping drive a flock of sheep to Baltimore, and while asleep in the Negro house of a tavern, he was seized, gagged, bound, hurriedly placed in a covered carriage, and taken to Virginia, where he was sold to a man named Holland.

Holland, who was now on his way South, had stopped over a few days at his home, which was in this neighborhood. Levi reported the case to a trusty Negro, who agreed to take Stephen the next night to the home of Levi's father, and give him an opportunity to hear Stephen's story. After listening to it, Friend Coffin wrote at once to Edward Lloyd concerning the matter. In about two weeks' time Lloyd arrived, having traveled many weary miles by stagecoach, but he found that Stephen had been taken further South.

The next day, Lloyd attended the meeting of Friends at New Garden and informed them of the circumstances. George Swain and Henry Macy agreed to accompany him in pursuit of the boy. Friends contributed money for the expenses, as well as a horse and saddle and other necessary equipments for the journey. They found Stephen in Georgia, where he had been sold. The purchaser gave bonds to deliver him when proof should be given that his mother was a free woman at the time of his birth, and in due time our friends returned and Stephen was ready to testify against his kidnapper, who had been arrested and given bonds to appear for trial; but rather than meet Stephen in court and abide the judgment, he forfeited the bond.

This was Levi Coffin's first experience in the liberation of slaves. In his father's woods he often met the hunted Negro, and "many times," he says, "I sat in the thicket while they devoured my bounty, as I listened to their tales about hard masters and cruel treatment, or in language glowing with native eloquence, they spoke of the glorious hope of freedom which had animated their spirits in darkest hours and sustained them under the lash."

During his young manhood he was often engaged in some way for the benefit of the slaves. He organized a school for them, which was at first encouraged by some of the slaveholders, but was afterwards closed, as they considered it dangerous for the slaves to be educated. He often examined, in person or by proxy, coffles of slaves; and it is surprising how many he found among them who had been kidnapped, although kidnapping was said to be strongly opposed by slaveholders. Many were released as a result of his efforts.

He married the daughter of a neighboring Friend, and in September, 1826, moved to Indiana, where he began business as a merchant and manufacturer of linseed oil. There was quite a settlement of free colored people at the place, whose parents, if not they themselves, had been settled there by the committees of North Carolina Yearly Meeting. These colored people were often called upon to harbor and forward those who had escaped from their masters, but on account of their inability to manage properly, the owners sometimes regained possession of the fugitives.

Levi Coffin tried to interest his neighbors in this subject, but met with little encouragement, at first. Even if they wished to help, they were afraid of the penalty of the law. Levi told them that when a boy in North Carolina he had read in the Bible that it is right to take in the stranger and administer to him in distress, and he believed that it is always safe to do right; that the Bible, in bidding us to feed the hungry and clothe the naked, said nothing about color, and that he should try to follow out its teachings.

The colored people soon came to understand that in him they had a friend, and that a stranger knocking at his door would be admitted. Without advertising it in the newspapers, it soon became known by those interested in aiding the fugitive, that if his house could be reached safety was assured, and fugitive slaves began arriving before he had lived a year in his new home.

The Underground Railroad was not a deliberately organized institution, with capital stock publicly subscribed and officers annually elected at large salaries. Trains did not run from certain public places on schedule time, yet they made good connections. The collection of fares was no part of the conductor's business. It was his duty to receive all who came to him fleeing from the land of bondage, in pursuit of "liberty and happiness." If needful, they must be warmed, fed or clothed, then conveyed to the next most suitable station on the road to Canada, without charge. They were, with a degree of caution, passed from one friendly hand to another. Sometimes they were kept in schoolhouse lofts where, perhaps for days, they were the unobserved listeners to the children's recitations. Sometimes they were hidden in hay mows, straw ricks, or between feather beds in some good housewife's chamber, and in all sorts of ways kept from the eager eyes of their pursuers.

Levi Coffin's house soon became a Union station for those coming by various lines from the South, converging at Newport, Indiana. Some of his friends became much concerned for him. They said that his business interests would suffer, that his very life was in danger, and that his duty toward his family and friends demanded that he should cease his connection with so hazardous and disreputable a business. Levi and "Aunt Kate" had long before counted the cost. They knew all the dangers better than their advisers. They had deliberately and intelligently reached the conclusion that the pathway of duty was plain before them, and they steadfastly pursued the right, leaving business interests, personal safety, and all with Him who, they believed, had called them to this special work.

When his views and practices became generally known, his business interests did suffer for a time, for men declared that they would not patronize such a man; but others came to him, and his business prospered. He needed an increased income. Horses and wagons must be always on hand to convey guests ten, twenty, thirty, or forty miles on short notice, as they were likely to appear at any time for passage on the Underground Railroad.

At this station it sometimes occurred that several trains arrived in the course of one night. At no time on retiring were Levi Coffin and his wife sure of an uninterrupted rest. The gentle tap might be heard at any hour of the night, and when heard, Levi would silently open the door, give a whispered invitation to come in, and, leaving the sitting room door open, return to his wife and tell her of the hungry company needing refreshments. After the passengers had entered, the doors were closed and the windows curtained, that no spy from the outside might see what was going on within. Lamps were lighted, fires built, and soon the smell of hot coffee and cooking would indicate that a satisfying portion was in preparation for the ragged, hungry, shivering travelers. When warmed and fed they were put away to rest as circumstances would permit.

Levi Coffin was often threatened with hanging, shooting, and the burning of his property, but he feared not, and often said, "Barking dogs never bite." On one occasion a letter was received from Kentucky which stated that on a certain night an armed body of men was coming to Newport to burn the town. Levi Coffin's store, porkhouse, and dwelling were to be the first fired, and if they were successful in getting him they intended that his life should pay for the crimes he had committed against Southern slaveholders. He was advised to leave town. Most of the inhabitants were Friends and non-combatants; they raised no resisting force to meet the invaders, placed no pickets outside the town, but retired to rest as usual. None showed any fear except one poor laboring man who had built a little cabin in the woods a mile and a half from town. Upon hearing the springtime music of the frogs he thought that the Kentuckians were coming, and hastened to town to give the alarm.

Levi Coffin states that the largest company of fugitives ever seated at his table at one time was composed of seventeen men, women and children, varying in color from the light mulatto to the coal black Negro. They were from Kentucky, and the next night after reaching the Ohio side of the river, when near a road, they heard the sound of horses' feet, and soon saw their pursuers close upon them. Hurriedly entering a large cornfield across the road, they ran for liberty and life, closely pursued by fifteen or twenty armed men. The negroes scattered in the wilderness of tall, full-bladed, bottom-land Indian corn, which afforded a good shelter. The pursuers called to them to stop or they would be shot. Some recognized the voices of their master, but did not incline to obey. They had a taste and a hope of liberty, and these were already giving them a spirit of independence. Several shots were fired, which they heard cutting the friendly maize around them. They ran several miles before stopping to collect their company. All could not be easily found, but it was very important for them to leave the cornfield before day; it was now nearly morning.

They entered the woods near by and secreted themselves in the bushes. Soon they heard the sound of wood-chopping, which again alarmed them, but by careful observation they discovered that the chopper was a friendly Negro. He conducted them to a safe hiding-place and furnished them with food, as the bundles of clothing and food with which they had started had been lost during their hurried flight. They were afterwards conducted to a station on the Underground Railroad, where their lost companions soon appeared. Two of them were wounded, one with shot in his back, the other with a bullet wound several inches long, in his side. Two covered wagons were appropriated to their use, and early one morning, "Aunt Kate," of *Uncle Tom's Cabin* fame, was called to the door. Upon asking who was there, she was told, "All Kentucky." "Well, bring all Kentucky in," was the ready response. Breakfast was soon ready and they were told to eat all they wanted, for they were among friends and in no danger of being captured in that neighborhood of abolitionists. They were soon at their ease, and "did all eat and were filled."

In this case Levi Coffin called some of the neighbors in to see this valuable lot of property, the worth of which he estimated to be at least $17,000. They remained for two days. The shot were taken out of the man's back, and the wounded side was dressed. Needed clothing was furnished, and all were sent on their way rejoicing to the house of John Bond, twenty miles away.

The next morning a messenger came from Richmond, Indiana, with word that fifteen Kentuckians were there hunting fugitives. Levi Coffin quickly sent this message to John Bond with word that the colored people better be scattered. Thinking it safe to travel in that country by day, John had sent them forward immediately upon their arrival. He now mounted a horse, pursued and overtook them, and had them secreted with different Friends, where they remained in hiding for several weeks, until the hunters had given up the chase. They were then forwarded to Canada.

Meanwhile, the Kentuckians had hired a lot of roughs to aid them in finding their property, who formed parties and started out in different directions. The party searching the town of Newport entered one or two at a time to avoid suspicion, and inquired of the children in the streets if any fugitive slaves had been in town lately. They were told that a lot of them had been at Levi Coffin's, but had gone on to Canada. This information was given at the meeting of the company shortly afterward, and two divisions were sent to the lakes to watch for the crossing of the fleeing slaves to Canada. The slaveholders hired more men, with whom they proposed to search every Friends' community in that region. All their efforts proved futile, so that, discouraged and angry, they swore they would burn Levi Coffin out, shoot him at sight, or hang him to a limb, if it cost $10,000.

A friend of Levi Coffin's who overheard the threats, and thought that they started for Newport, mounted a horse, and with pistols in his pockets hurriedly rode to give Levi warning and help him to fight. He called Levi out of bed and excitedly told his story. Levi replied that if they had really intended to do such a thing they would never have told of it; and added: "Now, thee put up thy pistols. We have no use for them here, as we do not depend upon firearms for protection." The well-meaning visitor was persuaded to retire, and Levi went to bed and to sleep.

Soon the hunters returned South, but before going they conferred an honorable and lasting title upon our friend. They said they could get no trace of their slaves on top of the ground, after they reached Levi Coffin's house; and declared that there must be an underground railroad of which he was president. This story they took pleasure in repeating several times in the city, as a good joke, and it became the talk about town, so that when Levi went to Richmond he was asked by his friends if he knew of his late promotion, and was told of the title given him. Levi said this was the first he had heard about an underground railroad, and it was doubtless the origin of the term.

For more than twenty years in Newport, Indiana, and for about ten years in Cincinnati, Ohio, his home was the refuge of the fleeing slave. On an average for each of the twenty years, one hundred and six fugitives were received, cared for, and forwarded from this station; and more than three thousand in all were fed at his table. Many of them were clothed and shod, the sick were nursed, medical attendance was provided, and sometimes the stay of the slaves was prolonged to weeks and months. In all this time he never lost a passenger.

―――――――

"Hurrah for Quakerism!"

[FROM *Memories of Old Friends*]

CAROLINE FOX

[Memories of Old Friends *belongs on the same shelf with Percy Lubbock's* Earlham *and Julius Hare's* The Story of My Life, *books which depict the life of the upper middle classes in Victorian England. Excerpts are included here because they reflect the change which had come over Quakers in the two hundred years since the children of the light first took heed of Richard Howgill's admonition, "Return home to within." And because many Quakers, by the middle of the nineteenth century, were themselves members of the wealthy upper middle class, Caroline Fox*

(1819–1871), while showing us how far the Quakers have traveled from "within," shows us at the same time the rich complexity of Victorian life.

What a world! "Hurrah for Quakerism!" cried this girl of twenty-one, happy to believe that Barclay had never been refuted, that Fox had done some good; and to comment upon the "struggling nature of earnest American thought" as demonstrated by Emerson. Would she have hurrahed, we wonder, in the days when Quakers were hunted "like butterflies on the fells"?

In her day and time she hurrahed, and found time to set down the experiences which give us pleasure to read today. Hurrah for Caroline Fox.]

―――――

August 24.—J. Pease gave us a curious enough account of a shelf in the Oxford library which is the receptacle of all works opposed to the Church of England, which are placed there to be answered as way may open. Barclay's Apology, and Barclay's Apology alone, remains unanswered and unanswerable, though many a time has it been taken from the shelf controversial, yet has always quietly slunk back to its old abode. Hurrah for Quakerism! . . .

London, May 19, 1840.—Returned with Harriet Mill from Carlyle's lecture to their house in Kensington Square, where we were most lovingly received by all the family. John Mill was quite himself. He had in the middle of dinner to sit still for a little to try and take in that we are really here. A good deal of talk about Carlyle and his lectures: he never can get over the feeling that people have given money to hear him, and are possibly calculating whether what they hear is worth the price they paid for it. Walked in the little garden, and saw the Falmouth plants which Clara cherishes so lovingly, and Henry's cactus and other dear memorials. Visited John Mill's charming library, and saw portions of his immense herbarium; the mother so anxious to show everything, and her son so terribly afraid of boring us. He read us that striking passage in "Sartor Resartus" on George Fox making to himself a suit of leather. How his voice trembled with excitement as he read, "Stitch away, thou noble Fox," etc.

June 3.—Spent the evening at the Mills', and met the Carlyles and Uncle and Aunt Charles. Conversation so flowed in all quarters that I could not gain any continuous idea of what took place in the most remarkable ones, but what I did catch was the exposition of Carlyle's argument about the progressive degeneracy of our lower classes, and its only obvious remedies, education and emigration: about Ireland and its sad state, and how our sins towards it react on ourselves; but it was to the Condition-of-England question that his talk generally tended. He seems to view himself as the apostle of a certain democratic idea, bound over to force it on the world's recognition. He spoke of George Fox's "Journal:" "That's not a book one can read through very easily, but there are some deep things in it, and well worth your finding." . . .

February 2, 1842.—Cousin Elizabeth Fry sends a simple and characteristic account of her dinner at the Mansion-House on the occasion of Prince Albert's laying the foundation-stone of the Royal Exchange: "I think you will be interested to hear that we got through our visit to the Mansion-House with much satisfaction. After some little difficulty that I had in arriving, from the crowd which overdid me for the time, I was favored to revive, and when led into the drawing-room by the Lord Mayor I felt quiet and at ease. Soon my friends flocked around me. I had a very satisfactory conversation with Sir James Graham, and I think the door is open for further communication on a future day. It appeared most seasonable, my then seeing him. I then spoke to Lord Aberdeen for his help, if needful, in our foreign affairs. During dinner, when I sat for about two hours between Prince Albert and Sir Robert Peel, we had deeply interesting conversation on the most important subjects. With Prince Albert upon religious principle, its influence on sovereigns and its importance in the education of children; and upon modes of worship, our views respecting them—why I could not rise at their toasts, not even at the one for the queen, why I could rise for prayer; also on the management of children generally; on war and peace; on prisons and punishment. I had the same subjects, or many of them, with Sir Robert Peel. The kindness shown me was extraordinary. After dinner I spoke to Lord Stanley about our colonies, and I think I was enabled to speak to all those in power that I wanted to see. I shook hands very pleasantly with the Duke of Wellington, who spoke beautifully, expressing his desire to promote the arts of peace and not those of war; he said he was not fond of remembering the days that were past, as if the thoughts of war pained him. Although this dinner, as numbers I have been at, may not in all respects accord with my ideas of Christian simplicity, I have felt, and feel now, if on such occasions I seek to keep near to my Guide and in conduct and conversation to maintain my testimony to what I believe right, I am not out of my place in them, when, as it was the other day, I feel it best to go to them."

April 20, 1842.—At Meeting a Friend spoke very sweetly, but, from circumstances over which she had little control, her sermon forcibly reminded me of "going to Bexico to zee de Bunkies."

May 28, 1842.—Called at Cheyne Row, where Carlyle and his wife received us with affectionate cordiality. He looks remarkably well and handsome, but she has not at all recovered the shock of her mother's death. He wanted to know what we were doing at the Yearly Meeting, and what were its objects and functions, and remarked on the deepening observable among Friends; but when we told of the letter to the queen recommendatory of peace in Afghanistan, he was terribly amused. "Poor little queen! She'd be glad enough to live in peace and quietness if the Afghans would but submit to her conditions." . . .

Carlyle gave me a number of the "Dial," which Emerson has marked and sent him as a good sample of the tone and struggling nature of earnest American thought; also an American pamphlet on Capital Punishment, with some of his own characteristic notes in the margin. Carlyle does not like capital punishment, because he wishes men to live as much and as long as possible; he rejoices in the increasing feeling that it is a right solemn thing for one man to say to another, "Give over living!" But on my characterizing it as a declaration that though God could bear with the criminal, man could not, he said, "Why, there are many things in this world which God bears with: he bears with many a dreary morass and waste, yet he gives to man the will and the power to drain and to till it and make oats grow out of it. But you'll make no oats grow out of men's corpses. This pamphlet-author is oddly inconsistent; with all his enthusiastic feeling for the value of individual life, he is quite in favor of going to war with England, thus willing to sacrifice thousands of brave fellows, while he would save the life of a miserable rascal like Good, who cut his wife into pieces and stuffed them into a coach-box." Carlyle's laughs are famous fellows, hearty and bodily. . . .

June 11, 1842.—Elizabeth Fry took us to Coldbath Fields Prison. Asked her concerning her experience of solitary confinement: in one prison, where it was very limitedly used, she knew of six who became mad in consequence of it. Met the Duchess of Saxe-Weimar (sister to our queen-dowager), her two pretty daughters, and Lady Denbigh. The survey of the prison was exceedingly interesting. It is, on the whole, the best of our houses of correction, though a severe one, as whipping and the treadmill are still allowed. It was sad to see the poor exhausted women ever toiling upward without a chance of progress. The silent system is enforced with as much strictness as they can manage, but of course it is sometimes evaded. It was beautiful to hear Cousin Fry's little conversations with them; her tone of sympathy and interest went to their hearts. She had no reading, owing to the High Church principles of the directors and chaplains of the prison, but she craved leave to tell them a story of the effect of one passage from the Bible on a poor prisoner, which melted many of them to tears. The tact with which she treated the two chaplains who went round with us was inimitable, telling them that if the duchess was very anxious for a reading she would propose to turn out all the gentlemen except her brother, for they had said it would be impossible to be present at worship which they did not conduct. The duchess was much pleased, and with her unaffected daughters drove off to Chiswick.

July 27, 1842.—John Sterling is interesting himself much about George Fox, whose life he means to write. He sadly misses his earnest, prophetic spirit in the present day, and thinks Carlyle the only one who at all represents it. . . . Speaking of the old Puritan preachers, Carlyle comments on the excessive fun which bursts out even in their sermons, and says that he believes all really great men were great laughers too, and that those who have the gravest capacity in them have also the greatest fun; therefore he cordially hails a hearty guffaw even from a Puritan pulpit. . . .

Falmouth, January 4, 1846.—I have assumed a name today for my religious principles—Quaker-Catholicism—having direct spiritual teaching for its distinctive dogma, yet recognizing the high worth of all other forms of faith; a system in the sense of inclusion, not exclusion; an appreciation of the universal, and various teachings of the Spirit, through the faculties given us, or independent of them.

June 3, 1846.—Paid the Carlyles a visit. . . . He asked about Yearly Meeting and the question of dress. I told him that the clothes-religion was still extant; he rather defended it as symbolizing many other things, though of course agreeing on its poverty as a test. He said, "I have often wished I could get any people to join me in dressing in a rational way. In the first place, I would have nothing to do with a hat; I would kick it into the Serpentine, and wear some kind of a cap or straw covering."

February 18, 1847.—A damsel belonging to Barclay's establishment being here, I thought it right "to try and do her good"; so I asked her, after many unsuccessful questions, if she had not heard of the Lord's coming into the world. "Why," she said, "I may have done so, but I have forgot it." "But surely you must have heard your master read about it, and heard of it at school and church and chapel." "Very likely I have," said she, placidly, "but it has quite slipped my memory!" and this uttered with a lamb-like face and a mild blue eye.

May 20, 1847.—Carlyle wandered down to tea, looking dusky and aggrieved at having to live in such a generation; but he was very cordial to us notwithstanding. Of Thomas Erskine, whom they both love: "He always soothes me," said Mrs. Carlyle, "for he looks so serene, as if he had found peace. He and the Calvinistic views are quite unsuited to each other." Carlyle added, "Why, yes; it has been well with him since he became a Christian." We had such a string of tirades that it was natural to ask, "Who *has* ever done any good in the world?" "Why, there was one George Fox: he did some little good. He walked up to a man and said, 'My fat-faced friend, thou art a damned lie. Thou art pretending to serve God Almighty, and art really serving the devil. Come out of that, or perish to all eternity.' This—ay, and stronger language too—had he to say to his generation, and we must say it to ours in such fashion as we can. It is the one thing that *must* be said; the one thing that each must find out for himself is that he is really on the right side of the fathomless abyss, serving God heartily, and authorized to speak in His name to others. Tolerance and a rose-water world is the evil symptom of the time we are living in: it was just like it before the French Revolution, when universal brotherhood, tolerance, and twaddle were preached in all the marketplaces; so they had to go through their Revolution with one hundred and fifty a day butchered—the gutters thick with blood, and the skins tanned into leather: and so it will be here unless a righteous intolerance of the devil should awake in time. . . . Then another man who did some good was Columbus, who fished up the island of America from the bottom of the sea; and Caxton,—he too did something for us; indeed, all who do faithfully whatever in them lies, do something for the universe." He is as much as ever at war with all the comfortable classes, and can hardly connect good with anything that is not dashed into visibility on an element of strife. He drove with us to Sloane Square, talking with energetic melancholy to the last.

"The Blood of Christ . . . No More Effectual than the Blood of Bulls and Goats"

WALT WHITMAN

[George Fox said, "I should have a sense of all conditions, how else should I speak to all conditions." And Walt Whitman (1819–1892) says, after one of his characteristic listings of persons: "All this I swallow, it tastes good, I like it well, it becomes mine, I am the man, I suffered, I was there." Whitman described himself as, "stout as a horse, affectionate, haughty, electrical," and all these characteristics, the "haughty" too, in the opinion of those to whom he would not truckle, belonged to Fox. Friends generally have not recognized the Quaker elements in Whitman because he speaks of something they have been taught to be silent about: sex. But it would be very difficult, with the exception of such passages in Whitman (and these also, in their truthtelling) to find in him lines which do not reflect Quaker influence.

Whitman's memories of Elias Hicks (1748–1830) are written with great tenderness. They are suffused with that peculiar and affecting light which results when winter focuses once again on spring. Whitman is remembering not only the old black-eyed preacher but himself when young, and a Brooklyn kitchen at sunset where his father says, "Come, Mother, Elias preaches tonight." For Whitman this was a memory. For most of us today, "Come, Mother, Elias preaches tonight," is spoken out of an America which passed before our time.

"Hicks," says Elton Trueblood, whose essay on Whitman and Hicks follows, "was pleading for a real experimental knowledge of God and Christ," and was warning against "confidence in a mere traditional or historic belief." But to an age already responding to hymns like "There is a fountain filled with blood," and "Washed in the blood of the lamb," Hicks's view of the actual blood of Christ was horrifying, and his comparison disgusting. But early Quakers, who went naked for a sign—or, as did the elegant Barclay, walked the streets of the city in sackcloth and ashes—could have digested such language and accepted *such meanings without repugnance, certainly without any such break-up of the Society as Hicks's words helped forward.]*

———

Prefatory Note.—As myself a little boy hearing so much of E. H., at that time, long ago, in Suffolk and Queens and Kings counties—and more than once personally seeing the old man—and my dear, dear father and mother faithful listeners to him at the meetings—I remember how I dream'd to write perhaps a piece about E. H. and his look and discourses, however long afterward—for my parents' sake—and the dear Friends too! And the following is what has at last but all come out of it—the feeling and intention never forgotten yet!

There is a sort of nature of persons I have compared to little rills of water, fresh, from perennial springs—(and the comparison is indeed an appropriate one)—persons not so very plenty, yet some few certainly of them running over the surface and area of humanity, all times, all lands. It is a specimen of this class I would now present. I would sum up in E. H., and make his case stand for the class, the sort, in all ages, all lands, sparse, not numerous, yet enough to irrigate the soil—enough to prove the inherent moral stock and irrepressible devotional aspirations growing indigenously of themselves, always advancing, and never utterly gone under or lost.

Always E. H. gives the service of pointing to the fountain of all naked theology, all religion, all worship, all the truth to which you are possibly eligible—namely in *yourself* and your inherent relations. Others talk of Bibles, saints, churches, exhortations, vicarious atonements—the canons outside of yourself and apart from man—E. H. to the religion inside of man's very own nature. This he incessantly labors to kindle, nourish, educate, bring forward and strengthen. He is the most *democratic* of the religionists—the prophets. . . .

The following are really but disjointed fragments recall'd to serve and eke out here the lank printed pages of what I commenc'd unwittingly two months ago. Now, as I am well in for it, comes an old attack, the sixth or seventh recurrence, of my war-paralysis, dulling me from putting the notes in shape, and threatening any further action, head or body.

W. W., CAMDEN, N.J., JULY, 1888

To begin with, my theme is comparatively featureless. The great historian has pass'd by the life of Elias Hicks quite without glance or touch. Yet a man might commence and overhaul it as furnishing one of the amplest historic and biography's backgrounds. . . .

Elias Hicks was born March 19, 1748, in Hempstead township, Queens county, Long Island, New York State, near a village bearing the old Scripture name of Jericho (a mile or so north and east of the present Hicksville, on the L. I. Railroad). His father and mother were Friends, of that class working with their own hands, and mark'd by neither riches nor actual poverty. Elias as a child and youth had small education from letters, but largely learn'd from Nature's schooling. He grew up even in his ladhood a thorough gunner and fisherman. The farm of his parents lay on the south or sea-shore side of Long Island (they had early removed from Jericho) one of the best regions in the world for wild fowl and for fishing. Elias became a good horseman, too, and knew the animal well, riding races; also a singer fond of "vain songs," as he afterwards calls them; a dancer, too, at the country balls. When a boy of 13 he had gone to live with an elder brother; and when about 17 he changed again and went as apprentice to the carpenter's trade. The time of all this was before the Revolutionary War, and the locality 30 to 40 miles from New York city. My great-grandfather, Whitman, was often with Elias at these periods, and at merry-makings and sleigh-rides in winter over "the plains."

How well I remember the region—the flat plains of the middle of Long Island, as then, with their prairie-like vistas and grassy patches in every direction, and the "kill-calf" and herds of cattle and sheep. Then the South Bay and shores and the salt meadows, and the sedgy smell, and numberless little bayous and hummock-islands in the waters, the habitat of every sort of fish and aquatic fowl of North America. And the bay men—a strong, wild, peculiar race—now extinct, or rather entirely changed. And the beach outside the sandy bars, sometimes many miles at a stretch, with their old history of wrecks and storms—the weird, white-gray beach—not without its tales of pathos—tales, too, of grandest heroes and heroisms.

In such scenes and elements and influences—in the midst of Nature and along the shores of the sea—Elias Hicks was fashion'd through boyhood and early manhood, to maturity. But a moral and mental and emotional change was imminent. Along at this time he says:

"My apprenticeship being now expir'd, I gradually withdrew from the company of my former associates, became more acquainted with Friends, and was more frequent in my attendance of meetings; and although this was in some degree profitable to me, yet I made but slow progress in my religious improvement. The occupation of part of my time in fishing and fowling had frequently tended to preserve me from falling into hurtful associations; but through the rising intimations and reproofs of divine grace in my heart, I now began to feel that the manner in which I sometimes amus'd myself with my gun was not without sin; for although I mostly preferr'd going alone, and while waiting in stillness for the coming of the fowl, my mind was at times so taken up in divine meditations, that the opportunities were seasons of instruction and comfort to me; yet, on other occasions, when accompanied by some of my acquaintances, and when no fowls appear'd which would be useful to us after being obtain'd, we sometimes, from wantonness or for mere diversion, would destroy the small birds which could be of no service to us. This cruel procedure affects my heart while penning these lines."

In his 23d year Elias was married, by the Friends' ceremony, to Jemima Seaman. His wife was an only child; the parents were well off for common people, and at their request the son-in-law mov'd home with them and carried on the farm— which at their decease became his own, and he liv'd there all his remaining life. . . .

Of a serious and reflective turn, by nature, and from his reading and surroundings, Elias had more than once markedly devotional inward intimations. These feelings increas'd in frequency and strength, until soon the following:

"About the twenty-sixth year of my age I was again brought, by the operative influence of divine grace, under deep concern of mind; and was led, through adorable mercy, to see, that although I had ceas'd from many sins and vanities of my youth, yet there were many remaining that I was still guilty of, which were not yet aton'd for, and for which I now felt the judgments of God to rest upon me. . . . I began to have openings leading to the ministry, which brought me under close exercise and deep travail of spirit; for although I had for some time spoken on subjects of business in monthly and preparative meetings, yet the prospect of opening my mouth in public meetings was a close trial; but I endeavor'd to keep my mind quiet and resign'd to the heavenly call, if it should be made clear to me to be my duty. . . ."

But we find if we attend to records and details, we shall lay out an endless task. We can briefly say, summarily, that his whole life was a long religious missionary life of method, practicality, sincerity, earnestness, and pure piety—as near to his time here, as one in Judea, far back—or in any life, any age. . . . During E. H.'s matured life, continued from fifty to sixty years—while working steadily, earning his living and paying his way without intermission—he makes, as previously memorandized, several hundred preaching visits, not only through Long Island, but some of them away into the Middle or Southern States, or north into Canada, or the then far West— extending to thousands of miles, or filling several weeks and sometimes months. These religious journeys—scrupulously accepting in payment only his transportation from place to place, with his own food and shelter, and never receiving a dollar of money for "salary" or preaching—Elias, through good bodily health and strength, continues till quite the age of eighty. It was thus at one of his latest jaunts in Brooklyn city I saw and heard him. This sight and hearing shall now be described.

Elias Hicks was at this period in the latter part (November or December) of 1829. It was the last tour of the many missions of the old man's life. He was in the 81st year of his age, and a few months before he had lost by death a beloved wife with whom

he had lived in unalloyed affection and esteem for 58 years. (But
a few months after this meeting Elias was paralyzed and died.)
Though it is sixty years ago since—and I a little boy at the time
in Brooklyn, New York—I can remember my father coming
home toward sunset from his day's work as a carpenter, and
saying briefly, as he throws down his armful of kindling-blocks
with a bounce on the kitchen floor, "Come, mother, Elias
preaches to-night." Then my mother, hastening the supper and
the table-cleaning afterward, gets a neighboring young woman,
a friend of the family, to step in and keep house for an hour or
so—puts the two little ones to bed—and as I had been behaving
well that day, as a special reward I was allow'd to go also.

We start for the meeting. Though, as I said, the stretch of
more than half a century has pass'd over me since then, with its
war and peace, and all its joys and sins and deaths (and what a
half century! how it comes up sometimes for an instant, like the
lightning flash in a storm at night!) I can recall that meeting yet.
It is a strange place for religious devotions. Elias preaches
anywhere—no respect to buildings—private or public houses,
school-rooms, barns, even theatres—anything that will accom-
modate. This time it is in a handsome ball-room, on Brooklyn
Heights, overlooking New York, and in full sight of that great
city, and its North and East rivers fill'd with ships—is (to specify
more particularly) the second story of "Morrison's Hotel," used
for the most genteel concerts, balls, and assemblies—a large,
cheerful, gay-color'd room, with glass chandeliers bearing myri-
ads of sparkling pendants, plenty of settees and chairs, and a sort
of velvet divan running all round the side-walls. Before long the
divan and all the settees and chairs are fill'd; many fashionables
out of curiosity; all the principal dignitaries of the town, Gen.
Jeremiah Johnson, Judge Furman, George Hall, Mr. Willoughby,
Mr. Pierrepont, N. B. Morse, Cyrus P. Smith, and F. C. Tucker.
Many young folks too; some richly dress'd women; I remember
I noticed with one party of ladies a group of uniform'd officers,
either from the U. S. Navy Yard, or some ship in the stream, or
some adjacent fort. On a slightly elevated platform at the head
of the room, facing the audience, sit a dozen or more Friends,
most of them elderly, grim, and with their broad-brimm'd hats

on their heads. Three or four women, too, in their characteristic Quaker costumes and bonnets. All still as the grave.

At length after a pause and stillness becoming almost painful, Elias rises and stands for a moment or two without a word. A tall, straight figure, neither stout nor very thin, dress'd in drab cloth, clean-shaved face, forehead of great expanse, and large and clear black eyes (in Walter Scott's reminiscences he speaks of Burns as having the most eloquent, glowing, flashing, illuminated dark-orbed eyes he ever beheld in a human face; and I think Elias Hicks's must have been like them), long or middling long white hair; he was at this time between 80 and 81 years of age, his head still wearing the broad-brim. A moment looking around the audience with those piercing eyes, amid the perfect stillness. (I can almost see him and the whole scene now.) Then the words come from his lips, very emphatically and slowly pronounc'd, in a resonant, grave, melodious voice, *"What is the chief end of man?* I was told in my early youth, *it was to glorify God, and seek and enjoy him forever."*

I cannot follow the discourse. It presently becomes very fervid and in the midst of its fervor he takes the broad-brim hat from his head, and almost dashing it down with violence on the seat behind, continues with uninterrupted earnestness. But, I say, I cannot repeat, hardly suggest his sermon. Though the differences and disputes of the formal division of the Society of Friends were even then under way, he did not allude to them at all. A pleading, tender, nearly agonizing conviction, and magnetic stream of natural eloquence, before which all minds and natures, all emotions, high or low, gentle or simple, yielded entirely without exception, was its cause, method, and effect. Many, very many were in tears. Years afterward in Boston, I heard Father Taylor, the sailor's preacher, and found in his passionate unstudied oratory the resemblance to Elias Hicks's—not argumentative or intellectual, but so penetrating—so different from anything in the books—(different as the fresh air of a May morning or sea-shore breeze from the atmosphere of a perfumer's shop). While he goes on he falls into the nasality and sing-song tone sometimes heard in such meetings; but in a moment or two more as if recollecting himself, he breaks off, stops, and resumes in a natural tone. This occurs three or four times during the talk of the evening, till all concludes. . . .

Indeed, of this important element of the theory and practice of Quakerism, the difficult-to-describe "Light within" or "Inward Law, by which all must be either justified or condemn'd," I will not undertake where so many have fail'd—the task of making the statement of it for the average comprehension. We will give, partly for the matter and partly as specimen of his speaking and writing style, what Elias Hicks himself says in allusion to it—one or two of very many passages. Most of his discourses, like those of Epictetus and the ancient peripatetics, have left no record remaining—they were extempore, and those were not the times of reporters. Of one, however, deliver'd in Chester, Pa., toward the latter part of his career, there is a careful transcript; and from it (even if presenting you a sheaf of hidden wheat that may need to be pick'd and thrash'd out several times before you get the grain) we give the following extract:

"I don't want to express a great many words; but I want you to be call'd home to the substance. For the Scriptures, and all the books in the world, can do no more; Jesus could do no more than to recommend to this Comforter, which was the light in him. 'God is light, and in him is no darkness at all; and if we walk in the light, as he is in the light, we have fellowship one with another.' Because the light is one in all, and therefore it binds us together in the bonds of love; for it is not only light, but love— that love which casts out all fear. So that they who dwell in God dwell in love, and they are constrain'd to walk in it; and if they 'walk in it, they have fellowship one with another, and the blood of Jesus Christ his Son cleanseth us from all sin.'

"But what blood, my friends? Did Jesus Christ, the Saviour, ever have any material blood? Not a drop of it, my friends—not a drop of it. That blood which cleanseth from the life of all sin, was the life of the soul of Jesus. The soul of man has no material blood; but as the outward material blood, created from the dust of the earth, is the life of these bodies of flesh, so with respect to the soul, the immortal and invisible spirit, its blood is that life which God breath'd into it. . . ."

Note. The Separation.—The division vulgarly call'd between Orthodox and Hicksites in the Society of Friends took place in 1827, '8 and '9. Probably it had been preparing some time. One who was present has since described to me the climax, at a meeting of Friends in Philadelphia crowded by a great attendance of both sexes, with Elias as principal speaker. In the course of his utterance or argument he made use of these words: "The blood of Christ—the blood of Christ—why, my friends, the actual blood of Christ in itself was no more effectual than the blood of bulls and goats—not a bit more—not a bit." At these words, after a momentary hush, commenced a great tumult. Hundreds rose to their feet. . . . Canes were thump'd upon the floor. From all parts of the house angry mutterings. Some left the place, but more remained, with exclamations, flush'd faces and eyes. This was the definite utterance, the overt act, which led to the separation. Families diverg'd—even husband and wives, parents and children, were separated.

Of course what Elias promulg'd spread a great commotion among the Friends. Sometimes when he presented himself to speak in the meeting, there would be opposition—this led to angry words, gestures, unseemly noises, recriminations. Elias, at such times, was deeply affected—the tears roll'd in streams down his cheeks—he silently waited the close of the dispute. "Let the Friend speak; let the Friend speak!" he would say when his supporters in the meeting tried to bluff off some violent orthodox person objecting to the new doctrinaire. But he never recanted.

"The Fullness of the Godhead Dwelt in Every Blade of Grass"

D. ELTON TRUEBLOOD

[*In Elton Trueblood's opinion, Whitman's poetry will be remembered when the separation of Quakers into "Hicksites" and "Orthodox" is forgotten. This may be true, but the pity is that today there are more Quakers who know about and practice the separation than there are Quakers who know and read Whitman.*

However that may be, the separation took place, and an account of it, too long to repeat here, may be found in John Sykes's The Quakers. *Sykes finds the Orthodox falling away "from the Quaker method," that is, away from meetings without hired clergymen and toward "hot gospel techniques" and an emphasis "on the depravity of man, naturally subject to the dominion of Satan, and on the atoning sacrifice of Jesus that, for those who believed, brought personal salvation." The Orthodox splintered further into Wilburites and Gurneyites; and so far did "Orthodoxy" go that in 1878 the Ohio Yearly Meeting declared, "We repudiate the so-called doctrine of the inner light, or the gift of a portion of the Holy Spirit in the soul of every man as dangerous, unsound and unscriptural." This amounts to a repudiation of Quakerism as first conceived and, until this time, practiced. The Ohio Quakers were then theologically in the position of Bishop Butler, who said to Wesley, "Sir, the pretending to extraordinary revelations and gifts of the Holy Spirit is a horrid thing, a very horrid thing."*

Sykes believes that what was at stake in this controversy was the nature of the meeting for worship. "Was it to be a renewal of insight through the creative experience of the group together, the mystic reality, or was it to be an ordained service accepting the ruling letter of Scripture and the saving act of the Crucifixion, the logical form for which, as ultimately among American Orthodox Friends, was a congregation being moulded by a pastor? Only the first of these was Quakerism as the Hicksites, the most firmly of all, maintained."]

The fact that Hicks inspired Whitman is very important, important for the understanding of both men. There is no reason to suppose that Whitman remembered what the old man said; in fact, he specifically says he did not remember, but the mood seems to have been formative in the boy's life. The fact that Elias was a great man in the eyes of the Whitmans made the sensitive boy the more receptive. Here was one of his own people who had achieved what seemed like fame. It was natural that the poetic mood of the old man should be contagious. Was it an accident that one Long Islander loved to say that the fullness of the godhead dwelt in every blade of grass, and another Long Islander called his poems *Leaves of Grass?*

The oratory of Hicks included passages which tended to fall into regular stress. The heavily accented periods were like the cadences of prose poetry which "approximate, without quite reaching, metrical regularity." When we realize that Hicks, like most Friends of his period, spoke in a singsong chant when impassioned, we begin to have a valuable hint concerning the origin of Whitman's verse. . . .

The evidence that the mood of Hicks was contagious is found not chiefly in similarity of cadence, but, far more, in the similarity of the dominant message of Walt Whitman and the dominant message of Elias Hicks. In a real sense it was a "Song of Myself" that the Long Island farmer had been singing for so many years. "Always," says Whitman, "E.H. gives the service of pointing to the fountain of all naked theology, all religion, all worship, all the truth to which you are possibly eligible—namely in yourself and your inherent relations. Others talk of Bibles, saints, churches, exhortation, vicarious atonements—the canons outside of yourself and apart from man—E.H. to the religion inside of man's very own nature." For the poet this became:

I hear and behold God in every object, yet understand God
    not in the least,
Nor do I understand who there can be more wonderful than
    myself.

If we print Hicks' words in the same way we have:

> Nor have I ever found a Saviour anywhere else
> But in the light, spirit, and grace of God in my own soul.

The boy who heard Hicks in Morrison's Ball Room was later to write:

> In the faces of men and women I see God, and in my own face
>   in the glass,
> I find letters from God dropt in the street, and every one is
>   sign'd by God's name,
> And I leave them where they are, for I know that wheresoe'er
>   I go,
> Others will punctually come for ever and ever.

But already Hicks had said:

> And the law of God is written in every heart, and it is there that
>   he manifests himself;
> And in infinite love, according to our necessities, states, condi-
>   tions.
> And as we are all various and different from one another,
>   more or less,
> So the law by the immediate operation of divine grace in the
>   soul,
> Is suited to every individual according to his condition.

When we try to understand Elias Hicks as a theologian we are balked at every turn. . . . The truth is that Hicks was not a theologian at all, but a rustic poet. In this lies the significance of his career, the reason for both his success and his failure. He succeeded because he had a simple and single message, the Song of Himself, which he gave with emotional power on all occasions. . . .

"... Too Late to Become an Abolitionist Now"

[FROM *Two Quaker Sisters*]

ELIZABETH BUFFUM CHACE

[*Elizabeth Buffum Chace's account of her sister Rebecca's visit with John Brown forms one-half of the volume* Two Quaker Sisters. *And it is not the treatment of John Brown nor the Quaker refusal to take a stand against slavery which forms the most distressing part of this book, but the account by another sister, Lucy Buffum Lovell, of the terrible upbringing and the death of her three oldest children. At two and a half, Caroline Lovell was taught of death, and her mother hoped that her first ideas of death were "pleasant." At three, standing on a coffee pot, Caroline refused to get off, saying, "Daughter don't feel able to stand on the floor." At three she was given the* Life of Reverend John Peak *for bedtime reading. At four she had memorized Luke 18 and desired frequently to hear "about those people that spit on our Savior." At four and a half she had hemmed a set of sheets and pillowcases. At the same age she became much interested in temperance, influenced by "the scenes of intemperance, with its awful results, in the* Temperance Almanack." *She prayed that all those who drank "rum, brandy, gin, wine, alcohol, whisky, and arrack ... give it up and become good sober men." At five she backslid and when asked if she hoped she was a Christian replied "I've no reason to think I am." She was dead before six, and though "during health" she gave her parents no "reason to hope that her heart had been renewed," her mother "rests in the belief that 'the blood of Jesus Christ which cleanseth from all sin,' was applied to her soul." Poor Caroline, and poor mother.*

These comments have no place here except as they illustrate the uneven progress of understanding. In the same household, one sister makes a dangerous trip to take her sympathy and understanding to John Brown, while another, child of her time, tortures herself and her gifted daughter through a misapprehension of what her religion requires of both of them.]

Several persons, in various parts of the country, were forcibly carried out of Friends' meetings, for attempting therein to urge upon Friends the duty "to maintain faithfully their testimony against slavery," as their *Discipline* required. A few meeting houses in country places, had been opened for Anti-Slavery meetings; whereupon, our New England Yearly Meeting adopted a rule that no meeting house under its jurisdiction, should be opened except for meetings of our religious Society.

During those years, I could not help feeling a sense of grave responsibility for these unrighteous proceedings, so long as I remained a member of the Society, and my mind was deeply exercised concerning my duty in the matter. Other Anti-Slavery Friends thought it was best to remain in the Society, and strive to reform these abuses. But we were few in number; and the great body of Quakerism in the country was against us. Our lips were sealed in the meetings, and out of meetings we were in disgrace,—"despised and rejected." One young Friend in Massachusetts had written a very earnest, open letter to Friends, in remonstrance for their pro-slavery position. He was universally condemned by all the powerful influences of the Society. Talking with one of the most influential members at our Yearly Meeting, who expressed strong condemnation of this young man's presumption, I said, "But is not what he says true?" And he replied, "Well, thee may be sure, it will certainly kill him as a Friend."

No belief in Papal infallibility was ever stronger in the Catholic mind, than was the assumption, not expressed in words, that the Society could do no wrong; and that, on this question of slavery, silence should be maintained; and no reproof, exhortation, or entreaty against the pro-slavery attitude of the Society, should be tolerated. The claim of Friends, that the transaction of their Society affairs, should be under the immediate inspiration and guidance of the Holy Spirit, so beautifully set forth in many of their writings and sermons, as well are required in their *Discipline,* was sometimes perverted to authorize proceedings and actions which were far from being holy. . . .

When John Brown attempted to free the slaves in 1859 by his attack at Harper's Ferry, our family was stirred by strong emotions. On the dark day, when the grand, but mistaken old man, was hung on a Virginian gallows, a solitary strip of black drapery on our door reminded our neighbors that, with us, it was a day of mourning.

A younger sister of mine, Rebecca Buffum Spring, lived then at Eagleswood, near Perth Amboy, New Jersey. Like all of our family, she and her husband Marcus Spring were active in the Anti-Slavery cause. Her husband was a very wealthy New York merchant and they had for years used their resources in aiding the cause of the Negroes.

On October 17, 1859 came the startling news that men, led by John Brown, had attacked the Federal arsenal at Harper's Ferry, Virginia. There had been loss of life and the raiders had been captured and imprisoned.

My sister was deeply agitated at the news for she felt that John Brown and his men had, although unwisely, taken the first positive step toward ending the impossible conditions under which the country was laboring.

On November 2, 1859 the Circuit Court of Jefferson County, Virginia, pronounced upon John Brown and his men, the sentence of death. Lydia Maria Child, the well loved Boston Abolitionist, had requested permission of Governor Wise of Virginia, to visit the condemned men, and had seen them.

When Rebecca heard of this visit she felt that she also must do everything in her power to comfort and help the captives. Although she had never met John Brown she was touched by his blind devotion to the Negro, his lack of malice, his honesty of purpose, and his high courage. She felt that she must go to see him and try to ease his path, which all knew, was now only to death.

At first, after the Harper's Ferry raid, Virginians and Southerners generally felt that it was the wild thought of one unbalanced brain, or at most the work of one fanatic representing only a small group of extremists. Governor Wise and the people of Virginia therefore treated the prisoners with considerable magnanimity.

By November fifth, however, an entirely different feeling pervaded the State, for in the week since the raid the Northern press had adopted John Brown as the champion of freedom and its columns were filled with burning denunciation of Virginia and its Governor. A leading Northern daily paper wrote that Pontius Pilate was gentle in comparison to Governor Wise. Ministers of the gospel throughout the North spoke in like vein and the mail of the Governor was filled with denunciation and abuse and threats of personal revenge.

Sentiment in Virginia changed from contemptuous annoyance to real and bitter hate, and the feeling became widespread that Northerners as a whole were antagonistic and furiously determined to wreak vengeance on the officials and body politic of the State.

It was just at this time that my sister Rebecca decided to go to see John Brown. Accompanied only by her young son, Edward, nineteen years old, she left Eagleswood on November fourth, for Charlestown. Rebecca has written her recollections of this trip and I include them as she wrote them.

"When I decided I must go to Harper's Ferry to see John Brown my husband, Marcus, entreated me against it. The way was full of dangers, he urged, and I could never get there. I answered, 'We have talked against slavery all these years. Now somebody has done something. These men have risked their lives. I must go.' 'It would kill me,' he replied; and so I gave it up. Later, while on a trip to New York, he sent this message back:

" 'Mrs. Child has gone to see the prisoners, by permission of the Governor of Virginia; what a pity you didn't go with her!' Taking this for consent, before he returned home, my young son and I were on our way South. . . .

"We reached the Wager House, at Harper's Ferry, at about nine o'clock; and as the night was cold, drew near the fire. A gentleman called to see a lady staying at the hotel. They sat directly behind my chair. The lady remarked to her visitor that the ladies in the hotel felt like prisoners since the raid (October 16–17), the streets being full of soldiers and men in arms. She told of a night when they were awakened by fearful cries and the firing of guns. They had thought it an insurrection of the slaves, she said, and that they should all be murdered. She told how the citizens in the fight of the seventeenth had brought a wounded raider into that very room; and how the sister of the landlord stood before the captive and begged them to leave him to the law, and how, as she would not let them kill him there, they dragged him out and one of them killed him on the bridge, close by. And she said, 'I wanted to kill them all.'

" 'Who killed him?' I asked, starting to my feet. 'How cowardly to kill a wounded man!'

"The lady and all the people hurried away. Only the gentleman stopped to answer:

" 'Madam, it was one of our citizens. He would not have done it, but our Mayor had been shot down in the street.' Then he, too, left.

"We took the morning train for Charlestown, the county-seat, eight miles from Harper's Ferry. Many rough-looking men were hanging about the station there, and I was thankful that I had no need to ask questions, but had only to give my checks to a porter and walk up to the Carter House, the principal inn of the place.

"There the courteous landlord could not tell me where Mrs. Child was stopping, and even stated that no such lady had arrived. I insisted, and added that I came to join her. As he could tell me nothing of her, however, I set out to find Friend Howells, to whom I had been recommended by my Baltimore acquaintance. He lived at the other end of the village. The streets were filled with formidable-looking men, but no one spoke to us; yet I was glad to reach my destination. A servant conducted us through a hall to the dining-room, where several people were at table. The Friend received us very graciously and asked us to dine.

" 'I met thy friend Edward Stabler in Baltimore,' said I, 'who told me thee could give me important information. Can thee tell me where Mrs. Child is?'

" 'Mrs. Child?' he asked.

" 'The lady who has come here from Boston, by permission of the Governor, to see the prisoners.'

"The Friend flew into a most unfriendly rage. Starting to his feet, he shouted: 'I have nothing, and will have nothing to do with these things.'

" 'Neither have I, but I thought I might ask for my friend in a Friend's house without giving offense,' I replied.

" 'I have nothing to do with it. Let her stay in her own country and mind her own business.'

" 'I even thought she might be in this house.'

" 'I wouldn't receive her if she came.'

" 'I rather think John Woolman would.'

" 'I don't care what John Woolman would. I know David Howells wouldn't.'

"I reminded him of some of the principles of the Friends, but he only raged the more. So, stepping up the one step into the hall, I said: 'Peace be to this house,' then turned and walked to the entrance.

"He followed, muttering about dangerous times. When the light came in through the open door I was shocked to see the change in the man. He trembled, his lips were blue, his face twitched nervously. I was sorry for him; and my way seemed dark.

"The street, on the return, was still more crowded with sinister-looking men. When we reached the hotel, I asked for the landlord; but as soon as he came the room filled with men. He thought I would better come out on a back piazza. But instantly that, too, was crowded, while listeners pressed in every door and window. I said:

" 'I went to see the Quaker man, and he was cross as a bear. And I can't find Mrs. Child.'

" 'Why don't you go to see Brown's physician?' asked the landlord. 'He is a gentleman and will be civil to you.'

"To the physician's house we went. The servant said he was at home, and a kind looking gentleman came and assured me that Mrs. Child was not in town. After a little talk, he explained that he was not the doctor, who was too ill to see me.

" 'You have answered as the doctor—who are you?'

" 'I am a justice of the peace.'

" 'Then open the prison door for me.'

" 'Only Sheriff Campbell can do that.' He advised me to write to the sheriff, and actually walked up the street with me. Passing the prison, he pointed out a kind-looking man of powerful frame, standing on the platform before the door, as the jailer, Avis. At my request, the justice called Avis down, but instantly there was such a rush of men, thrusting their faces between us, that we could not talk; so Avis said that he would call at the hotel to see me. He came and from that time did all that he could to enable me to effect my wish, even using some strong words about it. Meantime, I had sent to the sheriff a note which, in due season, brought me the following reply:

November 6, 1859.

Mrs. Spring: Dear Madam—I received your note late last night requesting an interview with Capt. Brown. I am sorry I cannot grant your request; public opinion is very much excited by your coming here, and our object is to allay that excitement. I also understand from Capt. Brown that he does not wish to see you, or any one else. My responsibility is very great. If anything should occur in consequence of my granting you, or any one else, an interview, I should be censured by the whole community. I must therefore deny your request.

Yours respectfully,
J. W. Campbell, *Sheriff*

"While waiting for the reply I had sent toilet articles and other comforts to Capt. Brown, by my son, until the landlord said it was dangerous for him again to go through the mob to the prison. When I told the landlord that the sheriff had refused my request, he advised me to see George Sennott, the Boston lawyer, of counsel for Brown and his men, who was then at the hotel. I sent for him, and here at last found a true friend and helper. On the second day, Sunday, November 6, of my stay in Charlestown, Mr. Sennott obtained from the judge of the court an order for my admission to the prison at three o'clock, and he brought a message from Capt. Brown that he should be glad to see me.

"I had not dared to leave the house for fear of losing just such a chance. We now decided to take a walk. With my son I walked to a grove of forest trees, where I gathered leaves of rich autumn tints and fastened them together with thorns.

Returning to the hotel, I told the landlord that I now had permission to enter the prison and asked him to give me a half-opened rose that I saw in the garden. He answered: 'Yes, that, or anything else.'

"At the hour appointed we were admitted to the guard room in the prison to wait for the jailer, then engaged in the court room across the street. Presently I saw men bringing a man, apparently dying, from the court house into the prison. This was Aaron D. Stevens, Brown's lieutenant, desperately wounded in the Harper's Ferry raid. He had fainted several times during his trial, and the judge had ordered him returned to his cell. Avis, the jailer, accompanied him, and I was glad to think my waiting over, but Avis said that he must forthwith return to the court house with Cook, another of Capt. Brown's imprisoned men.

" 'Will you go back to the hotel, or wait for me here?' he asked.

" 'I will wait here,' said I.

"Some dozen men occupied the guard-room. Their talk was rough. The stoveheated air was suffocating, and it was not a pleasant half-hour for my son and me. At last Avis returned and led us into the prison-room. On one bed lay John Brown, on the other, Stevens. Mr. Brown attempted to rise, but could not stand. I gave him the rose, which he laid on his pillow. I looked for a nail on which to hang my leaves. Mr. Brown said they had taken out every nail. The window had strong iron bars; behind the bars I put the bright leaves. He looked pleased, and his wife told me afterwards that I could not have carried him a better gift, for he loved the woods. We drew our chairs near Mr. Brown's bed; the jailer sat on a bench back in a corner; I unrolled some worsted work and began to knit; Brown looked gratified and was inclined to talk. . . .

" 'I want to ask you one question,' said I, 'not for myself, but for others. In what you did at Harper's Ferry were you actuated by a spirit of revenge?' Brown started, looked surprised, then replied:

" 'No, not in all the wrongs done to me and to my family in Kansas did I ever have a feeling of revenge.'

"The shyness that I believe he felt in the presence of strangers was wearing off. He spoke several times to my son and looked at him tenderly. He was becoming more cordial and communicative when a loud voice called, 'Avis!' It was Sheriff Campbell. The crowd had become impatient and threatened violence if I were allowed to stay longer. The sheriff, alarmed, twice called the jailer. Avis hastened out and returned instantly with the verdict that I must leave. I shook hands with Brown on parting. 'The Lord will bless you for coming here,' said he.

"The great, tall sheriff opened the door and hurried out a little woman and a boy into the face of a furious mob of the worst-looking men I ever saw. We stood for a moment on the little platform at the top of the steps, and looked down over a sea of angry eyes and clenched and threatening hands and I did not feel afraid! I, who dare not pass a cow and who have such a terror of great dogs, was so uplifted in spirit that I had lost all feeling of fear, and walked through the mob, which opened just wide enough to let us pass, without thinking of the mob at all. I believe I was safer because I was not afraid. It was when Peter was afraid that he began to sink. It is good sometimes to get a glimpse of the power within us.

"Mr. Sennott brought me constant news of Capt. Brown. He improved steadily. Seeing nothing more that I could hope to do, I was intending to return home, when on November 8th Mr. Sennott desired me to see Mr. Brown again, in order to take a message from him to his wife, then in Philadelphia. I sent for Judge Parker, presiding judge of the Circuit Court, then in session, who not only granted me the permission I asked, but gave me his arm to the prison.

"What a different man I now found! Capt. Brown was sitting at a table, writing. He looked well; his hair, that had been matted with dried clots of blood, was washed and brushed. Thrown up from his brow, it made a soft white halo around his head. His high white forehead expressed a sort of glory. He looked like an inspired old prophet. He had just finished a letter to his wife and children. This he requested me to read and take to his wife, to whom he sent many messages. The last farewell was a silent one. Our hearts were too full for words. Stevens lay on his bed, apparently dying, but his great eyes shone, and his face was full of joy.

"Capt. Brown stood by the table as I left the room—a commanding figure, the white halo about his high head, on his face a look of peace. For twenty years he had believed himself divinely called to free the slaves. He had tried and failed. The slave power seemed stronger than ever; his little band of earnest young men were scattered, dead, or imprisoned, and he himself was condemned to die on the scaffold. But his faith never flinched.

"On November 24th John Brown wrote to me, 'I am always grateful for anything you do or write. You have laid me and my family under many and great obligations.'

"John Brown died on December 2nd and four of his men on December 16th. Aaron D. Stephens and Hazlitt were sentenced to die in March, 1860. I wrote many letters to these boys that winter and sent them many boxes of food and clothing." . . .

In the year 1865 while the Friends of Rhode Island were contributing liberally, and working devotedly, for the relief of the freedmen, the Yearly Meeting committee having charge of the Friends School in Providence, refused admission to a boy and girl, the children of a respectable colored physician of Boston, who was to be sent by a philanthropic association to look after the welfare of the emancipated slaves in New Orleans, and who wished to place his children in a good school during his absence. The committee were solicited to show their interest in the freedmen by receiving these motherless children into the school, but they replied that "the time had not yet come to take such a step," and our appeals fell on deaf ears.

My own convictions, long since established, were confirmed by these and other similar experiences, that it is not right for me to give any countenance or support to charitable or educational institutions maintained exclusively for colored people. The colored people are here, by no choice of their own—members of our body politic; and the sooner they are admitted to all the privileges of citizenship, and estimated solely by their merits and qualifications, the better for all concerned. It is a baneful policy to undertake to support two distinct nationalities or muncipalities in one commonwealth, or two distinct social fabrics, on any basis except that of mental and moral fitness.

All these experiences were an important feature in the education of our children of which, circumstances being as they were, I would by no means have deprived them. For there is no better influence toward the building up of a strong virtuous manhood and womanhood, than the espousal in early life of some great humanitarian cause as a foundation. By such preparation men and women are made ready to take up all questions which concern the advancement of mankind. The slavery of the black man is abolished, the shackles have fallen from his limbs and he is crowned with the diadem of citizenship. It is too late to become an Abolitionist now but in the process of overthrowing one great wrong there is always laid bare some other wrong, which requires for its removal the same self-sacrificing spirit, the same consecration to duty, as accomplished the preceding reform. . . .

The Little Iron Soldier

or, What Aminadab Ivison Dreamed about

[FROM *Margaret Smith's Journal*]

JOHN GREENLEAF WHITTIER

[*"It is my sober judgment," wrote Rufus Jones, "that John Greenleaf Whittier grasped more steadily, felt more profoundly, and interpreted more adequately the essential aspects of Quaker life and faith during the fifty years . . . 1830 to 1880, than did any other person in the American Society of Friends. . . . I am unable, furthermore, to think of any English Friend of the same years who saw as clearly or who expressed with equal wisdom and balance the universal religious significance of the central Quaker principles."*]

Whittier (1807–1892) himself told a boy, "My lad, if thou wouldst win success, join thyself to some unpopular but noble cause." Following his own advice, Whittier joined not one but two unpopular and noble causes: poetry and abolition. The cause of poetry is always suspect; and abolitionists in the pre-Civil war period were about as popular as Freedom Riders in the sixties. Whittier won considerable success in both the causes he joined; but because (I hope) poetry will outlast polemics, he is remembered chiefly as a poet.

Whittier is one of the few persons who can write religious poetry without becoming either mawkish or grandiloquent. He can be dry and pedestrian; but when speaking of the ineffable, wings are a pleonasm, anyway. His "I know not where His islands lift their fronded palms in air" may not be the equal of Vaughn's "My soul, there is a country far beyond the stars"; but, like it, Whittier's poem does not wear out with repetition. And poems like "Snow Bound" and "Telling the Bees" should survive for at least as long as we have any memory of, or regard for, the people we once were.

In this volume Whittier is chiefly represented as neither poet nor abolitionist, but as a fabulist, writing of still another Quaker concern: war. He was anti-war, as he was anti-slave and pro-poetry. And if he were alive today, he would certainly have joined a third noble and unpopular cause, that of outlawing war by other ways than preparing for it.]

———

Aminadab Ivison started up in his bed. The great clock at the head of the staircase, an old and respected heirloom of the family, struck one.

"Ah," said he, heaving up a great sigh from the depths of his inner man, "I've had a tried time of it."

"And so have I," said the wife. "Thee's been kicking and threshing about all night. I do wonder what ails thee."

And well she might; for her husband, a well-to-do, portly, middle-aged gentleman, being blessed with an easy conscience, a genial temper, and a comfortable digestion, was able to bear a great deal of sleep, and seldom varied a note in the gamut of his snore from one year's end to another.

"A very remarkable exercise," soliloquized Aminadab; "very."

"Dear me! what was it?" inquired his wife.

"It must have been a dream," said Aminadab.

"Oh, is that all?" returned the good woman. "I'm glad it's nothing worse. But what has thee been dreaming about?"

"It's the strangest thing, Hannah, that thee ever heard of," said Aminadab, settling himself slowly back into his bed. "Thee recollects Jones sent me yesterday a sample of castings from the foundry. Well, I thought I opened the box and found in it a little iron man, in regimentals; with his sword by his side and a cocked hat on, looking very much like the picture in the transparency over neighbor O'Neal's oyster-cellar across the way. I thought it rather out of place for Jones to furnish me with such a sample, as I should not feel easy to show it to my customers, on account of its warlike appearance. However, as the work was well done, I took the little image and set him up on the table, against the wall; and, sitting down opposite, I began to think over my business concerns, calculating how much they would increase in profit in case a tariff man should be chosen our ruler for the next four years. Thee knows I am not in favor of choosing men of blood and strife to bear rule in the land: but it nevertheless seems proper to consider all the circumstances in this case, and, as one or the other of the candidates of the two great parties must be chosen, to take *the least of two evils*. All at once I heard a smart, quick tapping on the table; and, looking up, there stood the little iron man close at my elbow, winking and chuckling. 'That's right, Aminadab!' said he, clapping his little metal hands together till he rang over like a bell, 'take the least of two evils.' His voice had a sharp, clear, jingling sound, like that of silver dollars falling into a till. It startled me so that I woke up, but finding it only a dream presently fell asleep again. Then I thought I was down in the Exchange, talking with neighbor Simkins about the election and the tariff. 'I want a change in the administration, but I can't vote for a military chieftain,' said neighbor Simkins, 'as I look upon it unbecoming a Christian people to elect men of blood for their rulers.' 'I don't know,' said I, 'what objection thee can have to a fighting man; for thee's no Friend, and hasn't any conscientious scruples against military matters. For my own part, I do not take much interest in politics, and never attended a caucus in my life, believing it best to keep very much in the quiet, and avoid, as far as possible, all letting and hindering things; but there may be cases where a military man may be voted for as a choice of evils, and as a means of promoting the prosperity of the country in business matters.' 'What!' said neighbor Simkins, 'are you going to vote for a man whose whole life has been spent in killing people?' This vexed me a little, and I told him there was such a thing as carrying a good principle too far, and that he might live to be sorry that he had thrown away his vote, instead of using it discreetly. 'Why, there's the iron business,' said I; but just then I heard a clatter beside me, and, looking around, there was the little iron soldier clapping his hands in great glee. 'That's it, Aminadab!' said he; 'business first, conscience afterwards! Keep up the price of iron with peace if you can, but keep it up at any rate.' This waked me again in a good deal of trouble; but, remembering that it is said that 'dreams come of the multitude of business,' I once more composed myself to sleep."

"Well, what happened next?" asked his wife.

"Why, I thought I was in the meeting-house, sitting on the facing-seat as usual. I tried hard to settle my mind down into a quiet and humble state; but somehow the cares of the world got uppermost, and, before I was well aware of it, I was far gone in a calculation of the chances of the election, and the probable rise in the price of iron in the event of the choice of a President favorable to a high tariff. Rap, tap, went something on the floor. I opened my eyes, and there was the little image, red-hot, as if just out of the furnace, dancing, and chuckling, and clapping his hands. 'That's right, Aminadab!' said he; 'go on as you have begun; take care of yourself in this world, and I'll promise you you'll be taken care of in the next. Peace and poverty, or war and money. It's a choice of evils at best; and here's Scripture to decide the matter: "Be not righteous overmuch." ' Then the wicked-looking little image twisted his hot lips, and leered at me with his blazing eyes, and chuckled and laughed with a noise exactly as if a bag of dollars had been poured out upon the meeting-house floor. This waked me just now in such a fright. I wish thee would tell me, Hannah, what thee can make of these three dreams?"

"It don't need a Daniel to interpret them," answered Hannah. "Thee's been thinking of voting for a wicked old soldier, because thee cares more for thy iron business than for thy testimony against wars and fightings. I don't a bit wonder at thy seeing the iron soldier thee tells of; and if thee votes tomorrow for a man of blood, it wouldn't be strange if he should haunt thee all thy life."

Aminadab Ivison was silent, for his conscience spoke in the words of his wife. He slept no more that night, and rose up in the morning a wiser and better man.

When he went forth to his place of business he saw the crowds hurrying to and fro; there were banners flying across the streets, huge placards were on the walls, and he heard all about him the bustle of the great election.

"Friend Ivison," said a red-faced lawyer, almost breathless with his hurry, "more money is needed in the second ward; our committees are doing a great work there. What shall I put you down for? Fifty dollars? If we carry the election, your property will rise twenty per cent. Let me see; you are in the iron business, I think?"

Aminadab thought of the little iron soldier of his dream, and excused himself. Presently a bank director came tearing into his office.

"Have you voted yet, Mr. Ivison? It's time to get your vote in. I wonder you should be in your office now. No business has so much at stake in this election as yours."

"I don't think I should feel entirely easy to vote for the candidate," said Aminadab.

"Mr. Ivison," said the bank director, "I always took you to be a shrewd, sensible man, taking men and things as they are. The candidate may not be all you could wish for; but when the question is between him and a worse man, the best you can do is to choose the least of the two evils."

"Just so the little iron man said," thought Aminadab. "'Get thee behind me, Satan!' No, neighbor Discount," said he, "I've made up my mind. I see no warrant for choosing evil at all. I can't vote for that man."

"Very well," said the director, starting to leave the room; "you can do as you please; but if we are defeated through the ill-timed scruples of yourself and others, and your business pinches in consequence, you needn't expect us to help men who won't help themselves. Good day, sir."

Aminadab sighed heavily, and his heart sank within him; but he thought of his dream, and remained steadfast. Presently he heard heavy steps and the tapping of a cane on the stairs; and as the door opened he saw the drab surtout of the worthy and much-esteemed friend who sat beside him at the head of the meeting.

"How's thee do, Aminadab?" said he. "Thee's voted, I suppose?"

"No, Jacob," said he; "I don't like the candidate. I can't see my way clear to vote for a warrior."

"Well, but thee doesn't vote for him because he is a warrior, Aminadab," argued the other; "thee votes for him as a tariff man and an encourager of home industry. I don't like his wars and fightings better than thee does; but I'm told he's an honest man, and that he disapproves of war in the abstract, although he has been brought up to the business. If thee feels tender about the matter, I don't like to urge thee; but it really seems to me thee had better vote. Times have been rather hard, thou knows; and if by voting at this election we can make business matters easier, I don't see how we can justify ourselves in staying at home. Thou knows we have a command to be diligent in business as well as fervent in spirit, and that the Apostle accounted him who provided not for his own household worse than an infidel. I think it important to maintain on all proper occasions our Gospel testimony against wars and fightings; but there is such a thing as going to extremes, thou knows, and becoming over-scrupulous, as I think thou art in this case. It is said, thou knows, in Ecclesiastes, 'Be not righteous overmuch: why shouldst thou destroy thyself?'"

"Ah," said Aminadab to himself, "that's what the little iron soldier said in meeting." So he was strengthened in his resolution, and the persuasions of his friend were lost upon him.

At night Aminadab sat by his parlor fire, comfortable alike in his inner and his outer man. "Well, Hannah," said he, "I've taken thy advice. I didn't vote for the great fighter today."

"I'm glad of it," said the good woman, "and I dare say thee feels the better for it."

Aminadab Ivison slept soundly that night, and saw no more of the little iron soldier.

Part Three

QUAKERS

IN THE

WORLD

CHILDREN OF
BIRTHRIGHT QUAKERS

. . . their respectable and orthodox successors.
—LOGAN PEARSALL SMITH

"Social Layers of Increasing Splendor"

[FROM *Unforgotten Years*]

LOGAN PEARSALL SMITH

[*"If we shake hands with icy fingers, it is because we have burnt them so horribly before." So says Logan Pearsall Smith (1865–1946) in "Afterthoughts," which forms a part of his wonderful collection of— and one wonders what to call them—paragraphs and sentences entitled,* All Trivia.

Had Logan Smith had his fingers burned as a child by his father who, carried away by mid-century revivalism, preached with such success that he frequently confused message and message-bearer? It is impossible to say. In any case, Logan Smith, born in a Quaker household, writes of Quakerism as Strachey wrote of Queen Victoria: a dear queer old thing which we have, thank God, outgrown.

His writing is placed before that of his mother, Hannah Whitall Smith, because his mother was too involved in life to stand aside from it and make historical generalizations about it. Logan made a career

363

of standing aside from life. This may have helped his sentences; it harmed his life. "In complete devotion to his art," says his former secretary, he had, "taken for granted all the ease and comfort which his companions gave him. Those companions had gradually become for him no more than the sources of all that made his life smooth and easy; as separate live beings they were ceasing to exist for him. The punishment for selfishness is to turn the world into a solitude."

In such a solitude Logan Pearsall Smith died. The result, it frequently appears, of living like an artist is that one gets the habit, and so must also die like one. However this may be, Logan Pearsall Smith's life, and that of his parents and sisters, illustrates the change that had come over Quakers and Quakerism.

———

The life of the Quakers in Philadelphia, where we lived as children, was that of a secluded community, carefully entrenched and guarded from all contact with what we called the "World"— that dangerous world of wickedness which, we vaguely knew, lay all about us. With that world and its guilty splendors we had no contact; of the fashionable American aristocracy (and every population has its aristocracy and fashion) we were not members; and I can make no claim, as Americans abroad are apt to claim, that I belong to one of what are called America's first families. With members of this greater world, like Edith Wharton and Mrs. Winthrop Chanler, I became acquainted only after I had come to live in Europe.

No, we spent our youth amid the evangelical plainness and the simple ways of living of the stricter Philadelphia Friends. And yet, those richly carved and velvet-covered chairs which adorned my grandfather's drawing-room at Germantown, those antlers which hung on the walls of his suburban residence— these seemed to tell a tale of richer experience, and tinged for me with gayer colors the past history and the European expeditions of the old gentleman who sat reading upstairs.

The theme of the American abroad has given rise to a considerable literature in recent years; its earlier documents are less well known, and it was with a good deal of interest that I recently read my grandfather's account of his experiences in Europe, and the authentic history of those trophies which had so impressed me as a boy. In my grandfather a tendency, which he bequeathed to his descendants, manifested itself at an early date, to make "jaunts," as he called them, to Europe; and in 1845 he had gone to England on a sailing packet, accompanied by my father. On his return he published in two volumes, under the title of *A Summer's Jaunt across the Waters*, an account of this journey. To boast of the distinguished acquaintances they have made abroad is one of the most legitimate satisfactions of returned Americans, and this was plainly one of the motives which inspired the composition of my grandfather's volumes.

The Philadelphia Quakers had always kept up a connection with the members of their sect in England, and this connection was frequently renewed by the visits of English Friends on holy missions. Some of these visiting Friends belonged to the highest sphere of the Quaker world—for all religious communities, however holy, are stratified in social layers of increasing splendor—and the impressiveness of their doctrine was much augmented by a sense of the plain yet brilliant world in which they lived, a world of Barclays and Gurneys and other rich English Quaker families which, like a Quaker Versailles, holy and yet splendid, shone for us across the Atlantic with a kind of glory—a glory which, to tell the truth, has never completely faded from my eyes.

My grandfather, though not interested in their doctrines, was by no means indifferent to the country houses and opulent tables of these English Quakers; he tells of dining with Samuel Gurney at Ham House, of meeting Elizabeth Fry, and of hearing her, in her feeble but honored old age, make a beautiful prayer from her large mahogany armchair in the meeting she attended. He tells also of being welcomed among a company of English Friends by a fellow Philadelphian and youthful acquaintance, Eliza P. Kirkbride, who had married, as his third wife, the eminent and opulent Joseph John Gurney.

But the great glory of this jaunt abroad of my grandfather was his visit to Stoke Park, then the residence of Granville Penn, William Penn's great-grandson and heir. Granville Penn, learning, according to my grandfather's account—and I dare say by a note from my grandfather himself—that a descendant of William Penn's secretary had come from Pennsylvania to England, sent him an invitation to Stoke Poges, which was accepted with alacrity. He relates how an elegant family carriage with liveried servants met him at the station; how he was conducted to the noble family mansion of the Penn family, where he spent some days, and in whose deer park he shot the buck of which the antlers afterwards adorned his suburban home; how his host drove him about the neighborhood in a coach with four horses, and took him to Oxford, where they dined at a raised table in the hall of Christ Church, and where, he tells with undisguised elation, all the guests except Mr. Penn and himself were lords. . . .

The echo of these glories, the sight of these antlers and royal chairs, must have seemed evidences of a "gayness" they could not but deplore to the stricter Quakers of Philadelphia, to whom my mother's family belonged, and among whom my sisters and I spent our childish years. But into the hearts of these most unspotted of the Chosen People had not the spirit of the world found an entrance, though unsuspected by themselves? No dreams, indeed, of dining with lords, of opera boxes, or of being mistaken for foreign princes, troubled, I am sure, their meditations in their silent Meetings; but when some opulent Friend from England came to preach the gospel to them, was not the impressiveness of his or her doctrine tinged and deepened by a sense of the sanctified splendor of such English Friends? Had they not indeed among them a living representative of that splendor in the Eliza Kirkbride who had reigned at Earlham, and with whom my grandfather had dined in England, and who, after the decease of her husband . . . had returned to her native city, where, preaching with great acceptance, she now reigned as a kind of Quaker queen, with many courtiers to listen to her holy boastings? Among these courtiers, one of the most assiduous was my mother's mother, Friend Mary Whitall, who was in our childhood always holding up before us the figure of Friend Gurney as the glass of Quaker fashion, and the very mold of form among the stricter Friends.

Thus into my boyish heart the spirit of the World found its entrance in various disguises, and intimations were also not wanting of those other enemies of our souls, the Flesh and the Devil.

It has become of late the fashion to speak with great frankness on sex matters, and many eminent authors dwell with especial emphasis on the first awakenings in them of a consciousness of this kind. Why should I not follow their example? These awakenings often come to innocent youth in troubled ways, and my first awareness of the allurements of what we call the Flesh was derived from circumstances of an unusual nature. Barnum's Circus came to Philadelphia in my boyhood, rousing considerable excitement in the youth of that quiet city; and among the Quakers the question was much debated whether their children should be allowed to witness this entertainment. While it was admitted on the one hand that the sight of the elephants and the other exotic animals would help to enhance their conception of the wonders of creation, there were grave fears on the other hand that the spectacle of the scantily clad female acrobats on the tightropes might sully the innocence of their childish minds. The compromise finally arrived at, at least in our family, was that the children should be taken to the circus and allowed to see the animals, but should sit with closed eyes while the acrobats were performing.

So there we sat, a row of Quaker children, staring with all our eyes at the performing elephants, but with our organs of vision closed and our hands before them during the less seemly interludes. But one little Quaker boy permitted himself a guilty peep through his fingers, and gazed on a show of muscular limbs moving, slowly moving, in pink tights. What he was gazing at was, he knew, the spectacle of Sin; and so striking was the impression that his concept of that word became colored in his imagination for a long time with the pinkness of those slowly moving legs. It was only long afterwards that he came to understand why he had been forbidden to gaze upon them, and the grave danger he might have thereby incurred.

While notions of the World and the Flesh reached me in hints that I hardly comprehended, I had no doubts about the

Devil; his activities were present to my apprehension in visible forms, about which there could be no mistake. The godly community of Philadelphia Quakers, going their ways and attending to their affairs in peace and quietness, would, to an observer from outside, have seemed a uniform community of pious people, all dressed in the same garb, all speaking the same language, all living in the same houses, all sitting in the same meditative silence, or listening to the same doctrines in the same square, unadorned meetinghouses. To such a superficial observer, William Penn's ideal of brotherly love, which he had expressed in the name of the city he had founded, would indeed have seemed to have been realized among them. As a matter of fact, however, this pious folk was divided into two bitterly hostile races, each of which regarded the other with holy abhorrence. There were two sets of meetinghouses, two sets of burial places, two orders of preachers of the Quaker faith; and between the adherents of one sect and those of another no relations could ever occur. This gulf was the result of a doctrinal earthquake which early in the nineteenth century had shaken the foundations of Quakerism in America and split it into two bodies—the orthodox sect on one side of the gulf, who clung to the stricter Trinitarian theology, and on the other the followers of Elias Hicks. . . .

Both my father's and my mother's families were adherents of the orthodox or conservative party, and the Hicksite Quakers were to my boyish apprehensions undoubtedly nothing less than children of the Devil. Even now, when I see my friend John Balderston, I shudder a little at the thought that though Samuel Kite, one of the most orthodox of the preachers in Germantown Meeting, was his grandfather, he himself played as a child with Hicksite boys in the street. But he was a bad boy, I fear, from his birth, and that he should end up at Hollywood need not surprise us. I remember climbing the wall that surrounded one of the Hicksite meetinghouses, and gazing in on those precincts with all the horror of one who gazes into Hell. Never since have I looked upon any object with such feelings of abomination.

This theological horror was accompanied, among the orthodox at least, by an immense sense of social superiority: ours were the high places, we felt, in this world as well as the next. This feeling that the Hicksites were outcasts and untouchables and social pariahs, though it had no foundation in fact, for they were as well off and as well descended as we were, and probably a more enlightened and cultivated set of people—this sense of social superiority is the main religious feeling which I still retain; and even now, when, as sometimes happens, I meet in London Philadelphians with the taint in their veins of Hicksite blood, I seem to know them at once, as by a kind of instinct, by a subtly mingled sense of theological and social repugnance, which I find it extremely difficult to overcome. . . .

The old doctrines of the corruption of man and his inevitable doom unless he finds salvation in the conviction of sin, the gift of grace, and a sudden catastrophic, miraculous conversion—this evangelical theology, though I was nourished on it in my youth, and tasted its joys and terrors, has now become utterly alien and strange to me. I cannot reconstruct in imagination that melodramatic world of hopes and terrors. I know, of course, that this body of convictions has an important place in religious history, and that, as a scheme of salvation, millions have fervently believed in it.

My parents, dissatisfied with what they considered the spiritual deadness of Quaker doctrine, welcomed the new outburst in America of revivalism, into which they plunged as into a great flood of life-giving water; and their evangelical activities formed for many years the absorbing interest of their lives. They went to revivalist meetings, they preached, they both wrote innumerable tracts, they converted souls, they lived in constant expectation of the Day of Judgment; and this highly colored world, with the heights of Heaven above them and the abysses of Hell beneath—this, and not their commonplace and commercial surroundings, formed the environment in which they lived with such feverish excitement. We children naturally caught the infection of this excitement; and were encouraged to embark in our tender years upon these spiritual adventures.

There can be no doubt that I was born a vessel of wrath, full to the brim of that Original Sin we all inherit from that crude apple that diverted Eve. I was, as my mother's letters of the time bear witness, greedy, given to fits of temper, and, as she expressed it, a gorilla for screaming. Against this old Adam in me one of the kindest and best of mothers strove with all her strength, but strove in vain. "Logan and I," she writes when I was four months old, "had our first regular battle today, and he came off conqueror, though I don't think he knew it. I whipped him till he was actually black and blue, and until I *could not* whip him any more, and he never gave up one single inch." In this state of sin I remained till I was four years old, when, however, I was rescued from it by my elder sister, now Mrs. Bernard Berenson, who, at the age of six, following the example of our parents, began the career of an evangelist, which she has since abandoned. I, who was then two years younger than herself, was the first object of her holy zeal. One memorable day she and a like-minded maiden named Fanny Potts led me to our bathroom, and there they prayed and wrestled with my carnal nature, until the great miracle of Conversion was accomplished in me.

"O Lord," prayed the future Mrs. Berenson, "please make little Logan a good boy; and don't let him tell any more lies!"

And then little Fanny Potts also lifted up her voice in prayer. "Lord, please give Logan a new heart."

Their prayer was granted, and a new heart was bestowed upon little Logan. But this heart, though purged of all former sin, was by no means immune from temptation in the future. He had in fact reached on this occasion the state of Justification only, not that of Sanctification, which, according to evangelical theology, renders us immune from sin. Again and again Satan would enter into his heart, and he would fall into sin again. In vain were his efforts to keep good by the force of his own will alone; and it was only after three years of spiritual struggle, lasting from the age of four to that of seven, that he renounced these Pelagian attempts to conquer Sin and Satan by his own carnal struggles, and realized that only by Grace, and unmerited Grace alone, and by no "deadly doing," could he attain the conquest that he sought.

All these facts I learn from a tract of my father's which I recently found among some old papers. The history of my struggle and salvation I had half forgotten, though I could still remember my infant agonies. This tract had an unusually large circulation, and, penetrating to the Western districts of America, made a powerful impression on the remaining tribes of Red Indians, who were converted by it in their thousands. Such, at least, was our family legend; and I remember the pride I took in the conversions thus accomplished; and believing, as I then believed, that each of us should wear as stars in our diadems in Heaven the souls which we had saved on earth, I took a holy delight in the prospect of shining in the courts of Heaven with the radiance of these rubies of the West.

I sometimes wonder if the children I see today playing about partake of the rich experiences of my childhood. Do they feel that they are disporting themselves on a thin crust above the flames of Hell; and when they are taken home do their mothers beat them black and blue to drive out the old Adam from within their tender skins? Do they strive, as we used to strive, to keep out Satan from their hearts, and pass their young years tormented as I was by the grim fact of sin and the dire necessity of grace? If not, many pains are no doubt spared them, but many joys and exaltations also. The glorious certainty that they are sanctified among millions doomed to Eternal Torment can never fill their hearts with holy pride, nor can they rejoice—as all my life I have rejoiced—in the consciousness that they can commit no wrong. I may do, I have undoubtedly done, things that were foolish, tactless, and dishonest, and what the world would consider wrong, but since I attained the state of Sanctification at the age of seven I have never felt the slightest twinge of conscience, never experienced for one second the sense of sin. . . .

When our parents had first arrived in England, they had been invited to a drawing-room meeting of leading Evangelicals, which was summoned to judge whether their doctrine was perfectly sound according to the strictest standards. All was well save on one point, about which there were dreadful whispers. From something my mother had said or written, it had come to be suspected that she was not altogether sound on the doctrine of Eternal Torment.

Hell, it was known, she believed in, but did she hold that its torments were destined to endure forever? As a matter of fact, she didn't; and although my father, and her friends besought her to conceal this heresy, when the crisis came and the question was put plainly to her in that London drawing-room, with that large company gravely waiting for her answer, a sudden impulse came upon her to tell the truth. She knew that her own and perhaps her husband's career as expositors of the Gospel might be ruined by this avowal; she had agreed that it would be wiser to give evasive answers on this point; but she suddenly felt that if she was questioned she must say what she thought, whatever might be the consequences; and if she had been capable of using such a profane expression she would have told herself that she didn't care a damn.

She could not, she avowed to the assembled company, believe that the God she worshiped as a God of love was capable of such awful cruelty; sinners, of course, He punished, but that He had decreed that their torments should be unending was to her a horrible belief. Her auditors were inexpressibly dismayed by this declaration; the myrtle, in Keat's phrase, "sickened in a thousand wreaths"; the company was on the point of breaking up in confusion when from the depths of that great drawing-room there floated forward, swathed in rich Victorian draperies and laces, a tall and stately lady, who kissed my mother, and said, "My dear, I don't believe it either."

This dramatic moment was, perhaps, a turning point in my life, since, if it had not occurred, our family would no doubt have soon returned to America, and the ties and friendships which drew us all back again to England would never have been formed. For this lady who thus intervened and took my mother under her protection was, as it were, the queen of evangelical Christians; and her acceptance, afterwards confirmed by that of her husband, William Cowper Temple, silenced all opposition and no further objections were suggested.

The Cowper Temples, owing to their great wealth and high position, were by far the most important people in the world in which my parents were, so to speak, on trial. Cowper Temple was in law the son of Earl Cowper, but said to be the son of Lord

Palmerston, who had long been Lady Cowper's friend, and who married her when Lord Cowper died. Their son had inherited Lord Palmerston's estates and great house at Broadlands; and the problem of this double paternity, if I may put it so, which was the gossip of the time (gossip which sounded strangely in our Philadelphian ears), had been successfully regulated by the young William Cowper's adding Lord Palmerston's family name of Temple to that of Cowper in a double appellation. After acting as secretary to his unavowed father, he served in several posts in the governments of the time and was raised to the peerage as Lord Mount Temple in 1880. His wife, who had corroborated my mother's view of Hell, is known in the history of art as the friend of the Pre-Raphaelites, and above all as the Egeria of Ruskin, who describes in his *Praeterita* how, when in Rome in 1840, he had first seen the beautiful Miss Tollemache (as she was then), and how, though he never met her, he had haunted the Roman churches on the chance of catching a glimpse of her sweet and statuesque beauty—a kind of beauty which had hitherto been only a dream to him—and how the thought of seeing her, if but in the distance, became, he tells us, the hope and solace of his Roman sojourn. It was only fourteen years later that he was introduced to her in London and became her friend.

Her friendship with my mother lasted till her death in extreme old age. She became a beautiful old saint, in whose character my mother could find only one flaw, if flaw it could indeed be called. Lady Mount Temple could never grasp the difference between right and wrong; when no cruelty was involved she couldn't see why people should not do what they liked. My mother would try to explain moral distinctions to her, and though Lady Mount Temple would say at the moment that she understood them, they soon faded from her mind.

When Oscar Wilde was out on bail between his two trials, she wrote him a friendly letter, inviting him to pay her a visit, by which letter, Oscar Wilde tells us, he was greatly touched. Her family, the Tollemaches, were a wild family, much given to misbehavior, and when one or another got in disgrace she would invite the offender to her home and would often send for my mother, as one familiar with right and wrong, to come and help the erring one back to the righteous path. I remember my mother's telling of one occasion when a Tollemache, married to a foreign prince, had run away from him with a lover, and then had been placed under Lady Mount Temple's roof to be made to realize the impropriety of her conduct. My mother was as usual summoned, and arrived in her Quaker garb and with her Bible, to help in this work of moral reformation. The Bible was read, there were prayers and exhortations, and all seemed to be going on in a most satisfactory manner, till one day, entering the old lady's writing room, my mother noticed that she was trying to conceal a piece of paper, and, when questioned, she confessed that she was composing a telegram for the lover of the erring lady to come and join them, since, as she put it, she felt that Matilda was feeling so lonely without him.

In her old age, Lady Mount Temple fell under the almost intolerable domination of a pious cook, and my mother was appealed to by the family to try to free her from this tyrant. But when my mother informed her of the fact (which she had ascertained) that this holy woman was the mother of a large family of illegitimate children, the only answer she received was, "My dear, I am so glad poor Sarah has had some fun." My mother, seeing that a charge of misconduct made no impression, thereupon visited the eldest of this irregular family, and suggested to him that as his mother must have saved a large sum of money, it might be wise to remove her to his home, and thus probably inherit her savings when she died. The son saw the wisdom of this suggestion, and Lady Mount Temple was made free at last. . . .

My mother and father had more than once attended camp meetings in America, where, amid primeval forests or by the shore of some mountain lake, evangelicals had been accustomed to gather for holy jubilations (not always unaccompanied by hysterical outbursts in which the Chosen People would scream and dance and roll upon the earth); and as they often described to their hosts these outpourings of the spirit, it occurred to the good Cowper Temples to inaugurate a series of such meetings in their park upon the banks of the Test in England, and this project was successfully carried out. My father was an acceptable preacher at these meetings; but my sincere simple-minded mother, beautiful in her Quaker dress, with her candid gaze and golden hair, was given the name of "the Angel of the Churches," and her expositions of the Gospels, delivered in the great beautiful eighteenth-century orangery in the Park at Broadlands, attracted the largest audiences, and made those gatherings famous in the religious world.

They were unattended, however, by any of the wilder phenomena of the American camp meetings, with which my mother had no sympathy, and I cannot recall the spectacle of any English aristocrats foaming at the mouth or rolling in holy ecstasy upon those Hampshire lawns.

It is odd to me now to reflect that while these meetings were going on at Broadlands, quite possibly Dante Gabriel Rossetti was also in the house in person (while in spirit such immeasurable miles away), for he often, I believe, stayed at Broadlands, and painted some of his pictures and wrote some of his poems there. But on us, if we saw him (and we may have seen him), he made, and could have made, no impression at all.

The beauty of Broadlands, with its park and shining river and the great house, full of history and portraits, and crowded with eminent people earnestly seeking Salvation for their souls, had a great effect upon my childish imagination; and when I now recall this period of our lives I cannot but regard as a fantastic adventure this sudden transference of a family of plain-living, middle-class Philadelphia Quakers into circumstances and surroundings so different from what they had been accustomed to. . . .

My mother paid little attention to all the unaccustomed circumstances in which she found herself at Broadlands; those to whom she preached were in her eyes little more than souls she hoped she could help to a true knowledge of the gospel truths; but my father was immensely delighted by his sanctified success among the great ones of this earth. If his head was turned by it, one can hardly blame him; though a little worldly wisdom (but

what chance had he ever had of acquiring worldly wisdom?)
might have given him some notion of the fantastic character of
this adventure. Even the presence at Broadlands of a large black
evangelical Negress from America, named Amanda Smith, who
would also expound the Scriptures to the earnest but indiscrimi-
nating ears of the assembled company—even the concurrence
of this holy Negress (whom my mother came to like and made
a friend of) and the necessity of sharing his triumphs with this
dusky rival, though no doubt extremely repugnant to him, did
not in the least warn my father of the sandy basis upon which his
fairy castle was being built. Indeed, as its airy pinnacles rose
higher and higher in the sky, he became incapable of listening
to the warnings my mother gave him of the risks he ran.

How could he listen? Ruddy, handsome, with the fine
whiskers so admired at that date, rich from the proceeds of the
bottle factory at home, and, unlike other evangelists, paying his
own way in a lordly fashion, he became, as his fame spread from
Broadlands, more or less the rage in religious circles. His
photograph adorned the windows of the London shops: immense crowds flocked to his ministrations; his thrilling voice
held audiences of thousands in rapt attention. Soon his reputation as a preacher crossed the Channel; he was invited to Paris,
where he held many meetings; the wives of monarchs in Belgium and Holland welcomed him to those countries, and discussed the state of their royal souls with him in private inter-
views. In the churches thousands listened spellbound to the
doctrines he proclaimed. I have already spoken of the two steps
of my conversion, the first that of Justification, by which all my
sins committed in the past were washed away, and the second
step, that of Sanctification, which rendered me immune to sin in
the future. The doctrine of the separation, as by different
operations of the Spirit, between Justification and Sanctification
was widely held by the Wesleyans, who found much authority
for it, they thought, in the Scriptures. It was very prevalent in
America when my father began to preach it to the "miserable
sinners" of England. To believe that, by an act of faith, they had
become "dead to sin," as Saint Paul expressed it, was received
as the most glorious of good tidings. Proclaimed first by my

father in 1873, and then at Broadlands, it was decided to hold a great meeting at Oxford in the autumn of 1874, and the university city was filled with earnest Christians of almost all denominations, and many ecclesiastical dignitaries. Professor Warfield of Princeton has published, under the title of *Perfectionism* (Oxford Press, 1931), an admirable and scholarly account of the whole movement, and the part played in it by my father. The effect of the Oxford meeting was, he says, nothing less than amazing. Many foreign as well as English Christians were assembled there, and, above all, German theologians, who insisted that my father should come and proclaim the good news to that country. To Germany he went, therefore, in 1875, where he met with an almost royal reception. The Emperor lent him a church, he was granted an interview with the Empress Augusta, and the most distinguished theologians attended his sermons. My father knew no German, but the necessity of translation seemed only to increase his evangelical power. The old Pietist associations were revived, and the divine glow seemed to illuminate all Germany, where a religious sect was formed which, I am told, still exists with thousands of adherents.

To England my father returned for further triumphs. "There is nothing more dramatic in the history of modern Christianity," Professor Warfield writes, "than the record of this 'Higher Life' Movement," as it was called. Brighton was occupied with even more earnest Christians than was Oxford, more church dignitaries, and more famous foreign preachers; the Dome was filled to overflowing, and the sermons had to be repeated in the Corn Exchange. "All Europe is at my feet," Professor Warfield records my poor father as exclaiming when he stood on the platform of the Dome. But almost immediately an announcement appeared in the papers that he had been compelled to cancel all his engagements and to return almost at once to America. It was suggested that a fall from a horse some years before had led to the return of certain distressing symptoms which rendered absolute rest necessary. I must say that in the family we didn't believe in that horse; at least I am certain that my mother didn't. I don't think she ever referred to it at all, which made people suspicious, and so universal became the gossip that my father's friends felt it necessary to issue a further explanation. It had come to their ears, they stated, that my father had inculcated doctrines that were most dangerous and unscriptural, and that there had been conduct on his part which, though it was free, they were convinced, from all evil intention, had rendered it necessary for him to abstain from public work, and take the complete rest rendered necessary by the fall from his horse. That the doctrine of Sanctification and Deadness to Sin might lead to dangerous forms of Antinomianism was well known from the history of the past; whether it was an unscriptural doctrine has been much discussed by theologians. But this was not the doctrinal quadruped from which my father slipped at Brighton. It was a much more mysterious beast which he had also brought from America, so mysterious that even the learned and profound Professor Warfield seems never to have guessed at its existence. But my mother knew it well; she was constantly warning my father against it, and in her old age she wrote a book to tell the world of its dreadfully dangerous character. So strongly was she convinced of its prevalence that she said there ought to be a preacher stationed on the top of every steeple, to warn Christian worshipers against it.

What exactly was the nature of this doctrine? I cannot find that it has a name, so for convenience I shall call it the doctrine of "Loving-kindness." It is one of the most ancient of heresies; it seems to have existed from the beginning of Christianity, and it is based moreover on a sound psychological basis—on the fact, namely, that nature, in one of her grossest economies, has placed the seats of spiritual and amorous rapture so close to each other that one of them is very likely to arouse the other. Even the holiest of saints and most devoted of nuns—so exactly do these two forms of ecstasy feel alike—have sometimes found it extremely difficult to distinguish between them. From this fact it was only too easy to form the heretical belief that this heightening of religious experience, due to the mingling of the sexes, was God's own way (and His ways were mysterious and not to be questioned by carnal reason) of bestowing His blessing upon them. When a holy preacher sat near a sanctified sister, or a female penitent close to her confessor, they became more conscious of the Baptism of the Spirit; and, as my mother sardonically expressed it, the nearer to each other they sat, the deeper and richer this consciousness became. To describe this experience in carnal terms, indeed in any spoken words, was impossible; it could only find expression in holy endearments. That the love feasts of the early Christians were followed by such endearments was the universal view of the most enlightened pagans: we should recoil with horror, Gibbon says, from such a notion, did not the documents show that every sect of Christians brought this accusation against every other sect. . . .

As people grow old, it becomes very hard for them to keep clear in their minds the important distinction between Right and Wrong—outlines become dim and one thing fades into another. Certainly it is extremely difficult, especially for her unsanctified descendants, not to detect a touch of amusement in my mother's book; a kind of—what shall I call it?—well, a kind of holy fun in her descriptions of the pranks played by this amazing animal in the abodes of the "dear, deluded saints," as she calls them, who made it their pet.

At the time, however, my father found it wise, as I have said, to cease his ministrations; though to the Cowper Temples, I think—certainly to Mrs. Cowper Temple—all this fuss seemed incomprehensible and silly. If these good people wanted to kiss each other, what, she wondered, could be the harm in that?

In sackcloth and ashes my father recrossed the Atlantic, not, like his father, with song and dancing; no staghorns, no royal chairs, were among his luggage. However—and these coincidences are perhaps worth noting—my mother brought with her a haunch of venison from Dunrobin Castle, where she had been on a visit, which haunch, given her by the Duke of Sutherland, was consumed immediately on our return to Philadelphia by ourselves and our relations with more snobbish than gastronomical delight.

The toughness, the lack of savor, of this ducal haunch still linger on my palate, as my first taste—there have been others—of the vanity and insipidity of worldly things.

"I Am Broad, Broader, Broadest"

[FROM Letters]

HANNAH WHITALL SMITH

[Hannah Whitall Smith (1832–1911) was as happy in her old age as her son was sorrowful in his. She had perhaps been wrong about some things but she had never been selfish. Yet she had not, as we commonly gauge such things, had a happy life. Her firstborn children died. Her husband, Robert, had to retire from his career as a revivalist. Hannah Smith herself was to see that crowds responded in exactly the same way to an evangelism uninspired from within, as they did to what she knew (since she was in both cases the preacher) was the real thing.

In her own life and family she witnessed the truth of what Howard Brinton asserts in Friends for 300 Years: "For the evangelist," Brinton writes, "the religious service was focused on himself; for the older type of minister the sermon arose out of the united life of the meeting. The evangelist kept careful count of the number of conversions he made. The older Friends did not pretend to know what changes the Spirit might be secretly making in the hearts of their hearers. . . . The revival unsettled the meeting, produced a chaos of ecstatic testimonies and much running about, and the pastor was brought in to restore order."

Through this period of religious "running about" Hannah Whitall Smith lived, and her experiences are of value in tracing the history of Quakerism. History and Quakerism apart, she is a fascinating woman, incapable, it seems, of writing a dull word.]

TO HER PARENTS

Baltimore, Oct. 18, 1875 (Aet. 43)
We three sisters do enjoy so intensely being together. We stick close together, and are quite the admiration of the Meeting, for our wonderful likeness to each other, and the love and

unity that manifestly exists between us. Aunt Julia said it was such comfort on First Day, when poor dear Friends were screaming out their sermons, to look down at us three, and know how we sympathized.

TO MRS. HENRY FORD BARCLAY

The Cedars, June 3, 1876 (Aet. 44)

It is just a year since the great Brighton meeting, and the contrast between our lives then and now is certainly a very mysterious one. Personally I greatly prefer the utter quiet and seclusion of the present, but it makes my heart ache to look at my dear husband, and think of the blight that has fallen on him. . . .

We have come to our country home for 5 months. We absolutely decline all the urgent requests to hold meetings, etc. that come to us continually, and go nowhere. I sit mostly from morning until night in a little bay window that overlooks the children's croquet ground, and from where I can just see the dear parents' home across the lawn through the trees. It would be impossible for *you* to conceive of such a quiet secluded life, and I expect it would not seem pleasant to you, but if you had had such a heart-scald as *we* have, you would understand how thankful we are for such a refuge.

But I did not mean to write in this strain, for I have no feeling of complaining in my heart. My life is full of the dear children's interests, and of sweet cares for my husband and parents. A *commonplace* life is I am sure by far the most desirable life for a woman, and henceforth I shall seek to make mine such most emphatically.

Our children are having a happy summer. Mary and Logan have both been to a swimming school and have learned to swim, and there are several small lakes and streams near us where they can swim. They have a boat and a horse, and, more than all, the liberty of American children, which means more than you can imagine. They have just come up from a paddling excursion in the woods, where they have been reveling in mud and water, and all sorts of fun.

TO MRS. ANNA SHIPLEY

The Cedars, Aug. 8, 1876 (Aet. 44)

Now I am going to give thee a plain unvarnished statement of *facts*, and thee may make what theory out of them thee pleases. I confess I am utterly nonplused and cannot make any. First of all as to the plan and object of the meeting. It was planned by Dr. Cullis and its sole object was to reinstate Robert in the eyes of the church and the world. I always said it ought not to have been called a "Convention for the promotion of holiness," but a "Convention for the promotion of Pearsall Smith."

Neither Robert nor I approved of it nor wanted it held, but Dr. Cullis was so sure it was "of the Lord," and had so set his heart on it, that, as he had stood by Robert more nobly and grandly than any other human being, we both felt constrained simply out of gratitude to him, to yield to his wishes. To be fairly honest about it, we neither of us felt for a moment as if we were serving the Lord in the matter at all. We both have felt ourselves dismissed on to Dr. Cullis's team, and concluded the Lord would not be very angry with us under the circumstances, though I confess I often secretly thought it would serve us right if He should make the meeting a complete failure as far as Robert and I were concerned. And to tell the truth I did not care whether He did nor not. I only want the will of God done under all circumstances, and I really don't much care what His will is.

I felt utterly indifferent to the meeting in every way, except that it was a great trial to me to leave my home and the sweet children. Nothing ever made Christian work pleasant to me except the thought that I was doing the will of God, and now that that is gone, I find *no* pleasure in it whatever. So we made no preparations for the meeting, we neither studied, nor prayed, nor meditated, nor in fact thought about it at all. We had got it to do, and when the time came we meant to do our best, and the rest was in the Lord's hands. We both of us hated it cordially, and felt we should be only too thankful when it was over.

It was in no sense a religious or "pious" undertaking on our parts. We were neither fervent, nor prayerful, nor concerned, nor anything that we ought to have been. Thou sees I am telling the *honest* truth. And I really cannot imagine a meeting begun in a worse frame of mind than ours was, according to all one's preconceived notions of what is the right and suitable thing. And in precisely the same frame of mind we went through the meeting. It was all a wearisome *performance* to us. We did it as over an impassable gulf. The flood had come since the last time, and changed all things to us. There was no interest, no enthusiasm. The meetings were a bore, the work was like a treadmill. We counted the hours until we could get away, and hailed the moment of emancipation with unspeakable joy. And all pious chroniclers or church historians would have been compelled by the force of their logic to have added to this record, "and no wonder the meeting was an utter failure."

But still, to keep to *facts*, I am compelled to record that the meeting was a *perfect success*. There was just the same power and blessing as at Oxford or Brighton, only on a smaller scale, because of the meeting being smaller. There was every sign of the continual presence of the Spirit. Souls were converted, backsliders restored, Christians sanctified, and all present seemed to receive definite blessings. It is said by Dr. Cullis, and *to* him by many others, to have been the best meeting ever held in this country. And it really *was* a good meeting, even I, uninterested as I was, could see that. There was just the same apparent *wave* of blessing as swept over our English meetings. And Robert and I never worked more effectually. He had all his old power in preaching and leading meetings and the very selfsame *atmosphere* of the Spirit was with him as used to be in England. As for me, thee knows I am not much given to tell of my own successes, but in this case in order that thee may have all the *facts*, I shall have to tell thee that I was decidedly "favored" as Friends say. In fact I don't believe I ever was as good. All who had heard me before said so.

The fuss that was made over me was a little more than even in England. The preachers fairly sat at my feet, figuratively speaking, and *constantly* there kept coming to me testimonies of definite blessing received while I spoke. The second time I spoke a Democratic editor was converted and consecrated on the spot; and I could scarcely get a minute to myself for the enquirers who fairly overwhelmed me.

I hate to write all this, and thee must tear it right up, but how could thee know it unless I told thee, and the facts thee must have in order to see what a muddle it all is. For who would have *dreamed* of such an outcome to the indifference and want of every sort of proper qualification for their work, which I have described beforehand? I must say, it completely upsets all *my* preconceived notions, and I do not know what to make of it. They all talked to me most solemnly about how dreadful it was in me to *think* of giving up public work, but I was utterly unmoved, and both Robert and I came away more confirmed than ever in our feelings of entire relief from everything of the kind. *We are done!* Somebody else may do it now.

The one satisfaction of the meeting to *us* was this, and it *was* a satisfaction, that Robert was treated with all the old deference and respect. . . . Henceforth home and home life for us. To be a "good housekeeper" seems to me the height of honor now! We had to refuse lots of urgent invitations to hold meetings in various places, but we did it without a longing thought, only *too* thankful to be released.

And now, WHAT does thee think of it all? *I* think one of two things, but which one I think I don't know. Perhaps thee can tell me. Either I was awfully wicked in the whole matter, and God was not in it anywhere, and all the success was by force of natural gifts and talents. Or else I was awfully good, so good as to have lost sight of self to such a degree as to be only a straw wafted on the wind of the Spirit, and so consecrated as not to be able to form a desire even, except that the will of God might be fully done.

I waver about myself continually. Sometimes I feel sure I have progressed wonderfully, and that my present sphynx-like calm and indifference to everything whether inward or outward except the will of God, is very grand. And then again I think I am an utterly irreligious and lazy fatalist, with not a spark of the divine in me. I do wish I could find out *which* I am. But at all events my *orthodoxy* has fled to the winds. I am Broad, Broader, Broadest! So broad that I believe everything is good, or has a germ of good in it, and "nothing to be refused," if it be received with thankfulness.

I agree with everybody, and always think it likely everybody's "view" is better than my own. I hold all sorts of heresies, and feel myself to have got out into a limitless ocean of the love of God that overflows all things. My theology is complete, if you but grant me an omnipotent and just Creator I need nothing more. All the tempests in the various religious teapots around me do seem so far off, so young, so green, so petty! I know I *was* there once, it must have been ages ago, and it seems impossible. "God is love," comprises my whole system of ethics. And, as thou says, it seems to take in *all.* There is certainly a very grave defect in any doctrine that universally makes its holders narrow and uncharitable, and this is always the case with strict so-called orthodoxy. Whereas, as soon as Christian love comes in, the bounds widen infinitely. I find that every soul that has traveled on this highway of holiness for any length of time, has invariably cut loose from its old moorings. I bring out my heresies to such, expecting reproof, when lo! I find sympathy. We are "out on the ocean sailing," that is certain. And if it is the ocean of God's love, as I believe, it is grand.

But enough! Now what will thee do with it all? "Be not righteous overmuch" is a salutary check I think. But oh how sad, that the nearer we seek to approach our God, and the more we try to please Him, the greater our dangers! That is, not *sad,* since it is His arrangement, but very perplexing. I guess He means us to be good *human beings* in this world, and nothing more.

TO MRS. HENRY FORD BARCLAY

Philadelphia, April 13, 1877 (Aet. 45)
Friends here are enjoying Stanley Pumphrey exceedingly; I mean those we call *Gurneyite* Friends. Among the others he is most unwelcome because of the turndown collar of his coat, and they can hardly endure to see him in their galleries. Only this week he attended the Quarterly meeting at Haddonfield, which

is the meeting we attend when living at our country place, and as he was going in the door, a Friend met him and told him that the Elders had met and had decided to request him not to sit facing the meeting on account of his coat! So he had to betake himself to the side benches. Can thee imagine such darkness in this century, and only 6 miles from Philadelphia? . . .

I must tell thee such a smart thing about Ray (aged 8). The other night when I was just leaving her after her goodnight kiss in bed, she said in such an old fashioned way, "Well, mother, I have had my first doubt." "Thy first doubt," I exclaimed, "why what was it?" "Why," she answered, "Satan came to me and said, 'Ray, thee must not believe that Jesus loves thee, for he don't.' " "Well," I asked, "what did thee say?" "Say," she repeated enthusiastically, "why I just said, 'Satan I will believe it,' and then he went away." I was delighted to find how clearly she understood the right way of dealing with doubts, and encouraged her in it. . . .

She has been cured by Dr. Cullis's prayer of faith of a longstanding and very suffering dyspepsia. She went through quite a little conflict before she could come to the point of letting him pray and lay hands on her, but finally gave up and trusted, and has been perfectly well now for more than a month. She said to me the next morning, "Mother, Satan makes it very hard for me to believe that I am healed," but with this exception her faith does not seem to have wavered, and the cure is complete.

TO MISS PRISCILLA MOUNSEY

Philadelphia, April 10, 1878 (Aet. 46)

Dear friend, I have felt inclined to give thee a word of admonition, in noticing the recurrence again of thy old trouble of self-analysis and self-reflection. Thy inward dryness and barrenness, which so often trouble thee, are simply after all moods of feeling that may arise from a thousand surrounding causes of health, or weather, or good or bad news of outward things; and they have no more to do with the *real* attitude of thy soul toward God, than a headache does, or a fit of indigestion.

TO MRS. ANNA SHIPLEY

The Cedars, June 15, 1878 (Aet. 46)

As to "ups and downs," beloved, don't thee know that I am of the kind who never have any? My path seems to lie along a sort of *dead level* arrangement, that is very comfortable, but not at all glorious. My whole experience seems to be hopelessly commonplace always, except when I come in the way of fanatics, if they are fanatics. And even then the glamour of the fanaticism *will not* get into my life, do what I may. I see its heights, but cannot scale them, and have to trudge on in the homely old ways, like a poor stupid ox. I cannot even get any inward voices and never could. I remember when Anna Richards was in the depth of her mysticism, I tried hard to walk in the same paths, but in vain. Scruples *would not* come, although I tried to cultivate them assiduously. I even wooed a sugar scoop "concern," and caps and handkerchiefs, but it was all of no use. And just so it seems to be now. With the exception of that affair of novel-reading I do not find myself "called" into anything nor out of anything. Even my Christian work comes to me in commonplace ways, and with none of the romance of Quaker "concerns." I expect the poetry of mysticism is not for me, and I have got to plod on in the prose of commonplace life always.

TO HER SISTER, SARAH NICHOLSON

Sept. 18, 1880 (Aet. 48)

I have had a revelation about guidance that seems to make obedience a far simpler thing. It has come to me through seeing the fatally sad mistakes made by so many. It is this—that the voice of God comes through our *judgment*, and not through our *impressions.* Our impressions may coincide with our judgments or they may not, but it is through the latter *alone* that God's voice comes. And when people go by impressions in opposition to their judgments, they are turning from the true voice of God, to follow the false voices of self, or of evil spirits, or of morbid conscience, or of some evil influence from other people. It *is* said

in the Bible that He will guide the meek in judgment, and it is
not said that He will guide them in impressions or feelings.

I believe this going by impressions always leads either into
fanaticism as with S.F.S. and others, or into insanity as with the
Friends. While the people who are led by God through their
judgments make very few mistakes. Think of this and tell me
thy views. Now in the matter of novels thee and I only have
impressions to go by. Our judgment tells us that a moderate
reading of novels is a good thing as preserving the mind from
overwork in one direction. And as a *fact*, my best work both in
preaching and writing has been done while I was taking the
occasional recreation of reading good novels. When I was
writing "Frank" I kept a novel by me to read in whenever I grew
tired of writing.

TO HER SISTER, SARAH NICHOLSON

Germantown,   March 3, 1881 (Aet. 49)
But, Sally, you *cannot* love if you *do not*. You can so bring the
Lord in as to lose all sight of the person, and can be perfectly
sweet and compassionate towards the person, but as to loving or
respecting that which does not win love and respect and does not
observe it, you just *cannot*, and that is the long and short of it. For
instance, A.C., suppose it was my lot to live with her and bear
things from her, or M.O., I could so see the Lord in it all as to be
perfectly victorious, and also to be tenderly compassionate
towards them, but I *could not* love nor respect them.

TO HER SISTER, SARAH NICHOLSON

Yellowstone Park, Aug. 13, 1881 (Aet. 49)
I am awfully sorry M. has missed all this, and yet I am *sure*
she could not have stood it. It is simple misery to me, and I have
had a wretched time with my digestion. I really would have gone
to bed if I had been at home, but I just had to keep on and stand
it. . . .

As to there being no fruition in life, I am not worried about
that, for I do not think this life is meant for fruition. . . . Look at

Mother, for instance, she just lived the ordinary round, kept house, brought up her children, was kind to her friends, but this was all; she did no especial work, and made no mark anywhere; but I have no doubt she fulfilled her mission in this nursery stage, and it would have been folly for her to have bewailed herself.

I feel as if I had carried this camping-out party through by prayer. So many perils have beset us on every hand that I do not know what I could have done if I could not have prayed. So I have concluded I *do* pray about almost everything, though I had never especially noticed it. But *united* prayer with other people I confess I do not care for, and I have told Mrs. Little so and she doesn't expect it of me. She and Cad keep it up by the hour sometimes, but I tell them their prayers get answered upside down often. They and Sarah Smiley met *every day* one summer to pray that *I* might not become "Broad Church," and I kept getting broader and broader, and finally they got Broad themselves.

TO MRS. ANNA SHIPLEY

Germantown, Jan. 11, 1882 (Aet. 50)

Oh, Anna, my heart just aches for the misery, pure unmitigated misery, there is in this world. Thee sees *I* get below the surface and know. And as I sit in those meetings, and see the "old stagers," as thee calls them, come in, I know of the awful sorrows that lie hidden in those apparently calm lives, and I could cry for every one of them.

Only the other day I looked at a row of them who happened to be sitting together and every one of them *I* knew, though no one else did, had husbands who made their lives, as far as the earthly side of it goes, one long torture. What is invalidism compared to *that?* No, beloved, suffering is the universal lot, and we may well be thankful, it is no worse for us individually than it is.

Oscar Wilde is a "sell." He looks like two radishes set up on their thin ends. He does say now and then a fine thing about art, just about what I would say about religion. But his manner is so poor and his style so excessively "Rose Matilda" that I believe everybody is disgusted. Logan did not get *one* idea from him, but I got several. For instance, he said—"To the true artist there is no time but the artistic moment; and no land but the land of beauty." There is a meaning in this, but what could *Logan* make out of it? And such a Logan!

TO MISS PRISCILLA MOUNSEY

Germantown, Jan. 18, 1882 (Aet. 50)

The loneliness thou speaks of I know. For do not think, darling, that it is confined to unmarried people. It is just as real in lives that have plenty of human ties, husbands, and children and friends. It is the loneliness of this *world life*, the loneliness of hearts that are made for union with God, but which have not yet fully realized it. I believe it is inseparable from humanity. I believe God has ordained it in the very nature of things by creating us for Himself alone. And I believe He very rarely allows any human love to be satisfying, just that this loneliness may drive us to Him. I have noticed that when a human love *is* satisfying something always comes in to spoil it. Either there is death, or there is separation, or there is a change of feeling on one side or the other or something, and the heart is driven out of its human resting place on to God alone.

Sometimes God permits a little taste of a satisfying love to a human being, but I do not believe it ever lasts long. I do not mean that the *love* may not last, but separation comes in some way, and the perfect *satisfaction* is taken out of it. Now, darling, thy loneliness is not *only* because thou art unmarried and hast no very close human ties, it is the loneliness of a heart made for God but which has not yet reached its full satisfaction in Him. Human love might *for awhile* satisfy thee, but it would not last.

If thou can only see this and *settle down* to it, it will help thee very much. Thou wilt give up, as I have, any expectation of finding satisfaction in the creature, and will no longer suffer with disappointment at not finding it. And this will deliver thee from the worst part of the *suffering* of loneliness. Thee will accept it as a God-given blessing meant only to drive thee to Himself.

Thy loneliness is only different in *kind* but not in *fact* from the loneliness of every human heart apart from God. Thy circumstances *are* lonely, but thy loneliness of spirit does not come from these, it is the loneliness of humanity. Therefore *nothing* but God can satisfy it. No change of circumstances, no coming in of the dearest earthly ties even, not *my* continued presence even, could really satisfy for any length of time the hungry depths of thy soul. I am speaking, darling, out of the depths of my own experience when I say this, and thee may believe me.

TO MISS PRISCILLA MOUNSEY

Germantown, Jan. 22, 1882 (Aet. 50)
If I were with thee, my precious child, I would make thee give up all future *self-reflective acts*. By this I mean all thinking over either thy successes or thy failures. The moment the action is passed, forget it, and pass on to the next. If thee does not understand just what I mean here, tell me, and I will explain more fully. It is the rule of my life never to think over my past action. This saves me all temptations to self-elation, and all temptations to discouragement, and enables me to live continually in the present moment with God.

In the evening I preached to a great crowded church in the city and had to go all alone. I wanted *thee*, darling! And of course I left my gum shoes in the pulpit, and had to be run after out to the street by somebody to bring them.

TO MRS. LAWRENCE

Yosemite Valley, Aug. 5, 1882 (Aet. 50)
Carrie, do let us cultivate ourselves into being *nice* old people. One secret I am sure is always to take the part of the young, and I intend to do this more and more. Right or wrong, they shall have my *sympathy*, and help in the former. I wonder if thee could not come to an understanding with thy mother. I had to with mine. I just told her plain out that she must not interfere in my children's lives and I advised her not to criticize my management of them. I told her it would not change my management in the least, and it would only make unpleasant feelings. She cried, and it was very hard for me and for her, too,

but it worked like a charm and was far happier for her as well as the rest of us ever afterwards. That continual interfering ruins a household, and it gets worse as people grow older. I think Mother really loved me better after that than before. She laid down the *responsibility* of things, and it was a relief to her.

Is it not strange, Carrie, that in this world we cannot do really kind and Christlike things without getting into trouble? We may do a thing in a business way and it turns out a great success; but do the same thing as a kindness, and it is sure to make a muss somehow. I would love to open my house to all the distressed saints if I could, but if I did, it would just end in trouble, I suppose.

TO MRS. HENRY FORD BARCLAY

Germantown, Oct. 18, 1882 (Aet. 50)

The other day when I was fixing up Mary's room at College, she wanted me to buy her a leather covered arm chair. I did not think she needed it, and was going to refuse, when she coughed. Immediately I thought "Now perhaps she will die of consumption, and then how I shall wish I had bought her that chair." So forthwith I bought it. And when it came home I said, "There, daughter, thee coughed up that chair." I tell thee this that thee may know just what a foolish mother I am. I tell the children that their Heavenly Father will have to give them their discipline, for their earthly parents have not the heart to do it.

TO HER FAMILY

Martha's Vineyard, Mass., Aug. 30, 1883 (Aet. 51)

This is a place about like Ocean Grove, but the meetings must be much smaller, for the one last night was a very meager affair. The sermon was a *denunciatory* one that was calculated in my opinion to drive sinners away from the God depicted in it; and apparently it did, for with all their coaxing they could not get a single person old or young up to the altar. . . . Then he drew a blood-curdling picture of the awfulness of *thus* rejecting God's offers of mercy.

He certainly tried the "terror" plan, which David Updegraff says is the *only* effectual way, most fully and vigorously. It fairly made me heartsick, and I wondered how God could endure it to be so misrepresented, but the text came to my mind "the times of this ignorance God winked at" and it comforted me. Especially as I knew He had nothing much but ignorance to wink at in all of us all our lives long.

After the sermon, I was introduced to the preacher and determined to "upset his theology" by asking him my question. So I said that I had noticed he had said in the course of his sermon that the thing which distinguishes a man from a beast is his free moral agency, and I asked him if this free moral agency did not necessitate a knowledge of good and evil? "Most certainly it does," was his reply, "and that is just where man shows his divine origin," etc., etc. Then I said, "Why did God forbid man to come to that knowledge? And why is it called a 'fall' when he did come to it? Did not God Himself say after it was done 'Man has now become *as one of us* to know good and evil'?" For once the preacher was nonplused but rallying himself he said, "Oh, that only meant actually doing evil, it meant the experimental knowledge that comes from doing it. Of course man knew about good and evil before that." "Then," I said, "was that experimental knowledge the kind God had, for He said man had come to *His* kind of knowledge." "Yes," he replied, "it was." "What," I said, "had God actually *done* the wrong thing?" "Oh, no, I did not mean that," he answered. And then I took pity on him and said, "Well, thanks, that is something to think about. Good night," and walked off. He called out after me, "I never thought of the subject before so have only answered your questions off hand." "Well," I called back, "think of it now and see what will come to you about it."

TO HER SISTER, SARAH NICHOLSON

Germantown, March 12, 1885 (Aet. 53)
Thy letter dictated to Madge fell like a knell upon my heart. And I immediately made up my mind that I would let thee die if thee could, and would not be so hatefully selfish as to try to

keep thee in thy poor suffering body one day longer. But what I shall do without thee I cannot tell; for I assure thee, life looks like a dreary pilgrimage if I am to walk through the rest of it without my twin.

Poor Charles Coffin was here last night, and, oh Sarah, what trouble he has had and is having. Then Rendel Harris was here too and he has just sent in his resignation, and it is probable that he and Helen will have to take up their march again, and find a new home and new work. Then there was Robert—three *doctrinaire* men, all three quite eminent in the religious world, and all three under a cloud. It did seem rather odd. I told them the trouble with them was that they had all been righteous overmuch; they had not mixed in enough of the world in their religion. Thee and I have had such a spice of the old Adam in all our religion that we have never been able to quite turn the corner into the region of extra piety. I am sure that has been my salvation many a time. We were made to be human beings here, and when people try to be anything else, they generally get into some sort of scrapes.

TO HER FRIENDS

Berlin, March 7, 1886 (Aet. 54)

I went with Logan last evening to a concert. The music was very fine, Logan said, and it did sound nice, but my inward ear for music has never been opened yet, and I confess I did not particularly enjoy it. Logan says that is an evolution I shall have to get in Heaven. And I suppose I must, if I am to enjoy the harps there. At present, I confess, a very short exercise in harp playing suffices me.

Yesterday morning Logan took me to the picture gallery here, and I saw Rembrandts and Titians and Tintorets and Claud Lorraines, etc. etc. And I may as well tell the truth at once and say that *I do not like them!* I am sure if any modern painter were to paint such poor pictures now, he would be hooted out of the profession. I forgot to say that in Antwerp I saw several of Reubens' pictures, and they simply disgusted me. They were great fat masses of coarse flesh. The babies were like pigs for coarseness, and in one or two of his Christs, the anatomy was repulsive. I think of course the "Old Masters" were wonderful considering how long ago they painted, etc. etc.; but that is not the orthodox style of praise, I know, so I do not hope to build any reputation on it.

TO HER FRIENDS

Broadlands, Aug. 13, 1886 (Aet. 54)

The visit of Lady Pembroke and her friends, Lady Lothian and Lady Brownlow, was, I suppose, a very fair example of the way with such visitings among the aristocracy, and it was tiresome, I am sure, to everyone concerned. It appears to be the regular thing to take visitors first all over the show rooms of the house and descant on the pictures, statuary, etc., and then all over the gardens and as much of the park as they can drag themselves. So instead of sitting down and having a good talk, we all had to perform this painful duty. I confess I prefer my own way of having callers in my library at home, seated at my table with my "revolver" beside me, and my friends sitting in comfortable rocking-chairs before me. However, if I had Lady Pembroke and Lady Lothian and Lady Brownlow calling on me, I cannot tell what I might feel impelled to do! It evidently was the conventional thing to go over the house and grounds, and no one seemed to think for a moment of doing anything else.

I frankly confess if I *lived* in England I should want to belong to the aristocracy. My independent spirit would revolt, I fear, at the idea of having anyone Lord or Lady it over me. I always tell the aristocracy this, and they enjoy it greatly.

Archdeacon Summer wore a black alpaca *apron* all the time, and I was very anxious to know what it was for, so I asked him out plump and plain, to the great amazement of all the party. He said it was a remnant of the old cassock that the priests of Rome still wear, but I could not find out that it had any especial meaning. There was a High Church clergyman present who said they *ought* to be wearing the *whole* cassock, and that all Clergymen ought to wear it. These High Churchmen are a subject of great perplexity to me. How they can be as "High" as they are and not go over to Rome is incomprehensible to my uninitiated mind. But they all seem very holy men, and I expect our Father in Heaven does not mind *their* notions any more than He minds *ours*, whether aprons or coats.

TO HER DAUGHTER, MARY BERENSON

London, Feb. 22, 1905 (Aet. 73)

Yes, we did rejoice in the assassination of the Grand Duke, and we only hope there will be some more! I have always said that Quaker or no Quaker, if I had lived in Russia, I should have been a Nihilist! It is the only voice the people have. I will get that *National Review* and read that article, but I am afraid it will make me more furious than is comfortable.

Feb. 25, 1905

I must repeat that I *did* write "The Christian's Secret" at the point of the bayonet, as it were. I did not want to write it at all, and only did it at father's earnest entreaties. He had started a Paper, which I thought was a great mistake, and I declared I would not write a line for it. But he begged so hard that at last I said I would write one article and no more, if he would give up drinking wine at dinner. Then when that article was published everybody clamored for another, and father begged, and I was good-natured and went on, but under a continual protest. And the best chapter of all was written on a voyage over from America to England, when I was sea-sick all the time, and as near cursing as a person who had experienced the "blessings of holiness" could dare to be! So tell B.B. books can be successful even if they *are* ground out with groans and curses, and I feel very hopeful of his book. The great point is to have something to say, and this he has.

I enclose thee a sample of Ray's Mathematics that thee may get a little idea of what the child is doing. It seems incredible that this is the child of whom thee and I felt very doubtful whether she could ever learn to eat a bun!

I wish I could give thee my philosophy of life which has carried me through my 70 years without any serious quarrels with anyone, and has given me the universal reputation of being a peacemaker. Even through all the mazes of theological controversy, which is quite as quarrelsome a matter as "Kunst-fussing," I always managed to be at peace with my opponents, and I cannot remember ever having had what I considered an enemy, although others might have thought I ought to have considered them as such. And as a fact some of my apparently worst enemies have become in the end my warmest friends.

I came across a book that taught that the true secret of the philosophy of Jesus was to become a King by being the Servant of all, and it carried such profound conviction to my soul that I have always tried to act on it. It struck me as being not so much religion as the most profound common-sense. And such it has proved to be throughout my whole life. Even through all the fights in the Women's Christian Temperance Union and the British Women's, it has worked with almost magical power.

The girls went to Confession last evening, so had to get up early to go to Church before breakfast this morning. It seems a bother, but I feel it is more of a comfort than a bother, for to have your conscience cleared and all your sins cast into the depths of oblivion once a month would certainly be very conducive to one's peace of mind, if one could only believe in it, as no doubt they do. And fortunately there is nothing *contrary* to my religion in it, although it does not quite go to the length of mine. For I believe you can do the same thing every day, or every hour, or whenever you feel a need, and that too without the intervention of any Confessional Box or any Holy Father. To me the Box and the Father would be nothing but a hindrance, but to many people no doubt a tangible Box and a materialized Father are genuine helps, and I have no fault to find with them.

Babies *are* fun, but I am done with them, thank goodness.

TO HER DAUGHTER, MARY BERENSON

London, Nov. 17, 1905 (Aet. 73)
Almost any school with a lot of girls would be more fun for Karin than your grown-up (not to say middle-aged) atmosphere.

Look at Ray, what bliss all the nonsensical fun they have at Newnham is to her. It is evidently the divine order, and there is no getting out of it. They must have their fun just as kittens must, and not with their mothers, but with other kittens. . . .

Thee need not feel the slightest delicacy about always telling me how B.B. feels. My experience of life has taught me to look upon the vagaries of the male portion of our race as one looks upon avalanches or earthquakes—things that cannot be stopped nor altered, but must simply have way made for them, with as little personal inconvenience to one's self as possible. And just as one would always be glad to know when avalanches or earthquakes are coming, so I always like to know what the men of my acquaintance feel about things, or what they want, in order that I may get out of the way.

I am afraid Willie's continual smoking has so undermined his moral nature that he really does not know right from wrong, poor fellow.

TO HER DAUGHTER, MARY BERENSON

London, Feb. 15, 1906 (Aet. 74)

I send thee a belated birthday present—a telescope Cigarette holder. Thee need not advertise that it is a present from the author of the "Christian's Secret of a Happy Life"! But I think it may save thee from a little of the poison of thy cigarettes, of which I have a few fears.

TO HER DAUGHTER, MARY BERENSON

London, Feb. 22, 1906 (Aet. 74)

I do not wonder thee was "jiggered" over that cigarette case. I felt rather jiggered myself. But as thee is too old for me to forbid thee to smoke, and so I am entirely delivered from responsibility, I want, since thee *will* smoke, to help thee do it as comfortably as possible. I do not understand it, unless it is that the mother in me gets the better of the reformer sometimes! And I happened to see that little holder at one of those moments. Such are the frailties of poor human nature!

I feel quite awed at the thought of Ray being nineteen so soon. When I was 19 I got married, like the ignorant idiot I was. And what worries me is that I had no more thought of doing such a thing than she has, and had not the slightest fondness for men. It all came on me like the earthquake on San Francisco last week, and in one day my life was overturned. And why may it not be the same with Ray? It would be *too* awful!

TO HER DAUGHTER, MARY BERENSON

Iffley, Feb. 2, 1907 (Aet. 74)

I wonder if you *ought* to urge B. B. to write when he feels so unable to do it. If you spur him on too far, all his machinery may give out, and thee may have him a helpless invalid on thy hands. Let him lie absolutely fallow for a while; and then, if he has anything to say, and any power to say it, he will feel an inspiration, and it will be easy. I read a very striking story of a man with a great deal of brain power, whose wife urged him on and on to do a certain piece of work when he felt unequal to it, and as a result his brain gave way, and he was a semi-idiot the rest of his life—I advise thee to be careful, but do not tell B.B. all this.

TO HER DAUGHTER, MARY BERENSON

Iffley, Nov. 15, 1907 (Aet. 75)

Poor dear Emily—her illness is *too* dreadful, and I am afraid she has no religion to comfort her. You people without religion have no idea what a dreadful loss it is. Instead of its being meritorious on the part of anyone to believe in the God of the New Testament, it is the greatest piece of self-indulgence possible, for there is no comfort in the universe to equal it. . . .

TO HER DAUGHTER, MARY BERENSON

Acland Nursing Home, Oxford, Nov. 13, 1908 (Aet. 76)

Mrs. Rollings and I are comfortably settled into this Nursing Home, waiting for a doctor from London to make an examination. I inform the doctor that, as a specialist is going to examine me, he is sure to find what he is looking for, and of course I shall have to have an operation of what he finds. They all say it will relieve me entirely, but I doubt it. However, by the time this reaches thee, it will all be settled and done with. If I *should* die, which of course is always possible, what I would like would be to be cremated, and no funeral, and no weeping relatives to gather around my bed. Thee must not think of coming over no matter what happens. I do not expect to make an edifying deathbed, and I would far rather no one should "gather around" it.

TO HER DAUGHTER, MARY BERENSON

Oct. 4, 1909 (Aet. 77)

I told Logan and Ray at dinner last night with great glee that sometimes I have a lovely whizzing or buzzing in my head that I *hope* means apoplexy, and it quite heartens me to think that the time may be shorter than I fear.

TO HER DAUGHTER, MARY BERENSON

Iffley, Dec. 14, 1909 (Aet. 77)

Men are by nature unreasonable and have to be cajoled. They cannot be driven but must be coaxed. One feels undignified in descending to such methods, and yet I feel sure it is the best way. From the fact of their position of Lordship, encouraged at first by the wife's self-abnegation, they get to a place where they *have* to be managed; and the wives I have known who have made a success of marriage have always been women to pet and coax their husbands. No man can resist petting and coaxing.

It is one of my uncomfortable days, and I cannot write much. I do not believe there is such an all-absorbing occupation to be found anywhere as the one I am kept busy with, namely waiting on my "Mistress of Ceremonies." There is not a single five minutes in the day when she is not making some demand or other; and she is only quiet when I fall asleep for two or three hours in my chair at night. It really does seem a ridiculous occupation for a woman with brains!

It really is amazing how your "Woes" continue to be unending! It must be intended to teach you the unalterable imperfection of all human things; and I believe in the end you will have to settle down to it, and consent to stop short of perfection. I long ago had to do this, and it has produced such a feeling of being only a stranger and a pilgrim here, with my real home beyond, that it has relieved me immensely. Poor B.B. will just have to *settle down* to having things wrong, and then he will not mind, and it will not make much difference in the end.

Life, I find, is full of "settlings down," and nothing really matters except one's own spirit, and one's health. But as long as you have "woes" to relate we *must* hear them, and shall never be tired of hearing. You have certainly had at least 150 by this time, or even 200. We go with thee step by step in all thy experiences, and daily letters are the principal excitements of our day. They are like a serial story in the morning paper.

This sentence expresses my Theology in a few words: "It is enough to know that God's responsibility is irrevocable, and His resources limitless." This covers the whole ground of my heresies. By-the-bye, when I say it is foolish to try to be pious when God only wants us to be happy, I mean of course by pious that side of religion that consists in emotions, and pious feelings, and religious performance. I do not mean being *good*. Good we must be, or we cannot be happy, but some of the very best people I know are not pious at all. They are just plain common-place *good*, and to be good is necessarily to be happy. There is no happiness in the world equal to the happiness of being good.

TO HER GRANDDAUGHTER, RAY COSTELLOE

Iffley, March 22, 1910 (Aet. 78)

I cannot help feeling that to be without any real faith in God, and without knowing of His love and care, is an irreparable loss to the soul, and to all the higher nature; and opens the door to miseries and unhappiness that could not possibly enter into a heart that hides itself in the keeping of a loving God. Don't shut thyself out too determinedly against what long years of experience have taught me is by far the purest joy our hearts can hold. At least, darling Ray, keep an open mind, and listen to the still small voice of God that I am sure speaks to thy inner self. To His loving care I commit thee, and, even though thee may not yet thyself know Him, He will always surround thee with His love.

"Had Jesus What Thee Calls Common Sense, James?"

[FROM *A Quaker Childhood*]

HELEN THOMAS FLEXNER

[Helen (Whitall) Thomas Flexner is another member of the large and gifted Whitall tribe. She too, a birthright Quaker, was brought up amidst Friends like her father, whose failure to test "tradition against principle," in an era in which all the principles but not all of the traditions of Quakerism were still relevant, made life for young Quakers—more aware of "changed social conditions" than their elders—difficult. They saw their parents, from whom they had learned their Quakerism, failing to practice what Woolman had said was necessarily its core: that is, in Woolman's words, "to take hold of every opportunity to lessen the distress of the afflicted and increase the happiness of the creation . . . to turn all that we possess into the channel of universal love."

I do not know of any more affecting account of the relationship of a mother and daughter than that which is given in A Quaker Childhood. It is pitiful to find this relationship filled, finally, with so much sorrow. To the mother, dying of cancer, and at her request, is brought a "faith healer." About his presence both mother and daughter feel guilt. But except for the change in Quaker practice, no guilt need have been felt,

nor need someone have been "brought in." Early Quakers were them-
selves "faith healers." That is, they, and Fox in their forefront, had
faith, prayed, and healing frequently resulted. Tradition and principle
here agreed, and both were forgotten.]

———

At home when I was a small child there had been little to
suggest to me the restriction placed upon women in the outside
world. Our family sitting room was presided over by a large steel
engraving of Elizabeth Fry in Quaker cap and flowing Quaker
dress. When I joined the family group around the fire after
supper there she hung, an imposing figure on the wall above me.
We all honored her because she had visited the cruel British
prisons of her day and reformed them. According to Quaker
theory women were the equals of men, the two sexes facing each
other "with level-fronting eyelids," a phrase I often heard. And
in practice twice a week at the Sunday and Thursday morning
meetings for worship I saw my mother sit opposite, even though
a little below, my father in the raised gallery for ministers and
elders. On the one occasion when I attended a joint business
session of the Men's and Women's Monthly Meeting, as I
pushed open the door at the far end of the room I saw my mother
and my father seated side by side in solitary state before a long
table littered with papers. They performed respectively the
duties of the clerk of the Men's and clerk of the Women's
meeting. I remember the sharp stab of pride I felt at I stood in
the doorway to look at my parents. . . .

When I search among childish impressions for facts significant of my mother's real position, I find only a few and those of
the homeliest sort. First there is the scheme to get a new nursery
carpet. . . . It was my father's consent, not my mother's, that had
to be obtained. This I obviously accepted without question as
entirely proper. Then on several occasions I heard my father
complain to my mother of the expense involved in employing a
protégée of hers to help with the cleaning—an old woman and,
as he thought, not worth the wages paid her. My mother's
answer to these remonstrances was to keep Mrs. Webster, who

needed help, out of my father's sight—as I well remember, since I was cautioned not to speak of her in his presence. I should have understood from this that my father had control of the family pocketbook, and probably did understand, though I thought nothing of it. Before I was old enough to have any real knowledge of the power of money, my grandmother Whitall's death had put my mother in possession of her inheritance, freeing her from a sense of economic dependence. I did notice that my father showed a greater sense of being in the right when he criticized my mother, her preaching in particular, than she showed in her comments to him. But she was in every way gentler and less easily excited than my father. Visiting friends agreed more often with him than with her, asking his opinion rather than hers. I merely thought them stupid. I heard her regret her lack of education, since at sixteen she had finished the course at the best girls' school in Philadelphia, and there was no woman's college then in existence to which she could go. After her marriage my father had begun to teach her Latin, which she passionately desired to learn, but Carey's birth put a stop to that. My mother's powerlessness to get the education she desired was a signpost I should have paused to consider, but I speeded by, no doubt because my mother seemed perfectly well educated to me. . . .

Carey herself had been forced to fight for the privilege of receiving an education, not only against the general social prejudice but against my father's veto. Conventional both by temperament and training, my father accepted the ideas of the group into which he had been born. Like nearly all Quakers, he was proud of Quaker principles and traditions without feeling any great necessity to test the one against the other afresh in changed social conditions. His grandfather had not counted the cost of freeing the slaves brought him by a Southern wife—that was incumbent on every Quaker of his period who came into the possession of slaves. During the Civil War my father himself— though a passionate abolitionist and supporter of the Union— had automatically refused to join the army medical corps. The equality of the sexes was as much a matter of principle with Quakers as pacifism, but it did not operate as effectively for reasons perhaps not difficult to understand. Their noncooperation with government forced Quakers to live a life apart, forming as it were a state within a state, persecuted at first, tolerated later. As time went on the men gradually began to take a man's part in government. John Bright in England was a power in parliament, though not without suffering severe criticism from his fellow Quakers. Living more and more cooperatively with the communities in which they were settled, Quakers had to make some sort of practical terms with the prevalent customs and in so doing were influenced by them. This was especially the case with the men, whose activities took them outside the family and the religious groups.

In the seventeenth century the founders of the Society of Friends had valued inspiration in both men and women far more than education, of which few possessed very much. However, they soon began to set up special schools for the training of their children. It is fair, I think, to assume that in these early schools a sincere effort was made to educate the girls as thoroughly as the boys. But in the course of time, along the Atlantic seaboard of the United States, at least, this original equality of the sexes in education was lost. A settled life in one community had brought prosperity to many Quaker families. They had become landed proprietors of a sort or successful merchants and manufacturers, and they began in their schools and colleges to follow the general rule of the people about them in giving greater educational advantages to their sons than to their daughters. My father himself, and all three of his half-brothers, had received a college education, but neither my mother nor his sister had enjoyed a like advantage. Thus he was dreadfully shocked by Carey's determination after she left school to continue her studies at a non-Quaker, coeducational college where she felt she could get the best training. He set his face against it and a severe struggle ensued between my father on the one hand and Carey, supported by my mother, on the other. Since I was a child three years old and still in the nursery when this battle raged, I possess no knowledge of it at first hand, but none the less from hearsay and contemporary letters I have formed a vivid idea of the way in which it was fought.

My father's objections to Carey's going to Cornell University were threefold—social, domestic and religious. It would be disadvantageous to her first because she would there be thrown with all sorts of people and would probably fall in love and insist upon marrying some unsuitable fellow student or professor. If she escaped this danger, which seemed highly improbable to my father, years of study would unfit her for happiness in domestic life where women's true happiness lies; and most terrible danger of all, her religious faith might be undermined, destroyed even, in a non-Quaker, all-too-probably free-thinking atmosphere. Driven from one position, my father took up another and finally entrenched himself behind the impregnable bulwark of expense. He could not afford to send Carey to college. Such an outlay for four years was not to be thought of, he said. Carey assured him she would cut down the four years' course to two years. She was sure she would be able to do it. The expense even for two years was more than my father felt he could meet. Though it was true that he utterly disapproved, his disapproval would not be considered the deciding factor, he declared. He simply did not have the money to do as Carey and my mother desired. Further discussion was useless.

From the beginning the odds were in my father's favor. The whole community was back of him, an invisible but strong support, and the members of his own family in the midst of whom we lived day by day sympathized with him and pitied him openly. Overburdened as he already was with the support of eight children, including Frank who was then the baby, how could he agree to further unnecessary outlay?

"Poor Brother James," I can imagine Great-Aunt Julia or Aunt Mary or Uncle John exclaiming with sad headshakes. "Carey asks altogether too much of her father."

Had the education of a son been in question, my father's family, highly conservative and sufficiently well-to-do, would have felt differently about the expense. A daughter was another matter in their eyes. Carey and mother appeared to be beaten. My mother, however, still had a weapon in reserve.

"Nothing is left for us but tears," she told Carey. "I have used every argument I can think of in talking with thy father.

Reason will not move him. Now we will see whether he can stand out against our weeping. We shall both have to cry day and night, thee as well as I."

Carey was ready even for that. So together and separately they wept and they wept. My father pled with them, lost his temper, called them unfair, shut himself up, stayed away from home, all to no purpose. They accepted his reproaches in silence and in silence continued to weep whenever he appeared. Worried and distressed beyond endurance by their red eyes and wet faces, my father surrendered at last.

"Since nothing else will satisfy thee," he said to my mother, "I will somehow find the necessary money, almost impossible as that will be. But," he added, turning to Carey, as she herself recounted the story, "only for two years. After two years thee will have to return home whether thee has been able to get thy degree or not."

"I told my father not to worry about my degree. I would attend to that myself. No one believed I could do four years' work in two. I had to cover the freshman and sophomore years while I was attending junior and senior classes. Often I worked all night long. In the winter when my room grew terribly cold at night I took my books down to the cellar and sat in front of the furnace. By opening the furnace door and crouching down near it on the janitor's chair I managed to get a glow on my page bright enough for reading. I had to keep watch for the janitor, who was a lazy fellow and often slept late. Only by using every moment was I able to get my degree in the time allowed me by my father."

It was in some such words that Carey used to tell the story of her going to college. . . .

I greatly admired the energy and intelligence displayed by my sister in getting a college education, while my father's utter helplessness against the unquenchable weeping of his wife and daughter produced a comic effect that somewhat mitigated my condemnation of his behavior. But my mother was the real heroine for me. It was she, and she alone, who had won the battle by her amazing steadfastness and ingenuity. I thought above all of my mother. The knowledge that she had been forced to employ a method so alien to her noble courage was dreadfully painful to me. Without suffering that indignity she should have been able to give her talented eldest daughter, on whose career her heart was set, the education she herself had longed for and been denied by destiny. That my father, loving her as I knew he did, should have forced streams of tears from my mother's eyes was a terrific proof of the power exerted by prejudice on the men of his generation.

However many children might be at home my parents' life continued dedicated day by day to doing God's work in the world. With this purpose in mind my father practiced his profession and my mother managed her family. A hitch in our routine rarely occurred. The children each went his or her own way, making such combinations with the others as naturally arose. From Monday to Saturday we ran along different levels, as it were, attending different schools and cultivating different friends for the most part. Sunday on the other hand was devoted to religion by us all as a family group. The morning began with prayer and reading of the Bible. No excuse other than illness was accepted on Sunday for absence from this rite. After Bible reading followed the decorous walk through the quiet streets to meeting, and the long hours of quietness within the meeting-house walls. Midday dinner, plentiful and luscious, slowly consumed and slowly digested, offered an interval restorative rather than enlivening. Then my father accompanied by a daughter of suitable age took the long streetcar ride down to the Boys' Mission School he conducted in South Baltimore, while my mother rested—her only period for rest during the entire week. My brothers for some reason did not teach in my father's mission school. What they did on Sunday afternoons I do not know. They were never at home. A meeting for worship again filled the evening hours. No driving, no playing, no reading of stories was allowed: only the hushed rooms at home, the high, evenly lighted hall of the meeting house over which God brooded.

These Sundays followed one another throughout the winter months, their solemn monotony piling up for me, until when spring came around again the restlessness they induced rose by mid-afternoon to an irresistible tide. Then the big house about me was completely silent, as if deserted. Though I listened intently not a sound from my mother's room or the kitchen reached my ears. No longer able to stand staring through the windows, I used sometimes to rush out by myself and wander alone far off through the poorer quarters of the town, past rows of small houses, with three white-painted wooden steps leading up to a closed wooden door. I found some uncomprehended solace in those rows of houses and in these people on the streets who were utterly strange to me. Always I returned home quieted and appeased, and for many years when depressed or lonely I continued to seek equilibrium of spirit by wandering alone through strange streets or along unfrequented country roads.

Any variation in the Sunday routine had for me in my childhood the force of an explosion. Once an English boy scarcely older than I, thirteen or fourteen perhaps, rose up from his seat beside his mother on the women's benches at our formal meeting for worship. With amazement I saw him stand there, erect but small above the high back of the bench. I could hardly believe my ears when in his lilting English voice he urged that solemn congregation to trust in the Lord. Quickly I turned my eyes to the gallery where the authorized preachers and elders sat, but the faces ranged above me were immovably quiet and composed; no smallest change of expression could I detect on even my father's face or my mother's. Surely they could not have failed to hear Roger. When meeting was over and I could find my way through the crowd of slowly departing Friends to my mother's side, she checked my excited whispering with a gently uplifted hand. Not a comment was made until we had reached home, then at last she said in her quiet way that Roger was too young to preach in meeting, and began at once to talk of something else. What subsequently took place I learned from chance remarks. The boy's parents were visited by the head elder of the meeting, old Cousin Edward Morrison, and were advised to restrain Roger. This they failed to do. He preached the next Sunday and the one after that. Perhaps they did earnestly endeavor to control him, or perhaps they may even have believed their son inspired, as the Bible said. "Out of the mouths of babes and sucklings hast thou ordained strength" and again Christ's words, "Thank thee, O Father, Lord of heaven and earth, because thou hast hidden these things from the wise and prudent and hast revealed them unto babes" were texts often quoted even in our family where the self-expression of babes and sucklings was shut off with firm discipline. Whatever the feeling of Roger's parents may have been, they were finally told to keep him away from meeting and this order was obeyed. Roger was clearly an abnormal boy, a case for a nerve specialist. Years later in one of our Western states he ended his own life after shooting a girl who refused to marry him.

More exciting than Roger's preaching even was another strange event that broke the decorous routine of Sunday morning meeting. A visiting woman friend seated in the gallery above my mother began slowly to untie the strings of her Quaker poke bonnet of plum-colored silk. I watched her slowly take it off and lay it on the seat beside her, then rise up to speak. Her face framed only in the thin white ruffle of her undercap shone pale and her eyes gleamed, as she stood for a moment in silence to dominate the congregation. Then speaking in a low intense voice she called to repentance two souls on the benches before her, in the torments of unconfessed sin. As she continued to speak her exhortation became more impassioned, until her voice filled the large room with its thrilling vibrations. Though I knew that Hannah Milbrook's words were not meant for a little girl like me, I also writhed on my seat with the sense that I had committed some dreadful sin. . . .

Since I entered Miss Bond's school with my chum, Peggie White, I had no sense of strangeness because I was the only Quaker among the pupils. Indeed, I doubt whether I was ever conscious of that fact. I was well used to Episcopalians and the Episcopal service, since I often went to evensong with Peggie at the parish church in our neighborhood. I enjoyed the singing and the beautiful prayers and collects, some of which I learned by heart through constantly repeating them, but the service never moved me as did the silence and simplicity of our meeting. After I had made friends with other girls at school I sometimes went with them to the churches they attended. I even saw the sister of one baptized by immersion inside a hideous dark church. A tank of artificially heated water struck me as a ridiculous substitute for the River Jordan and I felt that it was far more in accord with the Gospels to omit the outward symbolism of baptism, as Quakers did. To my friend however I made no such comment and the internal sense of superiority I surely had was perhaps somewhat mitigated by being referred to my parents.

Once I did experience a moment of fierce religious antagonism. I was walking peacefully home with a girl whose parents happened to be zealous high-church Episcopalians. Our books under our arms and our hair hanging down our backs in neat braids, we chattered and laughed as we walked, mulling over school gossip. Suddenly changing the subject, Edith broke out:

"My mother says no one can go to heaven without being baptized. Everyone who hasn't been baptized goes straight down to hell when she dies."

Edith's tone was triumphant. It excited in me a violent upsurge of anger. So that was what Edith had been thinking all the time! How about my mother? Had Edith's mother been talking about my mother? Was she to go to hell? These questions went through my mind like a flash of lightning. I stopped short where I was on the pavement to confront Edith, but instantly the calm, beautiful face of my mother rose up before me. My mother in hell! Impossible! Without deigning to answer Edith by a single word I walked on again, my head in the air. With angry eyes I scrutinized her pretty round face, her dark hair, the tiny pearls in her ears.

"How silly Edith looks," I thought to myself, "with holes burned through her ear lobes to stick pearls in! How terribly silly!" . . .

During the first winter after Carey's return home in November, 1883, or it may have been the second winter, a national convention of the Women's Christian Temperance Union was held in Baltimore. My mother, who was president of the Maryland Branch, entertained as many of the delegates as our house would hold. . . .

This was the first, and I think the only time I saw Frances Willard, the leader adored by so many earnest women of my mother's generation and in particular by my Aunt Hannah. She was a slim woman with a narrow pale face and eyeglasses astride a small nose. The lusterless blond hair that bounded her ivory-white forehead on either side was artificially waved, I noticed at once. This artificial waving of Miss Willard's dust-colored hair struck me as out of keeping with the intense gaze she fixed on me through her eyeglasses. The impression of extreme concentration she produced on me put me off.

My mother, however, promoted the cause of Temperance with no less zeal than did Miss Willard herself. Since God had created Man in His own image, my mother believed that men and women were really capable of virtue. Christ's admonition to his disciples—"Be ye therefore perfect even as your father in heaven is perfect"—she cited not only as a command but also as a promise. Believing thus in the possibility of perfection for human beings, she hated drunkenness as the most powerful cause of depravity. With terrible quickness drink could extinguish the divine spark in man, she asserted, reducing him to the level of the beasts. His very body was destroyed by it. To show the dreadful physical effects of alcohol, my mother possessed a set of charts which she displayed at meetings and also at home to her children. I found it hard to believe that the discolored, shapeless mass of putrescence labeled "Drunkard's Stomach" on the chart could be the same organ as the smooth, pink pouch assigned to the "Total Abstainer." Comparing the two, I felt that only an idiot would knowingly give himself a stomach like the drunkard's stomach.

For my mother total abstinence was not a question merely of protecting others weaker than herself—"Cause not thy brother to offend." She had experienced the temptation of drink in her own person, she explained to us. Once long ago in the early years of her marriage the doctor had ordered for her a daily glass of champagne to recruit her strength after a difficult confinement, and she had found herself looking forward to her dinner with greater and greater impatience until one day, lifting her glass to her lips, she perceived as in a flash of revelation the true cause of her eagerness. It was not food for which she longed, it was the champagne that went with it. Back down on the tray she put the glass she had so eagerly seized and, trembling with a sense of the awful danger that confronted her, she determined then and there never so long as she lived to drink another drop of intoxicating liquor. Had it not been for this sudden revelation my mother would have been a drunkard. Gazing at her face I could not believe in any such possibility, but my mother's earnest voice left no doubt of her own conviction. She felt it a sacred duty, she said, to save others, especially young people, from the temptation she herself had experienced. The Women's Temperance Campaign in Maryland, of which my mother was the leading spirit, proved highly effective. They even succeeded in having anti-alcohol propaganda, as we should now call it, inserted in the physiology textbooks used throughout the state in our public schools. This victory was a cause of great satisfaction to my mother. . . .

I was now the eldest child and the only daughter at home, but it took me some time to realize the advantages of my new supremacy. Indeed, so far as my father was concerned, it was of little consequence since he already had the habit of taking me about with him and Frank, of course, still remained first in his affections. The absence of my three older sisters did, however, make a great difference in my relations with my mother. Now when she had a free afternoon it was I who went with her for the drive in the park which was almost her only recreation and rare at that. I remember the joy of sitting beside her in the open carriage, but nothing of what she said. At home in the late afternoons she was more likely to talk seriously with me, I found, and I made a point of wandering into her room after I got back from my walk, or had finished my lessons perhaps. . . .

Very often she talked to me of Tolstoi, whose book, *My Religion,* just translated into English, lay on her desk. She herself believed that the Sermon on the Mount should be put literally into practice. Tolstoi's account of his experience was a great comfort and inspiration to her. "We should all re-examine our conduct in the light of what Tolstoi has been able to do," I heard my mother say to my father, and she became more scrupulous than ever in doing what she thought was right. Finally my father remonstrated with her.

"It is very foolish, Mary, to give to every beggar who comes along," he said one day at luncheon. "The man I saw waiting in the hall this morning was obviously a drunkard. Any child would know that he wanted money to get a drink."

"I warned him against doing that," my mother replied. "I told him that Christ had died to save just such sinners as he is from their temptations. He kneeled down and prayed with me before he left."

My father said nothing more on that occasion. But the stream of derelicts that flocked to our house in constantly increasing numbers was more than he could bear with patience. No doubt he argued with my mother about the matter in private, and one day he broke out again at table.

"Do show a little common sense," he urged her in an irritated tone. "Those rascals of thine tell each other where they can always get money for a drink. Thee does not sufficiently consider the consequences of what thee is doing. I admire Tolstoi in many ways, but he has no common sense, and he lives in the country."

My mother looked genuinely hurt and grieved by this remonstrance and her voice when she answered had a note of reproach in it. "The Society of Friends has always held that Christians should obey the teachings of Christ literally. Tolstoi is doing in Russia only what we are trying to do here. Christ commanded us to give to him that asketh. He did not tell us to take thought for the consequences in this world. Had Jesus what thee calls common sense, James?"

My father made no reply to this question but I thought he looked annoyed rather than convinced.

Finally my mother herself must have decided that it was a mistake to give money at the door. Instead of dimes she began to hand out tickets for food and lodging at a charitable lodginghouse, but she still accompanied every gift with a serious exhortation. "At least they are forced to listen to me," she once said with her gay smile, but seeing Frank and me about to laugh she added quickly, "it really is no joking matter. Sometime in some crisis one of them may remember my words and be helped by them. Words are like seeds, they take root."

Under the new treatment my mother's beggars soon began to decrease in number until finally no more at all came. This seemed to prove that my father was right, but somehow I felt it did not prove that my mother was wrong. I recognized in her a spiritual sincerity that I respected. She made a determined effort to obey Christ's commands and she had complete faith in his promises. My father's way was somewhat different. He said much the same things that my mother said, cited the same texts from the Bible, but he seemed able to make an easier adjustment between beliefs and actions. He was not bothered by inconsistency as my mother was bothered. The beggars were frauds, of course, and a horrid nuisance crowding the hall, but for me they symbolized my mother's goodness.

I did not attempt to piece all these impressions together; I had not yet got to the point of considering the effect, whether for good or evil, of unattainable ideals on human character; my mother's constant effort to live by a counsel of perfection fostered in me a dislike of living as though one's ideals and one's actions belonged to two different worlds. Even as a child I saw people valuing themselves for their beliefs, however much they failed to live by them. This I called hypocrisy and judged with all the harshness of inexperience. For my father, it is true, I made instinctive allowances. I knew him to be really good and kind in spite of certain obvious contradictions, but I drew no general conclusions from this fact. I was entirely capable of taking advantage of his tolerance toward my shortcomings while I condemned the concessions that made his leniency possible. I relied on his sympathy and enjoyed sharing my pleasure with him.

"... A Unique Laboratory Experiment
Which Worked"
[FROM A Small-Town Boy]

RUFUS M. JONES

[In 1932 Henry J. Cadbury, brother-in-law of Rufus M. Jones, wrote, "There is in America a huge dull mass of denatured Quakerism which is not conscious of its difference from other churches and even less of its international affiliations." Except for the influence of Rufus Jones, Quakerism in America would have been, in 1932, even duller, more denatured, and less aware of its truths and of their international application.

Rufus Jones (1863–1948) united in himself the two chief strains of Quakerism: mysticism and practicality. He was a professor of philosophy at Haverford College and a leading authority on mysticism. At the same time he chaired for many years the American Friends Service Committee, whose practice it is, to postpone religious exercises—to the dismay, still, of some fundamentalist Friends—to feed first and without any question except "Are you hungry?"

Harry Emerson Fosdick lists Rufus Jones's accomplishments thus: He was (1) the leading historian of mysticism, (2) a great teacher of philosophy, (3) a reformer in the Society of Friends, (4) the outstanding leader in the extension of Quaker service around the world, (5) an interpreter of vital religion to multitudes in many countries and all churches.

These were some of his accomplishments, and they explain, in part, why the Quaker of the twentieth century has been moved to try to recover for himself the principles of seventeenth-century Quakerism.

Others are capable of listing and evaluating Rufus Jones's accomplishments as a re-vitalizer, in his day and ours, of the Religious Society of Friends. But no one else is able to write with his own humor and charm of the Quakerism of an earlier America.]

A Quaker Meeting of the type which prevailed when I was a boy was a unique congregation, which would certainly have perplexed a visitor from the planet Mars, if he had happened to parachute down and had landed in time for Meeting. Charles Lamb has described in a memorable Essay the essential aspects of a Quaker Meeting as he knew it in London, but our Meeting was composed entirely of farmers and their families, and it had, as it was bound to have, a rural aspect which would have been unfamiliar to the famous essayist.

The plain-looking meeting-house with unpainted seats and undecorated walls stood on a sightly hill from which we could see the Kennebago Mountains of Western Maine, eighty miles away. It formed the center of a small community of houses and farms, surrounded by a fringe of ancient forests in which, at least to my imagination, roamed deer and moose and bears, and where "loupcervies" and catamounts and plain wildcats were waiting to pounce upon anyone who ventured into its depths. We lived three miles away from the Meeting and could reach it only by a drive in wagon or sleigh through the "dangerous" woods. Thither on Thursdays and Sundays we always went. In the winter there was a huge hot soapstone under the buffalo robe, and I used to slip down and sit on it or near it as we creaked through the snow. There were many other boys in the group, as the neighbors from near and far gathered to fill the meeting-house, which in my youth seemed to be of vast dimensions. There was no bell, no organ, no choir, no pulpit, no order of service, no ritual. There was always silence and then more silence. It was strange that these hard-working toilers kept awake through these long hushes, but they did keep awake, for it was "unbecoming behavior" to nod or to doze. For them this "silence of all flesh" was a sacrament of awe and wonder. They were in faith and practice meeting with God, and the occasion called for all their powers of mind and spirit. It might be supposed that a little boy, keyed to action and charged with animal spirits, on a hard bench, with feet unsupported, would have hated this silence and would have longed for a chance to hit the boy in the next seat over the head. But that was not the case.

Sooner or later the boy would get hit no doubt when the proper time came for it. But the silence came over us as a kind of spell. It had a life of its own. There was something "numinous" about it, which means, in simpler non-Latin words, a sense of divine presence, which even a boy could feel. It was almost never explained to us. There was very little said about it. No theories were expounded. No arguments were promulgated. We "found" ourselves in the midst of a unique laboratory experiment which *worked*. A boy responds to reality the moment he feels it, almost quicker than an adult does. He has not yet travelled so far inland from "the immortal sea that brought him hither," and he hasn't yet been "debauched" by commonplace words and phrases and the dull mechanics of life. Anyway that experiment with silence in the far-off period of my youth, sitting in the hush with the moveless group, concentrated on the expectation of divine presence, did something to me and for me which has remained an unlost possession.

A little country boy near my home was gazing out of the window with his eye fixed on the sky, and his mother asked him what he was looking at. He said with simple confidence: "I was thinking how I could go up there where God is. There are a number of questions I want to ask Him and some things I want to talk over with Him!" I was as artless and naive as that, only I had got over the sky-idea very early in life and thought of God as a Presence in the midst with whom I could commune without any ladder. He came to our meeting with us, and we did not need to go somewhere else to find Him. I cannot remember when I first discovered that there was a meeting place within, where Spirit met with spirit and where the Above and the below belonged together. I knew it certainly as early as I knew that the water in our lake was buoyant and held up the young swimmer instead of drowning him. The two things came together. I learned to swim and to enjoy silent worship at about the same time. Almost always the silence was broken in the early part of the meeting by a vocal prayer.

> Haply some one felt
> On his moved lips the seal of silence melt,

as Whittier has expressed it. The prayer always came out of the silence and was more or less the expression of the group-feeling. The prayer was tremulous with emotion and it voiced for the waiting group the yearning for fellowship and communion. We all stood with bowed heads as the spontaneous prayer was being poured out. I was glad to get my little feet on the floor for a few minutes change of position, though I felt even then, and more emphatically later, that the act of rising and sitting down again disturbed the attitude of hush and reverence. But as soon as we were seated again the silence took on a new depth of penetration. The whole burden of worship was thrown upon each individual soul. One could be vacant and unconcerned with empty mind, *or* one could mount up as with wings of eagles into the heavenlies and find the Fatherland to which he belonged. Whatever was done in this period of silence had to be done by the person himself. It was once more like swimming. Nobody could do it for you. You either did your swimming or your worshipping *yourself*, or it wasn't done. There were no substitutes to perform for you in either of these activities. But silence never filled the whole duration of the meeting. In front of us and facing the main body of the congregation there were two raised seats on which sat two rows of gifted weighty Friends, who were more likely to be "moved" to bring a message to the meeting than were the rank and file who filled the rest of the meeting-house, though no one ever knew in advance where the "inspiration" would break out. At the head of the upper row of women Friends sat a woman of unusual grace and dignity. She wore a bonnet of the usual Quaker type; underneath it a white muslin cap, and over her shoulders a neatly folded silk scarf or shawl. One could see that she was becoming tremulous, and I knew in advance that she was being inwardly "moved" to rise with a message. The first visible sign was the untying of her silk bonnet strings, then the graceful removal of the bonnet, which she passed to her nearest companion on the upper seat. Then she arose to her full height, and we felt at once the stateliness of her form and the queenliness of her presence. She had been to Africa in a sailing vessel as a missionary to Liberia. She had carried her message of love and healing to Ireland, Great Britain,

Norway, Germany, France, Syria and Palestine. She had visited almost all the Quaker meetings on the American Continent. Here she was in her home meeting, probably the most widely known Quaker woman minister, rising to speak to these assembled farmer folk. Her voice was soft like the wind in pine trees, but with a musical cadence and a carrying power which reached every listener. There was a slight change of position on the part of the hearers, and all eyes turned to the woman who had arisen. She began almost in a whisper, but we all heard every word of her Scripture text: "He brought me to His banqueting house and the banner over me was love." The amazing, seeking, pursuing love of God was always her theme. She was profoundly evangelical and preached to win souls from sin to a consciousness of salvation. The reality of heaven as the home of the redeemed was as sure and as vivid as was Mount Blue, which we could see from the Meeting-House hill. With a mounting voice—still as clear as a bell—she described the glories of the heavenly city. She had in her home a case containing specimens of the twelve stones in the foundations of the celestial habitation, and one could *see* the eternal home of the soul as she rapturously portrayed it. Then she swept our hearts with the lines which she loved to quote:

> "Oh, well it is forever,
> Oh, well for evermore,
> My nest's hung in no forest
> Of all this death-doomed shore."

As she sat down and put on her bonnet and tied its strings, a deep hush spread over us and the canopy of love became a real covering.

Nobody felt like breaking that silence until it had done its perfect work on our minds. It was pretty sure to be broken finally by a man near the top of the upper row on the men's side of the house. He was the husband of the woman who had spoken. He was as gifted and as widely travelled as was his wife. He was richly endowed with practical wisdom and clear common sense. He understood human nature, and he knew with remarkable insight what would reach and interest a boy. His voice had a nasal quality which amounted almost to impediment, but after the first few sentences that was forgotten, for we were caught and carried along with a distinct fascination and a narrative style of address. Bible heroes lived again as we listened. Incidents of travel, pictures of the Holy Land, illustrated his message. First, and last and all the time it was about life here and now. How to live a good life, how to be a true citizen, how to meet the trials and temptations which beset us all, and how to come through valiantly and triumphantly. "Fight the good fight, lay hold on the life which is life indeed," rang out at the end like a trumpet call. Young as I was, I knew that that was the gospel for me. Every time that this man spoke he built something into the fiber of my life. I wanted to be ready for the heaven I had heard about, but I didn't want "to be an angel just then and with the angels stand." I wanted to be a good boy and be a man like that stirring speaker and *do things.* . . .

But, alas, not all who spoke were of this high quality. They could not be expected to be. The cream never goes all the way down to the bottom of the pan! Every country neighborhood has its "seconds," and it is fortunate if it does not have a few queer specimens. We had our share of the "seconds" and the "queers." A Quaker Meeting of the free type is a pure democracy, and no talent, however small, is wrapped in a napkin and hidden away. Many of the one-talent exhorters, or per-adventure quarter talent speakers, were "repetitive," and we all knew in advance what they would say and how long it would take them to say it. The volume of voice rose in the reverse of the significance of what they communicated, and their gestures were frantic in the same proportion. "The question isn't," a certain earnest speaker would say, "whether or no or not we darsent, no, not by no means." I have no idea what it was that we didn't dare, but the speaker left no doubt of our lily weakness in daring. Another of our urgent speakers called for spade work: "We must know of a digging deep. Yes deep, down to that foundation which is beyond the reach of human scrutiny. Yes, scrutiny. And we must know of a riding through the gates. Yes, gates!" It never got me anywhere. It slipped off and left me unenlightened.

"The trouble with this meeting," a critical-minded Friend who wore a white beaver hat would say, "is that we have no Caleb and Joshua to bring back the grapes of Eschol, and so the women have taken to wearing bunches of them on their hats—yes hats!" With the text in Deuteronomy, "Jeshurun waxed fat and kicked," he would dwell upon the worldliness of these degenerate days and the decline of God's true people. "Only a small remnant of the faithful remains. The rest have gone back to the flesh-pots of Egypt and even to the leeks and onions thereof." And a woman speaker would tell us what would "make a dying bed as soft as 'downing' pillows are."

Two fair sisters who were members of the meeting came under the spell of "the bloomer cult" of that period. They came to meeting wearing bloomer trousers. It created a great sensation as they walked up the aisle with as great determination as though they were storming the Bastille. They did not "testify" or give us propaganda about their "cult," but, like the man in the Bible who "talked with his feet," they preached with their legs, which at that period were modestly called "lower limbs." They made no converts, but for many years they were silent witnesses to the coming freedom of a new day.

But the story does not end there. We used to have an amazing list of itinerant visitors coming from all parts of the Quaker world. This custom of intervisitation was one of the most unique features of our religious fellowship. Those who came were for the most part the "pillar Friends" of the regions from which they came, and they brought to our remote village the ideas, the ideals and the spiritual leaven of the most favored sections of world-wide Quakerism. Instead of leveling down to a commonplace status of a single inbred community, we leveled up to the height of the best there was in our far-flung Society. It was an instance of cross fertilization through a waft of spiritual pollen from many fields of culture. The first visitor that I remember vividly was Stanley Pumphrey of England. I can still *see* him standing in our Minister's gallery, clothed in a pepper-gray suit of foreign cut, pouring forth with odd accent and peculiar phrase his thrilling message, which caught and arrested and fascinated the small boy who had ridden through the woods to hear him. Next came William Wetherald of Canada. He had been a professor at Haverford College. He was a scholar and spoke like one. He had been through a series of shifts and changes of religious experiences and had at last *found himself* on a high table-land of life, and I dimly knew that I was listening to an expert. But our "Jeshurun man" disagreed with him and challenged him on the spot and plunged into a vigorous debate. It went too deep for me to follow the lines of it, but I was all for the visitor and against "Jeshurun," who, by the way, on his way home from Meeting one day was thrown from his wagon head on against a tree, but his high-crowned beaver hat broke the fall and saved his life.

Then came Rufus King of North Carolina, who, during the battle of Gettysburg where he fought on the Southern side, was convinced that war was wrong. He made his way to Philadelphia after the battle, became a Friend and travelled far and wide as a minister, and came to us with his droll and humorous way of speaking, but at the same time with a note of high reality, and his words stayed in the mind long after he was gone south with the wild geese. With him came Dr. James E. Rhoads, later President of Bryn Mawr College. He was one of the most dignified men I ever saw, with unforgettable grace of manner. There was an unusual power to his speech and a tenderness in his approach. He put his hand on my head and "prophesied" about me. It made a great impression on my family who thus got some assurance at that time in my boyish career, and it probably had an effect upon me, at least I never forgot it. I cannot catalogue the long line of visitors who came in slow succession, but I must mention John Y. Hoover of Iowa, the uncle of Herbert Hoover. He was tall and gaunt, with an Abraham Lincoln type of build. He was a revivalist preacher, and one of the first to bring us word of the fresh "going in the top of the mulberry trees." Caroline Talbot of Ohio was another extraordinary character. Her peculiar strain was that of prophecy. She could see and reveal "states," and she would suddenly tell you what was going on in your mind. I hardly dared to think while she was speaking for fear that she would fish out all my thoughts and my secret feelings.

Once each month in the middle of the week we had "monthly meeting" for business affairs. There came first a meeting for worship of the usual type, only larger than common. . . .

The Sense of the Meeting

[FROM *A Boy's Religion from Memory*]

RUFUS M. JONES

"If Friends' minds are easy, I apprehend it may now be a suitable time to lower the shutters and proceed to the business of the meeting." As the venerable elder at the head of the meeting spoke these words, slowly and solemnly, he raised his broad-brim and put it on his head with considerable dignity, and we children knew that the "first meeting" was over. In these modern days a dinner is served "between the meetings," but in my boyhood days no such thing ever happened. Not even the hungry boy got a bite until the affairs of the Church were properly settled. Creak, creak, creak—we heard the middle "shutters" coming down from above to divide the men from the women. I could never imagine how it was done! No human instrument was ever anywhere visible. The ancient elder spoke, and lo, the wonder worked! Later, when the investigating age was upon me, I crawled up a ladder into the loft and solved the mystery; but in the early period it seemed as though the same spirit which "moved" the solemn man to put on his hat was also in the descending shutters which no visible hand touched!

I used always to sit on the "men's side," but I sat close up by the partition, and ever and anon I caught the notes of a woman's voice breaking in upon our "business" with a strong outpouring of prayer or the earnest word of counsel, for the women had less "business" than the men, and hence "religious exercises" filtered all through their "second meeting." It was somewhat so on the men's side, though to a less extent. But even here it was impossible to draw any line between "business" and "religious exercise." A solemn religious tinge colored everything, even the driest items of business, and I believe the spiritual tide often rose higher in the "second meeting" than in the first—particularly if there was a visiting minister present.

By the "world's" methods, all our business could have been transacted in twenty minutes. We often spent two hours at it, because every affair had to be soaked in a spiritual atmosphere until the dew of religion settled on it! Above, in the "high seats," sat two men at a table fastened by hinges to the minister's rail. This table was swung up and held by a perpendicular stick beneath. On it lay the old record-book, a copy of the "discipline," and papers of all sorts. The "clerk," the main man of the two at the desk, was another one of those marvelous beings who seemed to me to know everything by means of something unseen working inside him! How could he tell what "Friends" wanted done?—and yet he always knew. No votes were cast. Everybody said something in his own peculiar way. A moment of silence would come, and the clerk would rise and say: "It appears that it is the sense of the meeting," to do thus and so. Spontaneously from all parts of the house would come from variously pitched voices: "I unite with that," "So do I," "That is my mind," "I should be easy to have it so." And so we passed to the next subject.

Occasionally there would be a Friend who had "a stop in his mind," or who "didn't feel easy" to have things go as the rest believed they should go. If he was a "weighty Friend," whose judgment had been proved through a long past, his "stop" would effectually settle the matter; but if he was a persistent and somewhat cantankerous objector, the clerk would quietly announce that the "weight of the meeting" seemed decidedly favorable to action.

The longest stretch of business was always over the "queries." These were original inventions of the Quaker, and they have no parallel in any other religious body. Like many other things, the "queries," with their carefully rendered answers, have undergone a change. They take a less important place now, and the boy of today may not tell of them when he gives his impressions to the next generation. But in my day they were still alive, and the meeting took them seriously enough.

"Are all meetings regularly held?" "Are Friends careful to observe the hour?" "Do Friends keep from all unbecoming behavior therein?" "Are tale-bearing and detraction guarded against?" "Do Friends pay their bills, settle their accounts, and live within the bounds of their circumstances?" "Do they read the Holy Scriptures in their families, and bring up their children in the nurture and admonition of the Lord?" "If differences arise, are measures taken to end them speedily?" "Is the discipline administered timely and impartially?"

Each separate meeting sent its special set of answers for this public confessional. "Love and unity are not so well maintained as we could wish." "Some Friends do not observe the hour." "Mostly kept from unbecoming behavior, though a few cases of sleeping in meeting have been observed." "Friends *generally* bring up their children in the nurture and admonition of the Lord." I had no idea what that meant, though I supposed it meant "to be good."

After the answers were read, we listened to grave preachments on these various lines which "were queried after," as the phrase used to run. What got said on these occasions was not very juicy food for a boy, though the standard of life which was set up in these times of examination did, after all, have a silent influence which left a good deposit behind.

There were two transactions which were always exciting, and I used each time to live in hope that they would come off. One was "the declaration of intentions of marriage." When such an event occurred the man and woman came in and sat down together, facing the meeting in the completest possible hush. It was an ordeal which made the couple hesitate to rush into marriage until they felt pretty sure that the match was made in heaven. Solemnly they rose, with the parents standing on each side, and informed us that they purposed taking each other in marriage, and the parents announced their consent. The meeting "united," and permission was given "to proceed." The marriage itself came off at an even more solemn meeting, when the man and woman took each other "until death should separate." I remember one of these occasions, when the frightened groom took the bride "to be his husband," which made the meeting less solemn than usual.

The other interesting event was the liberation of ministers for religious service "in other parts." If the minister was a woman Friend, as often happened in our meeting, she came in from the other side with "a companion." They walked up the aisle and sat down with bowed heads. Slowly the bonnet strings were untied, the bonnet handed to the companion, and the ministering woman rose to say that for a long time the Lord had been calling her to a service in a distant yearly meeting; that she had put it off, not feeling that she could undertake so important a work, but that her mind could not get any peace; and now she had come to ask Friends to release her for this service. One after another the Friends would "concur in this concern," and the blessing of the Lord would be invoked upon the messenger who was going forth.

Some of these occasions were of a heavenly sort, and the voices of strong men choked in tears as a beloved brother or sister was equipped and set free. From this little meeting heralds went out to almost every part of the world, and the act of liberation was something never to be forgotten—only to be surpassed by the deep rejoicing which stirred the same company when the journey was over and "the minutes were returned."

It is all very well now to sit down at a comfortable desk and write of what happened in those long business meetings. But the kind reader will please remember that the uncushioned seats were hard in those days, and that a boy's stomach will not be fed with "considerations on the state of the Church!" Long before the "concluding minute" was read a rebellion was well underway within. The vivid picture of that steaming dinner which was (to the boy) the real event of those days, blotted out the importance of preserving love and unity, or any of the other desirable things which concerned the elders. At length the happy moment came—"We now separate, proposing to meet again at the usual time and place, if the Lord permit."

With this began the invasion of the homes in the neighborhood. Every dining-room had its long table, and an elastic supply to fit the rather reckless invitations which all members of the family gave with little or no consultation. Here was one place where a boy counted as much as a man! In the meeting he had no part to play, he was not considered, but the havoc he wrought on the dinner made him a person of some importance! If he got crowded out to the second table the delay only made him a more dangerous element to reckon with!

No boy who has had the fortune of being taken to monthly or quarterly meeting in the good old days of positive religion and genuine hospitality will forget what it meant, so long as he remembers anything.

I Go to Philadelphia

[FROM *Finding the Trail of Life*]

RUFUS M. JONES

One of the most important features of the association with my new-found "uncle" and "aunt" was the fact that their home was, in Yearly Meeting Week, one of those old-fashioned centers of hospitality which was so elastically expansive that it could house and feed an unbelievable number of relatives and Friends. Here on these occasions I met almost literally "Friends from everywhere." I found myself all unexpectedly plunged into a living nucleus of pure and unalloyed old-time Quakerism, such as I had before only read of in books or heard of from descriptions given by "the oldest living inhabitant." It was an extraordinary experience, one that could hardly have been duplicated then, and one that could no more be found on earth today than could the dodo in his native habitat.

Yearly Meeting, which came then in April and coincided with the annual visit to the city of the circus and with the usual week of rain, was the yearly gathering of the "orthodox" Friends of Pennsylvania, New Jersey and Delaware. It convened in the Arch Street Meeting House and brought together, at that period, about a thousand men and twelve hundred women, who met for their business sessions in different meeting rooms. The men for the most part wore coats with straight collars—the "shad-belly" type—and they were crowned with broad-brimmed beaver or silk top-hats which they kept on their heads until after they had taken their seats in the meeting house. The women, and even the girls in many instances, wore the old-time "sugar-scoop" bonnets, while those who were slightly more "gay" wore a neat "shun-the-cross" bonnet. One would hear, after meeting or at dinner, a comment like this about some woman Friend who had been appointed on some important committee: "What dost thou think of appointing——— on a committee like that? Why, she has a cape on her bonnet!" I remember how on one occasion a venerable visiting Friend from England who had been twice around the world "in the love of the gospel" expressed a "concern" to visit the women's meeting in order to give them a message of truth and life, and the meeting decided that "way did not open" for the Friend to go. I expressed great surprise at this decision when we were sitting at dinner. "Didst thou suppose," a friend replied, "that a man with a beard like that would be approved!" . . .

The centerpiece of the exercises of Yearly Meeting in those days was the reading of a list of "Queries" which were designed to reveal the moral and spiritual condition of the members and the meetings of the Quaker flock. They were searching questions about the life and conduct, "the walk and conversation," of the membership. These Queries were admirably fitted to form a silent "confessional" for the individual soul, and if they had been read effectively and then left upon the soul and conscience of the listener to be silently faced and meditated upon, they would have produced a powerful impression. But the custom had grown up to have them formally answered in writing and to have the answers *weightily* considered. This operation usually took two days. It is difficult enough for a man to diagnose his own soul and report honestly the findings, but to formulate public answers on the moral and spiritual state of a religious body approaches the impossible, and becomes largely an elaborate play of words. In any case it does not promote the life and health that are undergoing diagnosis. I very early revolted from this method of investigation as unproductive and tedious, and I felt that the "preachments" that followed each Query and Answer were dull and stereotyped. I debated the problem vigorously with the older friends. Isaac Sharpless was a stout advocate of the ancient custom, maintaining that it had done much to produce the careful, tremulous, guarded moral life of the Society; while Thomas Chase held with me that it would be more effective for each individual to balance his own accounts in a silent confessional and review, in the hush, his own spiritual assets and liabilities. So far as I know, the Society of Friends is the only Christian body in the world that diagnoses its state and condition by means of Queries, and the unique and curious method of introspection has always deeply interested me.

I felt that everywhere the emphasis on garb and speech and Quaker badges of plainness was excessive. It seemed to me a bondage and a burden, a load and a yoke, instead of a way of joy and freedom. The uniform note was negative rather than positive. "Do not" was too much in evidence. The puritanic strain was woven through the web. I remember the awful seriousness with which a prominent Friend warned us to beware of falling into the pernicious custom of tipping the hat when meeting one another in the street, and of saying, "Mr. So and So," or "Miss So and So." And finally, in an extraordinary rhythmic quaver he added with a burst of emotion, "We must guard against a great and growing evil, which is extending over the length and breadth of our broad land and has now reached the Allegheny Mountains—I mean baseball!"

The Mysticism of Rufus Jones

[FROM *Friend of Life*]

ELIZABETH   GRAY   VINING

[*Many Americans know Mrs. Vining through her books about Japan, where she was from 1946 to 1950 tutor to the Crown Prince. She is also a novelist and the biographer of Rufus Jones. In the selection that follows she writes with understanding of Jones's conviction that "Whatever your mind comes at | I tell you flat | God is not that."*]

———

It was through reading Emerson in college that Rufus Jones first became aware that the religion in which he had grown up, with the dew of which he had been sprinkled from morning till night, the religion of his beloved Aunt Peace, was actually a mystical religion, a part of a great spiritual movement. By that realization and through the influence of Pliny Chase his mind was directed toward the study of mysticism from a historical viewpoint, and his first written treatment of the subject was his graduation essay, "Some Exponents of Mystical Religion."

It was, however, his own mystical experience at Dieu-le-fit which at the age of twenty-four turned him from one who had some knowledge about mysticism and who sought to know more, into one who had knowledge of mysticism through his own experience. It changed the direction of his life, provided its consuming interest, opened his understanding of the mystics of whom he was to write, and gave him an unfaltering conviction of the reality of God.

This was the first but not the only such experience in his life. Even more impressive to him was that which he had on the ship going to England when unknown to him Lowell was dying, and he felt himself "surrounded as by an enfolding presence and held as though by invisible Arms," when his entire being was "fortified for the tragic news that awaited him on landing." In this experience, even more than in the earlier one, he was aware of the overwhelming love of God and of his own response to it.

He recognized also a still different kind of experience, in which there was "no single moment of invasion of uprush" but after which he discovered that new life and power had come without his knowing exactly when. Such an experience, which he called "a case of quiet mystical receptivity" occurred after his automobile accident in 1922. Though he acknowledged the exhilaration of returning health when he had thought life was ended, he was convinced that he had received also a spiritual revitalization resulting in a new level of life. He was evidently referring to this experience when he wrote in 1936, "There is a type of *organic mysticism* which is much more common than highly conscious mysticism is."

It was an experience, he said in the Introduction to W. C. Braithwaite's *Beginnings of Quakerism*, "not merely emotional, not merely intellectual, not merely volitional, through which the soul finds itself in a love-relation with the Living God. There are all possible stages and degrees of the experience of this 'relation' from simple awareness of the soul's Divine Companion to a rapt consciousness of union with the One and Only Reality."

The significant features of this experience he described many times. In the Introduction to *Spiritual Reformers* he noted "the consciousness of fresh springs of life, the inauguration of a sense of mission, the flooding of the life with hope and gladness and the conviction, amounting to a certainty, that God is found as an environing and vitalizing Presence." To these he added later, the integration of the personality, "the closing of chasms and cleavages" whereby "the divided will, the divided mind, the divided heart become fused into a unity." A further characteristic of the experience is its incommunicability. In spite of the mystic's certainty that he has been in communion with God, be is unable to tell in words what he has received, and he is unable to bring back "concrete information about the nature and character of God."

Rufus Jones was firm in maintaining that mysticism was not the whole of religion. "It [religion] is essentially bound up with all the processes of the intellect and with all the deeper issues of the will as well as with these first-hand intimations of the soul's vision. The present-day revolt from doctrine is in many ways superficial. There can be no greater religion without the interpretation of life, of the universe, of experience, of mind, of God. What we ought to revolt from is traditional dogma." And again, "Mystical experience is not a substitute for the moral and rational processes of everyday life."

In the course of his life he defined mysticism over and over again in books and articles, in addresses, in innumerable question periods. At the end of any lecture on mysticism, he commented, someone was sure to rise and say appealingly, "Will the speaker kindly tell us in two or three plain words what mysticism really is?" The number and beauty of his definitions make a choice of a single example difficult, but one of the simplest is that given in *The Trail of Life in the Middle Years:* "The essential characteristic of it is the attainment of a personal conviction by an individual that the human spirit and the divine Spirit have met, have found each other, and are in mutual and reciprocal correspondence as spirit with Spirit." The phrase "mutual and reciprocal correspondence," a favorite phrase of his, is borrowed from Clement of Alexandria, who was from his youth one of his spiritual heroes. In 1910 he published a little book of *Selections from the Writings of Clement of Alexandria.* In his *Luminous Trail,* in 1947, he repeated the definition that he gave in 1909 in his *Studies in Mystical Religion* and which evidently he considered the most satisfactory of his formulations: "Mysticism is the type of religion which puts the emphasis on immediate awareness of relation with God, on direct and intimate consciousness of the Divine presence. It is religion in its most acute, intense and living stage." "Mysticism may, and I think should, stand for that type of experience in which a person feels an overmastering conviction that actual contact is attained with a divine, life-giving, joy-bringing Presence," he wrote in *Pathways to the Reality of God.*

Throughout his life he made a distinction between affirmative mysticism and negative mysticism. Here he parts company with many writers on the subject, to whom the negative is the classic type and indeed the only real mysticism.

The *via negativa*, as Rufus Jones saw it, called for withdrawal from the world, from all that is finite and temporal, in order to lose oneself in that which is infinite and eternal. The naughting of the self, the elimination of the I, the me, and the mine, the extirpation of all desire, the quenching of all thought, the merging of the individual personality in the divine Whole is necessary if union with the divine is to be achieved. Plotinus's often quoted phrase, "the flight of the alone to the Alone," expresses this summit experience. Ecstasy is the goal of the follower of this way.

The affirmative mysticism, to the interpretation of which Rufus Jones gave his life, was a "milder and more normal correspondence of the soul with God." The affirmation mystic, he declared in *Social Law in the Spiritual World*, "seeks union with God, but not through loss of personality." On the contrary, his personality is fulfilled in God. Saint Paul's statement, "It is no longer I that live but Christ liveth in me," Rufus Jones understood as "no negation of personality but a triumphant type of immensely expanded personality." The mark of the affirmative mystic is a transformed personality, radiant, vital, filled with energy, who finds, as he said in *Social Law in the Spiritual World*, obedience to the vision more important than the vision and who seeks to serve God in this world.

Ecstasy in itself he distrusted, as being related to symptoms of hysteria, auditions, bodily changes and hypnosis. Trances and ecstasies have an element of abnormality and are not the best part of mysticism. He considered it a weakness of the negation mystic that he encouraged men "to live for the rare moment of ecstasy and beatific vision, to sacrifice the chance of winning spiritual victory for the hope of receiving an ineffable illumination which would quench all further search or desire." Thirty-four years later he put it even more strongly: "I am equally convinced that the emphasis upon ecstasy which the Neoplatonic strain of thought introduced into Christian mysticism was an unfortunate and very costly contribution, and quite foreign to the mysticism of the New Testament. In fact for many interpreters ecstasy came to be thought of as the *essentia* of mysticism: "No ecstasy, no mystic!" He qualified this statement somewhat by making it clear that he was thinking of ecstasy chiefly as a semi-pathological state marked by an abnormal autosuggestibility and hysteria. "There is a type of ecstatic state, of inspiration and illumination, which seems to me to be a most glorious attainment and very near to the goal of life—a state of concentration, of unification, of liberation, of discovery, of heightened and intensified powers, and withal, a burst of joy, of rapture and of radiance."

The source of negative mysticism he found in the belief in a wholly transcendent God, unknowable, wholly other, abstract, and characterless. He was fond of quoting in this connection the lines,

> Whatever your mind comes at,
> I tell you flat
> God is not that!

This God of the negation mystic, the "nameless Nothing" of Eckhart, the "Divine Dark" of Dionysius the Areopagite, the "fathomless Nothingness" of Tauler, Rufus Jones characterized as the "Abstract Infinite." "The long struggle of man's mind with the stern compulsions of this abstract infinite is, I think, one of the major intellectual tragedies of human life. . . . It is easy to see how that theory of the abstract (i.e. characterless) infinite would lead the mind of a mystic to expect his experience of God to terminate in a mental blank, an everlasting Nay."

To him God was a Concrete Infinite. He used the term for the first time in the introduction to *Spiritual Reformers* and continued to employ it to the end of his life. "No ancient or medieval thinker," he wrote in *Testimony of the Soul,* "ever dealt adequately with what we have learned to call 'the concrete infinite,' an infinite revealed in and through the temporal and the finite." The great symbol of the concrete infinite he finds in Saint John's figure of the Vine with its many branches. "In that figure we have the suggestion of an Infinite that goes out into multitudinous manifestations and finds itself in and through its interrelated and finite branches. Perfection is not through isolation and withdrawal but through self-surrender and sacrificial limitation." In the *Luminous Trail,* after interpreting John

IV, 24, to mean, "God is essentially Spirit and man can join with Him in vital fellowship, for he too is spirit," he went on to say, "This report means that religion is founded on a concrete Infinite, for Spirit is a concrete Reality, not on an abstract and 'naughted' Absolute, and intercommunion is an intelligible process of Like with like."

The affirmative type of mysticism he traced first to Saint John and Saint Paul, who, he said, had been often disqualified as mystics by New Testament scholars who assumed that mysticism meant withdrawal from all that is finite and temporal. With the Renaissance and the recovery of New Testament models, a new type of mysticism came to birth, more Pauline and Johannine than the medieval type had been. The medieval view of God and man was broken by the new humanism, not the modern humanism of naturalistic philosophy that "reduced man to a natural creature" but the luminous humanism of Erasmus and the Renaissance thinkers, who discovered with joy the glorious potentialities of the human mind and spirit. "The focal idea of this new type of mysticism," he wrote, "is the glowing faith that there is something divine in man which under right influences and responses can become the dominant feature of a person's whole life. The favorite text of the exponents of the affirmation mysticism was that noble oracular fragment in Proverbs already quoted: 'The Spirit of man is a candle of the Lord.' This line of thought goes back for its pedigree, without much doubt, to the humanism of the Renaissance."

To this humanism, "at heart deeply Platonic and mystical," was added the Reformation's rediscovery of the primitive message of Christianity and its insistence on the responsibility of the individual in the sphere of religion. "The center of religion was no longer thought of as being an external imperial organization; it was felt to be the inner life of the individual man. This shift of attitude was like the coming of the vernal equinox and with it came a new outburst of mystical life." From the strand of mysticism of the Friends of God, the humanism of Erasmus, the inward religion of Luther's early insight, and the glowing message of the New Testament came, as Rufus Jones showed in his historical studies, the mysticism of Caspar Schwenkfeld, Hans

Denck, Sebastian Franck, Sebastian Costellio, and Jacob Boehme, the spiritual reformers whom he believed to be the forerunners of the Quakers of the seventeenth century.

Thomas Traherne, the seventeenth-century poet, he cited as a brilliant interpreter of affirmative mysticism, and he considered William Law its chief exponent in the eighteenth century. William Blake was, he said, the "most notable mystic" of the latter century, but in none of his books did he care to tackle the elucidation of Blake. Nor was Blake one of the many poets whom he frequently quoted.

Although he insisted upon the distinction between affirmative and negative mystics, he declared with equal emphasis that there were both affirmative and negative elements in both types of mysticism. The difference between the two types was a relative difference. "There have been no negation mystics who were not also affirmative, and there neither are nor will be any important affirmation mystics who do not tread at some point the *via negativa*—the hard and dolorous road."

All the great mystics up to the Reformation were, he felt, negative because of the prevailing metaphysics but affirmative in their experience. Again and again he paid tribute to their lives and their personalities, to the good that they did in the world. He loved them and he wrote of them in book after book, Meister Eckhart, whom he called "the peak of the range," Plotinus, the anonymous author of the *Theologia Germanica,* Saint Bernard of Clairvaux. Even Dionysius the Areopagite, whom he considered responsible for much of the more extreme form of negative mysticism, he spoke of as "this dear man."

This question of the classification of different types of mysticism is discussed by Thomas H. Hughes of the University of Edinburgh in his *Philosophical Basis of Mysticism.* He finds the division into Mild and Extreme Types, into Cognitive and Conative Mystics, and into Affirmative and Negative Mystics not "a sufficiently distinctive classification since it rests on a principle which is not essential to the mystical Faith." In preference he would use Rudolf Otto's Soul-mysticism and God-mysticism, or Dean Inge's Speculative, Practical, Devotional, and Nature Mysticism, though these do not allow for overlapping. The most generally accepted grouping, according to Mr. Hughes, is Philosophical, Nature, and Religious Mysticism.

Nature Mysticism is rooted in divine immanence, Philosophical mysticism in divine transcendence, Religious mysticism at its best combines the two: union with the Personal God, for transcendence and immanence are reconciled in personality.

By this classification, Rufus Jones clearly belongs with the religious mystics. God to Rufus Jones was personal in the sense that we can enter into a relationship with him. To use Martin Buber's term, He is not the God of the Philosophers, but the God of Abraham, Isaac and Jacob, to whom we can say, "O Thou!"

Beyond that, Rufus Jones's mysticism is profoundly Quaker. It is colored by the Quaker strain that has come through his home and the meeting, through his reading of Quaker sources, through his knowledge of the New Testament and the primitive Christianity to which seventeenth-century Quakerism was a conscious return. Though he found immense inspiration in Plotinus, in Eckhart, Tauler, the *Theologia Germanica*, and Ruysbroeck, he was happiest with them when they were expressing, in other terms, ideas which were Quaker ideas; also when they moved away, he was obliged to say sadly, as he did of the author of the *Theologia Germanica*, "I go most of the way in joyous company with this dear man whom, not having seen, I love. But I cannot finally be satisfied with any system of thought which empties this world here below of present spiritual significance or which robs the life of a human personality of its glorious mission as an organ of the Life of God here and now, and which postpones the Kingdom of God to a realm where the Perfect is a One with no other."

His rejection of the negation mystic's withdrawal from the world is characteristic of Quaker thought and practice. "True godliness," wrote William Penn, "does not turn men out of the world, but enables them to live better in it and excites their endeavors to mend it." Quakers marry, engage in business, occupy themselves with a hundred activities to improve the world. In their meetings for worship and in times of private meditation, it is true, they withdraw from distractions, even the religious distractions of ritual and sacred music, but the insights which they receive at such times they return to the world to put into effect as best they can. "The history of the Society of Friends," writes Howard Brinton, "shows that acceptance of the principle of withdrawal in worship has not resulted in any attempt at final or complete withdrawal. The negative journey to the Light was invariably followed by the positive journey to the needy but good world." "Those who see God," said Rufus Jones, "must gird for service. Those who would have a closer view of the divine must seek it in a life of love and sacrifice."

George Fox was to Rufus Jones pre-eminently the type of the affirmation mystic. "He thought of man, raised to his full spiritual height, as an organ of the life of God. The early Friends, his followers, knew of no limits to what God could do through a man or a woman, raised by His power to stand and live in the same Spirit that the prophets and apostles were in who gave forth the Scriptures. They made conquest of their fears, they were released from a sense of danger, they became concentrated and unified spirits dedicated to the task of building the Kingdom of God according to the pattern in the Mount."

Ascetic practices, characteristic of medieval mysticism, have never been part of Quaker discipline. The testimony of temperance comes from social and moral reasons, not from a desire to mortify the flesh. Quaker simplicity in dress and speech arose out of a concern for truth and sincerity. Good food has always seemed to Friends one of the God-given pleasures of life which there is no reason to put aside except as by cutting down one's own supply one can share with those in need. Rufus Jones himself had always a healthy, human interest in food. His letters home often report on good meals he has enjoyed or bad ones he has suffered from, and lobsters and new peas were high among the joys of his summer home in Maine.

His view of mysticism was also strongly colored by the Quaker idea of the sacraments, of which a brief statement may be found in *Faith and Practice*, the book of Christian discipline published by the Philadelphia Yearly Meeting. "With full appreciation of the help which has come through the outward forms to countless generations of Christians, Friends symbolize by their very lack of symbols the essentially inward nature of the sacraments. Friends' testimony is not a negative protest but an affirmation of the sacramental nature of the whole life when it is under the leading of the Spirit." The Eucharist, which Rufus Jones sometimes accepted when he was with other religious groups, was to him a moving ceremony but in no way a necessary door to communion with God. His admiration for Evelyn Underhill was tempered by his disappointment over her inability to understand the Quaker point of view on the sacraments and her insistence on the necessity of the communion service. "I have just read the proof for the American edition of Evelyn Underhill's *Worship*," he wrote to Violet Hodgkin Holdsworth. "It is an important book, but she is quite unable to appreciate or even to understand the full meaning of Quaker worship without sacraments. I have talked with her frequently about this, but can never make her see what it means to us. She grows more high Church as she grows older and that side of her religious life overtops everything else; but she is a great soul." The affirmation mystic, Rufus Jones insisted, found God revealed in the finite. To him everything was sacramental. "Nothing now can be unimportant. There is more in the least event than the ordinary eye sees. Everywhere in the world there is stuff to be transmuted into divine material. Every situation may be turned into an occasion for winning a nearer view of God."

Perhaps the most striking difference between Rufus Jones's mysticism and that of the classical mystic, whether affirmative or negative, and at the same time the most essentially Quaker element in it, was his conviction that mysticism flourished best in groups. Preparation must be made in the individual heart but the heightened receptivity of the group waiting in silence helped many to enter into an experience with God which they would not have attained alone. There are many expressions of this fundamental Quaker principle, from Robert Barclay's statement in the seventeenth century: "As many candles lighted and put in one place do greatly augment the light and make it more to shine forth, so when many are gathered together into the same life there is more of the glory of God and His power appears to the refreshment of each individual, for each partakes not only of the light and life raised in himself but in all the rest," to Howard

Brinton's brief sentence "Quakerism is peculiar in being a group mysticism, grounded in Christian concepts."

Rufus Jones too found many ways and occasions to restate this truth. More than any other scholar he has studied and written about mystical groups; it is perhaps his most important contribution to the history of mysticism.

"Mysticism flourishes best in a group," he wrote in *New Studies in Mystical Religion*, "and it can, if left to itself, produce out of its experience a type of organization that favors its growth and increase in depth and power."

"The great fact remains," he had said even earlier in *The American Friend*, "that there is no greater gift than the gift of listening to God, and that there is no greater spiritual power than that which comes when a whole congregation is fused and melted in silent waiting and soul-worship before the living God, when God's presence can be felt and His voice heard so distinctly that no audible words are needed."

Early Quakers, and many modern Quakers also, used the terms Light Within, Christ Within, Light of Christ, Seed of God, the Inward Teacher, That of God in every man, interchangeably. Rufus Jones seldom used the term "Christ Within." He used instead Spirit, Divine Spirit, the Spirit of Truth, the Holy Spirit, Presence, the Over-World, and Emil Boutroux's term, "the Beyond that is Within." He believed that Christ who was both human and divine had come primarily to lead people to a new experience with God. "The greatest single thing about Christ," he said in China to the eager crowds that heard him there, "is His *experience* of God and His transmission of the life of God into the lives of men." "Christ was concerned to have men's lives flooded with the consciousness of God, to have them become 'rich in God.'" "The most unique thing to my mind about the Jesus of history is, not a new ethics or a new interpretation of society or a fresh message about the Kingdom of God, important as these are, but a new and most wonderfully rich experience of God that apparently had been growing and deepening all through those silent background years."

A further question about Rufus Jones's own type of mysticism to be considered is this: Did he regard the mystical experience as open to everyone, or did he think it was a special gift or capacity determined by the individual psychic make-up or bestowed by God's favor?

There are to be found in his writings passages in which he seems to waver in his opinion or even to contradict himself wholly. "Some degree of this experience ... is probably present in us all," he wrote in *Social Law in the Spiritual World*. "Even the most prosaic of us are haunted by a Beyond." When he wrote *Spiritual Reformers*, after long study and research on mystics who were spiritual geniuses, he seemed to change his mind. "It is an experience that is by no means universal. It is not, so far as we can see from the facts at hand, an experience which attaches to the very nature of consciousness as such, and indeed one which is bound to occur even when the human subject strains forward all the energies of his will for the adventure, or when by strict obedience to the highest laws of life known to him he *waits* for the high visitation." He goes on to describe persons "as serious and earnest and passionate as the loftiest mystical saint," who appear "impervious to divine bubblings," and he says that to make mystical experience the only way to God would be to set up an "election as rigid as that of the Calvinist system, one determined by the peculiar psychic structure of the individual."

Later, in *New Studies of Mystical Religion*, he returned to a modification of his original position. "Mysticism is a normal trend of the soul and can be cultivated," he said. The capacity for mystical experience was normal, in the sense that it was not pathological or unbalanced or evidence of a diseased mind. It was, however, he sadly conceded, not universal, in the sense that it came naturally to everybody. "Probably in the last analysis the psychical disposition of the individual himself is the crucial factor," he said. "It comes only to those who can meditate, who can stop living by clock-time and space-speed and center down into that interior hush where the human spirit touches the skirts of God."

Still later he asserted without qualification, "When I talk mysticism I mean something fundamental to the normal essential nature of the soul." And his final word, in *A Call to What Is Vital*, was: "The mystical trait—and I mean by it the consciousness of direct relation with God, existential religion—is not in any true sense confined to a small chosen list of religious geniuses, but is a feature of the democratic laity as well as of the high pulpit class that form the usual lists." In this he differs from his friend Dean Inge, who said categorically in his *Christian Mysticism*, "Everybody is naturally either a mystic or a legalist." He did, in the Prologue to *The Flowering of Mysticism*, make a half-hearted attempt to differentiate between two distinct types of men, the biological man who has no interest in the Beyond and the man for whom the walls of separation between the seen and the unseen are thinner, but he quickly concluded that the distinction is "one of degree rather than type," that the gift of "correspondence" is present in "all normally endowed persons" but rises to a higher level in those with special gifts.

The greatest mystics, Rufus Jones believed, have been religious geniuses. "They make their contribution to religion in ways similar to those in which the geniuses in other fields raise the level of human attainments and achievements." "All of the great capacities of the soul come to light best of course in persons who are geniuses." But he believed that there are far more mystics of the milder sort than is commonly supposed. "I am convinced that a great many of these so-called 'ordinary persons' have a sense of contact with spiritual forces that give their lives an extraordinary effectiveness." Indeed, he even went so far as to say that many were mystics without knowing it. "By far the larger number of mystics probably live and die without explicitly knowing they are mystics ... They quietly manifest in acts that energies not their own and incursions of power from beyond themselves are coming through them." One of his favorite topics, which formed a chapter in his last book as well as several articles, was the mysticism of ordinary persons. Wherever he went he met people who had felt themselves "in contact with an environing Presence and supplied with new energy to live by," and among his papers are some remarkable letters from otherwise unknown people telling him of experiences they had had.

Though he believed that the capacity for such experience could be cultivated, and indeed in one place characterizes the mystic as one who "has cultivated with more strenuous care and discipline than others have done the native homing passion of the soul for the Beyond," there are no handbooks of mystical training to be found among Rufus Jones's fifty-four book titles. The classic "ladders" of ascent he considered suitable only to the few; to many these were "unreal and artificial." Though at one time he declared that it required a "training analogous to the athlete's," he was for the most part dubious about techniques and well marked roadways, "convinced that the mystic way will always remain a way of surprise and wonder."

He did nevertheless in several of his books give some hints and suggestions as to how the mystical aspirant may best pursue the serious business of his life, which is "to seek, to find, to love and to be in union with God." Though he did not use the word *purgation* he did regard the process of overcoming selfishness, of organizing the instincts and emotions, sublimating the old springs of action and energy and developing new habit tracks as primary and essential. He did not minimize the importance of concentration. "Training in concentration," he pointed out, "is the first step toward any difficult goal in life. Meditation is simply concentration in a special field."

"Preparation through appreciation of *beauty*, learning to sound the deeps of *love*, formation of purity, gentleness, tenderness of heart, freedom from harshness of judgment, absolute honesty of purpose and motive—these positive traits and qualities of life are far more important steps on the inner pathway than are artificial techniques of discipline."

The right use of great spiritual literature and the fellowship of "spiritually contagious persons" he also counted among the important aids to the deepening of the mystical capacity.

Beyond these general suggestions, which apply as much to any person who wishes to live a good life in accordance with the will of God as to him who longs to achieve mystic union, he does not go. The technique of Yoga or of Zen Buddhism, which he recognized as being a "discipline of a very high order for the control of sense, of muscles, of imagination, of wandering thoughts, of human passion," did not, he believed, achieve the end which he saw as the desirable one. "Routine, cut-and-dried systems of discipline may help to make a Stoic temper, or to prepare a climber of Mt. Everest, or"—and here he makes one catch one's breath—"to forge a mystic of the type of Saint John of the Cross, but these disciplines seem to me to be too doctrinaire and too remote from life to be satisfactory ways into the heart of divine reality."

To many people any routine that could forge a mystic like Saint John of the Cross would appear to leave nothing more to be desired. In another book Rufus Jones explained further what he meant about the Spanish saint. "If one wants to see a man who has climbed clear above the pleasure line and who lives in a height in which the pleasure spur is forgotten and has been left behind as though it did not exist, let him read Saint John of the Cross. I admit that it sometimes seems to me as though, in leaving behind all reference to aspects of preference, of like and dislike, Saint John has also left behind our human way of life and has withdrawn almost into a vacuum where exists very little of the air we mortals breathe. . . . I feel a sense of hush and awe in the presence of these tremendous lovers of God" (he was writing about Fénélon and Madame Guyon as well as Saint John of the Cross) "but in my critical moments I am convinced that they are endeavoring to do what cannot be done and, I am bound to add, what ought not to be done. They propose to eliminate all the springs of action which characterize us as men, to obliterate all the concrete clues from human experience which serve as practical guides for us, and to walk only by a supernatural pillar of cloud and fire from above."

A mysticism, however lofty, which left humanity behind was foreign to Rufus Jones's thought. "I am interested," he said, "in a mysticism which brings life to its full rich goal of complete living, with radiance and joy and creative power." A mysticism, furthermore, that did not find expression in creative service, remained to him incomplete. In describing John Woolman, who was to him the best expression of the ideal of Quaker mysticism, he told how Woolman became extraordinarily tender to human need and sensitive to "every breath of wrong" which man does to man. "Here was a mysticism," he concluded "—and it was the type to which I dedicated my life—which sought no ecstasies, no miracles of levitation, no startling phenomena, no private raptures, but whose overmastering passion was to turn all he possessed, including his own life, 'into the channel of universal love.' "

THE CONVINCED (2)

I had found a place.

—CAROLINE STEPHEN

"Feeding upon the Bread of Life . . ."

[FROM *Quaker Strongholds*]

CAROLINE   STEPHEN

[At this juncture the viewpoint changes. We have been looking at
Quakerism through the eyes of those whose parents were Quakers and for
whom Quakerism was often either taken for granted or, as was the case
with Logan Smith, derided. There were many exceptions, of course, and
Rufus Jones was a notable one.

The section which follows is made up of the writings of those who
came to Quakerism not by "birthright" but by the force of their own
convictions. The "convinced" Friends at this period received their
convincement, for the most part, from the principles of early-day
Friends, rather than from the efforts of any evangelist. Some, like
William Hubben, had Quakerism first brought to their attention
through the works of the American Friends Service Committee. Others
had Quaker meetings at hand which they could attend, as Caroline
Stephen (1834–1909) did.

In 1890 she published Quaker Strongholds, "and showed to
many wavering and discouraged souls that they were despairing
prematurely of the future of 'our beloved Society.' " So writes Thomas

446

Hodgkin; and he finds the words which follow to be the most significant in this book, which has become a Quaker classic.

"The perennial justification of Quakerism lies in its energetic assertion that the kingdom of heaven is within us: that we are not made dependent upon any outward organization for our spiritual welfare. Its perennial difficulty lies in the inveterate disposition of human beings to look to each other for spiritual help, in the feebleness of their perception of that Divine Voice which speaks to each one in a language no other ear can hear, and in the apathy which is content to go through life without the attempt at any true individual communion with God."|

The notorious disinclination of Friends to any attempts at proselytizing, and perhaps some lingering effects of persecution, probably account for the very common impression that Friends' meetings are essentially private—mysterious gatherings into which it would be intrusive to seek admission. Many people, indeed, probably suppose (if they think about it at all) that such meetings are no longer held; that the Society is fast dying out, and the "silent worship" of tradition a thing of the past—impracticable, and hardly to be seriously mentioned in these days of talk and of breathless activity.

Some such vague impression floated, I believe, over my own mind, when, some seventeen years ago, I first found myself within reach of a Friends' meeting, and somewhat to my surprise, was cordially made welcome to attend it. The invitation came at a moment of need, for I was beginning to feel with dismay that I might not much longer be able conscientiously to continue to join in the Church of England service; not for want of appreciation of its unrivalled richness and beauty, but from doubts of the truth of its doctrines, combined with a growing recognition that to me it was as the armour of Saul in its elaboration and in the sustained pitch of religious fervour for which it was meant to provide an utterance. Whether true or not in its speculative and theoretical assumptions, it was clear to me that it was far from true as a periodical expression of my own experience, belief, or aspiration. The more vividly one feels the force of its eloquence, the more, it seems to me, one must hesitate to adopt it as the language of one's own soul, and the more unlikely is it that such heights and depths of feeling as it demands should be ready to fill its magnificent channels every Sunday morning at a given hour. The questionings with which at that period I was painfully struggling were stirred into re-doubled activity by the dogmatic statements and assumptions with which the Liturgy abounds, and its unbroken flow left no loophole for the utterance of my own less disciplined, but to myself far more urgent, cries for help. Thus the hour of public worship, which should have been a time of spiritual strengthen-ing and calming, became to me a time of renewed conflict, and of occasional exaltation and excitement of emotion, leading but too surely to reaction and apathy.

I do not attempt to pass any judgment on this mental condition. I have described it at some length because I cannot believe it to be altogether exceptional, or without significance. At any rate, it was fast leading me to dread the moment when I should be unable either to find the help I needed, or to offer my tribute of devotion, in any place of worship amongst my fellow-Christians. When lo, on one never-to-be-forgotten Sunday morning, I found myself one of a small company of silent worshippers, who were content to sit down together without words, that each one might feel after and draw near to the Divine Presence, unhindered at least, if not helped, by any human utterance. Utterance I knew was free, should the words be given; and before the meeting was over, a sentence or two were uttered in great simplicity by an old and apparently untaught man, rising in his place amongst the rest of us. I did not pay much attention to the words he spoke, and I have no recollection of their purport. My whole soul was filled with the unutterable peace of the undisturbed opportunity for communion with God—with the sense that at last I had found a place where I might, without the faintest suspicion of insincerity, join with others in simply seeking His presence. To sit down in silence could at the least pledge me to nothing; it might open to me (as it did that morning) the very gate of heaven. And since that day, now more than seventeen years ago, Friends' meetings have indeed been to me the greatest of outward helps to a fuller and fuller entrance into the spirit from which they have sprung; the place of the most soul-subduing, faith-restoring, strengthening and peaceful communion, in feeding upon the bread of life, that I have ever known.

"No Other Religion than the Will of God"

[FROM *The Vision of Faith*]

CAROLINE STEPHEN

TO MISS E. WEDGWOOD

December 9, 1872

Since you have been here the thought of your protracted crisis has been very much in my mind, and I feel, as I so often do, a longing for a few more words, though, strange as it almost seems to me, it is of myself more than of you that I want to write. . . . I did not feel as if I had been able at all fully to answer you when you asked in what sense I had gained by this summer, and yet I had, and have, a great wish that you should know how great the blessing is which has come to me since those days when I "discouraged" you by my feeling of the darkness, by telling you I felt my life had been a failure and had been wasted, and that I saw no reason to think the individual loss was a means to a good end. I did not and, in a sense, I do not, only I no longer want to see that or anything but the beauty which is independent of me, and in seeing that is a gain and a blessing such as I used not to be able to imagine and cannot describe. All life seems to me more beautiful since my own "personal" life seemed to me done with. I told you that I remember in those days I thought very likely when I had finished dying a certain kind of death I should find there was a new and better kind of life behind it; but I did not expect so soon to have such a vivid sense of it, and what I had not at all foreseen was the sense I should have of this better kind of life being there for everybody. I have such a sense of its being the solid ground underneath our feet, which is there whether we know it or not, to receive us when our own private edifices crumble away, so that I feel as if a great terror for all whom I love, as well as for myself, had passed away. I do not dread any misfortune so much as I used, because this sense of the unchangeable foundation seems to give me a hold on something beyond them. It is so entirely without any effort or any individual means that this peace has come to me, that I know it must be open to everybody. It was just when, because I saw no escape, nothing to wish and no reason to expect any good thing, I abandoned all effort—it was then that the mere necessity I fell back upon proved to be "the good and perfect and acceptable will of God" on which my soul could rest with a rest and peace that are better to me than any pleasure. I don't of course mean that it would be so if I had not been in the right road and wishing to be taught, and in particular if I had not faced the worst in the way of doubt as well as of pain. But that amount of honesty is all that seems to be required of us to secure our finding His will left to us as enough for us when all our own wishes are denied. . . . It is as if my painted roof had been smashed and, instead of the darkness I had dreaded, I had found the stars shining.

"Not Quakerism but Truth"

[FROM *Quaker Strongholds*]

CAROLINE STEPHEN

"By their fruits ye shall know them." It would ill become me to attempt any estimate of the fruitfulness of that branch of the Christian Church which I have joined as compared with the branch of it in which I was brought up. I feel bound, however, to say that I cannot reconcile the fact of the signs of life and spiritual energy which I find within as well as without the Society with the idea that either branch of the Church is really cut off from the root of the living Vine. Does it follow that our peculiar principles and practices are of no consequence?

I cannot myself believe that this is a legitimate conclusion from the admitted fact that undeniably holy and Christian lives are led within as well as without our borders. That fact does, I think, show at least that everything does not depend either upon the observance or the disuse of outward ordinances—it shows that either course may be pursued in good faith and without destruction to the Christian life; but it is not inconsistent with the belief that results of profound importance to the character of our Christianity are involved in this question of ordinances and orders, and that it therefore behoves us to seek the utmost clearness with regard to it.

This question is the very key of the position of the Society of Friends as a separate body. It is as witnesses to the independence of spiritual life upon outward ordinances that we believe ourselves especially called to maintain our place in the universal Church in the present day.

The importance of our separate position is perhaps somewhat obscured in the eyes of some amongst us by the fact that we can no longer assume the vehemently aggressive attitude of the early Friends, as against Christians of other denominations. They believed it to be their duty to attack the "hireling priests" of their day as guilty of "apostasy," and upholders of the mysterious powers of darkness. In our own day such judgments would imply either the grossest ignorance or else downright insanity. We cannot help knowing, and rejoicing to know, that a large proportion of the clergy are amongst the most devoted and disinterested of the children of light, using their official position, as well as every other power of body and mind, for the promotion of the kingdom of God and the spread of the gospel. . . .

In like manner, it would be impossible for Friends in these days to speak in the tone of the founders of the Society, as though we possessed a degree of light in comparison of which all other Christians must be considered as groping in thick darkness. The early Friends sometimes spoke of the "breaking forth of the gospel day" through the revelation made to them as of an event almost equal in importance to its original promulgation sixteen hundred years before. In these days we could not with any kind of honesty or justice claim a position so enormously in advance of our neighbours. . . .

There is thus, I think, a certain perplexity as to our relative position in the Christian Church which is a cause of some weakness amongst Friends. It is in some respects easier to maintain an aggressive attitude than one of mere quiet separateness; and it would be no wonder if some, especially of our younger members, in these days of free interchange of sympathy, should begin to falter a little as to the importance of our separate position. It is, indeed, one which will not be maintained except as the result of deep and searching spiritual discipline. The testimony against dependence on what is outward cannot be borne to any purpose at second hand. We must ourselves be weaned from all hankering after what is outward and tangible before we can appreciate the value of a testimony to the sufficiency of the purely spiritual; and that weaning is not an easy process, nor one that can be transmitted from generation to generation. Unless our younger Friends be taught in the same stern school as their forefathers, they will assuredly not maintain the vantage-ground won by the faithfulness of a former generation.

Some other causes have, I believe, tended to confuse our relation to the outer world, and make it important that Friends should look well to their path, and consider whither it is tending: whether we are really guarding the position which it is specially our business to defend, or allowing ourselves to be drawn off into the pursuit of less important matters. There are in the main stream of the Society many currents and counter currents, and its recent history has been one of change and reaction, so that it would be dangerous and presumptuous for a new-comer to attempt to foretell its course; but I may venture to point out some of the tendencies which are and have been at work amongst us, preparing the conditions under which our future work must be done.

It is well known that the Society, which sprang very rapidly into existence in the middle of the seventeenth century, began during the eighteenth to diminish in numbers, and was for many years a steadily dwindling body. Closed meeting-houses and empty benches are now to be found in all parts of the country where, in former days, the difficulty was to find room for all who came. Within the last thirty or forty years, our numbers have, however, begun slowly to increase, although the increase is so far from being equal to the rate of increase of the population at large, that in proportion to other denominations we may still be considered as in a certain sense losing ground. The actual increase, small as it is, is nevertheless a significant fact. . . .

With the new rising tide of fervent zeal and benevolence came a great change in the prevailing tone of religious feeling. The Bible, which, in their dread lest the letter should usurp the place of the spirit, had amongst Friends been almost put under a bushel, was brought into new prominence, and so-called "evangelical" views respecting the unique or exceptional nature of its inspiration began to be entertained. Gradually the idea of the necessity of teaching "sound doctrine" assumed an importance which had formerly been reserved for that of looking for "right guidance;" and in some quarters a visible tendency has, of late years, been manifest towards more definition of doctrines and popularizing of methods than would have been tolerated half a century ago.

Although these modern tendencies have undoubtedly been accompanied by, and have probably in some degree led to, an increase in our numbers, a strong protest has from time to time been raised against them by those who feel that Quakerism had its roots and its strength in a deep inward and spiritual experience which frees from all dependence upon outward things. In America the protest against (or, as those who protest would no doubt rather say, the introduction of) this modern phase of comparatively superficial religious activity has caused grievous schisms and troubles. About the year 1826, a large party, under the leadership of one Elias Hicks, in that country broke off altogether from the main body of Friends, and is suspected by the "orthodox" of having, under professed obedience to the inner light, become practically a Unitarian or rationalist body. In England, however, the two main currents have flowed side by side, and have not resulted in any considerable division of the stream.

Both parties claim to be taking their stand upon the original principles of the early Friends. Those who uphold above all things the doctrine of the inward light, and the primary necessity of immediate inspiration and guidance to the bringing forth of any good word or work, and especially to the performance of any acceptable worship, have abundant evidence to produce, in the writings of Fox, Barclay, Penn, Penington, and other fathers of the Society, that this was the foundation and the constant burden of all their teaching. Those, on the other hand, who are throwing themselves heart and soul into missionary and "evangelistic" efforts, say truly enough that the early Friends did not so "wait for guidance" as to be content to sit still and make no effort to lighten the darkness around them, and that it was the intermediate or "mediaeval," not the "primitive" teaching of the Society which exalted the individual consciousness into the supreme authority, thus developing, in fact, a claim to something approaching personal infallibility.

There are, of course, dangers in either extreme—in the over-valuation of visible and tangible activity, and in the undue intensity of introspective quietism. Too much "inwardness" seems to develop an extraordinary bitterness and spirit of judgment, under the shadow of which no fresh growth would be possible. It is obviously dangerous to sanity. Too much "outwardness" dilutes and destroys the very essence of our testimony, encourages a worthless growth of human dependence, and can hardly fail to be dangerous to sincerity. But yet the divergence is, I believe, a case rather of diversity of gifts and functions than of contradiction in principle. Both functions are surely needed. Where a living fountain is really springing up within, it must needs tend to overflow. The leaves and blossoms are as essential to the health and fruitfulness of a tree as its root. The secret, as I believe, of the strength of our Society, its peculiar qualification for service in these days, lies in its strong grasp of the oneness of the inward and the outward, as well as in the deep and pure spirituality of its aim in regard to both.

There is, I believe and am sure, a special and urgent need in these days for that witness to the light—light both within and without—which was the special office of early Quakerism. I am not equally sure that Quakerism, as it is, is the vehicle best adapted to convey that testimony to the present generation. If it be not so, it is largely the fault of our degeneracy as a body; of the lapse of our Society into a rigid formalism during the eighteenth century, and into a shallow seeking for popularity in the nineteenth. But, in spite of all such right-hand and left-hand defections, it seems to me that there is life enough yet in the old tree for a fresh growth of fruit-bearing branches. It seems to me that the framework of the Society has vigour and elasticity enough yet to be used as an invaluable instrument by a new generation of fully convinced Friends, were our younger members but fully willing and resolved to submit to the necessary Divine discipline. It is no new wave of "creaturely activity," no judicious adapting of Quakerism to modern tastes, that will revive its power in the midst of the present generation. It is a fresh breaking forth of the old power, the unchanging and unchangeable power of light and truth itself, met and invited by a fresh submission of heart in each one of us, which can alone invigorate what is languishing amongst us, and make us more than ever a blessing to the nation.

Had this power ever wholly disappeared from amongst us, there would be little use in dwelling fondly upon its deserted tenement. It is because a measure of the ancient spirit is still to be recognized amongst our now widely scattered remnant that I would fain stir it up, amongst our own members especially, and if possible also amongst others, by means of the experience actually acquired by our Society of the power of an exclusively spiritual religion.

It is, I hope, hardly necessary to repeat that it is not Quakerism, but Truth, that I desire to serve and to promote; the sect may no longer be what is needed, and may be destined to extinction, for aught I know. But that view of Truth which has found in Quakerism its most emphatic assertion—that purely spiritual worship and that supremacy of the light within which were set forth with power by Fox and Barclay and Penington— these things are of perennial value and efficacy, and the need for their fresh recognition seems to be in our own day peculiarly urgent.

_____

"Before They Find It, They Rest in Authority"

[FROM *Christ in Catastrophe*]

E M I L   F U C H S

[*The words that follow are taken from the Foreword to Fuchs's* Christ in Catastrophe.

"*Emil Fuchs, a man who has passed through great suffering, has walked among us and lived among us. He spoke to us with the authenticity of one who has seen Truth and heard it and felt it. . . . Now he has gone back to labor in Europe, leaving this writing for us; therefore we set down these words about him.*

"*Emil Fuchs was born in Germany. He was a minister in various places. . . . After 1921 he worked closely with the Social Democratic Party. . . . He became a member of the Society of Friends in 1925. In*

1931 he became professor of Religious Science at the teachers' college at Kiel.

"A period of great suffering followed. He was dismissed from Kiel when the Nazi party came to power. Shortly thereafter he was imprisoned. After he was released he was under the constant watch of the Gestapo, but until 1936 he was able, together with his sons, to assist the escape of refugees by operating a car-hire business. The vehicles were confiscated in 1936. His sons fled Germany. His daughter, a sensitive painter who had given herself to political work, helped her husband escape, but she did not know where he was or how she and her infant son could join him, and she began to suffer recurrent disturbance of mind. Finally she threw herself from a moving train to her death.

"Of all these things we know little, for Emil Fuchs did not talk of them much.... This writing which he has left with us is about his life and experience in Germany, but it is about all life and all experience. It is the witness of a man who is both saint and prophet."

———

How desperately people ask, "How can God be love, when all still happens that has happened in the world of men—and will go on happening in time to come?"

The same world with the same history cries out to me in a clear voice, "God is love."

If God is love and you hate your brother, you live without God. You live without the one creative power of life. Do you wonder that you live in a world of death? Three or four thousand years ago, a poet said:

> Thou sendest forth thy spirit; they are created.
> Thou hidest thy face, they are troubled.
> Thou takest away thy breath, they die,
> And return to their dust.

When men and whole generations of men and whole nations and civilizations seek their life from wealth and power and oppression and injustice, when they live without love in greed and hate, they separate themselves from God and return to their dust.

When nations and civilizations have to die, as in the times we live in, a stream of death and terror runs over the earth. It is not because God is far away, but because man in his hatred and selfishness does not reach out to him, does not reach out to the creative power around him, even within him. God asks more from us than to be small, narrow, selfish, respectable people going the way of money-getting and traditional righteousness. He asks us to be strong upright people who dare to give happiness and life for him and for his kingdom. He created man out of the animals by making him hear this call, and as long as we hear it, so long do we live as men, and his strength is in us. When we do not hear this call, we are living in nothing better than narrow selfishness. Great achievements and discoveries become mere instruments of this selfishness. Hatred and antagonism grow. Man and his civilization begin to die in all the torments of death.

God's love is in this, that he gave us a great goal. The challenge of God's love may therefore be a terror for man. We have to decide whether we pass through this terror into peace and certainty of life's meaningfulness or whether we shrink from it into destruction. Just as those who crucified Christ had to decide, so we also have to decide: whether we shall hear his challenge and seek the way of truth, love and brotherhood, or whether we will again crucify him in all his suffering brothers and sisters—and return to our dust.

CHRIST RE-CRUCIFIED

Sometimes we wonder why in the books, letters and testimonies of Jesus' time and immediately after, there is no mention of him. For the great men of Rome and Greece the happenings in Galilee and Jerusalem were as the news of the lynching of a Negro in an unknown township of the South is to people nowadays. They read, shudder a little and forget. And if a destitute Negro is lynched, or if a hungry child dies in China, or if a drunken man stumbles through the slums of Philadelphia, or if a rich man supports a Hitler or otherwise oppresses freedom and truth, sacrificing righteousness to profits: then in each of these events is Christ's challenge: how much of God may there have been in this your brother, your sister, whom you killed, starved, denied education and constructive living, or drowned in luxury?

"Inasmuch as ye have done it unto one of the least of these my brethren, ye have done it unto me. . . . Inasmuch as ye did it not to one of the least of these, ye did it not to me."

There are many in whom Christ's challenge mingles in a strange way with the traditional, inherited faith in force. Such people try to help their suffering brothers by fighting against those who oppress them. And there are other ways of trying to join obedience to Christ with obedience to tradition. There are the churches who try to speak his message clearly, and yet tremble to offend the easy-going, the comfortable and the influential. There are the millions of men who mingle the challenge they hear with an egoistic longing for a more comfortable life and for materialistic striving. But at the same time there is the growing number of those, very often trembling like the disciples, who are forced by a divine challenge to stand and struggle and work and speak, bringing people to a clear understanding of Christ's way and to a clear decision between him and tradition, injustice, self-deceit and force.

We must know, all of us, that we are fighting against him insofar as we hinder any of our brothers from finding his own constructive life. And we know that we stand for him—again, all of us—insofar as we stand for the rights of others, for understanding and peace and truth and justice, and—most important of all—insofar as we are prepared to sacrifice our comfort and our privilege for the lives and rights of our brothers.

EXPERIENCE AND AUTHORITY

Again and again men have tried to tell us various things about God: how he is and what he is and how he created the world and how Jesus became his revelation. Men have put together their accounts out of the Bible or out of their heads, and again and again we have to recognise that God is too great a mystery for us to comprehend. He is dwelling in the Light unto which no man can approach. The creative mystery of the world cannot be known through man-made doctrines and teachings. God put in the midst of history a simple man, pure in heart and strong in truth, giving in him the message of what we shall be and what mankind will be.

And behind this man stands the history by which God taught a nation to come to an understanding of a great goal roused in the inward being of its prophets and leaders. In this history the Bible tells us of Abraham, who had to go out from his father's house in a higher search; of Moses, who had to take the shoes from off his feet; of Isaiah, who saw God in the Temple; of Ezekiel, who saw him by the river Chebar; of all the prophets and poets, who denounced unrighteousness and sang redemption.

What all these men saw of God and can tell of him is the image of the eternal mystery in the human mind. We know that they experienced his challenge to them and his call to their people; we know that the continuing reality of his self-revealing leads to Jesus.

So we read the Bible, not to construct doctrines about God or laws about society, but to experience with men and women before us the way God spoke to them. We hear his message and we hear how the word, the terrifying challenge—came to them and how they obeyed, had to obey, and how the word became an overpowering force in their lives. We do not have to dispute with men about doctrines, and we do not have to argue whether this or that church or this or that religion is right; none of that matters. What matters is that people heard the word and tried to live obedient to the light of truth, hope and love in which the living God showed himself.

I like the song "Lead kindly light amid the encircling gloom." When I sing it I feel that the man who wrote it stands before the eternal Light and seeks guidance as I seek it. This man was a cardinal of the Roman Catholic Church. He became a Roman Catholic because he could not find peace and rest in his faith without the ancient sacred authority of the church behind it and behind his experience of God and Christ.

Very often people say to me, "How can you dare to stand so

entirely alone? We need the authority of the Bible and the authority of the church. Our own unaided experience does not give us the strength to risk our lives going on the hard way." But I had to go my way alone. When I was a young pastor, Christ showed me the spiritual distress and loneliness of the German labouring people, people who could not hear the message of Christ because the church defended the oppression under which they suffered. So I had to stand against the majority of the churches and the church people. When I was in distress and did not see what to do, the living Christ was there, and he showed me the next step, the one step needed.

I had to go through many struggles against church authority, tradition and prejudice. No words of the church, no explanations of theologians made my way clear. He himself spoke to me. Jesus of Nazareth became the message of God for me today. He taught me to accept my cross; he made me certain of his resurrection; he made me strong to stand alone. After a life of hardship, lonely struggling and difficulties, came the real decisive question, whether I could stand when all the foundations of life seemed to break and death was imminent.

Not the church, not the poor pastor who visited me in prison, not anything of authority was my help, but the living Christ. He made me clear that his goal is the truth. He made me certain that for me and my children it was better to take suffering than to deny conscience. He makes me certain again today when, in disappointment, I sometimes ask, "For what did we suffer if the people are again going the wrong way?"

I do not deny that people like Newman, the cardinal, can find the reality of Light where I did not find it. I do not deny fellowship to those who follow Christ in other words and doctrines, and who feel called to other tasks. But I often think that very many do not come to the full reality of God because, before they find it, they rest in authority. In catastrophe everything is changing. For millions of people the traditional words and doctrines and images of God are meaningless. How can we bring them the message if we ourselves are abound up in tradition and cannot show them God's presence, as it came to us, in words that make them understand?

We will never come to a full strength in God if we do not acknowledge the sin of our lives. But, for many good Christians, faith is so bound up with tradition that they never realise the deep sinfulness of custom. Luther, for instance, was so dominated by inherited feelings of reverence for mighty men and princes that he never realised the egotism of the princely revolution that destroyed Germany and made his own work an instrument for enslaving subject peoples.

Again and again the churches have been the last to see the injustices of tradition. Capitalist organization and technical development brought growing welfare for millions while at the same time it created slavery for other millions. The churches have been very slow. It is hid from their eyes that tradition is not sufficient to give truth and insight, that once more we must stand before God alone and hear his voice.

There are millions who are full of peace and strength because they have found God in tradition and authority. There are millions whose lives go on without consciousness of new need. But there are also millions who have lost the ability to live in old ways. The ethics of the past have become lies to them, its laws injustice, its faith deception. And there are those who see this fact, this need, and are called to seek a new foundation for man's life and work. They are those people to whom God says today, "Get thee out of thy country, and from thy kindred, and from thy father's house, unto a land that I will show thee."

He leads them through despair and loneliness and doubt and error and even through sin and helplessness and darkness. But he gives them new visions, new thoughts, new outlooks— and perhaps the power by which eternal truth again overwhelms the inward being of the millions. "Not by might, nor by power, but by my Spirit, saith the Lord."

At the end of a talk I gave in a German town, a man of perhaps fifty years came to me saying, "I must speak to you in private." We went aside, and he said to me with tears in his eyes, "For many years I have longed, Sunday by Sunday, to go to church to hear the old hymns and to serve God, but it has become impossible for me. When I come near the church, I see standing in the door the field chaplain who was with us in the war, and I hear again the words he said to us in 1914 when we were young men waiting for our first attack. He said, 'Shoot them, beat them, kill them. Win the attack.' So I cannot go into the church."

When the man had left I asked who he was, and I was told that he was a well-known man, chairman of the Communist Party of that district. In that moment I knew that the living Christ stood behind this man when he spoke to me, and that in this man is a challenge to all Christ's followers. Here is a man who cannot go into the church, cannot come to the worship of God because between him and the church is the war cry of a Christian pastor.

He is one of millions who cannot hear the message. This man, longing for what is eternal, went to the Communist Party. He longs for a world of justice, of peace. He lives in a world of hatred and privilege and oppression. In the Communist Party he hears a loud voice promising him a world of justice, peace and love in which property and economic antagonism can no longer set men against men. He is aware of the message of Christ that violence and hatred are not the right way. But at the same moment he sees Christians prepare for war to defend their privileges and their domination. And then, sad at heart perhaps, he hears alike from Christian pastors and Communist leaders the same hopeless teaching: man is such a wretched, such a sinful, such a greedy being that his passions will never be overcome. Always he will fight before giving up domination, privilege, nationalist ambition.

From both sides the same gospel of despair: in this world you must fight, fight even for the highest purposes. Christians believe that they have not only the right but also the duty to use things like the atomic bomb to realize ideals. And oppressed men conclude that they have not only the right but the duty to fight in the same way for their ideals. Both are so strongly dominated by unhappy experiences with other men, so involved in distrust, that they cannot see the human being in their opponent—the human being who would have no ideals or longing for love and fellowship were not the image of God in his innermost being. Such men dare not trust in the power of God. They have not the courage to speak to that of God in man, that of God in their antagonists. That is why they are helpless to overcome hatred.

Distrust of man is the essence of the outward history of man. History shows clearly that man defends privilege violently and tries violently to free himself from oppression. But for Christians can that be the reality of man and history? I hear the cry of Jesus out of the mouth of that Communist. I hear his challenge from all the helpless men and women who see no hope for themselves except in force and fighting. But I see great danger when such helpless, faithless people call themselves Christians. Jesus did not ask his followers to fight for him. He did not ask his heavenly Father to send him twelve legions of angels. He went to the cross and suffered, certain that suffering love would overcome the world. And yet Christianity identifies itself with one opposing power or another, not seeking justice but following tradition.

Let us hear the challenge of Christ. There may be hard disappointment and bitter suffering on the road he points to. He never promised quick or easy victory. Only by our suffering can we overcome prejudices bred in millions of people by the inability of Christians to speak to their times. Mahatma Gandhi led a great nation along his way of truth and came to a great creative success. When will the Christian conscience be strong enough to unite those who call themselves after Jesus in the building of a world of brotherhood? When will we be ashamed to call Christian those who trust in the sword?

IS GOD REAL? ARE WE REAL?

There were many good Christians, among them pastors and church leaders, who told me when Hitler came to power, "I cannot lose my position since I must care for my children, and they have to continue their education." Or they said, "My son cannot lose his calling. He must say, 'Heil Hitler.' What will he do if he loses his job?" They all thought that material existence was more important than conscience. What was their God? They had an idea of God, but the reality to which they trusted their lives was money and the getting of money.

I speak of Germany. There are today good Christians, pastors and church leaders, who in sermons, articles and pamphlets excuse themselves and their nation. From all history they search out the evil deeds of others and point to every mistake and injustice of other nations. "Look," they say, "they are no better than we are." When they speak of the terrible guilt which the German nation brought on itself during the last century, they look at others and compare themselves. They do not stand before God, and they do not try to bring their nation to stand before God. It seems to me that one of the decisive tasks of Christians in Germany is to bring people to realize the reality of God. If God is reality, then I know that I will never find a good way in the future, not happiness, not strength, until I find his forgiveness and his spirit to begin anew.

So long as God is an idea in which we believe only with the mind, whilst in real life our chief aim is earning money and winning influence and power, we will never overcome the inward weakness that is servility. We will never overcome that outward weakness, nationalism, so long as it is more important to defend the honour of a nation against accusation than to find the right relation to God in our conscience. And it may be that what is true of Germany is true of all mankind.

When we think of the future of our nations, do we trust in God or do we trust in weapons and armies and all the clever arts which have nothing to do with him? Is he real to us at all if, in important problems of life, we do not trust in him? What does it mean, this trusting in God? I think it means that we are certain that spiritual power is life's precious foundation. It means that we are called as nations and as individuals to take a great task, to lose our lives and to find the life and power which overcomes distrust and hatred and cowardice.

We look back to those whom catastrophe destroyed, those who could not live out their lives, those who gave them because they could not submit to that which was against their consciences. They gave their lives because they had heard Christ's challenge. They had to obey. Something of his eternity lived in them and made them forever his fellow workers, even though we cannot realize it now.

For now, when outward improvement comes, guilt and suffering are zealously forgotten. It seems as if poor and empty people will again win leadership and as if the nations will again run the way of momentary power and success. It is utter darkness if out of the catastrophe not only individuals but whole nations go on as poor and empty of spirit as before.

But the challenge of the living Christ is behind catastrophe; it is in it, beside it, through it. We had to suffer and risk our lives, and we have again to suffer and risk our lives in confronting more catastrophe. But by hearing his voice, hearing it in the midst of ruin, obeying his voice, taking our task in suffering, forgetting ourselves and becoming his instruments—thus we become real. His victory comes into our lives because we try to do his work. Eternity is in our lives overcoming fear and hatred, and giving us this great vision; that we are Christ's fellow workers on earth, united with him in his eternal being.

"... Invisible but Existential"

[FROM *Exiled Pilgrim*]

WILLIAM HUBBEN

[*William Hubben (1895—1974), born a German and a Catholic, was an American Quaker, and former editor of the* Friends Journal.

He tells of the place to which he has come and the spiritual journey he made to reach it in the two passages which follow. He prefaces his book with the first, which is taken from the writings of Richard Howgill, a Quaker of Fox's day.

"Return Home to Within: sweep your Houses all. The Groat is there, the little Leaven is there, the Grain of the Mustard Seed you will

see which the Kingdom of God is like . . . and here you will see your Teacher, not removed into a Corner but present when you are upon your Beds and about your Labour, convincing, instructing, leading, correcting, judging and giving Peace to all that love and follow Him."

This was the goal he reached. The journey itself he summarizes as follows: "In our time, a Catholic who changes his allegiance in matters religious will come to realize that he is leaping in big strides over weighty chapters of history even when his conversion takes years of search. He is far from the office of the Holy Inquisition in Rome, whose methods have considerably softened; a thirty years' war is spared him too; and when he is in haste to reach beyond Luther, Calvin and Zwingli, right over to the radical Protestantism of the Quakers, he is traveling over centuries. On the way he meets the Puritans and Presbyterians with their austere self-discipline and impressive strictness; there are Wesley and his followers, full of gentle enthusiasm; the attractive Pietists with their tender devotion, and the Quietists living in this world but not being of it. Upon seriously deciding to settle with the Quakers, he finds that the Friends of today are different from those of Fox's time. They have fitted themselves into a new world; they have done away with broad-brimmed hats and bonnets and have a place for the arts, for music and for literature. There is in the modern Friend a vivid awareness of his spiritual heritage and the sufferings of his forebears; the newcomer, as does the birthright Quaker, benefits from a record of good works and self-discipline that have helped to shape Western civilization and make the Friends first tolerated, and then respected."]

Our Youth Movement group, together with liberal Protestants, particularly members of our Mennonite Church, was active in adult education. We succeeded in getting good teachers and lecturers and our literary and philosophical discussions attained a high level. In the general mood of depression of the post-war years however, an unwholesome tendency to split into sectarian groups was noticeable. It was the age of cultisms. Any group was liable to be invaded by fanatics such as vegetarians, anarchists, reformers of our monetary system, sun worshipers, and psycho-analysts.

When meeting in the home of a member or in our adult school we would start out in a normal fashion but suddenly we would find ourselves involved in a heated debate, difficult to account for it afterwards. How did it start? Who had been first and what had been said? We only seemed to know that heat had been generated by light. And we were by no means young people only; bearded men and mature women showed the same tendency. There was one person who had surrendered to the oracles of the Siderian Pendulum as the key to universal knowledge, by which one could discover the sex of chicken eggs, oncoming diseases, and even dormant talents. Another preached a special diet to alter first the chemistry of the brain and then the disposition of man's mind. Mrs. Offerman, favorite counselor of Mother, seemed to have raised generations of disciples who firmly believed in phrenology and palm-reading; and soon, astrology appeared in Hirsch's necktie factory. An era of almost religious fervor for the alchemy of the twentieth century was flourishing. One heard of miraculous healings effected by a shepherd; a carpenter in the poorer section of our city had cured a hopeless case of consumption, and it became the fashion to apply clay or cottage cheese to any boils. The educated as well as the workmen had their fads. After rationalism had failed to reassure man in his belief in human omnipotence, the pendulum was swinging over to a blind readiness to believe in superstitions, which are the legitimate children of any rationalistic age.

A great many incidents were disquieting or plainly abnormal in the religious field also. Christian sects, which our town had hardly known before, were springing up and proclaiming the end of the world. Another war would break out; the Messiah would return and sit in judgment over mankind. Small circles or brotherhoods made one particular point of Christian teaching their specialty. We had among us extreme adherents of nonviolence, Gandhiists or Tolstoyans; after having been attracted to their meetings for a brief period, I soon felt estranged by their slavish imitation of foreign customs. Do we have to live on goat's milk or a rice diet to achieve meekness? Or go barefoot and in sandals in order to be humble? Would the cult of deep-breathing save our distraught generation? One of these sects, led by a tailor, outraged the church leaders when it became known that the members were kissing each other rather extensively before and after their services, and the "Hugging Chapel" brought defamation over sectarianism of any sort. In another group, the young men grew exactly the type of parted beards traditional in the pictures of Jesus. Did they feel more Christlike that way?

One could not help coming to contact with a number of such currents and undercurrents and I tried to recognize trends common to all. Wasn't the German mind in its early adolescence? After centuries under the tutelage of state and church, its first groping for a new vision was bound to be insecure. We were trained to think in collective terms of state affairs, of other nations, and of religion. Now, breaking loose, we shambled along as if half-drunk and without discipline. The picture in other cities was the same; everywhere, a note of longing for expression and for unity was pervading such groups, much as their sectarian methods divided them. As yet, the German mind was unable to realize it. And when finally unity was achieved under Hitler, force, suppression, violence, and intolerance mixed together into an eerie witchcraft, generating terror for the nation and the world. And vegetarianism, astrology, Youth Movement, apocalyptic prophecies, and the thousand minor recipes for salvation were feeding into Naziism and were gladly absorbed by the alchemy of Germany's darkest hour.

The most disquieting phase of these movements was their messianic universalism mingled with suspicion against opposition. The individual had no rating in discussions. It was the people, all peoples, all Germany, all Europe, all workers, all humanity that counted. A totalitarian solution must be found, and man as an individual no longer counted.

Did God?

In these discussions the center of man's endeavor surely was man. The starting point for all reforms, again, was man. The ultimate goal of whatever was to be done was man. The message of the churches, to be sure, called for repentance, but it too pointed toward man's organization as the refuge from all ills, toward the church itself, calling it a divine foundation, and arrogantly claiming for it unequaled rights and substantial privileges. I knew then and there that a higher reference was needed, an orientation toward an origin and an aim above man.

I still cherished dreams of a Christian community that might be all-embracing and truly catholic or universal, a fellowship of the Faithful of all races and social classes, worldwide and yet real. There ought to exist a brotherhood like this, that tries to live a Way of Life as exemplified by Jesus without the separating creeds of theology. And if it did not yet exist, it ought to be created. The world was longing for it and it was needed. Perhaps somewhere in other countries such a community was at work; perhaps in Germany itself this enlightened brotherhood was silently spreading its message and one day I would actually meet one of its members. . . .

Among my workers in the party, the employees in the factory, the parents of our children, and my Protestant colleagues—everywhere I found the same longing for brotherhood. Wasn't this in itself an invisible church, a temple without walls, but built in the hearts of men? Yet I could not go on longing for a community that might not exist anywhere, while every day was making its demands on time and energy. I had to find jobs for boys on probation, clothes and often food, too, for my retarded children. I had to teach, indefatigably to try again and again to make those invisible grooves in the minds of the weak that would fit them for life. There were plenty of other things to do. A newspaper editor approached me to write a weekly survey on international news. I accepted. A national educational periodical asked for book reviews. I promised to do them and I kept my word. The demands of graduate work were growing from week to week. The city's cultural opportunities in the fields of the arts, music, and lectures had never been so rich as now. I had dear friends among my colleagues and workers. And there were Father and Mother giving more to our family life than ever before. A hundred small things had to be done day by day. When would I find time to care for big things?

Perhaps some day, a conversion would come, one of those gracious moments of light giving the long expected message from heaven. I knew of such divine voices breaking through at the most unexpected times; I had read of people sitting in a church or communing with nature's still voice and abruptly finding themselves surrounded by an aura of Truth. Indeed, conversions of this order had almost attained a standardized form in literature: such a seeker was struck by a ray of sunlight breaking through stained glass windows and creating a peculiar feeling of trust, the sensation of homecoming, a mixture of remorse and happiness which signalized the beginning of a new life. I was frankly cynical about such descriptions. They had become trite. I knew too much of life's dark side to forget for a single moment war, revolution, famine, exploitation, and many other forms of suffering. No standard pattern would be able to stir me deeply enough toward another course of living. It had to be life itself; the testimony of personalities; a pure mind; a saint; a new attitude; something existential—in other words, a different reality that could turn the tide.

I was praying for this kind of experience.

The ways of the Spirit are not ours and its message is hard to read even for those eager to learn.

At that time, I did not realize that great things were happening every day right before my eyes and that, to a small degree, I was sharing in them.

Our school children were receiving a free daily meal from the child-feeding mission of the American Friends Service Committee (Quakers) and, without much thought, we teachers assisted in distributing the food during recess. In our ignorance about the donors we even adopted the jargon of our children, calling the meal itself "a Quaker," and remarks like, "Have you had your Quaker yet?" or "How was the Quaker today?" were quite in order. *"Quakerspeisung"* (Quaker feeding) became a household word all over Germany, where, at the peak of the relief work, 1,100,000 children were under the daily care of Friends.

One day, while supervising a class of children when they were receiving food, I casually looked over one of the meal tickets. It said,

To the Children of Germany:

A greeting of friendship from America, distributed by the Religious Society of Friends (Quakers), who have, for 250 years, and during the several years of war just ended, maintained that only service and love, and not war and hatred, can bring peace and happiness to mankind.

The Society of Friends? Quakers? I had seen them mentioned in the literature of the Mennonites and in Tolstoy's religious writings, and yet, somehow, the popular notion that a Quaker was an expert in children's diet still lingered in my mind. I called Ferber's attention to the words on the meal ticket. His quick reply was, "The Americans beat us down with one hand and offer us food with the other." Nevertheless, I began searching for material about the Quakers, but it was not until I discovered the address of their Berlin center that I availed myself of a few pamphlets and small books written by the Friends themselves.

What I read then about the Society of Friends stirred my innermost hopes, temporarily abandoned, of finding a community of Seekers. Here was a family of Christians who had a faith without a creed, inclusive and not exclusive as creeds used to be. . . .

Was it possible that this was the answer? Did divine messages come this way—by mail and during ordinary hours of work? Would a new cathedral of faith quietly open its doors without the music of solemn organs and of bells pealing?

Yet—conversion by five-cent pamphlets? Something in me rebelled against this form of "revelation." A mere set of tracts appeared so inadequate a guide to steer me into a better faith and future. But then were these pamphlets designed to convert anyone? I could not find the slightest trace of proselytizing. They made no mention of joining the Friends. Wasn't it true that they merely addressed those seekers who already had drawn in themselves the marks of a new faith with the timid pencil lines of hope? Wasn't religious experience the response to a search; the home offered to the homesick; the rays on the sensitive film of the soul finally evolving into a picture?

So I read again and again the three or four pamphlets. They spoke of a Double Search—Man's search for God and God's longing for Man. Friends considered God no longer a stern judge but a loving Father whose presence we may experience everywhere. Life itself is a Temple where spiritual laws reign and all are called upon to perform priestly duties. Our actions ought to be sacramental, imparting a divine element to daily living. We are to celebrate transubstantiation daily by injecting a Holy Spirit into life, raising it to the level of Sanctity. We are One Body of Brethren, a Family of Love, One Invisible Church.

Such a simple message, I thought, I had found scattered in numerous creeds and groups. Every sect and church had one or several elements of it; yet I had been unable to gather things in this lucid way presented by the Friends.

When I returned to my classroom work, everything appeared new, in a miraculous sense of God's nearness. There were the same children at work and we went about it as we had done yesterday. Yet our room was infinitely larger. Life itself suggested space and light everywhere and an indescribable atmosphere of joy lent a new aspect to the small trifles of the hour. More than ever was I one with my pupils and, as if by magic, the differences of age and talent had disappeared. Life was clear and infinitely meaningful. I looked with a sense of wonder upon everything that had formerly happened to me in this building. Here I had started as a first grader with fear and awe and had returned to the same classroom as an erratic seeker. The Church of St. Mary's, in whose shadow we children had played and whose services had disciplined our spirits, was only a hundred yards away. Yet the majestic building seemed to have been removed forever to a different continent. I was in another church, catholic because it embraced all living souls; sacramental in its active spirituality; priestly in dignifying our everyday lives. And the whole scale of theological differences from Lutheranism to the tenets of extreme sects was shrinking to nothing but a color scheme of compromises. There was only the Catholic church at one end, with its historic claims and rigid antiquarianism, and at the other end was the equally universal Brotherhood of the Friends, invisible but existential. God was let out of the captivity of a church building into life. His revelation continued here and now, beyond the pages of the Book, sacred as its contents were. Galilee, Jerusalem, and Mount Tabor were here as they had been in the village of my childhood days. Creation and resurrection were no longer a record of the dim past. Once more, they became contemporary and eternal as in the tales of Grandmother.

Bit by bit, my eyes opened to the wealth of life. I understood Jakob Boehme's, the mystic's, words that heaven was a state of the soul and not a locality. The Early Friends spoke of "openings" as the revelation leading to harmony and vision. Now I saw why Friends had come to feed our children. Until yesterday America and Germany had been at war and quietly they came to right a wrong. And all they were willing to say about themselves were the few words on the meal tickets. Obviously, then, silent service was more than a form of worship.

True communion with God and the spirit of reconciliation are overwhelming experiences, and words are inadequate for their expression. Love for the enemy—hadn't it always sounded strained and hadn't I looked upon it with a fair degree of skepticism? Here, in the work of the Friends, evil was overcome by good in the Sacrament of Action. Action? Was this to be the answer to the problems of evil? Was Quakerism largely service-minded? Or was it the function of evil and suffering in war, crime, mental debility, and exploitation to create love and to call for devotion? I again read my pamphlets. Service was little emphasized. It was considered a natural outflow from brotherly love between men, and internal change was all that mattered.

And slowly this changed outlook also altered the picture of the past. The many experiences of peace and war time had been necessary; those friendships with laborers, artists, and teachers; the insight into the superstitious minds of the peasants as well as their wisdom; the British soldiers; the vision of the decomposed masses in revolution and in the inflation; the fear and longing of the present days; the Mennonites; the long line of personalities from a heretically inclined Grandmother to prominent priests or agnostic labor leaders—all had been challenging and meaningful.

I travelled the forty miles to the nearest Quaker Meeting for Worship with a depressing sense of inadequacy. What would these Friends look like? Their literature had an almost supernatural flavor. Vaguely I imagined a race of angels in plain clothes, traveling incognito under the guise of Friends and being so ethereal that their meetings would resemble a celestial congregation.

In this, I fortunately was disillusioned. The two Americans in charge of the Essen center were unassuming members of a body of thirty worshippers and their messages, spoken in the surroundings of a business office were equally unpretentious. It seemed symbolical that Elizabeth T. Shipley was a prominent social worker from Pennsylvania and Alfred Lowry a teacher. Their German, too, was excellent, as our conversation after meeting proved.

Silence, at first, was less gripping and prophetic than I had expected; it had something provocative and trying about it. Only after repeated attendance did this mode of worship appeal to my desire to find a divine-human harmony, producing the assurance of God's presence and removing doubts. And what more could the "Voice of God" be than assurance and the courage to venture forward trusting in His guidance? In one more respect my early contacts with the Friends proved revealing. If these Quakers ever were imagined to be angels, then, with all due respect, they were domesticated angels, at home in the realm of human problems and foibles, yet striving faithfully and with gracious patience to inject a spiritual note into every situation.

One day Alfred Lowry rose and gave a brief message on faith in God. At first I thought I had heard similar sermons, a thousand times, but when he closed saying, "We may forget to do His will. We may resist. But we must never give up believing," his words struck me with a peculiar force and, as if by an invisible hand, the hundred parts of life's puzzle were moved together into a significant whole.

To believe in God!

It sounded like a shopworn phrase from the vocabulary of the catechism, but beneath its naive expression was the secret of living. It was more than asking for an intellectual assent of reason; it touched upon the huge dislocation of man away from the center of life to the periphery of his own self. It meant to live in the awareness of God's existence and to keep one's faculties tuned to His presence. It raised the trivialities of home, work, and recreation to a new dignity, and a strange term like George Fox's "The earth took on a new smell" became meaningful. Indeed, everything took on a new sense of clarity and scope when belief was practiced. More than that: realizing God's presence called for unconditional surrender. Jesus' petition in the Lord's Prayer stood out like a completely novel message. "Thy Will be done." How relieving! Hadn't I been doing my own will; the party's will; the will of groups; the will of public opinion; the will of everybody except His Will? Probably the busy execution of all these wills was at the bottom of our uncertainty, of the recurring waves of depression and moods on which the psychologies of various persuasions were thriving. The blind were leading the blind and all men complained about the perennial darkness surrounding us. To follow God's voice might entail wandering into the Unknown and the dimensions of mystery, so much missed in many a Protestant service, would again have their rightful place; but this Unknown would not be darkness. No more generous advice could be given than to discard our self-made burdens and to accept the light and easy yoke. Why did we not do so?

Such simple thoughts impressed themselves upon me with an inexplainable power; happiness mingled with astonishment that everybody else was not under the same spell of this liberating truth. When I saw people's unhappy faces in the street, I had to control myself against approaching them with a consoling word. I had to be on my guard not to start preaching to my colleagues when the daily run of complaints filled our conversations; no command over words could possibly convey my vision. The midstream of Life itself carried me without human effort beyond the borderline of doubt, but my attempts at sharing my experiences with others were feeble, perhaps confused.

When, after an extended period of contacts, I joined the small group of German Quakers, I felt again that in the light of

Friends' history, a story full of suffering and sacrifice, it was almost too easy to become one of their family. What was to follow? Would life be different now that a greater impulse to serve and share had become articulate?

The letter notifying me of my admission into membership expressed a brief word of welcome. I read it over and over again. It was as if my room suddenly was visited by the silent ancestors whose company I had been claiming: George Fox, the enlightened shoemaker; William Penn, friend of the Indians; John Woolman, emancipator of Negroes and Indians; Elizabeth Fry, the "angel of the prisons"; and their spiritual brethren in German history, the Mystics and Pietists—strange visitors in a necktie factory. Outside a detachment of Belgian infantry marched by. I was living in a Catholic city of the Catholic Rhineland. What would be the consequences of my "Apostasy" from the Roman church? How could a testimony of friendship and peace be maintained in the midst of suppression, need, and religious intolerance? Had I been too hasty in joining the Society of Friends? It might not be easy, after all, to be a Friend.

My silent visitors, however, not only raised questions such as these; their presence also brought inspiration and confidence. The words of John's gospel came to me "You are my friends if you do whatsoever I command you." They held a great promise.

"... if you do...!"

THE CONVICTIONS (2)

We are nothing, Christ is all.
—SIR GEORGE NEWMAN

"The Society of Friends Does Not Hide its Light under a Bushel"

[FROM *Roads to Agreement*]

STUART CHASE

[*Stuart Chase's conclusions, drawn from his observation and study of Quaker meetings for business, both at first hand and in Francis, Beatrice, and Robert Pollard's book,* Democracy and the Quaker Method, *are somewhat on the order of an outsider's suggestion that the principle of the prayer wheel might be used in lifting water. Chase himself is aware of this and is careful to suggest that there are differences between the Society of Friends and the board of directors of the Standard Oil Company of New Jersey, in their goals at least, if not in their practices.*

However, as William James suggested fifty years ago, by acting "like," one "becomes." And it is possible that through the use of "cooling off techniques," "silent periods," "learning to listen," and "considering the facts," all for purposes of increasing the dividends, one might, in spite of oneself, move away from the oil barons and nearer Woolman. It seems a roundabout way, however.

This report on the uses of the "techniques" of the Quaker meeting for business, as given by Chase, may be interestingly and instructively

478

compared with Rufus Jones's earlier report on the same subject. One might attend, one feels, many meetings of the board of directors of the Standard Oil Company of New Jersey without perceiving an inkling of that which the boy Jones felt to be present in the Quaker meetings for business he attended.|

Quaker meeting-houses vary in size but are always plain, and many are ancient. Benches face a low gallery where some older members sit. There is no organ, no choir, baptismal font, stained glass, pulpit, or altar. Perhaps this is why they reject the name "church." There is no doxology, no sermon in the traditional Friends' meeting, no supplication, collection, or benediction.

What does one find then? "The effective worship of Almighty God," says William Wistar Comfort. "No other form of worship makes such demands upon the spiritual resources of those present." Ambition, self-seeking, ideas of power and domination are resolutely put aside. The meeting for worship on Sunday morning opens with a period of silence, lasting several minutes, while members seek the inner light, purging their minds of outside matters. This concentration, they feel, gives the silence a special vitality. "Dead" silence, says Comfort, where people are merely quiet but not concentrated, is valueless.

In Britain, the business meeting usually follows Sunday morning worship, but in America it may be held on a weekday once a month. It is the business meeting which primarily interests us, for here mundane matters are discussed and agreements reached—sometimes very difficult and far-reaching agreements, as when the Philadelphia Yearly Meeting had to decide whether members should own slaves.

Suppose we look in at a typical monthly business meeting, described by the Pollards. As it takes place in England and in the afternoon, it begins of course with tea. The only officer for this executive group of men and women is the Clerk. He is the only officer in any Quaker meeting though sometimes he may have assistants. He bows his head, and the regular period of silence opens the meeting. He then reads the minutes, and if there are no corrections, proceeds to a report on deaths, marriages, transfers, and appointments. A list of applicants for membership usually brings out the first discussion.

After everyone has had his say, the Clerk drafts a minute— the famous "sense of the meeting" minute in which group opinion is summarized. He reads it to the members for their assent or modification. *There is no formal voting.* Nobody, I am told, has voted in any Quaker meeting, in any country, in three hundred years—except where the law requires it on specified documents. The challenge of the Clerk to the members on the minute, and their response, can perhaps be interpreted as a kind of voting. But when a policy or an action is decided upon, there is no division between majority and minority; the decision is invariably unanimous.

Next on the agenda, at this particular British meeting, is a statement of the group's opinion about atomic energy. Discussion is general and prolonged. Finally, the Clerk sums up the sense of the meeting in a minute which is accepted by all. Shall the resolution be given to the Member of Parliament representing the district? Would a letter to the press be better? Or should a public meeting be called? More discussion, and then a unanimous decision in favor of a letter to the press.

The Clerk proceeds to ask a member to give his ideas on the closed shop in union contracts. The others listen carefully; there is no discussion. Another member describes relief work in Greece, again without action by the group. These are apparently reports for information only. The agenda completed, the Clerk bows his head for a final period of silence, and the meeting stands adjourned.

I had the privilege of attending a Friends' business meeting in a neighboring town in Connecticut. Except that it was held in one of the community centers instead of a meeting house, the procedure followed the pattern just described. Perhaps fifteen members were present. The Clerk was a local physician, tired that evening but alert. He kept his voice clear and low as he read the minutes and invited comment on the agenda. He scrupulously refrained from imposing his own views; never once did he say, "I think we should do this or that." From time to time, in the same low voice, he carefully summarized other people's views.

I found the atmosphere peaceful, almost relaxing. One or two of the older women were knitting industriously—even while they talked. No emotions came to the surface. Committees reported on foreign relief, on a delegation to Hartford, on applications for membership, on a public meeting to present the Quaker plan for the control of atomic energy. The Clerk called members by their first names, and so did all the others—which seemed a curious touch of informality in a procedure so dignified and ancient.

After the period of silence and adjournment, the Clerk told me that a really stirring issue divided the group, though no visitor could have guessed it. The issue was whether or not to build a meeting house. "We have had to ask for periods of silence when that comes up," he said. "Feelings are strong; but it will be settled, and settled right."

"Unanimously?" I asked.

"Unanimously," he replied with the utmost confidence.

Some years ago, the Pollards tell us, the burial ground of an English meeting house filled up. The business meeting had to decide where to inter the rest of the congregation when their turn came. Certain members wanted to enlarge the present ground to give everyone a fair chance to be buried comfortably close to the meeting house. Others observed that if this were done it would cut down the playground area of the Quaker school. Deep feelings were aroused—school and children versus a resting place for loved ones, a theme to engage a Thomas Hardy.

As emotions flared in the first meeting, the Clerk called for silence, and then, when he found the atmosphere still electric, held the matter over for a month—put it, as it were, into the refrigerator to cool. The second meeting showed little sign of cooling, however, and back to the icebox the subject went. It took six months for temperatures to get suitably low, but agreement when it came was unanimous, with no resentful minority or jubilant majority. The solution followed a pattern

common in Quaker business meetings and profoundly significant to our study. *The issue was not compromised but moved up to
another level where a new plan was evolved—a plan in nobody's mind
at the beginning of the discussion.* The burying ground was enlarged
but in a special manner which did not limit the playground or the
school. A good many technical facts had to be brought out and
digested before the solution was found.

Quakers have the usual business problems which confront
all churches; budget, upkeep of property, trust funds, charities,
new members. They also have special Quaker schools, and they
have their extraordinary missions of relief and social service here
and abroad, including at least one experiment with psychiatric
treatment of delinquents. In wartime, conscientious objectors
are a special concern. The Friends look after boys of other
pacifist organizations as well as their own.

The Society was early interested in prison reform and in the
improvement of intolerable conditions in insane asylums—
movements which later became worldwide. It helped to set up
Utopian communities, like Robert Owen's "New Lanark." It
was one of the first to take an interest in the condition of
American Indians. William Penn was always their friend, treating them as fellow human beings, not "savages."

The Society has never hesitated from the beginning to take
a position, often an exposed position subject to much crossfire,
on highly controversial matters. The London Meeting raised
the red-hot question of peace with France in 1802, as Napoleon
soared up the horizon. (Our feelings for Stalin in 1950 were
relatively amiable compared with British feelings toward Napoleon in the early 1800s.) More than a century later, in 1920, the
same Meeting called on British dock workers to stop the help
they were giving to Soviet Russia; the next year the American
Friends' Service Committee was aiding victims of the Russian
famine. Today the Society is deeply interested in better
American-Soviet relations. Quakers are always concerned with
disarmament and peace, and always oppose conscription.

At any time a meeting may have to consider such questions
as these:

Shall we take government grants for Quaker schools? What shall be the testimony on Palestine and the Arabs? How shall we assess the proposed bill to nationalize the land of Britain?

I mention these subjects to show the variety of thorny problems which a meeting may be called upon to handle. The Society of Friends does not hide its light under a bushel and never has.

At least nine major principles and procedures appear in Quaker business meetings, though not necessarily all in any one gathering. I saw perhaps half of them in the meeting I attended. All nine are directed to a specific goal, namely: *How can we settle this problem so that it will stay settled, so that it is settled right?* "Right" to the Quakers always has a deeply religious significance. We must not forget that they start on the basis of an ethical "inner light."

Here are the principles; as in most categories, there is some overlapping.

1. *Unanimous decisions.* There is no voting, no minority to nourish grievances and so prevent a real settlement.

2. *Silent periods*, always at the opening and closing of meetings, and whenever two opposing parties begin to clash.

3. A *moratorium* (or cooling-off technique) for questions where agreement cannot be reached unanimously, where opposing parties start to form. If they are important questions, they will come up again at future meetings until disagreement ceases and unanimity is found. Slavery kept coming up in the Philadelphia Meeting year after year.

4. *Participation* by all members who have ideas on the subject. Experience has demonstrated, says the Book of Discipline, "that the final decision of the group is usually superior to that of the individual." Members pool their knowledge and experience.

5. *Learning to listen.* Again to quote the Book of Discipline: "It behooves them in their meetings to hear with attentive and tolerant minds the messages and views of all members present." Quakers do not go to meetings with minds made up; they go to learn, expecting the right solution to crystallize from the experience of all.

6. *Absence of leaders.* The Clerk does some steering, but he must not interpose his ego or take a dominant role.

7. *Nobody outranks anybody.* Rich and poor, men and women, old and young, have equal status and are expected to participate equally. Everybody has had past experiences, and so everybody has something to give.

8. *Consider the facts.* As emotions are at a minimum, facts and their cool consideration can be at a maximum.

9. *Keep meetings small.* The best size for solving problems is a face-to-face group of not more than twenty persons. Yearly meetings of several hundred, however, are able to use the method.

From the beginning, Quakers have realized the conflict and trouble which a human ego on the loose can raise. Their meetings are specifically designed to keep the ego in its place, to encourage "we-feelings," discourage "I-feelings." Members try to think about the reaction of the group to the problem rather than about their personal reaction to it.

The Pollards in their book have raised some interesting questions about the relationship of Quaker methods to recent findings in psychology and social science.

Take the matter of ego, for instance. Many of us find it difficult to accept other people freely, but this is often much easier, psychologists say, than accepting oneself. Organized into small, permanent groups, Quakers have gone far to help one another face the reality of oneself—to stop fighting one's ego, trying to escape from it. After this internal conflict diminishes, it becomes easier to get along with other people.

Again, the Quakers recommend an attitude they call *"integration,"* rather than dominating or submitting to domination. Most of us are prone to one extreme or the other—indeed, there is a pre-human parallel. Psychologists describe the famous "pecking order" found in barnyard fowl as evidence of domination—who pecks whom. They compare it with the behavior of humans in a so-called "dominance-submission scale"—who outranks whom. By integration, of course, the Quakers do not mean submission but rather the power to cooperate, to act together in groups without domination. Integration implies even more: "a growth phenomenon that involves a change in the functions of an organism through the confronting of differences." Fusing differences may result in new and sounder conclusions all around.

Such "integrative" or "permissive" behavior by X is likely to be contagious. It also tends to make Y and Z feel more secure, as they recognize that X accepts them as they are, with no desire to dominate them. "The Friends' witness," say the Pollards, "has always been against dominative relationships of all kinds." People are accepted for themselves, not for pictures of themselves, and that makes for friendly relations. The Society of Friends has tried to live up to its name.

The Quakers have found a road to agreement and obviously a wide one. You can use some of their methods in the next meeting you attend, in every meeting for the rest of your life. But before you can use the total approach, a definite structure must be in place.

To begin with, Quakers are like-minded people, coming mostly from the same sub-culture in society, the "upper-middles" and the "lower-uppers," as W. Lloyd Warner might classify them. They know each other well; many are born in the faith— "birthright" members. They are not in so much of a hurry as most Americans; they can afford to let the right decision make itself known in due time. Their motto seems to be: When in doubt, Wait!—while the American hustler counters with: When in doubt, Act! And as we said earlier, Quakers begin with a religious conviction that it is their duty to find agreement.

Quakers meet usually in small face-to-face groups—a great help in problem-solving. As we have seen, they have learned a high degree of control over their egos and have all but banished from their gatherings the loud-mouthed, dominating type. They know how to listen, a function much neglected by most Americans. They respect the judgment of others, hoping to find there a new dimension for group judgment. This is not so much neglected by the rest of us as unheard of.

The most suitable bodies to make use of Quaker methods, say the Pollards, are executive committees, boards of directors, meetings of not more than a score of persons whose personnel remains fairly constant. One can call to mind various groups which already practice the rule of unanimity and others that have used silent periods. Comfort reminds us, for example, of the international conference in San Francisco in 1945, where the United Nations was born. The Secretary of State opened this conference by asking for a period of silence. With more than fifty nations represented, many of them non-Christian, any spoken prayer would have been out of place.

In February, 1950, a regional conference of fifty-five non-governmental bodies was held in Bangkok, the capital of Thailand. Representatives came from Australia, Burma, India, New Zealand, Pakistan, the Philippines, and other eastern countries. They adopted a resolution "recognizing the value of periods of silence as a spiritual force in the solution of controversial issues."

The General Assembly of the U.N. also favors a short period of silence to begin its sessions. If the international delegates are also able to empty their minds of preconceptions and prejudices, as the Quakers try to do, this should be a valuable device. The Quakers, incidentally, in spite of being Christians, are less culture-bound than other religious groups and almost free from national prejudices. Their sympathies are worldwide, going out to all mankind.

As for the rule of unanimity, I know of one board of directors that tries to practice it—the Standard Oil Company of New Jersey. The twelve directors meet once a week, and the executive board of five within the larger board meets every business day. All twelve are drawn from the active operations of the company—production, sales, personnel, but not the legal department. They seldom take a vote. If disagreement develops—say over a project to build a new refinery—the technical staff is called in, equipped with charts and statistics. The board listens to the facts. When the final decision is made they are all in it. Nobody says later on, "I told you so."

The anthropologists have some testimony running parallel to the Quaker method. Clyde Kluckhohn tells me that a Navaho community will fiddle around all day discussing a matter which any up-and-coming business executive would settle in fifteen minutes. It seems to Western eyes like dawdling nonsense. But when the Navahos finally settle the matter, the whole community has participated, *and it stays settled*.

Councils of the Solomon Islanders do not vote but come to unanimous agreement. William Penn wrote that Indian councils in America forego formal rules of order and "do not speak two at a time, or interfere in the least, one with another." George P. Murdock, who developed the famous Cross-Cultural Index at Yale, says that unanimous agreement is the rule in the councils of many primitive societies. The ancient Russian village organization, the *Mir*, used to hold open discussion of community problems and in some cases insist on unanimous agreement for a new policy.

The Quaker meeting is thus not an isolated case. It follows a deep groove, carved by many cultures, ancient and modern. But no other modern group of men and women has developed methods of group consensus to a comparable extent, while applying them so long and so successfully.

―――――

"To Serve Christ, Not to Feel Christ . . ."

[FROM *The Appeal of Quakerism to the Non-Mystic*]

WILLIAM LITTLEBOY

[*William Littleboy (1853–1936), an English Friend, wrote a number of essays notable for the quiet lucidity with which they present uncommonly acute insights. Among them are: "Our Beloved Dead," "The Meaning and Practice of Prayer," and "The Day of Our Visitation."*

In The Appeal of Quakerism to the Non-Mystic, *first published in 1916, Littleboy was saying, of the love of people for God, what Eric Fromm and others have more recently said of the love of men and women: that the test of the existence of love is not ecstasy. A suffusion of delight is a happy bonus which may or may not accompany love. One may brim with exultation, yet fail in every act by which love is expressed. The immature may even feel that, without some visible bone-shaking transports, love cannot exist. God, whatever else we may assume about Him, is surely not immature. In His sight, as Littleboy says, love is not evidenced by rapture, but by "faith and obedience."*

Those persons fortunately endowed by nature, and George Fox was one of them, may be faithful and obedient, and also know rapture. But there is no coefficient by which one equates rapture with love. The measure of the love of God is not emotion.

Jesus, as reported in the Scriptures, was not one to suppress what Littleboy calls "emotional enjoyment." Yet there is no record of His ever having said, "O ye of little rapture," as He said, "O ye of little faith."

"If ye love me, keep my commandments," He said. And there is no commandment enjoining ecstasy, rapture, and visions. As Littleboy remarks, the love of God is shown by a "following not a feeling. . . . Love must express itself in an act—otherwise it is barren. . . . And we are sure that in the sight of God the most ecstatic outpouring of adoration is, in itself, of less account than the lowliest act of unselfish service done by some diffident disciple who would not dare to assert, I love God."]

———

Has Quakerism a universal message; or is it an esoteric cult which may indeed have its place in the religious life of the nation as witness to the truth of an important principle, but which can never make a direct appeal outside a select circle, a spiritual aristocracy of persons largely endowed with the mystic temperament? Has it anything to say to those for whom the spiritual world, which stands ajar for some, is closed and padlocked?

To us who believe that the Quaker ideal involves the loftiest and most spiritual conception of the whole gospel of God's self-revelation to man, the question assumes a more personal aspect, and we ask: Does God indeed speak to *all* men, or are His direct appeals confined to a few saintly and sensitive souls? Can *I* who never consciously heard the inward voice, who am not of those to whom it is given to see visions and dream dreams—*dare* I believe that a real and intimate relationship exists between God and my own dull and earth-clogged soul? Upon the answer to our question stated in this personal form, depends I believe the hope and peace, the character of the whole outlook, of multitudes of anxious spirits.

Quakerism is not a system of theology or of ethics. It is a religion of the spirit—a religion of the inward way. . . .

Quakerism is thus, above most other religious types, the exponent of the mystical idea in religion. And here let us define what we mean by this expression—a matter of no small importance in view of the loose manner in which the word "Mystic" and its cognate terms are commonly used. The Mystical then "is a type of religion—in which all the deep-lying powers of the personal life come into positive exercise and function, so that there results an experience, not merely emotional, not merely intellectual, not merely volitional, through which the soul finds itself in a love-relation with the Living God. There are all possible stages and degrees of the experience of this relation, from simple awareness of the soul's divine Companion to a rapt consciousness of union with the One and Only Reality. *The term 'mystical' is properly used for any type of religion which insists upon an immediate inward revelation of God within the sphere of personal experience."*

Quakerism comes within the scope of the last clause. It insists on the reality of that "inward revelation of God in the sphere of personal experience," and not content with the exposition of a theory, it seeks to apply its fundamental principle, both in the God-ward and man-ward relations—in worship and in conduct.

It is needless to dwell here upon the application of this principle in congregational worship. We all of us agree, in theory at least, that we come together to meet with God and for fellowship with one another in His presence. What is true of public worship is true also of our personal relationship with God. If He meets us in the synagogue, He meets us also in the inner chamber of the soul. The "Inward revelation of God in the sphere of personal experience" is a process of illumination which must be constant. We are called to live in the companionship of Christ, and learn daily of Him in fuller measure than was possible to Peter and James and John in the days of His flesh. He is "closer than breathing, nearer than hands and feet," and constant communion with our divine Friend is essential to a full and worthy spiritual life.

All this is I think involved in the distinctive Quaker Gospel. Is it then a universal message, or is it meant for a select circle only? Is it for my neighbour with his peculiarly mystic or psychic type of soul, or is it for me too?

Now if we are to be guided by the voices of the majority of our teachers we shall be driven to adopt the more limited view, and take our place in the outer circle who worship from afar and must be content with second-hand relations with God. Men are always pre-disposed to make their own experience the standard for their judgment of others. One of life's hardest lessons is that there is no justification for expecting that our neighbour is to traverse precisely the same path as that which we ourselves have followed. The varieties of religious experience are probably far greater than any of us suppose. The difficulty a man has in grasping this truth is increased in proportion as his own experience has been vivid and clearly defined. One who has been lifted out of the horrible pit, has had his feet set upon a rock, and a new song put into his mouth, finds it hard to believe that another who has arrived quietly and without crisis, with no strong consciousness of guilt and no corresponding ecstasy of deliverance can really be a disciple at all. And he whose life is illumined with the brightness and joy of a heavenly companionship can with difficulty believe that his brother who walks in the shadows may yet be a humble and single hearted follower of Jesus Christ.

It happens inevitably that most of our teachers—the men who minister to us in speech and in writing—are those who can speak out of the fulness of a conscious experience. They speak that which they know and bear witness of that which they have seen. The fact that a man's spiritual progress has been colourless and uneventful makes it *prima facie* unlikely that he will hear the prophetic call. He thinks—it may be quite falsely—that he can have nothing to impart. He has never been caught up to the third heaven like Paul, nor can he say with Bernard of Clairvaux "Jesus, the very thought of Thee with sweetness fills my breast," and so he keeps silence. But this means that most of those to whom we look for instruction are drawn from a minority, that they have little conception of the spiritual atmosphere in which the majority live and move, that they constantly assume in their teaching a type of experience in their hearts which these do not possess, and that without dreaming that they may be hurting a tender conscience that they frequently postulate as essential to a true life in Christ experience corresponding to that which has befallen themselves, and in so doing rule out of the kingdom many of the poor in spirit for whom, as we may venture to believe, in reliance on Him who *never* misunderstands, its door stands open wide. Or again some mercurial person of our acquaintance gifted by nature with a sunny disposition, discourses to us on "the duty of joy," and cannot understand how any *Christian* can fail to feel and display the exhilaration of a pilgrimage to which the Valley of Humiliation is unknown.

So it comes to pass that in the teaching of many of our most honoured leaders there is at least an implicit suggestion that no one can walk with Christ without being aware of it, or hear His voice without recognizing it; and although most of them would hasten to disclaim any such intention, they do in fact leave the impression that our nearness to God is to be measured by the standard of conscious fellowship with Him and the emotional enjoyment of His presence.

This is a hard saying to the non-mystic. He, it may be, has no clear consciousness of God. No inrush of joy has flooded his spirit; no heavenly voice has spoken to his soul. He walks in spiritual twilight; there has been nothing dramatic in his experience; and that which has appealed irresistibly to another has had no message for him. When he seeks to lift his heart in prayer he feels as if he were speaking into a void; the eye of faith cannot pierce the mists which surround him. There is no voice, nor any to answer, nor any that regard. He believes in God;

falteringly indeed yet sincerely he tries to obey Him; he spends his life in His service. Yet the great emotional experiences of love, rapture, perfect peace, which come to others are denied to him. His whole soul goes out in a passionate cry for feeling. Or it may be that the experience of half a lifetime has convinced him that these spiritual luxuries are for some hidden reason not for him, and he has come to acquiesce with what grace he may in winter skies and a grey and featureless landscape, hoping that haply some better thing may be reserved for him when the veil of the flesh is withdrawn.

To such a one, whose case calls above all for sympathy and encouragement, comes the easy declaration from pulpit or press that every true disciple of Christ must needs have *some* consciousness of, and joy in, His companionship—how in reason can it be otherwise? It may be that the understanding and sympathetic Christ, who bore his griefs and carried his sorrows, may speak with another voice.

It is a fundamental mistake to assume that mystical experience (first hand communion with, and revelation from, God) is equivalent to, or necessarily accompanied by, strong emotion, or even clear consciousness of His nearness. Mysticism insists on the *fact*, not on the *method*, of the divine revelation to the soul. It is true that most of the great mystics dwell strongly on the emotional aspect of that divine intercourse which to them has been the greatest reality in life. Nevertheless it is clear from the writings of some of them that emotion is not, in their view, of the essence of the mystical relationship.

The fact is, as we have already said, that under the influence of longstanding Christian tradition we habitually overemphasize the place of the emotions in the spiritual life. We speak as if love (in the sense of conscious affection), rapture, overflowing peace were in themselves the essential characteristics of the life in Christ rather than the attitude of the soul towards God indicated by the qualities of faith and obedience. When the Gospel of Jesus was first proclaimed in a society which appeared to be rotten beyond hope of renewal, it evoked an enthusiastic emotional response—a joy unspeakable and full of glory, which is vividly reflected in the Acts and Epistles, especially in those of Paul. Since the Reformation at least, until within the last half-century, the Apostle of the Gentiles has been the dominating personality in the New Testament taking precedence for practical purposes of our Lord Himself; and it has been assumed that the experience of Paul—so shot through with emotion and with conscious relationship with the Fountain of Life and Light—is to be the type to which all Christian experience must conform. Yet it is not reasonable to expect that after twenty centuries of Christian Light, and amongst those who from their cradles have known the name of Jesus and have heard His Gospel, there should be the same sense of joyous exhilaration and rapture of response as when the glory first struck across a dying world.

And after all to be a Christian consists not in feeling, but in following; not in ecstasy but in obedience. The human factor that dominates the situation is not the emotions but the *Will*. The purpose of Jesus was undoubtedly that the hearts of his disciples should be untroubled and their joy be made full. A careworn and anxious demeanour is unworthy of a Christian and is an unfaithful witness to the world. Nevertheless Jesus rarely, if ever, made any emotional demand upon those who came to Him. His tests were always practical: "Follow Me"; "Take up your Cross"; "Go and publish abroad the Kingdom of God." The proof of love lay not in adoration but in action. "If ye love Me, ye will keep My commandments"; "He that hath My commandments and keepeth them, he it is that loveth Me." "To *serve* Christ, not to *feel* Christ, is the mark of His true servants: they become Christians in proportion as they cease to be interested in themselves and become absorbed in their Lord." The life of Jesus Himself was clouded, and as the end drew on, the strain became almost too great at times to be borne. "I have a baptism to be baptized with and how am I straitened till it be accomplished"; "Now is my soul troubled." His divine goodness shone in nothing more brightly than this; that He never allowed the inward conflict to interfere with His service for others. They who so lightly appealed to Him for relief, little knew the burden which rested on His own spirit. They tell us we ought to "feel like singing all the time." A far higher attainment is to sing when you *feel* like weeping.

That lack of sensitiveness to the divine Presence which we deplore is often chiefly a matter of temperament. It means that we are without that mysterious psychic quality by means of which some are able to see and hear things of the spiritual realm which are hidden from ourselves. But in so far as this is the cause it is clearly one for which we are not responsible, and to suppose that we can be at any ultimate disadvantage therefrom is to renounce our faith in a God of perfect goodness. But it may well be that the non-mystic has a deeper consolation than any of a merely negative character. Perhaps there is in his disability a great positive purpose. "Master," asked the disciples once, "Who did sin, this man or his parents, that he was *born blind?*" "Neither did this man sin nor his parents," replied Jesus, *"but that the works of God might be made manifest in him."* Even Jesus for a moment experienced the desolation of feeling Himself to be deserted. Do we not read that we may enter into the fellowship of His sufferings, that we may fill up that which is lacking of the afflictions of Christ for His body's sake which is the Church? This inability to feel is a heavy burden, harder to bear it may be than physical pain, for it is hidden from sight, and the troubled spirit does not receive the human alleviations which come to the suffering body. But it may be fruitful in bringing forth a rich harvest of sympathy and helpfulness for others in like need, and in this as in other things, it is more blessed to give than to receive. And beyond all this may we not venture to hope that this suffering may have its part, in a deeper sense than we can understand, in winning the world for Christ? We may at least be sure that He has need of the non-mystic to complete the harmony of a redeemed world.

"For Him That Is Joined to All Living There Is Hope"

[FROM *Work and Contemplation*]

DOUGLAS V. STEERE

[*In many instances practices first instituted by Quakers have been adopted—or adapted—as useful by other groups. Joseph Tuke's eighteenth-century plan, much in advance of its time, for the care of the insane of York became a model for reforms throughout the world.*

Douglas Steere's pamphlet on the Quaker work camp was published in 1942. Fifty years later we have in the Peace Corps an adaptation of that plan with national-political coloring. The Quaker name, "work camp," was less pretentious, eschewing both military echoes and prophetic overtones. The work camps, and the meetings for business, were a means for the expression of love in the "outward"; not, in the one instance, for purposes of reaching with minimum friction decisions of maximum expedience for profit-making; nor, in the other, of practicing anti-fission methods of living abroad while the nuclear devices at home were rushed to completion.

No matter what the motives may be behind such adaptations of Quaker practices, it is likely that persons practicing harmony rather than bickering, construction rather than destruction, will be, at the conclusion of such experiments, on better terms with themselves— whatever the case of their relations with "natives" or the stockholders may be.

The Quaker work camp members were not concerned with either political ideologies or profit-making. They were to think of their work as being, "not of dust or earth, or of flesh, or of time, but of God." And to strengthen this concept, the members practiced corporate contemplation: that is, they took part in what amounted to early Quaker silent meetings.

The knowledge of the interrelation of physical effort and spiritual awareness is an old one. But the Quaker work camp, while recognizing the interrelation, did not make one a means and the other an end. The contemplator was a better worker, the worker a better contemplator. Work was "love made visible." And love was the prerequisite of "great contemplation." One did not exhaust the body in order to have visions, nor have visions in order to be strengthened for increased physical efforts. Both activities were expressions of the whole man.

E. M. Forster in Howards End *cries out, "Only combine the passion and the prose." The work camp has been one Quaker attempt to heal this wound of division in the self; a place where the individual could learn "to work with this contemplation in him." While neither work nor contemplation, thus practiced, was a "means" but together formed the expression of a loving, and thus an integrated, person, the work camp itself may be a means: the means by which any individual, having practiced wholeness in the microcosm of a work camp, may depart to a larger work camp, the world, and there also be "a fellow workman with God."*]

In these days we are in the way of recovering some of the satisfactions that come from work with the hands and the body. The widespread interest and participation in handicrafts and gardening, the revival of native handicrafts in the Appalachian Mountains, the use of the crafts by occupational therapy as a way of restoring a sense of validity to those suffering from nervous tensions, the use of work with the body as the basic foundation of the whole educational technique in certain advanced schools on the continent, these are all weather-vanes that point in that direction. Nowhere is this satisfaction in labor more genuinely experienced than in the voluntary work camps in this country where young men and women donate a summer of physical work to help provide some much-needed service that will improve the standard of life in some hard-pressed community. . . .

WORK WITHOUT CONTEMPLATION IS BLIND

There is, however, a realization among the more thoughtful members of the work-camps that the whole story of work has not been told when this elemental goodness of work itself has been witnessed to. . . .

Five years ago the American Friends Service Committee established a work camp in western Pennsylvania for preparatory school boys where they were to build a much-desired road for the Westmoreland Subsistence Homestead. After the boys had got the work on the dirt road well along, the engineers employed by the government on the project discovered that they had made a mistake in placing the road and gave the word to begin it in another place. It was a difficult matter after that to get these boys to work with spirit. If they and their work had had so little worth and meaning as to be trifled with by faulty and careless planning, why should they exert themselves again as they had before? The frame of meaning of the work having been seriously damaged, the goodness seemed to bleed out of the work. . . .

Doestoevsky, who for suspected revolutionary activities spent four years as a young man in a prison camp in Omsk, Siberia, and suffered the torture of the "made-work" he found there, wrote later in the *House of the Dead:* "I have sometimes thought that the way to crush and annihilate a human being completely would be to set him to do an absolutely senseless and useless thing. If he were condemned to pour water from one tub to another and back again, or to pound sand in a mortar, or to carry a heap of earth backward and forward, I am convinced that he would either commit suicide within a few days or murder some of his fellow sufferers in order to suffer death at once and be delivered from his moral torture, shame and degradation." This secret of the way meaningless physical work can swiftly destroy the fiber and even the nervous stability of men is not unknown in some of the punishment camps in the world today.

Ade Bethune writes of work, "When any work is deprived of its contemplation, it becomes mere physical labor. The workers who are not able to think responsibly of what they are doing are no more than slaves chained to a meaningless action." It becomes increasingly clear, then, that for normal men and women, not action alone but sufficient contemplation to reveal the frame of meaning in which the work is done will be a decisive factor in whether their work acts creatively or destructively upon them. We neglect the frame of meaning only at our peril. To learn and practice contemplation, to discover, to enlarge, to renew the purposes for which we work, the frame of meaning within which we work, the frame of our relationships with our fellow workers, becomes, then, not an accessory or a luxury, but a central concern for those who understand most deeply the nature of work. . . .

It has been quite natural then that from the beginning the work camps of the American Friends Service Committee have given an important place to the practice of the direct act of contemplation and have regarded the corporate cultivation of this practice as a discipline that was integrally connected with the work experience of those it recruited to share in its camps. In the period of corporate silence in which the members of each work camp gather in the early morning before the manual work begins, it is a common experience that members report they have recovered the frame of meaning of their lives and of their work. They have often mentioned that they have become aware of incongruities, in the work or in the community or in themselves or between themselves and other members of the camp, that must be straightened before the work can become truly creative. In these periods of silent meditation, of waiting, they have felt the cold, icy capsulation in themselves and in their personal claimful demands melting down and a new and living sense of fellowship with, and responsibility for, the wider community springing up in them. And they have been brought to know by inward experience what the book of Ecclesiastes means when it says, "For him that is joined to all the living, there is hope." At times there has come a new sense of inward responsibility for the minute details of their work.

> And he sang as the threads went to and fro,
> Whether 'tis hidden or whether it show
> Let the work be sound for the Lord will know.

THE PRACTICE OF CORPORATE CONTEMPLATION

There is no single set of instructions for learning to use these periods of contemplation helpfully. There are those who would refuse to give any instruction for a week or two and simply let the newcomer make his own adventure in the silence, believing that the way to begin to contemplate is to begin to contemplate, not to study instructions on the subject; that only after you have begun and then actively come seeking help will the help be of the least value. There is much truth in this, and anything that could be written here will take on different meanings as the newcomer gathers his own experience; and since what is suggested here is most elementary, it may become quite obsolete and be pushed aside very early in each person's own experiencing if he finds he has come into a freer use of the silence.

The body should be got out of the way in meditation by getting it settled in a position that is comfortable enough to keep it from intruding on consciousness but not in such a relaxed position as to induce a vegetative state of half slumber.

Stilling the octopus of the mind by calling in its tentacles so that it may act as a whole, so that it may be open to receive, is the counterpart of stilling the body. This is much more difficult. That it does not succeed all at once is not surprising. Distractions from sounds send a tentacle of the mind whipping out to ascertain the source, distractions from wandering thoughts that come floating into the mind or that insistently elbow their way in are both especially disturbing to the beginner in contemplation. The sounds can be quietly drawn into the meditation by using them as though they were reminders of what the mind was seeking to draw itself beneath in order to understand. The distracting thoughts need not be resisted but can best be simply acknowledged and ignored. Cloud masses are forever changing their position overhead but we are not compelled to keep watch of them.

In beginning to meditate many have found it a help to give some conscious guidance to the gathered mind and to lead it gently through some chosen areas. These areas each person may select for himself. It often helps to write them out in advance. A hint of several suggestive fields might include: What at bottom am I longing to accomplish through the summer's work? What in the day past has made me and my work fall short of this? Where will I find the source of strength for effecting the necessary changes? Why do I not draw upon this?

What would it be like to know the members of this camp and to know the employers of labor and the workers of this community, not as prejudice and opinion paint them, but to know them in that which is eternal? Is there honestly a center in even the most outwardly forbidding person "that is not of dust or of earth or of flesh or of time but of God?" How can I reach it? How can I answer to it? How can I hold it in my mind's eye and salute it? How can I appeal to it? In my work am I in each person I meet seeking to answer to it? What in me will have to go before I can answer to it? In what particularly crucial situation that I face today do I need help to answer to this center? Confront this situation in the meditation and draw on the source of strength for lifting this situation into a frame of meaning that can alter it.

What excess baggage am I carrying: of preconceived vocation, of stiff unchangeable plans and commitments, of material possessions or desires for possessions (Remember Bernard of Clairvaux's warning to his ascetic Cistercian monks who blamed the luxury of the monks of Cluny, "You blame their eating of flesh, but you yourselves are gluttons in the matter of beans."), of self-pampering, of neglected duties, of unfinished business?

In what conflict situation do I stand where I need to be elevated to a third point, where I can see not only my side or the opponent's side but the creative right side which is identical with neither the one nor the other? What would the situation look like from the third point? Do I quickly identify myself with one side or the other in existing conflicts or do I help draw the situation over into the third point? In discussions am I on defense or am I teachable, honestly listening, learning and exploring?

Now after gently conducting my gathered mind over one or more of these areas, do I dare simply to wait in the silence, quite easy, for any intimations or concerns, for the restoration of perspectives, for the rekindling of patience and humor? Do I dare simply to wait on the Source of strength in order to be simplified, in order that the many in me be made one, in order that I be refreshed and renewed, in order that the good in me may rise and the evil in me may recede?

At any point in this meditation the gathered mind may find itself taken beyond its own effort to contemplate and be fixed by the Source which it contemplates. When this happens it is the best of all and meditation has ceased and a state of inward prayer has replaced it.

Occasionally in the corporate meditation a member of the group may feel drawn to share some insight that has come and will speak it out quietly. The others need not open their eyes. When it is rightly given, such vocal expression during the corporate period of contemplation will be less a breaking of the silence than an articulation of the silence. Isaac Penington once wrote of such corporate contemplation, "For absolutely silent meetings (wherein there is a resolution not to speak) we know not, but we wait on the Lord either to feel Him in words, or in silence of spirit without words, as He pleaseth."

There will very naturally be a frank discussion of these periods of contemplation among the campers as they work together and many helpful suggestions may be exchanged in that way.

The daily period of corporate meditation in the work camps has seldom been more than twenty minutes. This may seem like a long time to some and there will be a temptation to shorten it at the beginning, a temptation that should be resisted. Anyone knows that when he steps from a brightly lighted room into the darkness of the night, it takes some minutes for his eyes to adjust to the change. After the adjustment to twilight vision is made, he can discern objects and go on his way quite safely. But if he despairs in the first moments of the darkness and turns back into the lighted room, he conceals from himself the powers he possesses. . . .

CONTEMPLATION WITHOUT WORK IS EMPTY

But important as contemplation may be to work, the reverse is equally true. For "without it (action) thought can never ripen into truth," and it is in work that contemplation finds both its proving ground and the body in which to incarnate itself. "Work," says Kalil Gibran, "is love made visible," and only if contemplation can overcome the stubborn resistance of nature and habit, which are present with all of their power in physical work, can it reveal itself. Work is a stern disciplinarian to any contemplative who has a tendency to feel an imaginary sense of mastery. "Anyone who makes a mistake in regard to his material, its composition or its resistance will be punished by the result of his labor. An error of judgment means a broken tool. A miscalculation may destroy a machine," to say nothing of injury to a worker's own body. "The greatness of contemplation can only be given to those who love," wrote Gregory the Great. It would seem as though this might apply equally to work, the visible manifestation of love. For just as work is the natural issue of contemplation, it in its turn searches out one who resists work and declares that great contemplation can only be given to those who will reveal it in work. "I went upstairs and tried to pray," wrote Katherine Mansfield in her Journal, "but I could not for I had done no work."

There is something in commonly exercised physical work that prepares and cements and opens a community for common contemplation. For work breaks through reserves, physical work exposes hidden surfaces in men's lives to each other as conversation and ordinary social intercourse can rarely do. Work reveals sham, it reveals generosity, it reveals endurance, it reveals genuine capacity to cooperate. Work reveals a common humanity that runs through its own natural hierarchy of skill. Physical work breaks down barriers of age, and class, and race, and forms an outer brotherhood that calls for further common exploration. Only upon rare occasions today is it possible for a working community to share common corporate contemplation. But there is nothing that prepares for corporate contemplation more effectively than a community of common work. The absence of such experiences may hint at one cause of the poverty of many formal services of worship today. . . .

It might be well to conclude this discussion of contemplation and work with an adaptation of Immanuel Kant's famous phrase and to declare that contemplation without work is empty and that work without contemplation is blind. But Meister Eckhart, a German predecessor of Kant's, has put the matter even better when he speaks of learning to work "not as if one were running away from the inner contemplation . . . but one should learn to work with this contemplation in him, with him, and emerging from him so that . . . one becomes accustomed to working collectedly . . . for then he becomes a fellow workman with God." To learn to hold work within its frame of meaning, to learn to unite work and contemplation, to learn to work collectedly is an objective that one summer's experience will not exhaust.

———————

"Go Straight at It without Leaning on Any Kind of Intermediary Help"

[FROM *Buddhist and Quaker Experiments with Truth*]

TERESINA R. HAVENS

[*Quakers, in a world which emphasizes differences, have increasingly tried to point out likenesses. Attempts to find likenesses between two such relatively undefinable groups as the Quakers and the Zen Buddhists may appear to be on a par with comparing handfuls of water: the more effort you put into it, the smaller the comparable residue you have left in your hand. But even that escapability from analysis is a likeness.*

Nancy Wilson Ross in her introduction to her anthology, World of

Zen, *says that the teaching of Zen "lies outside of words. . . . To know Zen, even to begin to understand it, it is necessary to practice it." Even so, Quakerism. The key to the understanding of Zen, says Miss Ross, "lies in the words 'direct immediate perception' or 'direct seeing into.' "* So, over and over again, have the Quaker leaders spoken. Fox cried out time and again against the "notional": that is, against cerebral knowledge as opposed to the "experimental" participation of the whole person in a relationship with God.

A British student of Zen said recently that, in total, Zen practices were no more than a form of "brainwashing." "Brainwashing" as a term, suffers from guilt by association; and those who use it to condemn forget that we owe whatever advances we have made as human beings to a series of "brainwashings." And the pity has been that those incapable of the "brainwashing" which new and truer concepts require have tried to cleanse the truth-bearers with blood baths. We have been "brainwashed"—i.e., our minds cleansed of the comfortably and falsely "notional"—by every great poet, explorer, inventor, and theorist who ever lived. It is clear that the brains of most of us must be cleansed from greeds, fears, and cruelties before we are capable of living together as brothers; or even, for that matter, of surviving as individuals. The important question to ask is not "Has the brain been washed?" but "What has been removed in the washing?" And, "What has replaced the content which has been removed?" Zen and Quakerism would agree on a number of matters to be removed. There would be less agreement about the purposes of the cleansing.

"*Foreign religions,*" says Alan Watts in Beat Zen, Square Zen, Zen, "*can be enormously attractive and highly overrated by those who know little of their own. That is why the displaced or unconscious Christian can easily use either beat or square Zen to justify himself. The one wants a philosophy to justify him in doing what he pleases. The other wants a more plausible authoritative salvation than church or the psychiatrists seem able to provide.*"

Quakerism is neither "plausible" nor "authoritative." It is mysterious and personal. Like the successful student of Zen, however, who, in Watts' words, "knows himself to be one with all," the Quaker feels himself to be a member of a universal brotherhood.

The Zen student comes to this knowledge by way of Ko-an, *the unanswerable question, and through Satori, an awakening. The Quaker*

comes to his or her knowledge by way of God, to whom there is no answer
outside of living, and through Christ, who awakens one to this living.]

———

Now consider, was not here something of God in these
heathens, that learned them to know God . . . though they had
no written gospel?   —Fox, *Doctrinals*

*   *   *   *

"HAVING SUBDUED ALL ATTACHMENT"

An ancient Hindu sage:
"A man who is free from desires sees the majesty of the Soul
by the grace of the Creator. That Soul cannot be gained by the
Veda, nor by intellect, nor by much learning. He whom the Soul
chooses, by him the Soul can be gained. But he who has not first
turned away from his wickedness, who is not tranquil, and
subdued, or whose mind is not at rest, he can never obtain the
Soul (even) by knowledge."

An American Quaker prophet:
"My own will and desire being now very much broken, . . .
and as mine eye was to the great Father of Mercies, humbly
desiring to learn what his will was concerning me, I was made
quiet and content." . . .

EXPERIMENTATION AND INQUIRY

It is only a short step from Upakosala, the pupil in the
Upanishads who found Awakening with a minimum of instruction, to young Gotama, later to become known as the supremely
Awakened One, who found only preliminary answers from the
gurus of his time. The difference is that Upakosala never lost
his faith in the necessity of an outer Master, whereas Gotama,
like Fox, after seeking out one renowned teacher after another,
was finally forced by the inadequacy of them all to discover the
truth independently. . . .

How then did they discover their own answers, these two seekers? In both cases, a careful reader of our precious early documents, written in the first person, can discover that the climactic illumination came as the peak of a long series of "openings."

The founder of Quakerism, though a less radical innovator than the Indian pioneer, was no less insistent upon first-hand experience. Fox accepted the basic framework of the Christian path to salvation, but re-experienced it for himself. The work of Christ came alive in Fox's own immediate experience so directly that it seemed to Fox that Christ came to him "without the help of any man, book, or writing."

The freshness and first-hand quality of the resulting religion in both cases is due in no small measure to this independence and originality which characterized both Gotama and George Fox. In the development of both religions this experimental approach has had certain important corollaries:

1. Rejection of the outward "machinery of salvation": ritual, priesthood, sacrifice, etc.
2. Rejection of all outward authority, including that of the Founder himself. In Buddhism this takes the form of extreme self-reliance. . . .
3. Priority on silent meditation as a method which encourages each seeker to discover new truth for himself.

BEYOND THINKING, OR HOW TO
SILENCE THE MIND

. . . . Both Buddhism and Quakerism in their original forms, recognizing the indispensability of Silence for inner realization, made of corporate Silence the primary and almost the only required group exercise. The other was Meetings-for-Discipline (Buddhist) or for Business (Quaker). This Silence in both movements was not infrequently broken by edifying messages, as the following passage shows:

"On the Sabbath of the full-moon at the end of the rains the Lord was sitting in the open in the moonlight, with the Brotherhood gathered around him, when, observing silence to reign among them all, he addressed the Almsmen in these words: 'In this vocation I find contentment of heart. . . . All talk is stilled in this assembly which is set (as it were) in a shining mere.' "

But in this Silence, the mind as well as the tongue must be stilled. And why? Some of the reasons have been considered in the preceding chapter: the mind's tendency to pride, to disputation, to preoccupation with irrelevant abstractions. Moreover, its very busy-ness tends to keep us conscious of our own efforts, instead of waiting for what may be "given" from the depths. As Penington warns:

"Therefore take heed of the fleshly wisdom; take heed of thine own understanding; take heed of thy reasoning or disputing; for these are the weapons wherewith the witness is slain. That wisdom must be destroyed, and that understanding brought to naught, and thou become a child, and learn as a child if ever thou know the things of God."

ANSWER WITH YOUR LIFE!

A Zen Buddhist Ko-an:

> When you meet a master in the street,
> Do not speak,
> Do not be silent.
> Then how will you greet him?

A Quaker Query:

Do you live in Christian love one toward another? Have you a living concern for the welfare of each member even to the sharing of one another's burdens? Do you seek for unity in the Divine Life underlying all differences of opinion and circumstance? (New England).

. . . . In a Zen training center each trainee in meditation receives from his meditation Master or "Spiritual Director" (Roshi) a ko-an—a question or baffling anecdote which has no logical answer. At frequent intervals—sometimes several times a day—he is supposed to report to his Roshi on his progress. The spirit of his search is indicated in the following Advices:

"What is needed in the beginning of your exercise is to stir up your spunky spirits and be most resolutely determined to go on with your task. Summarily making a bundle of all you have hitherto understood or learned, together with your Buddhist knowledge, your literary accomplishments, and your clever manipulation of words, sweep it off once for all into the great ocean; and never think of it again. Gathering 84,000 thoughts into a seat . . . , squat on it, and strive to keep your ko-an all the time before your mind. Once lifted up before the mind, never let it slip off; try to see with all the persistence you find in yourself into the meaning of the ko-an given to you, and never once waver in your determination to get into the very bottom of the matter. Keep this up until a state of satori (sudden awakening) breaks upon your consciousness. Do not make a guesswork of your ko-an; do not search for its meaning in the literature you have learned; go straight at it without leaning on any kind of intermediary help; for it is in this way that you can make for your own home. . . .

"If you feel dull and confused and unable to bring the thought to a focus, get down . . . and walk for a while somewhat briskly. . . . Suddenly . . . your ko-an rises on its own accord before the mind. . . . You do not then know whether you are walking or sitting, your 'spirit of inquiry' alone occupies the whole field. This is called the state of passionlessness or egolessness, but this is not yet an ultimate state; another strong whipping is needed, but you must double the effort. . . ."

In the . . . queries, it is our life which is being tested. Not primarily our ideas, not our conformity to a prescribed doctrinal pattern, but our state of awareness, our degree of inward growth constitutes the answer. The aim is to drive us to search for a deeper change in ourselves, rather than an answer in words. Not to be answered primarily by thinking, and never in imitation of any previous answer, each Ko-an and each Quaker Query is supposed to be answered directly out of one's own experience and one's own insight. The Zen Master judges whether or not the pupil will "pass," not primarily by his verbal answer only, but by the light in his eye, by his total bearing, by his response to shock-actions on the part of the Roshi. If he does not pass, back he goes to work on his ko-an for more days, weeks or months, sometimes years. Some never pass.

The Quaker Query differs . . . in that it is addressed to a group, not merely to an individual. It is designed to test the spirit of the corporate life of a Friends Meeting. As with the Zen ko-an, the real answer cannot be given in words, but is reflected in the spirit and actions of the members, in the way in which they treat each other throughout the week.

In our contemporary world of more and more specialized scientific tests of all sorts, from intelligence tests and aptitude tests to atomic tests, how rare and difficult to formulate is a test of one's inward growth, of the spiritual growth of a religiously concerned fellowship of adults! Yet how desperately needed!

Certain other interesting parallels between Quakerism and Zen follow from the basic tendency of both to judge by life rather than by words or doctrines:

1. Journals (Diaries) and letters rather than theologies as constituting the basic "sacred writings"—i.e. first-hand documents of spiritual pilgrimage, crisis, and awakening.

2. Anecdotes rather than sermons—usually with a humorous twist. The hearer can "get the point" but it cannot be "explained" in words without losing it—like Zen itself.

3. Encouragement of manual labor. Prolonged silent meditation is too intense to keep up without relief. Zen provided this relief, as did St. Benedict, by expecting all monks to share in the work involved in raising food and keeping the monastery clean. There are delightful stories of how the answer to his ko-an would come to a monk when he was tending the Chinese cabbage in the temple garden or scrubbing the kitchen floor!

"... A True Friend in a Totalitarian State"

[FROM *Reaching for the Stars*]

NORA WALN

[Nora Waln's observations, in the excerpt which follows, were written prior to the Second World War, but of a Nazi-dominated Germany. What knowledge the Germans had of Quakers had come to them, for the most part, after World War I through the work of the American Friends Service Committee; that is, through the gifts of food, clothing, medicine, and the like. Quakers are not all of the same mind about this work. Some of the more evangelically minded believe that there should be less feeding and more preaching—or at least that the two should not be separated as they now are in the work of the Service Committee.

John Greenleaf Whittier, who edited an early edition of Woolman, wrote of the Journal, *"In the preface to an English edition, published some years ago, it is intimated that objections had been raised to the* Journal *on the ground that it had so little to say of doctrine and so much of duty. . . . However the intellect may criticize such a life, whatever defects it may present to the trained eyes of theological adepts, the heart has no questions to ask, but at once owns and reveres it."*

Certainly the German heart, which, as Miss Waln says, had "locked the Quaker in," had no questions to ask. But of what value is the Quaker "locked in"? "Is it possible to be a true Friend in a totalitarian state?" Is the need now to be so true a Friend that totalitarian states become obsolete?

But on this point Thomas Kelly (1893–1941), perhaps the most eloquent of recent Quaker writers, has a warning. "There is a tendency today, . . ." he wrote, "to suppose that the religious life must prove its worth because it changes the social order. The test of the importance of any supposed dealing with Eternity is the benefits it may possibly bring to affairs in Time. . . . This is a lamentable reversal of the true order of dependence. Time is no judge of Eternity. . . . But in saying this I am not proposing a lofty scorn of this maimed and bleeding world."

Kelly concludes his essay on "The Eternal Now and Social Concern" with these words: "We have tried to discover the grounds of the social responsibility and the social sensitivity of Friends. It is not in mere humanitarianism. It is not in mere pity. It is not in mere obedience to Bible commands. It is not in anything earthly. The social concern of Friends is grounded in an experience—and experience of the Love of God and the impulse to Saviorhood inherent in the fresh quickening of that Life. Social concern is the dynamic Life of God at work in the world."|

———

And when the Germanic, the Nordic, man has set his foot upon the last strip of conquered land, he will take the crown of the world and lay it at God's feet, in order that he may be crowned by the Almighty.

From reading this I turned to reading Ibsen. That is a natural turn. Radio and press repeatedly stressed the Nazis' feeling of the necessity to cleanse themselves, and all other Germans throughout the world, of every characteristic which is not Nordic. The National Socialist Students' Union has been entrusted with the task of cooperating with the Nordic Society in the promotion of Nordic ideals. The plays of Ibsen are in the repertoire of nearly every theatre.

And this is what I read from Ibsen, in words not quite so simple as those of Matthew: "If you won all, but lost yourself, then your whole gain was nothing but a wreath around a cloven brow."

"We have struck the word 'pacifist' from the German vocabulary" is a remark which I heard frequently from people of the Reich who felt that way. They were using something coined for them by Herr Franz von Papen, last German Minister to Austria. A peculiar thing was that I often heard, even from those who used these words, another statement: *"Ich habe alle Quaker in mein Herz geschlossen"* (I have locked all Quakers in my heart).

This greeted me in castle and cottage. It was said by ardent supporters of Naziism, as well as by German men and women, who whispered their pacifism; and by folk who went courageously forward as pacifist until arrested, and then continued pacifism in prison. In fact, I got the impression that pacifism might be out of the vocabulary, but that the Germans have not done with its practice yet.

Pacifism has been a German tenet for a long time. I have seen letters and journals which show that similar revelations on the ethics of living came to practical mystics in Germany simultaneously with their receipt by George Fox and others in England. These yellowed pages record a generous exchange in which the Quaker faith received tenets from German thought. William Penn had no difficulty in getting Germans to join in his "holy experiment"—the founding of Pennsylvania. In a present-day Germany no one ever drew away from me because by the fortune of birth I belong to the Quakers. Quite the contrary happened. When Germans discovered that I am a Quaker they received me with a readiness to love me, and often treated me with a warmth far beyond my personal merit.

I do not think the Germans are a people of short memory. Whenever I was told by a stranger, "I have the Quakers locked in my heart," I always queried, "Why?" The answers, often from men in uniform, were all like this one: "When we were defeated and forsaken, the Quakers came to us. They fed starving children, but not only did they bring food, they brought us friendship. They were quick in love, they restored our faith in human goodness. They came as friends." I was humbled by this remembrance, ashamed where I had been impatient.

Narration of the reason for this twentieth-century Quaker action must begin with a "declaration from the harmless and innocent people of God called Quakers," presented to King Charles the Second of England on the twenty-first day of the eleventh month, 1660:

> We utterly deny all outward wars and strife, and fightings with outward weapons, for any end, or under any pretence whatsoever: this is our testimony to the whole world. And whereas it is objected: "But although you say that you cannot fight, yet if the Spirit move you, then you will change your principle and fight for the Kingdom of Christ," to this we answer: that the Spirit of Christ, by which we are guided, is not

changeable, so as to once to command us from a thing as evil, and again to move unto it: and we certainly know and testify to the world, that the spirit of Christ, which leads us in all truth, will never move us to fight and war against any man with outward weapons, neither for the kingdom of Christ nor for the kingdoms of the world.

This explanation must further include a minute of the Quaker Monthly Meeting of March 1760, which sets forth a testimony regarding victory:

As we cannot join in shedding the blood of our fellow creatures, neither can we be one with them in rejoicing in the advantages obtained by such bloodshed; as we cannot fight with the fighters, neither can we triumph with the conquerors.

On my desk as I write lies a small book which I have made for my personal use. It contains a selection from the testimonies of Friends' minutes on war passed by groups in every country where they have dwelt. From 1660 to the present day not one minute deviates from that position. In the crisis of last autumn (1938) the Society of Friends in Great Britain held a meeting at its headquarters in London to consider the Peace Testimony of the society and its implications and interpretation today. The meeting was the largest in the history of the society in Great Britain. The final minute, which reaffirmed the Quaker Peace Testimony, stated:

We have looked over the world and at home, and we have seen everywhere the denial of those standards of human relationships which Jesus Christ showed to us. Some evils stand out clearly, some we know that we are only just beginning to recognize. God has met us here, and in His presence we have reaffirmed the testimony of our society against all war for whatsoever purpose and have determined to make that testimony our own today.

Looking back across the centuries, I am thankful to the

thousands individually unknown to history who have held true to that belief. Friends neither take part in wars nor celebrate the victories of armed might.

Guided by this spirit, Quakers of the Allied victor countries did not rejoice in a victory for which they had not fought, nor did they tarry for peace terms to be arranged. They hurried across the frontiers to their friends, the Germans, to give what aid they could, both spiritual and material, bringing sympathy and loving reassurance as well as food.

They stood staunchly by the Germans through the sad time that followed. During the occupation of the Ruhr in 1923, English Friends sent a special mission which by intervention with the French military authorities obtained certain privileges for the imprisoned German officials. The Centres in Paris and Germany, through cooperation, were able to alleviate in some measure the tension between the two countries. Exchange of visits was also arranged between Germany and France of people of influence in their respective countries. Friends took considerable interest in the movement in both countries for improving Franco-German relations through school textbooks, and German Friends translated from French into German *The Struggle for the History Books in the Schools of France.*

In the years 1925–1928 the Warsaw and Berlin Centres planned together a series of Polish-German Conferences held in Danzig, Warsaw, and Berlin. These resulted in the forming of Polish study groups among students in Berlin and Konigsberg, and helped towards an unbiased understanding of such thorny problems as the Polish Corridor.

Through the medium of the Quaker Centres in Germany and other contacts, Friends were in a unique position to receive information on current tendencies in German thought and the economic situation of the country. As early as 1922 a statement was published on the "peril to all stabilized civilizations involved in the condition of Germany today." The increasing anxiety among members of the German Committee of the Friends' Service Council in London led them to arrange for the publication in 1931 of a series of leaflets by well-known authorities on the direct effects of reparations payments.

In 1933, through the intermediary of the Frankfurt Centre, a number of children of German unemployed were entertained by French peasants in Alsace. That year also marked the beginning of extensive work among German refugees after the coming of the Nazi regime. Within the Dritte Reich the Quakers have centres from which they give help to those in trouble; and a "Rest Home" where come many afflicted by the bitterness which so often accompanies great suffering when it is felt to be undeserved.

There again, as in the post-war era, something very beautiful has been shown in the German character. The thanks of these people are not so much for the good food, warmth, and freedom from financial cares, although these are mentioned with gratitude, as for having their faith in human goodness restored to them once more when it had been lost.

Outside Germany, many people have asked me if there are any German Quakers. Germany, the land that gave Thomas à Kempis to the world, has its practical mystics still, men and women who have seen a vision of the true way of life, and want to be true to that vision, cost what it may. Some of these people have their spiritual home among Friends.

It may seem to people in other countries that it is impossible to be a true Friend in a totalitarian state. They need to remember that this era in Germany is not the only time and place where a minority holding deep convictions on the way peace can be achieved have found themselves in opposition to the established order. Followers of Confucius faced that peril in the reign of Ch'in Shih Huang-ti—some were buried alive, others had "traitor" branded on their brows and, chained together, were taken north to toil at building the Great Wall of China. He who was born at Bethlehem, and gave us the Sermon on the Mount, did not have an easy time. Not so long ago men were burned at the stake for what they believed. Later, George Fox and other Quakers were in the English gaols in company with men and women of other sects courageous in suffering for their convictions. Neither side was kind to pacifists during the war of 1914 to 1918.

The coming of the Nazi regime in Germany has meant

difficulties for Quakers, as individuals, and for other Christians. But in times of suffering the spiritual feeling of true Christian groups rises. This is certainly true of the Germans. The sons of those Germans who preached against the occupation of Belgium protest from their pulpits with a courage that does not shame their fathers. Catholics, ably encouraged by the Pope, are fearless in devotion to Christ's teaching.

I have sat in Quaker Meetings in Germany in various places. What we call a "living" silence was seldom absent. God seemed more present than in meetings where life does not call for the bravery that it does here. The German Quakers go forward led by the Spirit—a loving fellowship strong in Inner Light, able to believe that virtue lies in every heart, even the hearts of those who oppose them.

I have been present when the door has opened and an official stepped in. I have never seen a German Friends' Meeting broken up. It has been my experience to have the official bow his head through what remained of the hour of quietness and inspired speech. In the time of persecution in England, meetings were ruthlessly disturbed—Milton writes of dust thrown on the silent worshipers. There are records of children who held meeting alone because all the grown-ups were in gaol.

It is the Quaker belief that peoples can be a society of friends living peacefully and profitably together in a frontierless and unfortified world. Those who are born to an environment where great thoughts are a daily commonplace often are not impressed by them until experience makes them real. As a child in the United States I had no contact with forts or frontiers—even when we went to Canada I did not notice any. The first sentence in this paragraph was to me but a copybook task—something written down by Grandfather which I must copy neatly twelve times before I could go skating. That was when I was what my niece Brenda calls "suffering an educa-tion."

While I lived in Germany, that copybook sentence became real to me and, although I saw in process the building up of the most powerful army the world has ever possessed, I did not get the impression that the Germans have done with pacifism. Instead, there grew within me a faith that Germans will be a powerful force in the making of a frontierless and unfortified world.

———————————

"The Earth Is the Lord's"

[FROM *Quaker Ways*]

A. RUTH FRY

[*Ruth Fry is a student of Bellers, and her "Ten Commandments for Nations" may have had their origin in her knowledge of his concern for national problems. They are, in any case, a reflection of an almost universal conviction: that if we are to survive as persons we must have a new moral life as nations.*

"An awful solemnity is upon the earth, for the last vestige of earthly security is gone," writes Thomas Kelly. "It has always been gone, and religion has always said so, but we haven't believed it. And some of us Quakers are not undeceived, and childishly expect our little cushions for our little bodies, in a world inflamed. Be not fooled by the pleasantness of the Main Line life, and the niceness of Germantown existence. . . . For the plagues of Egypt are upon the world, entering hovel and palace, and there is no escape for you or me."

No escape, he continues, except that "some of us have to face our comfortable self-oriented lives all over again. The times are too tragic, God's sorrow is too great, man's night is too dark, the Cross is too glorious for us to live as we have lived in anything short of holy obedience. It may or it may not mean change in geography, in profession, in wealth, in earthly security. It does mean this: Some of us will have to enter upon a vow of renunciation and of dedication to the 'Eternal Internal' which is as complete and as irrevocable as was the vow of the monk of the Middle Ages. . . . Little groups of utterly dedicated souls knowing one another in Divine Fellowship. . . . Our meetings were meant to be such groups, but now too many of them are dulled and cooled and flooded by the secular. But within our meetings such inner bands of men and women internally set apart, living by a vow of perpetual obedience to the Inner Voice—in the world, yet of the world—obedient as a shadow, selfless as a shadow. Such bands of humble prophets can recreate the Society of Friends and the Christian church and shake the countryside for ten miles around."]

———

The morality of the nations must be as the morality of the individual writ large, therefore,

I. The State shall not exalt the false gods of national glory, national pride, national greed, for the Lord God is a jealous God, visiting the disobedience of the fathers upon the children, upon the third and upon the fourth generation of those that neglect Him, and showing mercy unto thousands of those that love Him and keep His commandments.

II. Every State shall acknowledge that all men are equally the children of God, and recognize the brotherhood of all men and the rights of primitive peoples.

III. The State shall not bear false witness against its neighbours, for Christ has said, "Love your enemies, bless them that curse you, do good to them that hate you and pray for them who despitefully use you and persecute you."

IV. The State shall do no murder, nor order its subjects to kill.

V. The State shall not steal, nor keep what it gains by force, for Christ has said, "It is more blessed to give than to receive." "Give, and it shall be given unto you, good measure, pressed down, shaken together and running over."

VI. The State shall not covet its neighbours' wealth, nor its neighbours' territory, nor anything that is theirs.

VII. The State shall not judge in its own case, for too often we fail to see the beam in our own eye, looking only for the mote in our brother's eye.

VIII. The Earth is the Lord's and the fullness thereof, and no State shall fear the prosperity of another, but rather rejoice in it.

IX. Thou shalt love the Lord thy God with all thy heart, and with all thy soul, and with all thy mind, and thy neighbour States as thine own country.

X. The State shall not seek its own life, for whosoever would save his life, shall lose it.

LOVE IS THE LAW OF LIFE. FOR GOD IS LOVE.

Comrade Ivan

TOM COPEMAN

[*Bernard Canter, from whose anthology,* The Quaker Bedside Book, *the account which follows is taken, traces "the thin line of Quaker contacts with Russia" back to 1697, "when Peter the Great was working in the Royal dockyard at Deptford as a shipwright. . . . Deputations of Quakers waited on him to urge liberty of conscience in his dominions, and they found themselves explaining their Peace Testimony and defending it against his criticism." This they are still doing.*

The existence of Russian "Quakers" raises the question as to what constitutes a Quaker. William Penn, never himself an official member of any Friends' meeting, wrote, "It is not opinion or speculation, or notions of what is true; or assent to, or the subscription of articles or propositions, though never so soundly worded that . . . makes a man a true believer or a true Christian. But it is conformity of mind and practice to the will of God, in all holiness of conversation, according to the dictates of this Divine principle of Light and Life in the soul which denotes a person truly a child of God."

So Penn defines "a true believer or true Christian" and the only Quaker emphasis in his definition is, "this Divine principle of Light and Life in the soul." There were and are those who can not subscribe to this. But Penn adds, "The humble, meek, merciful, just, pious and devout souls are everywhere of one religion; and when death has taken off the mask they will know one another, though the diverse liveries they wear here, make them strangers."]

The scene was Buzuluk in October, 1921, when the advance party of the Friends Relief Mission in the famine area consisted of Albert Cotterell, Nancy Babb and myself. At that time the railway yards were packed with crowds of refugees waiting, often in vain, for transport. Among them Albert Cotterell to his great surprise one day encountered a group of people calling themselves Quakers. Unfortunately he was shortly afterwards called away to Moscow and in his absence two or three of the Quaker refugees came to tell Nancy Babb and myself that they had obtained railway wagons and were leaving that day for the Kuban region. As we had a box of clothing waiting for them we suggested that ten of them should come to our quarters in the station buildings for a Meeting at which we would have our interpreter present.

As they sat on boxes and benches on the other side of the table we could not help being struck by their fine faces, especially the face of a matronly woman who sat silent with folded hands. They said they had always been called Quakers by other people, and according to tradition had been started "300 years ago by someone from England." In all they considered that (apart from other slightly different bodies) they numbered one million (!) but as they had neither any form of organization nor, apparently, any test of membership, it was hard to say.

They carried their disbelief in killing to such lengths that they did not even kill lice but "put them somewhere else." In the late Czar's time 609 of them refused to bear arms and most of them were imprisoned. At the beginning of the Kerensky regime their chains were knocked off and they were told to go and register. They, however, refused and said they would rather stay in prison. Released shortly afterwards, they had been excused military service by the Soviet Government but had eventually registered in the commune for agricultural work.

Questioned as to oaths, they said they did not believe in them but in brotherly words. They registered their marriages with the Government but believed that in marriage they were guided by the Spirit and that registration or oath was unnecessary. For the purpose of marriage they held a Meeting when "the brother declares to the sister that they will be married." If matrimonial troubles arose an elderly Friend was called in.

In the social order they seemed to be very near to Communism. In their religion they desired to be moved entirely by the Spirit and had no set forms. When a Meeting began they sang together or talked or sat in silence and believed that "the same brotherly feeling runs through them all." God was always with them, they said, and they gathered chiefly to express themselves and for fellowship.

After we had finished our questions we had a short period of silence and they sang a hymn. It was a most wonderful experience and I felt very near to them and I think they to us. I wished the Meeting could have been longer, but they were anxious to question us and put several heart-searching questions, one being whether English Friends accepted service under Government.

By this time they were in danger of being left behind, so we all shook hands and they took their box of clothing and went down to the train.

And that, so far as I am aware, was the last contact between English Friends and Russian Quakers. The estimate of their numbers given by the Russian Quakers can certainly be disregarded, and probably the date of their founding, for Russians in those days were weak at figures. The fact remains, however, that in 1921 there were in Russia groups of people called Quakers with a tradition of an earlier contact with English Friends.

"Unity, with Diversity"

[*When the members of the Friends' Mission to Russia returned to England after the presentation to the Soviet Peace Committee of the document which follows, they told English Friends what they believed must be done "if tensions are to be lessened and hopes of peace confirmed." Their recommendations follow in an abbreviated form.*

(1) *We must make a reality of our own Christian and democratic professions. We must respond "to the Communist challenge, not by a critical and defensive reaction but by a positive resolve to become better Christians and better democrats."*

(2) *". . . While fearlessly rejecting what we deem to be wrong or misguided in the policies and practices of the Soviet Union, to recognize what is good in its aspirations and achievements."*

(3) *". . . Avoid self-righteousness—and the expression in our-selves of the temper and practices we deplore and oppose in them."*

(4) *Resist moods of skepticism "where the peace declarations and approaches of the Soviet Union are concerned."*]

QUAKER FUNDAMENTALS   [*A statement presented to the Soviet Peace Committee in Moscow on July 16, 1951, by a member of the Friends' Mission to Russia*]:

The Society of Friends is a religious group of people, sometimes called Quakers, known principally for its Peace Testimony and for the relief work undertaken all over the world by its members.

One of its earliest members was John Bellers, born in 1654, who is known to all Russian schoolchildren as a pioneer in social reform. He said that war was the greatest enemy of the people and he appealed especially to teachers to work against war. Another early Friend was William Penn, the founder of the State of Pennsylvania.

For three hundred years Friends have worked for a genuine and lasting peace. They believe that social and individual justice (including racial justice) are essential to peace: and so is a spirit of good will to all men and of willingness to see good in those who differ from us, a spirit of reconciliation.

I want to tell you now what methods Friends believe should be used to achieve peace. But I cannot do that without saying something first about Friends' fundamental religious beliefs, about Quakerism, as it is sometimes called.

Friends believe that there is a plan in the Universe and a purpose behind it. Men are not just irresponsible puppets dancing for a short time in a meaningless void. But if there is a purpose there must be an authority responsible for that purpose, outside ourselves and beyond human authority, and we call that ultimate authority God.

To know the purpose of God implies a knowledge not only of the way in which the world works—which is what the scientist studies—but also of what it ought to be.

Friends believe that, in order to make the world what it ought to be, man needs to work with God, and God wants the help of man, but this cooperation must be free and not forced. Freedom is an essential part of the philosophy of Friends, freedom to choose; persuasion, not compulsion.

At the same time, Friends realize, of course, that freedom has a social as well as a political significance in practice just as it has a mental as well as a physical meaning. Men or women bound by poverty to a life of continual toil, and yet living in constant fear of unemployment, are not more free than the man who can be bought and sold. Men cannot think clearly when they are ill, hungry or afraid. To condition children by teaching, without at the same time developing their critical faculties so that they question what they are taught, is to turn them into slaves.

Friends, therefore, believe that we must overcome poverty, disease, fear, injustice and prejudice, and that to work for these ends is part of true religion. Friends believe, in short, that religion is something that has to be put into practice. It does not mean the repetition of certain acts or forms of words, but rather a sense that once we are sure that we know at least a part of God's purpose, then we must do something about it.

How can we know what to do?

Friends answer this by saying that there is something of God in everyone, that inspires them to aim at the highest, and urges them to respond to the highest. Everyone has the power to refuse; free will is an essential part of creation; but in his heart a man knows that good is right and evil is wrong in such a positive and certain way that no contradiction is possible.

Throughout the ages men have recognized certain qualities as the highest: truth, integrity, beauty, love, unselfishness and generosity. We believe that these are the qualities of God, that they have an absolute validity and that they are therefore bound, in the long run, to overcome error, hatred, suspicion, ugliness, greed, selfishness and the lust for power. These evils exist; they cannot be ignored, but the only way of overcoming them is to use truth, love, generosity, friendliness.

If we want to achieve peace it is useless to employ false-hood, to feel suspicion or hatred, or to be revengeful or resentful. Such methods as these are certain to fail to achieve good aims.

Friends believe that the character and methods approved by God are shown most vividly in the life, the teaching and the death of Jesus Christ. Quakerism is a Christian faith. It is not a superstition; it is a way of life. Friends accept Christ's teaching concerning the individual value of each man to God and our responsibility for one another.

Some of us may be more childish, more inexperienced than others and need special care. So do those who are particularly depraved or afflicted.

Friends, individually and collectively, have tried to put these beliefs into practice. They took a considerable part in the work for the emancipation of slaves and racial justice of all kinds. Through integrity in business some Friends prospered—people came to them as traders because they were honest and could be trusted—and these Quaker employers established a reputation for caring for and cooperating with their employees in the days when that sort of thing was an unheard-of innovation. Friends have always believed in education for all—boys and girls, rich and poor alike. Quaker schools were begun well ahead of schemes for universal education, but it was a Friend, Joseph

Lancaster, who developed the chain of schools that was expanded into a system of State education.

Friends founded a mental hospital run on modern lines as long ago as 1796, when the mentally sick were mostly treated like dangerous beasts. Their work for penal reform is best known through the name of Elizabeth Fry. Friends believe that all men, even criminals, should be cared for and humanely treated.

But in particular Friends strongly believe that war is never in accordance with the will of God, and this applies not merely to international war, but also to civil or class war. Friends have therefore tried to act as peacemakers in all human relationships, private and business, national and international. They believe that if changes of government are needed they can take place without violence, if men are willing to employ the time, teaching and patience that are needed for the success of non-violent methods. Friends are opposed to the training of youth for war; they regard military conscription as an offence to the human spirit and as inconsistent with the teaching and practice of Christianity. That Quaker pacifism is positive as well as negative is shown by the relief work undertaken by Friends almost since the beginning of their history. Relief work was done—as far as possible—on both sides. Friends Service Units have also worked in China and on a large scale again in the Second World War and after.

Friends have not been afraid to introduce Christianity into politics. They have used all legitimate means of peaceably influencing those who have the responsibility of government. They have tried to introduce non-violent methods of settling international disputes. Among other attempts at prevention of war (which is of course even better than relief of the sufferings caused by war), we may mention the visit of three Friends to the Czar of Russia in 1854, in an attempt to prevent the Crimean War.

Friends have also sent relief workers to assist in times of famine and other disasters not directly connected with war. Quaker relief in Russia was undertaken in the famines of 1892 and 1907, and again in the early years of the Revolution. At one time there were feeding centres in 280 villages in the Buzuluk district.

Friends have always believed also in small-scale experiments in understanding. They have established "Quaker Centres" in places where feelings ran high and friction was likely; centres where people of different habits, opinions, languages could meet in a friendly atmosphere. They have supported or initiated international work camps and seminars, attended largely by non-Friends. Friends believe that those who truly seek the will of God and wish to work with him can always find unity, even out of diversity. It is unity, with diversity, at which we must aim.

———

"Silence Helps the Spirit in Man"

[FROM *The World of Silence*]

MAX   PICARD

[*Max Picard, a Swiss philosopher and no Quaker, writes of silence like a Quaker.*

Of silence Thomas Kelly (once again) says: "Really powerful hours of unbroken silence frequently carry a genuine progression of spiritual change and experience. They are filled *moments, and the quality of the second fifteen minutes is definitely different from the quality of the first fifteen minutes. Outwardly all silences seem alike, as all minutes are alike by the clock. But inwardly the Divine Leader of worship directs us through progressive unfoldings of ministration, and may in the silence bring an inward climax which is as definite as the 'climax' of the Mass when the host is elevated in adoration. . . . [Words] should not break the silence but continue it. For the Divine Life who was ministering through the medium of silence is the same Life as is now ministering through words. And when such words are truly spoken 'in the Life,'* then when such words cease the uninterrupted *silence and worship continue, for silence and words have been of one texture, one piece."*|

———

There is a relationship between silence and faith. The sphere of faith and the sphere of silence belong together. Silence is the natural basis on which the super-nature of faith is accomplished.

God became man for the sake of man. This event is so utterly extraordinary and so much against the experience of reason and against everything the eye has seen, that man is not able to make response to it in words. A layer of silence lies between this event and man, and in this silence man approaches the silence that surrounds God Himself. Man and the mystery first meet in the silence, but the word that comes out of this silence is original, as the first word before it had ever spoken anything. That is why it is able to speak of the mystery.

It is a sign of the love of God that a mystery is always separated from man by a layer of silence. And that is a reminder that man should also keep a silence in which to approach the mystery. Today, when there is only noise in and around man, it is difficult to approach the mystery. When the layer of silence is missing, the extraordinary easily becomes connected with the ordinary, with the routine flow of things, and man reduces the extraordinary to a mere part of the ordinary, a mere part of the mechanical routine.

What many preachers say about the Mystery of God is often lifeless and therefore ineffectual. What they say comes only from words jumbled up with many thousands of other words. It does not come from silence. But it is in silence that that first meeting between man and the Mystery of God is accomplished, and from silence the word also receives the power to become extraordinary as the Mystery of God is extraordinary. It then rises above the order of ordinary words, just as the Mystery of God rises above the ordinary routine of things. It is as if words had been created for nothing else but the representation of the extraordinary. Thereby they become identical with the extraordinary, with the mystery; and thereby they have a power akin to that of the mystery.

It is true that man is able through the power of the spirit to give an elemental force to words, but the word that comes from silence is already elemental. The human mind has no need to spend itself in giving the word an elemental force that has already been given to it by the silence. The silence helps the spirit in man.

It is possible, too, that man could keep himself in the faith through the spirit, but the spirit would always have to be on the watch, always on guard, and faith would cease to be natural and effortless. And the effort required, not the faith itself, would then appear to be the important thing. A man who made such a great effort to believe might appear to himself as one to whom God Himself has directly committed the faith, as one saddled with the faith by God Himself. And he might seem to himself to be a prophet. It is true that the faith is extraordinary, but what is extraordinary is nothing to do with the external conditions of faith, not the effort required to believe. When the natural basis of silence is lacking, then the external conditions rise indeed to the level of the extraordinary.

The silence of God is different from the silence of men. It is not opposed to the word: word and silence are one in God. Just as language constitutes the nature of man, so silence is the nature of God; but in that nature everything is clear, everything is word and silence at the same time. . . .

"The Spirit of Seeking"

[FROM *Science and the Unseen World*]

ARTHUR STANLEY EDDINGTON

[*Pierre Cérésole (1879–1945), the son of a former president of Switzer-land, and an engineer, wrote when he applied for membership in the London Yearly Meeting, "I am of a scientific turn of mind upon the whole, and although I have always realized the essential importance of the Life of the Spirit—irreducible to the formulas of physics and mathematics—I have suffered within the restraints of a Christian orthodoxy which, in general, no longer really believes in its own dogmas. . . . God is seen, it seems to me, above all there where one makes a true and sincere effort to do his will. I feel uncomfortable and disturbed by every kind of special arrangement, attitude, discourse or silence by which one is supposed to approach God. It is in fact life itself, ordinary life as it is called . . . which is our essential and constant communion with God. . . ."*

It is by chance that this volume approaches its conclusion with the statements of two Quaker scientists. But in an age which may be terminated by forces discovered by science it is not inappropriate. However those who believe that it is science *which threatens us are mistaken. Science, as Arthur Stanley Eddington (1882–1944) observes, is only a method of seeking for truth. If what science discovers is used destructively, we are as silly in blaming science as is the woman who kicks her stove when she burns the stew.*

"There is only one match for these enormous astronomical distances," writes Cérésole, "these oceans of fire—the man who knows how to listen to the Eternal. Everything else is of absolute insignificance."

"Seeking," says Eddington.

"The Eternal," says Cérésole.

"Until," says Barclay, "all the kingdoms of the earth become the kingdom of Christ Jesus."

Such was George Fox's vision on Pendle Hill. Out of it, and sharing it, has come the Religious Society of Friends.]

In its early days our Society owed much to a people who called themselves Seekers; they joined us in great numbers and were prominent in the spread of Quakerism. It is a name which must appeal strongly to the scientific temperament. The name has died out, but I think that the spirit of seeking is still the prevailing one in our faith, which for that reason is not embodied in any creed or formula. It is perhaps difficult sufficiently to emphasize Seeking without disparaging its correlative Finding. But I must risk this, for Finding has a clamorous voice that proclaims its own importance; it is definite and assured, something that we can take hold of—that is what we all want, or think we want. Yet how transitory it proves. The finding of one generation will not serve for the next. It tarnishes rapidly except it be preserved with an ever-renewed spirit of seeking. It is the same too in science. How easy in a popular lecture to tell of the findings, the new discoveries which will be amended, contradicted, superseded in the next fifty years! How difficult to convey the scientific spirit of seeking which fulfils itself in this tortuous course of progress towards truth! You will understand the true spirit neither of science nor of religion unless seeking is placed in the forefront.

Religious creeds are a great obstacle to any full sympathy between the outlook of the scientist and the outlook which religion is so often supposed to require. I recognize that the practice of a religious community cannot be regulated solely in the interests of its scientifically-minded members and therefore I would not go so far as to urge that no kind of defence of creeds is possible. But I think it may be said that Quakerism in dispensing with creeds holds out a hand to the scientist. The scientific objection is not merely to particular creeds which assert in outworn phraseology beliefs which are either no longer held or no longer convey inspiration to life. The spirit of seeking which animates us refuses to regard any kind of creed as its goal. It would be a shock to come across a university where it was the practice of the students to recite adherence to Newton's laws of motion, to Maxwell's equations, and to the electromagnetic theory of light. We should not deplore it the less if our own pet theory happened to be included, or if the list were brought up to date every few years. We should say that the students cannot possibly realize the intention of scientific training if they are taught to look on these results as things to be recited and subscribed to. Science may fall short of its ideal, and although the peril scarcely takes this extreme form, it is not always easy, particularly in popular science, to maintain our stand against creed and dogma. I would not be sorry to borrow for our scientific pronouncements the passage prefixed to the Advices of the Society of Friends in 1656 and repeated in the current General Advices:

"These things we do not lay upon you as a rule or form to walk by; but that all with a measure of the light, which is pure and holy, may be guided; and so in the light walking and abiding, these things may be fulfilled in the Spirit, not in the letter; for the letter killeth, but the Spirit giveth life."

Rejection of creed is not inconsistent with being possessed by a living belief. We have no creed in science, but we are not lukewarm in our beliefs. The belief is not that all the knowledge of the universe that we hold so enthusiastically will survive in the letter; but a sureness that we are on the road. If our so-called facts are changing shadows, they are shadows cast by the light of constant truth. So too in religion we are repelled by that confident theological doctrine which has settled for all generations just how the spiritual world is worked; but we need not turn aside from the measure of light that comes into our experience showing us a Way through the unseen world.

Religion for the conscientious seeker is not all a matter of doubt and self-questionings. There is a kind of sureness which is very different from cocksureness.

"That Little Spark That Hath Appeared . . ."

ROBERT BARCLAY

If, in God's fear, candid reader, thou appliest thyself to consider this system of religion here delivered, with its consistency and harmony, as well in itself as with the scriptures of truth, I doubt not but thou wilt say with me and many more, that this is the spiritual day of Christ's appearance, wherein he is again revealing the ancient paths of truth and righteousness. For which end he hath called us to be a first fruits of those that serve him, and worship him no more in the oldness of the letter, but in the newness of the Spirit. And though we be few in numbers, in respect of others, and weak as to outward strength, which we also altogether reject, and foolish if compared with the wise ones of this world; yet as God hath prospered us, notwithstanding much opposition, so will he yet do, that neither the art, wisdom, nor violence of men or devils shall be able to quench that little spark that hath appeared; but it shall grow to the consuming of whatsoever shall stand up to oppose it! yea, he that hath arisen in a small remnant shall arise and go on by the same arm of power in his spiritual manifestation, until he hath conquered all his enemies, until all the kingdoms of the earth become the kingdom of Christ Jesus.

BIBLIOGRAPHY

Historical Background

Clark, G. N. *The Seventeenth Century.* Oxford: Clarendon Press, 1947.

Gooch, G. P. *English Democratic Ideas in the Seventeenth Century.* New York: Harper (Torch Book), 1959.

Knox, Ronald. *Enthusiasm.* London: Oxford University Press, 1959.

Miller, Perry. *The New England Mind in the Seventeenth Century.* New York: Macmillan, 1939.

Nuttall, Geoffrey F. *The Holy Spirit in Puritan Faith and Experience.* New York: Macmillan, 1947.

Trevelyan, G. M. *English Social History.* New York and London: Longmans, Green, 1944.

——. *History of England. The Tudor and Stuart Era.* New York: Doubleday (Anchor Books), 1953.

Wedgwood, C. V. *Seventeenth Century English Literature.* London: Oxford University Press, 1950.

Willey, Basil. *The Seventeenth Century Background.* New York: Doubleday (Anchor Books), 1953.

History of Quakerism

Besse, Joseph. *Collection of the Sufferings of People Called Quakers.* London, 1753.

Braithwaite, William C. *The Beginnings of Quakerism.* London: Cambridge University Press, 1955.

————. *The Second Period of Quakerism.* London: Cambridge University Press, 1961.

Brayshaw, A. Neave. *The Quakers: Their Story and Message.* New York: Macmillan, 1938.

Brinton, Howard, ed. *Byways in Quaker History.* Wallingford, Pa.: Pendle Hill, 1944.

Brinton, Howard. *Friends for 300 Years.* New York: Harper, 1952.

Comfort, William Wistar. *Quakers in the Modern World.* New York: Macmillan, 1949.

Drake, Thomas E. *Quakers and Slavery in America.* New Haven: Yale University Press, 1950.

Jones, Rufus. *Faith and Practice of the Quakers.* New York: Harper, 1927.

————. *Later Periods of Quakerism.* New York: Macmillan, 1921.

————. *The Quakers in the American Colonies.* New York: Macmillan, 1911.

————. *Spiritual Reformers in the 16th and 17th Centuries.* New York: Macmillan, 1914.

Lloyd, Arnold. *Quaker Social History.* New York and London: Longmans, Green, 1950.

Loukes, Harold. *Discovery of Quakerism.* London: Harrap, 1960.

Penney, Norman, ed. *The First Publishers of Truth.* London: Headley, 1907.

Raistrick, Arthur. *Quakers in Science and Industry.* New York: Philosophical Library, 1950.

Sewel, Willem. *History of the Rise, Increase and Progress of the Christian People Called Quakers.* London, 1722.

Sykes, John. *The Quakers.* Philadelphia: Lippincott, 1959.

Tolles, Frederick B. *Meeting House and Counting House.* Chapel Hill: University of North Carolina Press, n.d.

Vipont, Elfrida. *The Story of Quakerism, 1652–1952.* London: Bannisdale, 1954.

Wright, Luella. *The Literary Life of the Early Friends.* New York: Columbia University Press, 1932.

Journals and Biographies

Barclay, A. R., ed. *Letters of Early Friends*. London, 1841.

Best, Mary Agnes. *Rebel Saints*. New York: Harcourt Brace, 1925.

Brayshaw, A. Neave. *The Personality of George Fox*. London: Allenson, 1933.

Cadbury, Henry J. *George Fox's Book of Miracles*. London: Cambridge University Press, n.d.

Cadbury, M. Christabel. *Robert Barclay*. London: Headley, 1912.

Comfort, William Wistar. *Stephen Grellet, a Biography*. New York: Macmillan, 1942.

Ellwood, Thomas. *The History of the Life of Thomas Ellwood*. London: Routledge, 1885.

Flexner, Helen Thomas. *A Quaker Childhood*. New Haven: Yale University Press, 1940.

Fogelklou, Emilia. *James Nayler, the Rebel Saint*. London: Ernest Benn, 1931.

Forbush, Bliss. *Elias Hicks, Quaker Liberal*. New York: Columbia University Press, 1956.

Fox, Caroline. *Memories of Old Friends*. Philadelphia: Lippincott, 1882.

Fry, A. Ruth. *John Bellers*. London: Cassell, 1935.

Hodgkin, L. Violet. *A Book of Quaker Saints*. London: Foulis, 1917.

Jones, Rufus M. *A Small Town Boy*. New York: Macmillan, 1941.

Lambert, D. W. *The Quiet in the Land*. New York: Macmillan, 1956.

Lampson, Mrs. Locker, ed. *A Quaker Post-Bag*. London, 1910.

Newman, Sir George. *Quaker Profiles*. London: Bannisdale, 1946.

Nickalls, John, ed. *George Fox's Journal*. London: Cambridge University Press, 1952.

Noble, Vernon. *The Man in Leather Breeches*. New York: Philosophical Library, 1953.

Peare, Catherine Owens. *William Penn*. Philadelphia: Lippincott, 1957.

Penney, Norman, ed. *Experiences in the Life of Mary Penington*. London, 1911.

Pickett, Clarence E. *For More Than Bread.* Boston: Little, Brown, 1953.

Pollard, John A. *John Greenleaf Whittier.* Boston: Houghton, Mifflin, 1949.

Roberts, Daniel. *Some Memoirs of the Life of John Roberts.* Philadelphia: Friends Book Store, n.d.

Rogers, Horatio. *Mary Dyer of Rhode Island.* Providence, R. I.: Preston and Rounds, 1896.

Ross, Isabel. *Margaret Fell, Mother of Quakerism.* New York and London: Longmans, Green, 1949.

Smith, Logan Pearsall, ed. *Philadelphia Quaker: Letters of Hannah Whitall Smith.* New York: Harcourt, Brace, 1950.

————. *Unforgotten Years.* Boston: Little, Brown, 1939.

Strachey, Ray. *A Quaker Grandmother.* New York: Revell, 1914.

Van Etten, Henry. *George Fox and the Quakers.* New York: Harper (Torchbook), 1959.

Vining, Elizabeth Gray. *Friend of Life: The Biography of Rufus M. Jones.* Philadelphia: Lippincott, 1958.

Whitney, Janet. *Elizabeth Fry, Quaker Heroine.* London: Harrap, 1947.

————. *John Woolman.* Boston: Little, Brown, 1942.

Woolman, John. *The Tailor of Mount Holly.* London: Friends Book Center, 1926.

————. *Journal of John Woolman.* New York: Macmillan, 1903.

Faith and Practice

Aarek, Wilhelm. *From Loneliness to Fellowship.* London: Allen and Unwin, 1954.

Barclay, John, ed. *Selections from the Works of Isaac Penington.* London: Darton and Harvey, 1837.

Barclay, Robert. *Apology for the True Christian Divinity.* Wallingford, Pa.: Pendle Hill, 1942.

Barnes, Kenneth C. *The Creative Imagination.* London: Allen and Unwin, 1960.

Bownas, Samuel. *A Description of the Qualifications Necessary to a Gospel Minister.* London: Wm. D. Parrish, 1847.

Canter, Bernard, ed. *The Quaker Bedside Book.* New York: David McKay, 1952.

Cèrèsole, Pierre. *For Peace and Truth.* London: Bannisdale, 1954.

Dunstan, Edgar G. *Quakers and the Religious Quest.* London: Allen and Unwin, 1959.

Fosdick, Harry Emerson, ed. *Rufus Jones Speaks to Our Time.* New York: Macmillan, 1951.

Fuchs, Emil. *Christ in Catastrophe.* Wallingford, Pa.: Pendle Hill, 1949.

Grubb, Edward. *What Is Quakerism?* London: Allen and Unwin, 1940.

Havens, Teresina R. *Buddhist and Quaker Experiments with Truth.* Philadelphia: Religious Education Committee, n.d.

Hepher, Cyril, ed. *The Fellowship of Silence.* New York: Macmillan, 1925.

Hobling, Margaret B. *The Concrete and the Universal.* London: Allen and Unwin, 1958.

Jones, Rufus. *The Luminous Trail.* New York: Macmillan, 1947.

Kelly, Thomas R. *A Testament of Devotion.* New York: Harper, 1941.

Kenworthy, Leonard S., ed. *Quaker Leaders Speak.* Philadelphia: Friends Book Store, 1952.

Leach, Robert J., ed. *The Inward Journey of Isaac Penington.* Wallingford, Pa.: Pendle Hill, 1943.

Littleboy, William. *The Meaning and Practice of Prayer.* London: Friends Home Service Committee, 1937.

Lonsdale, Kathleen. *Is Peace Possible?* London: Penguin, 1957.

Loukes, Harold. *Friends Face Reality.* London: Bannisdale, 1954.

———. *Friends and Their Children.* London: Harrap, 1958.

Mather, Eleanor Price. *Barclay in Brief.* Wallingford, Pa.: Pendle Hill, n.d.

Maurer, Herrymon. *The Pendle Hill Reader.* New York: Harper, 1950.

Nuttall, Geoffrey F. *Studies in Christian Enthusiasm.* Wallingford, Pa.: Pendle Hill, 1948.

————. *To the Refreshing of the Children of Light.* Wallingford, Pa.: Pendle Hill, 1959.

Penn, William. *Fruits of an Active Life,* ed. William Wistar Comfort, Isaac Sharpless. Philadelphia: Friends Book Store, 1945.

Reynolds, Reginald. *The Wisdom of John Woolman.* London: Allen and Unwin, 1948.

Sessions, William H. *Laughter in Quaker Gray.* Philadelphia: Friends Book Store, 1952.

Steere, Douglas V. *On Listening to Another.* New York: Harper, 1955.

————. *Work and Contemplation.* New York: Harper, 1957.

Stephen, Caroline. *Quaker Strongholds.* London: Edward Hicks, 1891.

————. *The Vision of Faith.* London: Headley, 1911.

Tolles, Frederick B., and Alderfer, E. Gordon, eds. *The Witness of William Penn.* New York: Macmillan, 1957.

Tritton, Frederick J. *Prayer and the Life of the Spirit.* London: Friends Home Service Committee, 1954.

Vining, Elizabeth Gray. *The World in Tune.* Philadelphia: Lippincott, 1954.

Wilbur, Henry W. *Five Points from Barclay.* London: Friends General Conference Advancement Committee, 1912.

Wilson, Gladys. *Quaker Worship.* London: Bannisdale, 1952.

Wilson, Roger. *Quaker Relief.* New York: Macmillan, 1953.

Wragge, J. Philip. *The Faith of Robert Barclay.* London: Friends Home Service Committee, n.d.

ACKNOWLEDGMENTS

My first thanks for help in preparing this Reader go to the Napa County Library, its chief librarian, Dorothy Donahoe, and Pat Penland of her staff, who personally netted many an elusive volume for me.

I am also grateful to Edward Milligan, librarian at Friends House in London, and to Bernard Canter, editor of *The Friend,* for the loan of books and for helpful suggestions.

Paul Smith, President of Whittier College, put the Susan Johnson Memorial Library at my disposal.

Frederick B. Tolles, director of the Friends Historical Library at Swarthmore College, prepared the chronological tables.

My husband, Maxwell McPherson, transported tons of books between home, library, and typist. And in England he traversed hundreds of dangerous left-sided miles taking me to the hillsides, meeting-houses, and jails where Quakerism had its beginnings.

Mary Faville typed so many thees and thous, "you" still has a worldly ring for her.

Without the help of Denver Lindley, my editor at Viking, this book would never have taken shape; and even with his help, it is evident to me that, if you want a book, the easiest thing to do is to write, not edit, it.

Finally, I wish I could thank my mother, Grace Milhous West, who was the first person to say the word "Quaker" to me. Were she alive, she would find in this volume principles and precedents more akin to her own rich and exuberant nature than was the repressive Quakerism in which she was brought up; but which she nevertheless loved.

J. W., 1962

Eve Beehler deserves full credit for the desktop publication of a graceful and readable book.

I wish to thank Holley Webster, Carol Chapman and Liz Kamphausen for their faithful attention to proofreading text and to meeting due dates for copy.

And I am glad for Gay Nicholson's consultation and practical support in coordinating production of this reprint.

Rebecca Kratz Mays, 1992
Pendle Hill Publications Editor

Library of Congress Cataloging-in-Publication Data

The Quaker Reader/selected and introduced by Jessamyn West.
    p.   cm.
    Includes bibliographical references.
    ISBN 0-87574-916-X : $16.50
    1. Society of Friends   I. West, Jessamyn.
BX7615.Q36   1992
289.6—dc20   92-24943
                                              CIP